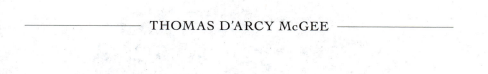

THOMAS D'ARCY McGEE

THOMAS

D'ARCY

McGEE

VOLUME I

Passion, Reason, and Politics
1825–1857

DAVID A. WILSON

McGill-Queen's University Press
Montreal & Kingston · London · Ithaca

© McGill-Queen's University Press 2008
ISBN 978-0-7735-3357-8

Legal deposit first quarter 2008
Bibliothèque nationale du Québec

Printed in Canada on acid-free paper that is 100% ancient forest free
(100% post-consumer recycled), processed chlorine free

This book has been published with the help of a grant from the Canadian Federation
for the Humanities and Social Sciences, through the Aid to Scholarly Publications
Programme, using funds provided by the Social Sciences and Humanities
Research Council of Canada.

McGill-Queen's University Press acknowledges the support of the Canada Council
for the Arts for our publishing program. We also acknowledge the financial support
of the Government of Canada through the Book Publishing Industry Development
Program (BPIDP) for our publishing activities.

Frontispiece: Thomas D'Arcy McGee, aged twenty-three. Copied by
William Notman from a daguerreotype, possibly by Leon Gluckman
(Notman Photographic Archives, McCord Museum, Montreal)

Library and Archives Canada Cataloguing in Publication

Wilson, David A., 1950–
Thomas D'Arcy McGee / David A. Wilson.

Includes bibliographical references and index.
Contents: v. 1. Passion, reason and politics, 1825-1857.
ISBN 978-0-7735-3357-8 (v. 1)

1. McGee, Thomas D'Arcy, 1825–1868. 2. Politicians – Canada – Biography.
3. Canada – Politics and government – 1841–1867. I. Title.

FC471.M25W54 2008   971.04092   C2007-906359-4

Set in 12/15 Bembo Pro with Cochin
Book design & typesetting by Garet Markvoort, zijn digital

TO EUGENE BALOGH

a legodaadóbb olvasóm

Contents

Illustrations

Introduction

As history it was nonsense, and as myth making it was not much better; nevertheless, it was a fascinating attempt to invent a usable past in the context of an uncertain future. The setting was a conference on "Canada and the Celtic Consciousness," held at the University of Toronto in February 1978. Against the background of the Parti Québécois' breakthrough electoral victory fifteen months earlier, and the growing possibility of separation, the conference organizers argued that English and French Canadians possessed a common Celtic heritage that could serve as a basis for national unity. Considerable effort went into demonstrating that many English-speaking Canadians had Celtic roots in Scotland and Ireland, that many French Canadians came from Celtic regions of France, and that they were all heirs to a glorious Celtic civilization that had once towered over Europe. A shared Celtic consciousness, from this viewpoint, could only help to keep the country together. At the same time, the conference also attracted a number of speakers who were not part of a national unity Celtic consciousness-raising agenda and who offered a series of perceptive insights about the history, culture, languages, and literature of the peoples of Ireland, Scotland, Wales, Brittany, and Canada. Some of these speakers, such as Owen Dudley Edwards and Conor Cruise O'Brien, were more into myth busting than myth making.

Hovering over it all was the ghost of Thomas D'Arcy McGee. For the myth makers, here was the ideal symbol of the Celtic contribution to Canadian nationality – an Irish Catholic Canadian who became the youngest of the Fathers of Confederation, who was widely regarded as an inspirational and visionary Canadian nationalist, and who articulated the concept of unity-in-diversity a century before it became the dominant motif of Canadian identity. To help things along, McGee had indeed argued that the Irish, "Highland Scotch," and French were all Celts together, and that their rapprochement with the Anglo-Saxons was a fundamental prerequisite for national unity.

Meanwhile, the myth busters approached McGee from a rather different angle. After giving a talk in which he challenged the central assumptions of Irish nationalism and dismissed the Easter Rising as the superfluous in pursuit of the unattainable, Conor Cruise O'Brien proposed a toast to D'Arcy McGee as the greatest Irishman in Canadian history and stated that a full-length scholarly biography of McGee was long overdue. And that was when the idea for this book was born. If no one else got there first, I thought, one day I would have a crack at it.

It was not surprising that O'Brien spoke so positively of McGee: in many respects, they were kindred spirits. Both men were first-rate writers and formidable polemicists who lived by their wits. They both rejected their early nationalism to become conservative admirers of Edmund Burke; indeed, McGee's interpretation of Burke anticipates many of the arguments advanced in O'Brien's biography of Burke, *The Great Melody*. And they both emerged as uncompromising opponents of revolutionary Irish republicanism; McGee in the nineteenth century and O'Brien in the twentieth century each became known as England's favourite Irishman.

Nor was it coincidental that O'Brien and McGee were subjected to virtually identical attacks. They were accused of being more interested in winning arguments than in seeking the truth, of being able and willing to make a speech on either side of any question, of adopting a confrontational approach that was ultimately counterproductive, and of drinking to excess. There were, of course, significant differences between the two men, not least in the area of religion; O'Brien was an agnostic, while McGee became a devout Catholic. And while O'Brien outlived numerous republican death threats, McGee manifestly did not. But coming to McGee via O'Brien proved to be a strange kind of reverse déjà vu; the controversy over Fenianism during the 1860s was remarkably similar to the debate over Irish republicanism during the 1970s.

As it turned out, a full-scale scholarly biography of McGee had already been written when O'Brien issued his call. In the summer of 1976, Robin B. Burns completed an excellent McGill University PH D dissertation entitled "Thomas D'Arcy McGee: A Biography." Meticulously researched and judiciously argued, Burns's biography dominated the field and seemed destined for publication; for the next twenty years, its presence deterred other historians from trying to emulate his achievement. But although Burns wrote some fine articles on McGee, he moved on to new areas of interest and left his thesis behind. It is one of the tragedies of Canadian historiography that when Burns died in 1998, his dissertation remained unpublished. Nevertheless, his work not only set a benchmark for all subsequent McGee scholars but also influenced the shape and scope of my own research. Everyone who writes about McGee owes a debt of gratitude to Robin Burns, and I am happy to record my own.

By the time that I began to think seriously about writing this book, political biographies had gone out of fashion within the Canadian historical profession – and particularly political biographies about people who were dismissed as dead white males. Given this reality, I am very grateful to the editors of McGill-Queen's University Press, Donald Harman Akenson and Philip Cercone, for their encouragement and enthusiasm. Similar thanks go to the Social Science and Humanities Research Council of Canada, which awarded me a generous three-year research grant. Without the support of McGill-Queen's, I would have been writing in the dark; without the support of the SSHRC, the research could not have been undertaken in the first place. The McGee Papers at Library and Archives Canada consist of only a handful of items. McGee's letters, lectures, and newspaper articles are scattered throughout a variety of archives in Ireland, the United States, and Canada. As a transatlantic figure, he demanded transatlantic research, and the SSHRC grant made this possible.

The SSHRC grant also enabled me to employ some talented and diligent research assistants who conducted a sweep of the Irish, American, and Canadian archives in search of McGee-related material. Todd Webb compiled an impressive collection of Canadian newspaper articles by and about McGee, pausing only to register his amazement at the vast resources of vituperation that were directed against McGee from Irish nationalists, Canadian Orangemen, a section of the Catholic press, and a kaleidoscopic variety of political rivals. When McGee made enemies, he made serious enemies. At times, Todd remarked, he seemed to be the most hated man in Canada. Thomas Richards tracked down every reference to McGee in the John A. Macdonald and George Brown papers at Library and Archives Canada. Anthony Daly scoured the Boston area for sources connected to McGee's editorship of the *Boston Pilot* and the *American Celt*; among other things, his findings helped to illuminate the personal and political dilemmas facing McGee just before his conversion to ultramontane Catholicism in 1851. Dana Kleniewski responded to my requests for specific information about hitherto unknown aspects of McGee's career in the spirit of an Irish folktale heroine following a *geasa*. All of them have made a significant contribution to this book, and I thank them accordingly.

I have also benefited from the comments and advice of friends and colleagues in the fields of Irish, Irish American, and Irish Canadian history. Kevin Whelan, Breandán Mac Suibhne, Gerard Moran, Gary Owens, and Kerby Miller pointed me towards important Irish archival collections that had been overlooked by McGee's previous historians. Jenny and Brendan Meegan followed the trail of McGee's sister, Dorcas, to Australia and unearthed important new information about McGee's early years in Ireland. Brian Lambkin opened up important questions about McGee's Young Ireland years. Timothy Meagher and Timothy Lynch directed me to some excellent sources in New York on McGee and the Fenians. From Buffalo, David Gerber generously gave me his research notes on McGee's controversial career in that city. In Canada, Peter Toner was equally generous in sharing his unrivalled knowledge of Irish Canadian nationalism; Cecil Houston offered some thought-provoking ideas about McGee's relations with the Orange Order; William J. Smyth commented extensively on an earlier draft; and Finn Nielsen supplied me with important forensic evidence in connection with McGee's assassination.

In the course of my search for sources, I received a great deal of help from dozens of librarians and archives. In particular, I thank Fernando Montserrat of the Fraser-Hickson Library in Montreal, Nancy

Marrelli and Vincent Ouellette of the Concordia University Archives in Montreal, David Sheehy of the Archdiocesan Archives in Dublin, Gillian Osley of the Archives of the Roman Catholic Archdiocese of Toronto, and William Cobert of the American Irish Historical Society in New York. I also thank the staff of the Archdiocesan Archives of Kingston, London, and Hamilton, the Columbia University Archives in New York, Library and Archives Canada, the National Archives of Ireland, the National Library of Ireland, the New York Public Library, the Archives of Ontario in Toronto, and the Public Record Office of Northern Ireland in Belfast. At the University of Toronto, Jane Lynch and the staff of the Inter-Library Loan department in the Robarts Library responded with efficiency, good humour, and persistence to my repeated requests for material.

At the Celtic Studies Program in St Michael's College, the University of Toronto, Ann Dooley, Máirín Nic Dhiarmada, Jean Talman, Jo Godfrey, and Mark McGowan have been a constant source of encouragement. I also thank Kate Merriman, Joan McGilvray, and Carlotta Lemieux for preparing the manuscript for publication, and the eagle-eyed Michael Power for compiling the index. A special word of thanks goes to Kyla Madden, deputy senior editor at McGill-Queen's University Press, whose cheerfulness, enthusiasm, warmth, and intelligence have made working with the Press an especially enjoyable experience. And then there is Zsuzsa, love of my life, who brightens up each day with her laughter and music, and who has always been there, during the bad writing days and the good writing days, providing sympathy and support, a sense of what is important and what is not, an encouraging smile and a catch yourself on, in the midst of all my McGeeing.

Not all the people listed above will agree with my interpretation of McGee and his world. But the generosity of spirit that I have encountered during the research and writing of this book has been nothing short of remarkable and has breathed new life into the old notion of a community of scholars. D'Arcy McGee would have approved.

McGEE FAMILY TREE

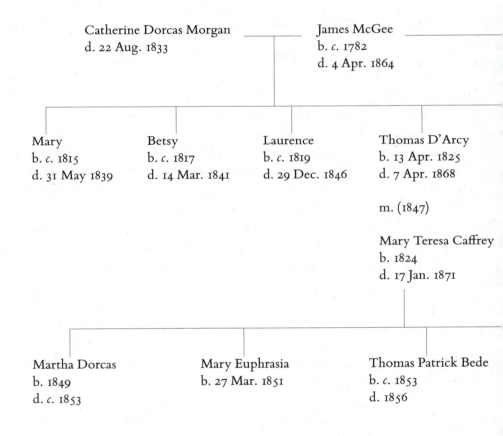

Catherine Dorcas Morgan
d. 22 Aug. 1833

James McGee
b. *c.* 1782
d. 4 Apr. 1864

Mary
b. *c.* 1815
d. 31 May 1839

Betsy
b. *c.* 1817
d. 14 Mar. 1841

Laurence
b. *c.* 1819
d. 29 Dec. 1846

Thomas D'Arcy
b. 13 Apr. 1825
d. 7 Apr. 1868

m. (1847)

Mary Teresa Caffrey
b. 1824
d. 17 Jan. 1871

Martha Dorcas
b. 1849
d. *c.* 1853

Mary Euphrasia
b. 27 Mar. 1851

Thomas Patrick Bede
b. *c.* 1853
d. 1856

Margaret Dea
m. 2 Mar. 1840

Dorcas
b. Dec. 1826
d. 27 Feb. 1887

Rose
b. 1827

Anna Maria
b. *c.* 1828–1829
d. 14 July 1868

James
b. 1830
d. 21 Feb. 1890

John Joseph
b. 6 Aug. 1840
d. 10 Apr. 1927

Rose
b. 1855
d. 1856

Agnes Clara
b. 6 Aug. 1857
d. 6 Jan. 1941

CHAPTER ONE

Day and Night Are the Whole World

Just after two o'clock in the morning on the night of 6–7 April 1868, Thomas D'Arcy McGee went into the saloon of the House of Commons and bought himself three cigars. Brushing past the people in the parliamentary lobby, where minutes earlier a solitary figure with red hair and a red beard had been pacing restlessly, McGee and his fellow Member of Parliament Robert MacFarlane walked south along Metcalfe Street on a mild night under a full moon. A few yards behind them was a group of four men, employees of the House of Commons. At Sparks Street, McGee turned off by himself towards Mrs Trotter's boarding house. One of the men, John Buckley, called out "Goodnight, Mr McGee." "Good morning," he replied. "It is morning now."[1]

As he walked slowly along Sparks Street, smoking one of his cigars, McGee had every reason to be in good humour. The "varicose ulceration of the leg" that had confined him to his room for almost the entire winter was healing, and McGee no longer jokingly referred to himself as a "cripple," even though he still moved with difficulty and used a cane. The heavy drinking that had alienated many of his friends and colleagues, and put a severe strain on his marriage, was now a thing of the past. "You will be glad to know that for now nearly twelve months I have been a firm teetotaler, and with God's blessing I intend to remain so for life," he had written earlier in the day to his former Young Ireland colleague and fellow member of the Royal Irish Academy, Father Charles Patrick Meehan. As MacFarlane later commented, McGee was "in excellent health and spirits" that night and had "addressed the house with great animation and a good deal of fire."[2]

In different circumstances, his address to the House of Commons would almost certainly have been forgotten. It was a good speech, retrospectively magnified into a great one, delivered by one of the finest orators in the English-speaking world. Speaking on national unity – a subject close to his heart – McGee challenged those Nova Scotia MPs who supported their province's attempt to leave Confederation. Much of the speech was taken up with a defence of Charles Tupper, who was currently in London to counter the work of an anti-Confederation delegation from Nova Scotia. It was true, McGee said, that the province had some relatively minor grounds for complaint, but such grievances could be dealt with "from a broad national point of view," in the same "spirit of even-handed fairness which we extended equally to Quebec, Ontario, or New Brunswick." The "unfailing exercise and exhibition of a high-minded spirit of fair play," together with "the mellowing effects of time," he argued, would ensure the ultimate success of the Union. At the close of his speech, McGee combined his adopted Canadian identity with the Burkean notion that public representatives must place the general good above the immediate interests of their constituents. "I ... speak here not as the representative of any race, or of any Province," he declared, "but as thoroughly and emphatically a Canadian, ready and bound to recognize the claims, if any, of my Canadian fellow-subjects, from the farthest east to the farthest west, as equally as those of my nearest neighbour, or of the friend who proposed me on the hustings."[3]

McGee's identification with Canada did not imply any weakening of his commitment to Ireland, the land of his birth. On the contrary, he believed that Canada could serve as a model for Ireland, and viewed himself as an authority on "the Canadian view of Irish misrule." Earlier in the day, McGee had completed a letter to the chief secretary of Ireland, the Earl of Mayo, in which he made a Canadian case for Irish reform. "Everything our emigrants find in Canada," he wrote, "is very unlike everything they left behind them." In Ireland, the landlord system reduced the majority of tenants to "hopeless penury"; in Canada, most Irish immigrants were moderately prosperous property owners. In Ireland, the Established Church ensured a privileged position for the Anglican minority; in Canada, there was "complete religious equality among all our churches." In Ireland, political power lay with the British; Canadians, in contrast, enjoyed "the fullest local control over our resources and revenues."

As a result, McGee asserted, the Irish in Canada were economically enterprising, politically conservative, and above all loyal to the British Crown. It was true, he added, that an insignificant minority supported the revolutionary nationalist Fenians, but they consisted of little more than "a few characterless desperadoes among the floating population of our principal cities." His conclusion was clear: "We are loyal because our equal civil and social rights are respected by this government, in theory and in practice. Were it otherwise, we would be otherwise." The chief secretary, McGee suggested, would be well advised to apply this example to conditions in Ireland.[4]

Along with Canadian and Irish politics, McGee had also been preoccupied that day with literature, one of his great loves. While he was laid up over the winter, he had been writing an "Irish American tale," based partly on his own experiences in New York and New England. Now that it was completed, he had written a letter to Charles Tupper, asking him to arrange for its publication in England. "It would form one pretty thick volume, 650 pages," he informed Tupper, "and must be anonymous, at least, at first." In his letter to Charles Meehan, written that same afternoon, McGee had discussed the possibility of publishing his latest poem, "Iona to Erin," in the *Nation* newspaper in Dublin – the paper for which he had written in his younger, more radical days and whose editorial assistant, Timothy Daniel Sullivan, had long admired McGee's poetry. If Sullivan reprinted the poem, McGee wrote, he should make sure that the correct word in one of the middle stanzas was "blent" and not "blend"; the attention to detail was typical. Other literary projects were broached. "I hope this fall to issue a volume of ballads at New York," he told Meehan. "What do you say to this title: 'Celtic Ballads and Funeral Songs'? You know I am an old keener, and half my lays are lamentations. It could not well be otherwise in this age with an Irish bard, if I am worthy to be called a Bard of Erin."[5]

All in all, it had been a good day – and one that encapsulated the central themes of his Canadian career. "Day and night are the whole world," said the Mac Óc in the Book of Leinster; the day and night of

6–7 April 1868 were a microcosm of McGee's world in the first year of Canadian Confederation.[6] His oratorical skill, his open-minded nationalism, his hope that the Irish Canadian experience could inspire far-reaching reforms in Ireland, his contemptuous dismissal of Fenianism in Canada, and his literary pursuits – all are exemplified in his speech and his letters. Running through everything is a sense of possibility, of optimism about the course of Confederation. "The breakers ahead have gone down," he informed Tupper, "and all is plain sailing at present."[7] His own future appeared equally promising; he planned to concentrate on his books and his poetry, and it seemed that the financial worries that had dogged his career would soon be over.

"There are only two things on Earth I fear – Death and Debt," McGee had told Mary Ann Sadlier the previous year. During the winter of 1867–68 his financial situation had reached the crisis point; he had incurred heavy election expenses, and his recent illness had prevented him from earning money as a public speaker. He was "penniless and pestered," his personal affairs were becoming "very oppressive," and he found himself in the humiliating position of asking John A. Macdonald for a $500 loan to stave off his creditors. Things could not go on like this, and in February 1868 McGee and Macdonald discussed ways out of the situation. Sometime in March they came up with a solution. Macdonald would appoint McGee commissioner of patents, an office with very few responsibilities, at the handsome salary of $3,200 a year; McGee would retire from political life, move from Montreal to Ottawa, and devote himself to writing. For the first time in his life, McGee would have a secure income, which would enable him not only to become a "Bard of Erin" but also to create a new literature for his new country.[8]

If the spectre of debt was being laid to rest, the fear of death lingered on. McGee's attacks on Fenianism had come at great personal and considerable political cost, and he had been receiving death threats in direct proportion to the intensity and extent of his anti-republican pronouncements. The fact that McGee had once been a revolutionary republican himself only increased the anger of his political enemies, who routinely accused him of betraying his earlier principles. At public engagements in Montreal, McGee was frequently protected by policemen, prompting one hostile observer to make sarcastic remarks about the "tramp tramp tramp" of his accompanying bodyguards. During the Montreal election campaign of 1867, some of his Fenian opponents fantasized about shooting him, and on New Year's Day 1868 there may well have been an attempt to assassinate him at his Montreal home. Two months later, McGee received a "hint about my public safety" from Macdonald and promised to stay on guard.[9]

Outwardly, McGee remained unmoved. "The threat of assassination covertly conveyed," he once remarked, "has no terrors for me." Inwardly, however, he was deeply troubled. The anxieties that he suppressed in his public statements came out in his dreams. On the afternoon of Sunday, 5 April, McGee was staying with James Goodwin and his wife in Ottawa. After working on his letter to the Earl of Mayo he had fallen asleep, only to awake in great distress. "I dreamt I was standing by the Falls of Niagara, and saw a boat containing two men sailing down the rapids, and approaching the brink of the cataract," he told the Goodwins. "Seeing their danger and their apparent ignorance of it, I rushed forward to warn them. The boat turned round and proceeded up the rapids, and I went over into the gulf beneath."[10]

At one level, the nightmare was triggered by the recent death of his close friend Lawrence Devany, whose twelve-year-old daughter had died four years earlier when trying to rescue two of her friends who had fallen through the ice on the Welland Canal. But there were other resonances as well. Fifteen years earlier, at the height of his anglophobia, McGee had used the Falls as a metaphor for his anger at the "blood stained" British flag flying on Canadian soil, in a poem so inflammatory that Mary Ann Sadlier omitted it from her collection of McGee's poetry. Later in life, when McGee had repressed and rejected such feelings, the image assumed a very different meaning; the pro-Confederation McGee warned Canadians that they risked falling into Niagara if they reached across to the United States for models of government. McGee had also been warning Irish Canadians about the dangers of falling for Fenianism, and he was currently in the middle of a letter that portrayed the Fenians as "enemies of Canada and enemies of Ireland" and as obstacles to much-needed Irish reforms. The fear of dying while trying to rescue others — and to rescue them from feelings that he had once held himself – was almost certainly connected to his underlying fear of Fenianism.[11]

And so McGee must have shuddered when he heard footsteps hurrying behind him as he hobbled towards Mrs Trotter's boarding house on the south side of Sparks Street. Exactly what happened next will never be known. There may have been one person waiting for him or there may have been two; the footsteps may have come from a gateway a few yards before Mrs Trotter's or from an empty house across the street. Either way, McGee knew that he was in danger; he quickened his pace, fumbled for his keys, found that the door was bolted from the inside, and drummed an urgent warning with his fingers on Mrs Trotter's windowpane. Mrs Trotter, who had been waiting up for her boarders, went into the hall and began to open the door. Suddenly, she was blinded by a flash, heard a shot, and smelt gunpowder. Turning back in shock, her first thought was that someone had set off a firecracker. As she picked up the hallway lamp, she realized that there was blood on her nightgown and in the doorway. Outside, she saw a slumped figure with blood gushing from the mouth; the face was unrecognizable. McGee had been shot at close range through the back of his neck.[12]

There have been other assassinations in Canadian history; one thinks of Pierre Laporte during the October Crisis of 1970 or the journalist Tara Singh Hayer, who was shot in 1998 after challenging fundamentalist Sikh nationalists. But McGee's case was unprecedented and unparalleled; the victim of the first assassination in Canada was a prominent federal politician, a former cabinet minister, and a Father of Confederation. The collective shock was palpable. The immediate reactions ranged from stunned disbelief to anger and an outpouring of public grief. McGee's funeral, held on what would have been his forty-third birthday, 13 April, was the largest that British North America had ever seen. Eighty thousand people thronged the streets of Montreal, and fifteen thousand participated in the funeral parade. It would be rivalled only by the funerals of George-Étienne Cartier and Pierre Elliott Trudeau.[13]

Right from the start, the murder of McGee produced the myth of McGee – that of the martyr who gave his life for Canada. Speaking in the House of Commons on the day of the assassination, and "struggling to repress extreme emotion," Macdonald was the first public figure to describe McGee as "a martyr to the cause of his country." Others quickly followed suit; McGee became known as "a martyr to British Loyalty" and "Canada's martyred Celt."[14]

Shortly after the funeral, a group of his admirers formed the Canada First movement, which drew inspiration from his memory and attempted to realize his vision of a "new nationality." Among them was William Foster, whose speech on *Canada First: or, Our New Nationality* became a foundation text of Canadian nationalism. McGee, wrote Foster, "breathed into our new Dominion the spirit of a proud self-reliance, and first taught Canadians to respect themselves." The assassination of such a gifted, genial, and patriotic man, he continued, had united Canadians in grief and made them realize how much they had in common. In time, the myth became magnified into Nietzschean proportions. "He always stood forth to me, in the light of a superman, one of those legendary beings, capable of doing everything and doing everything well," commented one of his admirers in 1925, during the centennial celebrations of McGee's birth.[15]

Against such inflated language, Irish republicans developed a countermyth of McGee as the archetypal "traitor to Ireland" who had sacrificed his earlier Irish nationalism on the altar of personal ambition. From this perspective, the praise of British and Canadian imperial politicians only underlined the extent of McGee's apostasy. "In reading his book of poems," wrote the Fenian Jeremiah O'Donovan Rossa in 1878, "I find a few verses where he prays for a dog's death should he ever desert the cause of Ireland; he did desert it, and a dog's death he got."[16]

Although there is no evidence that McGee's assassination was authorized by the Fenian leadership in New York, there is no doubt that many grassroots Fenians in the United States and Canada celebrated his death. Reports came in from Albany and Troy immediately after the assassination that the local Fenians were "quite jubilant" and "quite delighted" about the event, and similar sentiments surfaced in Canada.

"*Here's Long Life and Prosperity* to the *Man* that shot *Darcy McGee*," toasted a man named Michael Kelly in a Brampton tavern. In Prescott, where McGee had fought and lost a provincial election campaign the previous year, the brother of a candidate for the priesthood declared that "the shooting of McGee *was hard but honest*." And Luke Burns, a pumpman with the St Lawrence and Ottawa Railway, remarked that McGee was not really an Irishman, that he "deserved what he had got," and that "there would not be anyone sorry for it."[17]

Some others, who were neither loyalist admirers nor republican detractors, took a more cynical approach. When Dr Joseph Workman, the superintendent of the Toronto asylum, learned about McGee's assassination, his first reaction was one of fear and shock. "What, or who next?" he asked. "Who is safe? Who may not have on his track a wretch with a revolver in his pocket?" Workman had "a nasty sort of belief" that most Irish Catholics in Toronto welcomed McGee's death, and he reckoned that many of the politicians who publicly lamented it were privately relieved to see McGee gone. "He was an ugly fact," Workman wrote; "—a standing menace to either the party supported or opposed by him." But his reputation had been forever transformed by the events on Sparks Street: "The crowning act of his life has been his death. Had he lived a few more years he might have vanished from the stage, unwept and unhonoured – & left his wife and children in penury." McGee's assassination, it seemed, was the best career move he ever made.[18]

Of one thing we can be sure: in life and in death, McGee generated extreme reactions. And what a life it was. Against the background of famine and revolution in Ireland, immigration and nativism in the United States, ethnoreligious conflict and nation building in Canada, McGee moved through four different phases, each of which corresponded with a major component of nineteenth-century ideology – constitutional nationalism, revolutionary republicanism, ultramontanism, and liberal-conservatism. "Life does not count by years, but by events," he once wrote; "some men have lived as much at thirty as others at three score."[19] He started young – very young indeed. At the age of seventeen, a devotee of Father Theobald Mathew's temperance movement and a follower of Daniel O'Connell's campaign to repeal the union between Great Britain and Ireland, he moved to the United States. There, within weeks, he was a journalist with the *Boston Pilot*, the largest Irish Catholic newspaper in the country; two years later, on his nineteenth birthday, he became its editor.

In Boston he caught the eye of the folks back home, who invited him to become the parliamentary correspondent for the O'Connellite *Freeman's Journal*. Working in Dublin and London, McGee became increasingly attracted to the Young Ireland movement grouped around Thomas Davis and Charles Gavan Duffy. He joined their newspaper, the *Nation*, and moved with the Young Irelanders when they broke with O'Connell and formed their own political organization, the Irish Confederation, in 1847. McGee was still a constitutional nationalist – more radical than O'Connell but more conservative than John Mitchel and his followers. Under the pressure of the famine and inspired by the French revolution of February 1848, McGee and his fellow moderates in the Irish Confederation moved towards a revolutionary position; by July, he was on the revolutionary council that launched the rising of 1848.

Radicalized by his experience of revolution and repression, and driven back to the United States as a political exile, McGee defiantly proclaimed himself a republican revolutionary and traitor to the British Crown. From the summer of 1848 to the spring of 1849, his politics were virtually indistinguishable from those of the Fenians a decade later. But gradually, under the influence of Gavan Duffy, he came to believe that the time had passed for revolutionary politics, and he pulled back to his earlier moral-force position. At the same time, he became increasingly disillusioned with American life – its nativism, rampant materialism, excessive individualism, loose moral standards, violent crime, and urban degradation. It is one of the best-kept secrets of Irish American nationalism that many leading Irish American nationalists – John Mitchel, Michael Doheny, Richard O'Gorman, Thomas Meagher, for example – actually hated the United States.[20] What made McGee different was that he shouted from the rooftops what others had only whispered in the ears, and that his disillusion drove him to the ultramontane world of papal infallibility, exclusive salvation, the primacy of religion over politics, and uncompromising anti-Protestantism.

After his conversion to ultramontanism in 1851, McGee became one of the most conservative Catholic journalists in the English-speaking world, attacking all forms of Protestant heresy in the United States and hoping for a theocratic state in Ireland. His ultramontanism sharpened his antagonism towards Britain, which he viewed as the centre of an undeclared Protestant war on Catholicism in general and on Irish Catholicism in particular, and reinforced his sense of alienation in the United States. But it also made him view the British colony of Canada in a different light. As nativism peaked in the United States in 1854, McGee became increasingly impressed by the fact that French Canadians had secured a safe Catholic environment and had used their political power to advance the cause of separate schools in English-speaking Canada. Paradoxically, from his perspective, Irish Catholics were better off in British North America than they were in the Great Republic. Before long, he began to view Canada as a place of sanctuary for American Irish Catholics, and he helped to promote a colonization project that was designed to move hundreds of thousands of Irish Catholic immigrants from the squalor, degradation, exploitation, and corruption of American cities into the rural wilderness of Canada and the West.

Nothing came of the plans, but they raised McGee's profile and reputation among leading Irish Catholics in Canada, who invited him to Montreal in 1857; with their encouragement, he started up another newspaper, the *New Era*, and was elected a member of the Legislative Assembly of the Province of Canada. By this time, his ultramontanism had softened, although his adherence to Catholic teaching on such issues as Catholic education, religious marriages, and divorce remained firm. In Canada, he developed a national program that was strongly influenced by his Young Ireland and American experiences. His "new nationality" incorporated plans for economic integration, protective tariffs, railway development, western expansion, the encouragement of Canadian literature, and the entrenchment of minority rights —

especially, but not exclusively, Catholic minority rights. In the process, he aligned himself first against Canadian Orangeism and later against Canadian Fenianism, in a career that took him from the Reform party of George Brown and John Sandfield Macdonald to the Conservatives of John A. Macdonald, and that ended so abruptly on an Ottawa street in 1868.

McGee burned through life with a driving, restless energy, possessing a mind that was constantly "swarming with new thoughts," and approaching everything with what he called "my usual impatience." Incapable of standing still, he spent weeks and months of each year away from home, giving lectures, writing articles, and making contacts. When he was not on the road, he spent ten to twelve hours each day on his reading.[21] His output was astounding; he wrote a dozen books, made scores of parliamentary speeches, published upwards of three hundred poems, delivered well over a thousand lectures, penned an even greater number of letters, and wrote innumerable newspaper articles – all before the age of forty-three. In his first six years as a member of the legislative assembly, for example, he edited his own newspaper, went on annual speaking tours throughout British North America, took a law degree at McGill University, wrote his *Canadian Ballads and Occasional Verses*, along with a play entitled *Sebastian; or The Roman Martyr*, and completed an eight-hundred-page *Popular History of Ireland*.

Less visible, but at least as important, were the countless hours he spent on committee work. Among many other projects, he organized political clubs in Ireland, established adult education programs in the United States, and encouraged immigration projects in Canada. During his Young Ireland days, McGee served as secretary of the Irish Confederation, and threw himself into administrative work with a zeal that amazed his colleagues, pausing only for a four-day break after his marriage. "Tomorrow, I change my state & condition in life (get married)," he wrote to the Young Ireland leader William Smith O'Brien on Monday, 12 July 1847. "The Council are good enough to give me till Saturday. In the interim I go to Enniskerry ... I intend to work, very hard."[22] And work very hard he did, before, during, and after his career with the Irish Confederation.

In part, this energy may have been fuelled by insecurity. The death of his mother when he was only eight years old left him with a profound sense of loss and abandonment; emptiness could be filled with work, the desire to please could be transferred to his friends and colleagues, and public acclaim could compensate for private pain. McGee's early career was marked by a search for approval and a need to impress. "I might have liked him better," commented Thomas Davis after their first and only meeting, "if he had not so obviously determined to *transact* an acquaintance with me." The same tendency can be found in his first two books, where he lapsed into literary showing-off with florid and melodramatic passages.[23] As he became increasingly successful, the insecurities became less apparent and the prose settled into the plain style; nevertheless, his need to identify with political ideals, his continual alcoholism, and his continuous addiction to work all suggest that he was still trying to fill a very large gap. The resulting emotional drive, together with his remarkable intellectual abilities, propelled him into one of the most controversial, unusual, and unpredictable political trajectories in the history of the Irish diaspora.

Throughout his career, McGee's powerful passions were in a state of creative tension with his impressive intellect. His passions drove him to extremes; his intellect kept pulling him back to the centre. In his personal life, this struggle centred on his attitude to alcohol. As a teenager, he took the pledge of total abstinence and delivered dozens of lectures on temperance; in his thirties, he oscillated between teetotalism and alcoholic binges that were excessive even by the standards of mid-nineteenth-century Canadian politicians. Addressing an audience of teetotallers on St Patrick's Day in 1844, the eighteen-year-old McGee praised their victory over "deep-rooted passions" that threatened to become "stronger than your own human nature," and he acknowledged that the obstacles to total abstinence were "many and powerful." Twenty years later, at a dinner during the Quebec Conference, the young Mercy Ann Coles found herself sitting next to McGee. "Before dinner was half over he got so drunk he was obliged to leave the table," she recalled. "I took no notice of him. Mr. Gray said I acted admirably." No one felt the power of those "deep-rooted passions" more strongly than McGee himself.[24]

McGee's political enemies mocked his alcoholism, publishing reports of missed speaking engagements and retailing rumours that he had once passed out in a brothel. Some of his Canadian colleagues viewed with cynical amusement his efforts to break the addiction. "He has joined the Temperance Society," remarked Alexander Campbell in 1866, "and only gets drunk occasionally – what a really honest, well meaning, son of genius he is."[25] For his wife, however, there was nothing remotely humorous about the situation. On at least two occasions, she was called from Montreal to the Quebec City legislature to stop him from drinking, and she implored his assistants to keep him away from the whisky cupboard that he had installed in his office. In the middle of a letter to a friend about her husband's "unfortunate propensity," he staggered into the house: "He has just come in," she wrote, "& from his appearance, it is just a repetition of yesterday, so that I have given up all hope."[26]

The conventional wisdom is that McGee went through three bouts of heavy drinking in his life, each of which occurred at a time of acute political stress – his disillusionment with republicanism in America in 1851, his differences with the Sandfield Macdonald government in 1863, and his electoral contest with Bernard Devlin in 1867. It is clear from the Canadian evidence, however, that McGee had a constant battle with alcoholism from the early 1860s until the autumn of 1867. This was also the period of his fight against Fenianism, which unquestionably exacted a heavy personal toll.[27]

"With the passionate Celtic nature," McGee once remarked, "there is always a danger of running into extremes." "They err greatly who think that rude wit, and warm-hearted blundering, constitute the poles of Irish character," he wrote on another occasion. "Deep and terrible passions, noble and intense feelings, old and acute prejudices, strata upon strata, make it up. Humor is not the basis, but the relief upon the outer sides of the edifice." There was much personal projection in these comments; his own deep and terrible passions kept breaking through the carapace of reason and moderation. During his first conflict with American nativism in 1844, for example, McGee asserted in the *Boston Pilot* that the American Revolution would have failed without the Irish, and described native Americans as "cowards and sons of cowards." In doing so, he brought down a barrage of criticism upon himself, played right into the hands of his enemies, and alienated his allies; Bishop Benedict Joseph Fenwick of Boston was sufficiently offended to cancel his subscription to McGee's "inflammatory Paper."[28]

Equally passionate was McGee's response to the 1851 census, which revealed that Ireland's population had fallen by a quarter during the famine. Quadrupling the actual number of famine deaths, he accused the British government in general and Lord John Russell in particular of mass murder: "Gloss it over as ye will, statesmen and journalists of Great Britain, it is the foulest national murder since the time of Christ. Explain it, escape it as you will, for this year or next, the world is not to be so cheated by pretexts – the dead millions were foully murdered, and by you."[29] Channelling these revolutionary feelings to the far Catholic right, McGee during the 1850s and 1860s attacked republican nationalism with the same intensity that he had applied to American nativism and British policy during the famine. There was little sign of prudence or pragmatism in any of this.

Along with this intensity of feeling went a propensity towards paranoia and a predilection for conspiracy theories. McGee was brilliant on the details of political life, but his sense of subtlety, complexity, and nuance jostled with an equally powerful tendency to view politics as a grand morality play in which the forces of good struggled against the forces of evil. During his period as a republican revolutionary in 1848–49, McGee believed that the world was locked in combat between the "party of Reaction," led by the "hoary harlot Great Britain," and the "party of Revolution," consisting of American republicans and their European counterparts. By 1851, with his conversion to conservative Catholicism, the Manichean outlook remained, but the moral categories were reversed. McGee's new mission was to save Christendom from its secular, socialist, liberal, and republican enemies; the choice was now between "on the one side Red Republicanism and Socialism, on the other Authority and Law – on the one side KOSSUTH and 'my brother MAZINI' [sic], on the other, the Catholic Church."[30]

The one common factor in his republican and early conservative years was McGee's anglophobia. During the early 1850s, he placed Britain at the centre of an anti-Catholic conspiracy, with the Irish as its principal victims. The seventeenth-century land confiscations, the eighteenth-century Penal Laws, and the nineteenth-century shift to liberalism, he argued, were all part of the same sinister plot to wipe out Catholicism in Ireland. When liberalism failed, he continued, Britain used the weapon of famine; now that the famine had failed, Britain was reverting to the Penal Laws.[31] This was not McGee at his logical best. A similar conspiratorial outlook informed his opposition to secret societies in general and Fenianism in particular; during the 1860s, McGee became convinced that the Fenians were planning to subvert the Canadian state and to launch a revolution in Ireland. In this case, he was partially right in regard to Canada and completely correct in relation to Ireland.

Once he had taken a position, McGee maintained it with great skill, tenacity, and courage. This applied not only to his radical republican and ultraconservative periods but also to the liberal-conservatism of his Canadian career. At each phase of his career, McGee combined a coherent set of principles with a pragmatic, polemical, and passionate approach to arguments. Bishop John Hughes of New York, no mean polemicist himself, described McGee as "a theorist" who was "in the habit of subordinating the facts of a case to the fancies of his mind."[32]

There was some substance in the charge; through strategic silences and selectivity, through overstatement and understatement, through evasion and sometimes through invention, McGee employed a wide range of rhetorical resources in the service of what he conceived to be the greater good. On at least one occasion, at the height of his anglophobia, he published – and probably wrote – a forged letter to discredit the British ambassador to the United States, Sir Henry Lytton Bulwer.[33] Later in life, when he was excluded from the London Conference of 1866 on Canadian Confederation, McGee attempted to protect his political reputation by spreading false stories about the reason for his continuing stay in Canada; the illness of his colleagues, rather than a political decision, he said, had prevented him from travelling to London.[34]

One result of this approach, together with his changing principles, was that McGee left behind him a trail of former friends who became disillusioned and embittered enemies. In Ireland, the United States, and Canada, the same warning was repeated from different mouths: "Do not trust this man." John Dillon, one of McGee's allies in the Young Ireland movement, was among the first to register this opinion. In a letter to his wife from New York in 1849, Dillon wrote, "I have seen enough of McGhee [sic] here to make me think him capable of any thing – since the first day of his arrival on these shores his conduct has been one gross swindle." According to Dillon, McGee had misrepresented his own role in the revolutionary movement for the purposes of self-glorification and had deliberately falsified the past to shift the blame for its failure from Gavan Duffy to William Smith O'Brien. McGee, wrote Dillon, was nothing more than an "old schemer" and a "scoundrel," who told blatant lies whenever it suited him.[35] After McGee's conversion to conservatism in 1851, other old friends came to the same conclusion. Thomas Meagher, who had once written warmly of McGee's "sparkling little soul," was so enraged by the ultramontane McGee that his syntax cracked under the pressure of anger. McGee, he told Duffy, was "not to be relied upon – has no conscience, no goodness, no generosity – is a mere trickster in politics, is treacherous, and selfishness."[36]

Among the Canadians who came to share this view was George Clerk, the editor of the Montreal *True Witness*, who had supported McGee's colonization project in 1856 to relocate Irish immigrants from urban slums in the United States to the American and Canadian West. "I have no confidence in the man," he told Bishop Edward Horan in 1865. "He has deceived me once but he shall never deceive me again for I will never be so foolish as again to trust him ... The only interests which he cares for, are the interests of Mr. Thomas Darcy McGee."[37]

Given McGee's political oscillations, his formidable polemical style, and his erratic personal behaviour, such hostile comments are perfectly understandable. Yet they should not be taken at face value. Dillon was hypersensitive to the point of distortion; Meagher believed that McGee had betrayed liberal nationalism by becoming an ultramontanist; and Clerk was convinced that McGee had betrayed his ultramontanism by forming a political alliance with Canadian Protestants. None was an impartial observer, and their testimony must be treated accordingly.

Against such judgments, it should be remembered that McGee commanded great respect and admiration from an equal number of friends and colleagues. Gavan Duffy did not agree with McGee's conservatism and his repudiation of Young Ireland, but still declared, "If we were about to begin our work anew, I would rather have his help than any man's"; and he described McGee as "one who, in whatever else he had changed, had at least remained steadfast in his kindness to [me]."[38] James Moylan, editor of the *Canadian Freeman*, had a brief but intense falling-out with McGee in 1861, yet wrote glowingly of his "splendid abilities" after they were reconciled.[39] And Bishop Thomas Connolly of Halifax viewed McGee in 1868 as the Daniel O'Connell of Canada, "in all respects save that perhaps of his being a little prone to the bottle a fault which thank God he got completely rid of during the last six months of his eminently useful life."[40]

If the struggle between passion and reason, the conspiratorial mentality, and the driving energy were common features of McGee's changing career, there were also inner consistencies in the tone and temper of his prose, poetry, and oratory. McGee's ideas may have changed, but his style remained constant. His models, as he pointed out in 1848, were Daniel Defoe, Benjamin Franklin, Jonathan Swift, and William Cobbett, all of whom had been influenced by the eighteenth-century revolution in rhetoric that emphasized clarity of communication. Like them, McGee preferred a plain, direct, and concise writing style that hit the point in question, avoided "long introductions or perorations," and insisted that metaphors should function as adjuncts to arguments rather than as ends in themselves.[41] McGee became a master of metaphor, employed in conjunction with a wry sense of humour and a sharp satirical edge; it was entirely fitting that he registered his indebtedness to Swift and Cobbett.

In some respects, McGee seems remarkably similar to Cobbett. They were both self-taught men, had enormous energy, immersed themselves in the details of political life, measured reality against idealized notions of national identity, thought in terms of plots and conspiracies, travelled from one end of the political spectrum to the other, and moved through journalism into careers as members of Parliament. But where Cobbett moved to the left, McGee moved to the right and then to the centre; where Cobbett used a brilliant, bludgeoning satirical style, McGee employed a cutting wit; and where Cobbett viewed himself as the bluff and blunt personification of John Bull, McGee associated himself with the putative poetic imagination of the archetypical Celt. Cobbett and McGee may have shared a common idealization of the Middle Ages and a common antipathy to the Protestant Reformation, but one cannot imagine Cobbett writing poetry.[42]

For McGee, poetry was primarily but not exclusively a means of communicating historical, political, and moral lessons to a general audience; like his hero Thomas Davis, he believed that poetry could and should express the soul of a nation. Adopting familiar poetic forms such as the ballad and the sonnet, McGee wrote with a strong sense of rhythm, an aptitude for alliteration, and a striking use of imagery. He had the ability to paint pictures with words and to write simultaneously for the eye and the ear. His poetry was suffused with a consciousness of history, which was invoked to instill a sense of national pride and identity among the Irish at home and abroad; McGee's "Salutation to the Celts" and "Ossian's Celts and Ours" proved to be particularly popular in this respect. He adopted a similar approach in the service of Canadian nationalism, even though he had fewer historical materials with which to work. His poems on Jacques Cartier may not have been among his best but they struck a responsive chord, and were still being taught in Canadian schools up to the mid-twentieth century.[43]

Along with a romanticized view of the past, McGee's poetry generally expressed a sense of hope for the future, a belief in the possibilities of action. During the "days of shame" of the famine and the failed rising of 1848, a tone of anger and grim resolve preponderates; but in the United States the mood becomes more optimistic, as McGee projected his romanticism onto the rural West. Poems such as "The

Army of the West" and "Rise and Go" contrasted the supposed virtues of American frontier life over the urban squalor of the "self-conceited East" and encouraged Irish immigrants to leave the cities and clear homes for themselves in the wilderness. After his plans fell through in the United States, McGee's optimism assumed Canadian form and found poetic expression in his "Arm and Rise." Here, the immigration experience is portrayed in terms of energy, enterprise, opportunity, and independence; the prospect of fulfilment in Canada far outweighs the pain of leaving home.[44]

McGee's poetry was personal as well as political. Some of his poems display a mischievous sense of fun, in counterpoint to deeper strains of sadness about the death of friends or loved ones. Others express a sense of wonderment about nature (a theme that is particularly evident in his Canadian poems), or meditate about religious faith and the mystery of life. Most of these poems remain unread today; indeed, very few literary critics have taken much notice of McGee. Among those who have, the verdict is mixed. Seán Virgo has argued that McGee had an "extremely accomplished" technique but "wasted both time and talent on his Irish historical poems." In Virgo's view, McGee was at his poetic best when driven by a sense of outrage and indignation against social injustices – a judgment that says more about the critic than the poet.[45] Norman Vance, in contrast, described McGee as "a competent poet and a popularizer of genius," whose ultimate rejection of Irish nationalism turned him into an unperson in Ireland; McGee, asserted Vance, had been "edited out of conventional Irish literary history" for political rather than aesthetic reasons.[46]

There is no doubt that McGee has been largely forgotten in Ireland. Yet in his time, McGee's poetry was regarded as much more than "competent," and his Irish historical poems were singled out for particular admiration. Comparing him to the other Young Ireland writers, Samuel Ferguson declared that McGee was "the greatest poet of them all," ahead of Davis, Duffy, and James Clarence Mangan. In Ferguson's view, McGee's finest poems were "The Dead Antiquary, O'Donovan," "The Death of the Homeward Bound," and the historical "Salutation to the Celts." Duffy ranked McGee behind Davis and Mangan, but nevertheless argued that no one surpassed the "subtle charm" with which

McGee's poems and essays brought Irish history back to life. "I plunge into them like a refreshing stream of 'Irish undefiled,'" he wrote. Similarly, Mary Ann Sadlier declared that "the noblest of his poems are undoubtedly the historical," and commented that "his love for Ireland inspired Mr. McGee beyond all doubt with some of the very best and sweetest of his poems."[47] Because McGee's historical poetry has been ignored in Ireland and has lost much of its appeal in Canada, it is all the more important to recognize its significance to contemporaries, its role in the formation of national identity, and its centrality to McGee's mid-nineteenth-century reputation.

McGee was not only regarded as a master of the written word; he was also recognized by friends and foes alike as an outstanding orator. According to Duffy, McGee's speeches in the Irish Confederation of 1847–48 were "generally the best"; given the array of talent in the movement, this was high praise indeed. From New York, Richard O'Gorman in 1852 lamented McGee's conversion to conservatism but still believed that McGee would become the most successful Irish lecturer in the United States. In Canada, McGee's speeches left a deep and lasting impression among his hearers; more than half a century after his death, people still recalled the "charm of his eloquence" and the power of his performances in Parliament.[48] Born with the "gift of the gab," as he put it, McGee learned by listening. Among the political speakers whom he heard and admired were Daniel Webster in America, Daniel O'Connell in Ireland, and Robert Peel in England. His experience as a reporter at Westminster in 1846 also provided important lessons about parliamentary debate. But one of the greatest influences on his oratorical style was a brilliant, popular, and now largely unknown Irish American Unitarian lecturer named Henry Giles.[49]

"I got some of my first cues from hearing Giles," McGee wrote, "though I never could copy closely any man's manner." One of the first practitioners of the increasingly popular art of public lecturing, Giles spoke to packed houses in the towns and villages of New England, New York, and Canada; McGee was a teenager when he first heard him during the early 1840s. "The prime secret of his success," commented McGee, "was his earnestness"; with a voice that was "most flexible and musical in intonation," his arguments carried the audience along rhythmic waves, and culminated in a "perfect furor of excitement." Although Giles read his lectures, his delivery was so natural that "you were not aware after five minutes, whether he had a Manuscript before him, or not." The lectures generally made three or four serious points, punctuated by "sallies of wit," telling anecdotes, and "genuine sarcasm," with the result that they had "all the attractions of a novel or drama."[50]

Equally attractive to McGee was the oratory of the Irish nationalist leader Daniel O'Connell, whom he first heard speak at Conciliation Hall in Dublin in 1845. "His tone was low and conversational at first, and he used very little action," McGee recalled. "He kept his left hand fast in the right lapel of his over coat, while with the other he merely indicated his points. What struck me most was the facial accompaniment of the thoughts he uttered ... His voice changed with every change of topic, and though it never rose into vehemence, it still conveyed the full impression of strong internal emotion." McGee also admired O'Connell's pacing, his use of anecdotes, the spontaneity of his "denunciations," and the sonority of his voice. "As a master of the art of elocution," wrote McGee, "O'Connell seemed to me far more accomplished than any one I had heard."[51]

Although it is impossible to recapture the style and spirit of McGee's oratory, one can always follow the advice that he himself gave about the lectures of Henry Giles: "To judge them as compositions intended for oral delivery, they ought to be read aloud – an excellent practise which I always recommend, to those who would familiarize their ears to the best styles."[52] Reading McGee's speeches aloud can be supplemented by examining the testimony of McGee's listeners, which suggests a continuity of style from the 1840s to the 1860s, and demonstrates how deeply he was influenced by the examples of Giles and O'Connell.

The accounts sometimes begin with a description of McGee's personal appearance – his "unprepossessing" looks, his dishevelled clothing, his "uncouth" appearance – and register surprise at the contrast between his "flat and heavy" features and his soaring oratory. Sandford Fleming remembered the first time he saw McGee, at a packed St Lawrence Hall in Toronto, during the winter of 1861–62. Delayed by the train and aware of the audience's impatience, McGee strode onto the stage still wearing his buffalo coat. "The first impression was anything but pleasant," wrote Fleming. "Those around me thought that the uncouth looking person was a cab-man who had rushed on the stage to make known some dire calamity which had happened to Mr. McGee. All this was dispelled so soon as the unknown individual spoke a few sentences. It was the silver tongued McGee himself who charmed all present by his eloquence."[53]

McGee's listeners generally commented upon the conviction of his delivery, the "mellow richness" and "rhythm and cadence" of his voice, and the "unpretending and familiar" style of his speech. There were numerous reports of his playful humour, his "brilliant flashes of imagination and true Irish wit," and his "cutting sarcasm"; the parallels with Giles are immediately apparent. Like O'Connell, McGee realized that physical action was not necessary for effective oratory. "During the whole course of his two hours' address," wrote a Canadian admirer, "he stood fixed to one spot on the platform, with his hands clasped behind his back." Sometimes he spoke from a prepared script, and sometimes he did not; either way, McGee's delivery appeared so "natural" that it was widely assumed to be extemporaneous.[54]

In effect, McGee absorbed the lessons of Giles and O'Connell and incorporated them into his own approach, rather than trying to imitate their style. Central to McGee's oratory was the blending of "argument and fact and history," together with "articulate language and passion and poetry all combined." George Ross recalled that McGee's sentences contained "a poetical glow which awakened emotions and feelings never before touched by the human voice." The same feel for language that impelled McGee to write poetry also lay behind his oratory. Indeed, much of McGee's best poetry actually appears in his speeches, and he viewed his oratory as a modern version of ancestral poetic traditions. "As a lecturer," he wrote in 1855, "I am to [the Irish] what the ancient Bard was to their Fathers, a periodical visitor, freshening their feelings and elevating their tastes."[55]

For those who shared McGee's feelings and tastes, the periodic visits could be inspirational; for those who did not, McGee's bardic mission to improve a benighted people appeared pretentious and patronizing. His attitude towards the Irish in Canada, commented a Montreal

Irishman in 1864, "is that of a Parent to his children, of a Sovereign to his people, of a Roman Catholic Bishop to his flock. He assumes, or seems to assume, that the Irish are in a state of tutelage, if not of vassalage to himself; that they are intellectually and morally infants who must be looked after, and cared for, and done for, as incapable of taking care of themselves." Ironically, McGee had levelled exactly the same criticism against O'Connell some fifteen years earlier; the trouble with O'Connell's speeches, McGee had remarked in 1849, was that he "treated his hearers too much like children."[56]

Running through the continuities and changes in McGee's career were the underlying themes of Burkean conservatism, Celticism, and Catholicism. The connecting figure, and the man who loomed largest in McGee's intellectual world, was undoubtedly Edmund Burke. In McGee's view, Burke was the "greatest master of eloquence" in the English language, an outstanding prose writer, and a "profound political philosopher."[57] McGee studied Burke's speeches (no doubt reading them aloud), assimilated his ideas, and recommended that no student of politics should be "without Burke by his side or in his memory."[58] "If any young man present desired to contemplate the sublime of political science – the astronomy of affairs," he told a Montreal audience in 1856, "[I] would give him three authors: first, Burke; second, Burke; third, Burke."[59]

As a young man himself, McGee had held ambivalent views about Burke's political science. He admired Burke's liberal views on Ireland, America, and India, along with his foresight about the French Revolution, but felt that Burke's rhetorical powers "could not cover up the absence of that greatest requisite of greatness – practicability." When, later in life, McGee became more and more like Burke, his enemies flung these words in his face; in 1865 a correspondent of the *Irish Canadian* accused McGee of being "what he censures in the great Burke, (his cherished model) a man of genius without practical parts." By this time, however, McGee had not only dropped but reversed his earlier criticism. One of Burke's greatest insights, he now believed, was his view that "what is not possible is not desirable – that the possible best is the absolute best." The very practicability of Burke's approach had become the guiding principle of McGee's own political career.[60]

The road to this position was neither smooth nor straight. In the pre-revolutionary stage of his Young Ireland career, McGee adopted a Burkean emphasis on precedent and custom to strengthen his case for an Irish parliament with links to the Crown. But this approach was jettisoned during his republican period in 1848–49, when he either ignored Burke or quoted him in a highly selective manner. Burke's definition of a nation as a "moral essence," for example, was pressed into the service of McGee's Irish American nationalism, and Burke's dismissive views about "theological politicians" (actually aimed at Dissenters) were incorporated into McGee's argument that the Roman Catholic Church should leave politics to the laity. None of this had any organic connection to Burke's thought. McGee was using Burke's writings as polemical weapons rather than philosophical precepts. The result was as jarring as it would have been for Thomas Paine to have quoted Burke approvingly in the *Rights of Man*.[61]

All this changed in 1851, when McGee abandoned radical politics, aligned himself with European Catholic counterrevolutionary thinkers, and adopted Burke as his "great model." Even then, he had some misgivings to overcome. In March 1851, two months before he announced his conversion, McGee's admiration for Burke as "the Apostle of True Conservatism" was tempered by the caveat that Burke had become "crazed by his fear of an all-devouring Anarchism." McGee the moderate, it seems, was pulling back from Burke's more extreme anti-revolutionary pronouncements. But as McGee himself began to fear that "all-devouring Anarchism" was slouching through the United States and Europe, the qualification was soon dropped. Burke, he declared, was among those writers who taught him "to distrust sudden innovations, to respect old age and old institutions, even when imperfect, and to cherish a salutary terror of attempting to take the body of Society to pieces."[62]

From the autumn of 1851, the identification was total. McGee possessed his own "salutary terror" of revolutionary politics and projected his own experiences and aspirations onto those of his mentor. Burke, wrote McGee, had been deeply influenced by his mother, had made literature his "pathway to Parliament," and had been driven by "two strong passions: the pursuit of injustice in high criminals, and the exposition of justice towards all men"; he could just as easily have been writing about his own life and aspirations. When McGee championed the cause of justice within the British Empire, he consciously aligned himself with Burke's earlier attacks on the abuse of power. After the so-called Indian Mutiny of 1857, for example, McGee criticized "the East India Company's method of governing their conquest" by quoting extensively from Burke's speeches on the impeachment of Warren Hastings. More generally, the style and substance of McGee's anti-Fenian writings were very much in the tradition of Burke's anti-Jacobinism.[63]

Central to this identification was McGee's conviction that he and Burke shared a common consciousness of what it meant to be Catholic and Celtic in Ireland. Burke, of course, was nominally a Protestant; he could not have risen to a position of political power and influence had it been otherwise. But McGee was convinced, and with good reason, that Burke was actually a closet Catholic. Burke's mother and wife were both Catholics, he had been educated in part by a Catholic hedge-school teacher, he had a wide circle of Catholic friends ("the ornaments of a bygone Catholic generation"), and he probably received the last rites of the Catholic Church. This background, McGee argued, explained why Burke condemned the Penal Laws, supported the Catholic Relief Bill of 1778, and helped to establish Maynooth College, Ireland's Catholic seminary, in 1795. Burke's Catholic sympathies, McGee believed, not only pushed him in a radical direction against the Protestant Ascendancy in Ireland but also lay behind his conservative attack on the anti-Catholic ideology of revolutionary France. Having been grappling with his own radical and conservative tendencies, McGee came to place Catholicism at the core of his identity and defended the Catholic faith in a hostile Protestant environment. In Burke, he found a kindred spirit and a source of inspiration.[64]

If McGee claimed Burke as a Catholic, he also viewed him as a fellow Celt. "The fervor, the fire, the reverence, the deference for the past, exhibited in the 'Recollections on the French Revolution' [sic]," he argued in 1856, "were eminently Celtic – were noble illustrations of

Irish genius." He praised Burke for laying the foundation of "modern Celtic research" by bringing Gaelic manuscripts into Trinity College, and described Burke as one of Ireland's most distinguished Celts. Just as McGee placed Burkean conservatism within a Celtic framework, his own politics and personality were inseparable from his mythic construct of the Celtic character – a construct that was rooted in the Celtic Revival of the eighteenth century.[65]

The Celts arrived in Britain and Ireland in 1707, when Edward Lhuyd argued in his *Archaeologia Britannica* that the people of Wales, Scotland, and Ireland spoke a "Celtic" language, which had once been the dominant tongue of northern Europe. Before that time, there is no evidence that anyone in Britain or Ireland had ever described himself or herself as a Celt. Afterwards, it became possible for people who had been denigrated as "primitive" or "backward" speakers of an obscure language to re-imagine themselves as heirs of a great and glorious Celtic civilization. To identify oneself as a Celt was to invert negative stereotypes of savagery and superstition, and to assert the self-worth and superiority of traditional Welsh, Scottish, and Irish culture against English or American cultural arrogance.[66]

As a young man in the United States, McGee found such positive images appealing and useful. During the early 1840s, he countered American nativism by connecting the Irish with a magnificent Celtic past and by contending that the Celts were inherently republican and anti-imperialist. In this reading of history, the Anglo-Saxons were addicted to monarchy and conquest, while the "Celtic spirit" was "too proud, restless and intelligent in the masses, to bear with willingness the rule of kings." "The more truly Irish or Celtic we are," he asserted in 1845, "the more truly republican we must be, and consequently the more American."[67]

It was the kind of argument that an Irish Catholic looking for acceptance in the United States would want to cheer home, although quite where it left Irish Protestants remained unclear. Irish Protestants who had supported the American Revolution and had joined the United Irishmen were admitted as card-carrying Celts, while those who belonged to the Orange Order were kept out. At the same time, this political basis of inclusion or exclusion was implicitly contradicted by McGee's underlying racial assumptions about "undiluted Celtic blood." Not for the last time, he stumbled over the problem of accommodating Protestants within his Celtic concept of Ireland.[68]

One of the most intriguing aspects about McGee's concept of the Celt is its concertina-like quality; the meaning was expanded or contracted according to the melody he was playing. In his effort to establish a united Irish front against American nativism during the early 1840s, he opened things out so that Celtic equalled Irish minus the Orange Order. As a Young Irelander, however, he narrowed the definition in the service of pluralistic nationalism, arguing that the Celts were only one group among many within the Irish population. The Irish, he wrote, were a polyglot people; the "Celtic race" might have preponderated in Munster, but there were also Scots in the north, Spaniards in the west, and Anglo-Normans in the southeast, along with a smattering of Saxons, Danes, and Germans. Rejecting the "popular fallacy" that the Irish and the Celts were synonymous, he argued that intermarriage had made racial distinctions redundant, and insisted that the Irish should define themselves by their common cultural heritage.[69]

Although this argument fitted perfectly with the ecumenicalism of Young Ireland, it could not withstand the shock of 1848, when the failure of the revolutionary movement underlined the persistence of deep divisions within the Irish people. Back in the United States, this time as a republican refugee, McGee expanded the concertina: his Celts now embraced everyone in Ireland, including the "Scotch-Irish," whether they wanted to be embraced or not. As his consciousness of prejudice increased, the definition grew wider and wider. Reacting against comments in London newspapers that the Celts were "white savages," McGee countered that they were actually the "original inhabitants of Europe" – adding for good measure Gavan Duffy's statement that Cicero and "Michael Angelo" were "Celts with the O at the wrong end of their name."[70]

This position failed to blunt "Anglo-Saxon" attacks that equated the Celts with Irish Catholics and treated them as ignorant and superstitious peasants. In these circumstances, McGee drew in his lines of defence and prepared for battle. "A state of social hostility exists between citizens of Saxon and Celtic origin in the old Atlantic states," he declared in 1851. Neutrality was out of the question; the Irish were indeed Celts, the Celts were indeed Catholics, and they must break the Anglo-Saxon conspiracy before it broke them. "Catholicism," he asserted, "is the mark of the Celtic nations, and in proportion to their purity from admixture is their loyalty in faith." Irish Protestants, in McGee's view, had inflicted religious oppression and godless revolutionary republicanism on the Irish people, and were responsible for the failure of the risings of 1798 and 1848. Only a few years earlier, he had blamed the defeat of 1848 on the Catholic Church.[71]

At times, a consciousness of complexity threatened to break into this polarized view of the world, only to recede into the background. In a lecture delivered in 1852 on "The Celtic Race," McGee initially argued that national character was shaped by natural and conventional law, history, religion and language, and noted that "extravagant assertions upon one side had produced an ultra reaction on the other, and between both, truth and science, was sacrificed." By the end of the lecture, however, he had fallen into the very trap he had just warned his listeners against, drawing sharp contrasts between Saxon materialism and Celtic spirituality, and asserting that Irish Catholic Celts were on a providential mission to transmit the One True Faith to the New World.[72]

As long as McGee viewed Irish Catholics as an embattled minority fighting for survival in a hostile environment, this kind of "ultra reaction" would prevail. But when the context changed, McGee's defensive interpretation of the Celt changed as well. In Canada, the prospect of uniting different ethnoreligious groups within a common national framework meant that the politics of ethnic reaction gave way to an emphasis on compromise and cooperation. Each "racial" group had its own distinguishing characteristics, McGee now argued; it was more important to concentrate on their different contributions to the greater good than "to promote a dogged nationality." "The standard of conduct of these representatives of the Celtic element," he wrote, "should be that God had made of one blood all the nations of the earth."[73] In some respects, this marked a return to the position of his Young Ire-

land years, except of course that the Celts were now socially conservative liberals rather than radical democrats.

J.R.R. Tolkien famously wrote that "'Celtic' ... is a magic bag,
into which anything may be put, and out of which almost anything
may come."[74] This certainly applies to McGee's use of the term, for
he repeatedly redefined "Celtic" to correspond to his changing political outlook. At various points, McGee's Celts were naturally anti-
authoritarian or naturally law abiding; they were a distinct "race," or
they were a political or linguistic grouping; they were associated with
Irish Catholicism, or they embraced just about everyone in Europe;
they included Irish Protestants, or they defined themselves against
Irish Protestants. Beneath these different definitions lay a common
cluster of images. McGee consistently described the Celts as being
passionate, energetic, adventurous, courageous, spiritual, artistic, and
impulsive, and as a people who found it easier to begin projects than
to follow them through. If his oscillating political interpretation of the
Celts followed the trajectory of his career, McGee's description of the
"Celtic character" was remarkably similar to his sense of self. On both
the political and the personal level, McGee had created the Celts in
his own image.

This has wider significance. McGee was far from the only person
who thought and felt in this way, and Celticism became contested
ground among many other Irish who were making their own political
and personal projections onto an imagined Celtic past and Celtic character. The very act of conducting extra- and intra-Irish conflict within
a Celtic framework could only contribute to the dissemination of a
more general Celtic consciousness in North America. This consciousness was sufficiently vague and nebulous to encompass a wide range of
contradictory concepts while retaining generally positive connotations
among its Irish adherents – almost all of whom were Catholics.

The term was loose enough to have a broad appeal for Irish Catholic
immigrants, but it existed in an ambiguous relationship to Irish Protestantism. Such ambiguity was symptomatic of deeper dilemmas within
Irish nationalism. The Protestants could be seen as an alien "Anglo-
Saxon" presence, as Celts with a false consciousness, or as Celts insofar
as they were Irish nationalists. McGee at different times took each of

these positions. But whatever the word meant, most Irish Protestants wanted nothing to do with it. Given this situation, the concept was hardly conducive to national unity in Ireland. McGee, in common with other self-described Celts, was caught in the contradiction.

————

To be a Celt was to identify with an imagined global community. As someone who spent more than half his life in North America and was constantly on the move, McGee found in the Celts a sense of belonging, a connectedness with a wider historical and geographical world. In a different way, his Catholicism served a similar function; as well as providing spiritual nourishment, it helped to form his individual identity within both an Irish and an international context. Long before his conversion to ultramontanism, McGee took his religion very seriously indeed.

"I am, thank God, a Catholic," he wrote in 1847; " – I believe in my own religion – I learned it from a mother's knee – I was taught it by a father's example." His first non-fiction books celebrated O'Connell's campaign for Catholic Emancipation and attempted to rescue from obscurity the Irish Catholic writers of the seventeenth century. His earliest writings in the *Boston Pilot* defended the Catholic faith against its American Protestant detractors and maintained that Catholic authority, discipline, and morality provided a necessary counterbalance to the anarchistic tendencies of a Protestant democracy – a position that anticipated his subsequent religious conservatism.[75]

The central question facing McGee in his early years concerned the relationship between Catholicism and Irish nationalism. "If it came to a conflict between Religion and Patriotism, which would you sacrifice to the other?" McGee once asked a fellow Irish Catholic. The search for an answer produced what he called the "hardest internal battle" of his life.[76] As a liberal and as a revolutionary republican, he attempted to solve the problem by drawing a sharp line between the spiritual and temporal teachings of the church. "A man may be free and a Christian at the same time," he wrote in 1849; "... in all things temporal he may assert his private judgment, and yet be an irreproachable Catholic. And, among these things temporal, I include his domestic affairs, the education of his children, his manners, his temporal opinions, and his politics."[77] In this way, McGee was able to assert his intellectual independence and criticize the church's counterrevolutionary pronouncements, while embracing its spiritual and moral teachings.

Not surprisingly, an increasingly ultramontane Catholic Church strongly opposed this position, on the grounds that religious morality could not be separated from private affairs, education, and politics. Religious authority flowed from the Pope through the bishops to the priests and their flocks; there was no neat line beyond which Catholic teaching did not apply. Accordingly, liberal Catholics such as McGee were subjected to intense clerical pressure. In New York, Bishop John Hughes singled him out as a dangerous and destructive influence, and banned his newspaper from parish reading rooms. Conservative Catholic journalists denounced his writings as "sources of eternal damnation to all concerned," and described him as that worst of all Catholics, a "Protestant Catholic."[78]

McGee put up a strong fight. "If Catholics cannot separate the politician from the priest," he asked, "should we not be governed by priests? … If this be so, Theocracy, not Democracy, is the most perfect form of human government."[79] But the resurgence of American nativism, his growing skepticism about Irish nationalist politics, and his intellectual difficulties with a compartmentalized approach to Catholicism gradually forced him to re-evaluate his position. His conversion to ultramontanism in May 1851 seemed to come out of nowhere — and certainly took his readers by surprise. But it was the result of months of self-doubt, self-examination, and self-questioning — his "hardest internal battle." When McGee finally resolved his dilemma, all the complexities of his earlier position were replaced by an overwhelming sense of clarity: "What says our old Irish catechism? — 'Question. — For what end did God create you? Answer. — To love and serve him here on earth, and afterwards to see and enjoy him forever in Heaven.' This simple question and answer contains the whole Christian philosophy of public and private life. Never lose sight of it."[80]

Before 1851, McGee's separation of politics and religion had enabled him to put Irish nationalism above Catholicism; afterwards, he believed that Irish nationalism was inseparable from Catholicism. To suppose that there could be a "conflict between Religion and Patriotism," McGee now believed, was to "suppose an impossibility. In Ireland the real interests of the country are and must always be Catholic." Just as McGee's Celticism during the early 1850s excluded Irish Protestants, his ultramontane Catholicism triumphed over cultural pluralism. The Protestants, he wrote, were divided among a hostile Ascendancy class, republicans in the tradition of Wolfe Tone ("the most anti-Irish Irishman, in his philosophy of life and duty, that ever existed"), and well-meaning patriots such as Thomas Davis and William Smith O'Brien, who "never got at the heart of the land." Irishmen would only walk along the right path, McGee argued, if they kept their feet on "Celto-Catholic ground."[81]

McGee's own quest for "Celto-Catholic ground" eventually took him to Canada, where he supported improved separate school legislation, attacked the Orange Order, and attempted to inoculate his countrymen against the "disease" of Fenianism.[82] At the same time, he realized that the best way to safeguard and strengthen Catholic interests was through a process of accommodation – insisting that Catholics in Canada West should possess the same rights as Protestants in Canada East, reducing ethnoreligious tensions in English-speaking Canada (since such tensions could only hurt the Catholic minority), and forming pragmatic alliances with the loosely organized and constantly fluctuating political parties in the country.

On occasion, these alliances were strongly opposed by the Catholic Church in Canada. When McGee supported George Brown's Reformers in 1858–59, for example, he was denounced by almost every Catholic bishop in the country – a rather peculiar position for someone whose ultramontanism had drawn him to Canada. At other times, he worked closely and clandestinely with priests and bishops to influence the Catholic vote, on the grounds that Catholic unity meant Catholic strength. Not that there was anything inherently ultramontane about that: John A. Macdonald did the same thing, and he was an Orangeman. But that, in a sense, is precisely the point. In English Canada, the only way to advance Catholicism was through advancing minority rights, and the only way to advance minority rights was to embrace pragmatism and pluralism. In the process, the ultramontane McGee was transformed into the liberal-conservative McGee.

The changes in McGee's outlook and the fact that his career spanned three different countries have presented some serious challenges for his historians. How do they know if they have the "right" McGee? What weight should be given to the different phases of his career? Was he motivated primarily by personal ambition, or is he better understood as a political idealist? McGee's first biographers – Daniel Cobb Harvey, Alexander Brady, Isabel Skelton, and Josephine Phelan – agreed upon the answers: the "right" McGee was the Conservative Father of Confederation; the greatest weight should be placed on his Canadian career; and he was a great visionary, who stamped Confederation with its ideal and inspiring character and provided the new nation with its soul.[83] The full title of Harvey's biographical sketch perfectly captures the approach: *Thomas D'Arcy McGee, the Prophet of Canadian Nationality, being an account of how Thomas D'Arcy McGee, by precept and example, strove manfully to convert the abstract idea of Canadian nationality into a compelling sentiment of tolerance and goodwill among sects and races, of faith, hope, charity, and neighborliness among individuals.*

The McGee who emerges from the early biographies was a flawless human being whose domestic life was "happy in the highest degree" and who exhibited the highest moral qualities.[84] Skelton and Phelan even resorted to misquotations and elisions to present McGee in the best possible light; bowdlerization was employed in the service of deification.[85] The key words used to describe McGee were "prophet" and "martyr"; the overriding image is that of the Great Man who had been cut down in his prime by base men. According to Phelan, "All those who had written scurrilously of McGee – the newspapers that had published lies about him, the political enemies who had whipped up mob feeling against him, all those who let loose forces of hatred that they could not control – were guilty of his death."[86] McGee appeared as a Christlike figure, a virtuous moral teacher who was destroyed by the forces of evil but whose death confounded his enemies and whose resurrected spirit brought new life to a new nation.

One of McGee's great strengths, from this perspective, was his ability to steer Irish Canadian Catholics away from the snares of Fenianism and to ensure that they remained loyal subjects of the Crown. This interpretation was sometimes couched in unconsciously patronizing tones. Phelan, for example, viewed the Catholic Irish in North America as a quick, excitable, generous, simple people, rather like children, who were in need of a father figure to steady them down and set them right – someone, in fact, just like D'Arcy McGee.[87] This view of McGee has proved remarkably persistent and reached its apogee in *The Untold Story: The Irish in Canada*, a two-volume survey of over a thousand pages, published in 1988 and edited by Robert O'Driscoll and Lorna Reynolds.

A strange amalgam of scholarship, mysticism, and myth making, the book was replete with wild assertions, paranoid fantasies, and extravagant claims. The "clear air of Canada," it was maintained, "produced a psychologically calming effect on the Northern Irish Protestant and the Southern Irish Catholic." A fictional account of Grosse-Île was presented as a genuine historical document, amid dark hints that the "British Government" had paid "hush money" to cover up the "hidden holocaust" of Irish famine migration to Canada. The Fenian invasion of 1866 became "the most significant factor that led to the Confederation of Canada," rather than being one cause among many. And there, in this twilight of reason, stood D'Arcy McGee, the Celtic hero who supposedly saved Canada from its Fenian and American enemies and paved the way for Confederation.[88]

McGee was given the starring role in O'Driscoll and Reynolds's story of the Irish in Canada. He was featured in the frontispiece, his famous "Shield of Achilles" speech of 1860 provided the opening text, and he was the only Irish Canadian figure to receive his own separate section in the book. The editors incorporated him into a romanticized view of a past that existed only in their imagination. In advocating Confederation, they argued, McGee was "dimly remembering the great pre-classical Celtic Confederation of Europe, different blood-groupings held together by common ideals and a common culture, a

Confederation which the modern development of Canada has come to resemble."

Dimly, indeed. Even more perversely, the editors said the same thing of Ogle Gowan, the founder of the Orange Order in British North America. The section on McGee placed the scholarship of historians such as Robin Burns and William Baker in uneasy juxtaposition with the piety of Bill Davis, the former Conservative premier of Ontario. Burns and Baker notwithstanding, the general thrust of the book was that McGee commanded the support of most Irish Catholic Canadians and single-handedly ensured that they would remain loyal to the Crown − in contrast to their American counterparts. The Great Man theory of history was back.[89]

There was, however, one serious difficulty that McGee's loyalist hagiographers had to overcome − the fact that the Father of Confederation whom the Earl of Mayo described as "one of the most eloquent advocates of British rule and British institutions ... on the face of the globe" had once been a revolutionary republican whose self-proclaimed mission was "to rend the British flag − to blast the British name − to wreck the British edifice of power from cornerstone to cornice."[90] Faced with this problem, McGee's first historians treated his revolutionary period as an "erratic episode in his life," an immature response to unusual circumstances. "He did not stop to consider that he was a radical by accident and not from conviction," wrote Phelan. In Brady's view, McGee "had been a revolutionist largely by the accident of events." Harvey put it down to his "Celtic fervor and youthful ardor" − those Celts again − while Skelton contended that the conservative Catholic McGee was the "true McGee." Phelan agreed, remarking that McGee's anti-British writings "did not reflect his real mind."[91] It seemed that there had been a false McGee lurking in the shadows, who looked and sounded very much like the real McGee, except for his nasty habit of denouncing the British government and criticizing the Catholic Church.

Such an approach explained away rather than explained McGee's revolutionary republicanism and raised more questions than it answered. Treating McGee as an accidental revolutionary not only absolved him of responsibility for his own actions but also contradicted the biographers' dominant image of McGee as an intelligent and independent thinker. To ascribe his radicalism to immaturity and inexperience was to equate conservativism with wisdom and to adopt a patronizing attitude to his youth. When Mary Ann Sadlier compiled and edited McGee's poems in 1869–70, she reminded her readers that his anti-British "Song of the American Repealers" was merely a "boyish effusion." The middle-aged McGee viewed his radical past in much the same way. In his famous Wexford speech of 1865, he described the Young Irelanders (himself included) as "a pack of fools" and said that "no man need blush at forty for the follies of one-and-twenty."[92] It made sense for McGee and his Canadian admirers to treat his radical and revolutionary period as an aberration, safely sealed off within a cordon sanitaire of conservatism. But historians who follow this view are likely to miss a key component of his character and career, for his radical style was not confined to 1848–49; it ran through his entire career, assuming different forms in different circumstances.

From time to time, a few dissenting voices challenged the emerging orthodoxy. When Isabel Skelton published her adulatory biography of McGee in 1925, McGee's half-brother John Joseph was singularly unimpressed. Eighty-five years old, he had lived with D'Arcy McGee in Montreal and was a well-known figure in Canadian politics; he had become the clerk of the Privy Council and was the grandfather of One-Eyed Frank McGee, Canada's first hockey star. In later life, he had compiled material for his own life of D'Arcy McGee but could not afford the cost of publication.

Writing to John J. O'Gorman, an Ottawa priest who also was preparing a McGee biography, John Joseph maintained that Skelton's book contained some serious deficiencies. Skelton's critical comments about McGee's *History of the Irish Settlers in North America*, John Joseph declared, were "little short of down right bigotry." Her passing treatment of the Irish nationalist William Smith O'Brien's visit to Toronto in 1859 was "contemptible" and "appalling," and there was nothing in her book about Orange anti-Catholic violence in Canada. She had ignored the "Orange Lambs" of Bradford, who in 1860 had condemned McGee as a "traitor to his Queen and country" and threatened to shoot him if he tried to speak in their town. Nor had she mentioned the "outrages" at Peterborough in 1863, when the Orangemen "brought cannon to blow up the St. Patrick's day procession as it came out of Church." "It was only by a miracle that I myself escaped death," he added.[93]

In part, this reaction may have stemmed from John Joseph's position as a rival author, who believed that he had proprietorial rights to the McGee story; it may also have been that John Joseph had idealized his half-brother to the extent that any criticism, however mild, was anathema. But more than that was going on. This was the response of a man who reads a book describing events in which he was intimately involved and cries out, "It wasn't like that." And John Joseph did indeed identify two themes that McGee's first biographers had missed – the extent of ethnoreligious animosities in D'Arcy McGee's Canada, and the centrality of Catholicism to his career.

John J. O'Gorman was less critical of the early biographies, but he agreed that McGee's Catholicism had been ignored. Shortly after the McGee centenary celebrations of 1925, O'Gorman noted that "when so much was heard of what he did for Ireland and for Canada, nothing was said of what he did for the Catholic Church." It may not have been entirely coincidental that all of McGee's first biographers were Protestants. At any rate, O'Gorman was determined to redress the imbalance. "Thomas D'Arcy McGee," he declared, "was one of the greatest lay apostles that God raised up in his church in the nineteenth century."[94] O'Gorman elaborated upon this theme in numerous lectures, but his long-planned book never materialized.

Some fifty years after John Joseph McGee and John J. O'Gorman complained that the historiography was not hagiographical enough, Peter Toner came at McGee from the opposite angle, arguing that his reputation had been inflated beyond all proportion, largely as a result of his assassination. Toner's dissertation, "The Rise of Irish Nationalism in Canada," remains the best work on the subject, and it provided a useful and necessary corrective against starry-eyed views of McGee's life and influence. Far from being a "prophet," a "romantic," or a man of principle, Toner wrote, McGee had embarked on a "chosen course of self-advancement," which eventually cost him the support of his Montreal Irish constituency. To view McGee as being representative of the Catholic Irish in Canada, maintained Toner, was not only to exaggerate his significance but also to ignore the divisions within Irish Canadian Catholicism and to underplay the strength of Fenianism in the country. Nor did Toner accept the view that McGee had somehow saved Irish Canadians from Fenianism; it was much more likely, he said, that McGee's stand against Fenianism actually strengthened the movement it was intended to crush, by triggering a pro-Fenian reaction. McGee's anti-Fenianism, which went hand in hand with his Canadian careerism, pushed him farther and farther away from his earlier Irish nationalism: "The Fenian menace," Toner concluded, "produced in McGee a man who was almost anti-Irish."[95]

All this hit the romantic version of McGee like a bucket of iced water over the head. There was much substance in Toner's position. McGee was indeed concerned with "self-advancement," and a good lawyer for the prosecution would have little difficulty in assembling a series of McGee's private statements to support the case. But the "self-advancement" interpretation does not take us very far, and it fails to explain why McGee repeatedly took unpopular but principled stands throughout his career; his ultramontanism during the early 1850s, his colonization project of 1854–55, and his unequivocal anti-Fenianism during the 1860s are hardly signs of someone who put ambition above all else.

On the question of McGee's influence, Toner was undoubtedly correct to argue that McGee was not representative of Irish Canadian Catholic opinion in general – nobody could have been – and there is considerable evidence that McGee's strategy of isolating the Fenians backfired on him during the mid-1860s. As Toner argues, the view that McGee ensured that Irish Catholic Canadians would become or remain loyal to the Crown is just plain wrong. Nevertheless, McGee did enjoy the support of a substantial section of Catholic Irish Canadians, and Toner overstates the breadth (although not the depth) of the anti-McGee sentiment that developed in Montreal.[96] Toner was also right to argue that McGee's reputation was bolstered by his assassination, but he inverted the myth rather than transcending it, and wound up underplaying McGee's achievements. And Toner's view that McGee became "almost anti-Irish" is only sustainable if one adopts an ideological definition that equates Irishness with nationalism.[97]

The two most recent biographers of McGee broke with the hagiography of their predecessors without embracing Toner's critique of McGee's career and influence. In 1968 the Montreal lawyer Timothy Slattery published *The Assassination of D'Arcy McGee* – a rather misleading title, since the book was not actually about the assassination of D'Arcy McGee. A gifted and knowledgeable storyteller, Slattery was more interested in describing McGee's life than analysing his ideas or assessing their impact. While McGee's previous historians had assiduously avoided his drinking (with the exception of Skelton, who briefly addressed the issue), Slattery incorporated it into his narrative, including Macdonald's apocryphal remark: "Look here, McGee, this Cabinet can't afford two drunkards, and I'm not quitting."[98]

At times, Slattery's enthusiasm got the better of him, as he invented dialogue or embroidered scenes. The same problem occurred in his *'They Got to Find Mee Guilty Yet'* (1972), a book that actually was about the assassination of D'Arcy McGee and that focused on the trial of Patrick James Whelan for McGee's murder. Slattery the lawyer pointed out that "a reader cannot put himself in the position of a juror after a century. He lacks the advantages enjoyed by the juror who heard the witnesses, saw their hesitations, and studied their behaviour."[99] Slattery the storyteller happily ignored his own advice and provided imaginative recreations of how the witnesses sounded, looked, and acted. The difficulty with Slattery's books on McGee is that you can never be entirely sure where the lawyer ends and the storyteller begins. The great strength of his biography, however, lies in its detailed account of McGee's political career in Canada. Drawing on hitherto unused McGee correspondence, along with previously neglected archival and newspaper sources, Slattery's work marked a major advance over previous studies of McGee's Canadian career. What it lacked in analytical depth, it made up for in narrative breadth, at least as far as Canada is concerned.

While Slattery was preparing his books on McGee, Robin Burns was at the beginning of an eleven-year odyssey through McGee's writings. In his MA thesis, "D'Arcy McGee and the New Nationality," and his doctoral dissertation, "Thomas D'Arcy McGee: A Biography," Burns produced by far the best work on McGee's political career. The image of McGee as a "visionary" or "prophet," Burns argued in his MA thesis, obscured the fact that he developed a practical program for British American economic development, political union, minority rights, cultural independence, and constitutional change, and that he was an effective organizer as well as a brilliant orator.

In the highly fluid world of Canadian politics, Burns wrote, McGee's nationalist program transcended existing party divisions. To implement his ideas, McGee developed a strong base of support and formed a series of tactical political alliances that eventually brought him into the Conservative party and the pre-Confederation coalition, where he "realized many of his ambitions." In Burns's view, McGee was a shrewd and sophisticated politician, who was closely attuned to changing circumstances, approached politics as the art of the possible, and attacked the Fenians as latter-day Jacobins. McGee's "new nationality," Burns maintained, explained not only the emotive and intellectual power of his speeches and writings, but also his political pragmatism and his uncompromising opposition to Irish Canadian revolutionary nationalism. "His consistent and outspoken condemnation of Fenianism," Burns contended, "revealed the depth of his Canadian nationalism."[100]

The same search for consistency informed Burns's PHD dissertation, "Thomas D'Arcy McGee: A Biography," in which the focus was widened to include McGee's Irish and American careers. Both the breadth and the depth of his research were impressive; in his quest for sources, Burns spent almost as much time on the road as McGee had done himself. ("Good God!" cried his wife when she learned that years of research had taken Burns only up to McGee's twenty-third birthday. "Why didn't they assassinate him sooner?")[101] As well as providing a clear and compelling account of McGee's role in the Young Ireland movement, Burns was the first historian to explore fully McGee's American years from 1848 to 1857. In the process, he realized that the connection between McGee's Irish and Canadian nationalism was closer than he had previously thought, and that McGee's disillusionment with the United States was critically important in his transformation from radicalism to conservatism.

The key to understanding McGee's career, Burns concluded, lay in nineteenth-century romanticism; McGee, he wrote, "can best be understood as a romantic." All the central features of McGee's outlook – his historical consciousness, his idealization of the Celtic Middle Ages, his fascination with the sublime, his Catholicism, his nationalism, even his escapist ventures into alcoholism – were seen as typical characteristics of the romantic mindset. This underlying romanticism manifested itself in different ways, under the pressure of changing circumstances and possibilities. In Ireland, it found constitutional and then revolutionary expression through the medium of Young Ireland; in the United States, it was transformed into conservatism as McGee reacted against anti-historical, individualist, and materialistic social values. Having experienced failure and frustration in Ireland and America, McGee "found an emotional and intellectual home in Canada," where his romantic conception of the "new nationality" reflected and reinforced an emergent British American nationalism. "He died," wrote Burns, "with the knowledge that the romance of British America had become a reality."[102]

Burns's argument provided an elegant explanatory framework for McGee's career and neatly tied all the loose ends into a romantic package; in Burns's view, all the apparent contradictions in McGee's life were actually symptomatic of a deeper coherence. The trouble is, though, that the package is too neat. McGee's career cannot be subsumed under a single category, and the concept of romanticism can neither explain his specific responses to specific circumstances nor account for the inner tensions in his position – between passion and reason, principle and pragmatism, tradition and modernity, religion and nationalism, idealism and ambition, to name some of the major ones. And sometimes, as Freud might have said, a contradiction is just a contradiction.

In the pages that follow, I have tried to understand McGee on his own terms, to avoid the extremes of loyalist idealization and republican demonization, to situate McGee's writings in their immediate contexts, to provide a critical analysis of his developing ideas, and to discuss their impact on both sides of the Atlantic. I do not subscribe to the view that McGee was a "traitor to Ireland," unless it was traitorous to conclude that the best way of improving Ireland's condition was through far-reaching reform within the Union, rather than embarking on what he increasingly saw as a chimerical quest for national independence. Nor do I believe that McGee was the "leader" of Irish Catholics in Canada; to assume that he carried a homogeneous Irish Catholic community against Fenianism and into Confederation is to fall victim to a myth.

What he became, of course, was one of the most outspoken enemies of revolutionary republican nationalism, and a major voice for reform, the middle way, and the mutual accommodation of minority rights within the British Empire. Still, there was always something of the radical in McGee, even when he became a Conservative and even when he espoused moderation. This inner radicalism existed in a tense and ambivalent relationship with ethnoreligious conflict. On the one hand, McGee believed that the Irish in Canada should leave their hyphens behind them, reminding Orangemen that they were living on the St Lawrence, not the Boyne, and telling Irish Catholics that "we have no right ... to intrude our Irish patriotism on this soil."[103] On the other, his primary emotional identification was always with Ireland rather than Canada. Robin Burns was only partly correct when he argued that McGee's anti-Fenianism demonstrated the depth of his Canadian nationalism. In fact, the intensity of McGee's attack on revolutionary nationalism had as much to do with his Irish as his Canadian patriotism. Only by defeating Fenianism in Canada, he believed, could Canada serve as a model for Ireland.

In this sense, the contrast between McGee and Macdonald is instructive. After the Fenian invasion scares had passed, Macdonald in 1871 attempted to win over to the Conservative Party the pro-Fenian editor of the *Irish Canadian*, Patrick Boyle. "The paper might be as factious as it pleased about Irish home politics, or even as to New York movements, for all I would care," Macdonald told Frank Smith. "As long as it pursued that course it would keep up its present subscription list and influence."[104] For Macdonald, Canadian politics came first. If Boyle's newspaper supported the Conservatives in Canada, it could be as radical as it liked concerning Ireland; if such radicalism brought more Canadian Fenians into the Conservative fold, so much the better. McGee could never have taken such a position; it ran counter to his deeply held and long-standing belief that Fenianism was a menace to his religion and his country. Fenianism, he informed James Moylan in 1865, was "the worst obstacle, the Devil has ever invented for the Irish, an *irreligious revolutionary society*, in which patriotism takes the garb, of indifferentism, or hostility to religion. This is *the* enemy of the Irish Cause in our time; and it is that, every man should combat, *first and foremost*."[105] Compromise with such an enemy was out of the question.

McGee's anti-Fenianism cannot be explained only in political or religious terms; there was also a critically important psychological dimension to his position. He had himself heard the siren call of revolutionary nationalism and in the spring and summer of 1848 had moved from ideas to action. He had himself been an American-based republican who advocated armed struggle against all manifestations of monarchical government and who once argued that "Canada needs a revolution or needs nothing."[106] He had himself been intensely anglophobic, standing by Niagara Falls while a cataract raged in his breast, cursing the Union Jack across the border, and vowing vengeance upon the oppressors of his country. McGee knew better than anyone the powerful emotional appeal of Fenianism, since he had experienced something very like it himself. That is why he felt that Fenianism had to be engaged at an emotional as well as intellectual level, why he knew in his bones that the movement was "not to be put down, by half apologetic pleadings of 'good intentions.'"[107] And that is why his reaction against revolutionary nationalism was so intense, so extreme. As Richard O'Gorman put it in 1852, McGee was "energetically and angrily protesting against his former self and the dangerous Companions who led his young feet astray."[108]

It is no wonder that McGee became such a passionate enemy of Fenianism. He was trying to exorcise the Fenian within himself.

PART ONE

Ireland, the United States

I believe I am not prejudiced towards England. If you cast aside
the multitude of the political crimes perpetrated by her rulers,
I can look upon her literature, can admire her social institutions,
and do homage to the genius of her many illustrious children
with alacrity. But when I look upon her in connexion with
Ireland my indignation outruns my judgment.

McGee, *A SPEECH Delivered before the Repealers of Watertown, Mass., and the
Adjoining Towns, on the REPEAL OF THE UNION*, 1843

CHAPTER TWO

One of the Macs
April 1825 – April 1844

On Monday, 4 July 1842, the Boston Repeal Association met at the Marlborough Chapel to celebrate American independence and to support Daniel O'Connell's campaign for repeal of the Act of Union, which had united Britain and Ireland in 1801. Seated on the platform were the prominent figures of Boston's rapidly growing Irish Catholic community, and some of their leading American supporters; the speakers included well-known "friends of Ireland" such as John W. James and Lieutenant Lawrence Devlin of the U.S. Navy. Before an "exceedingly enthusiastic" audience, O'Connell was described as the "Washington of Ireland," and the Repeal movement was viewed through the lens of 1776: England could be driven out of Ireland, declared Devlin, only "at the point of the bayonet."[1]

In the middle of the proceedings, D'Arcy McGee was invited to the podium. He had arrived in the United States two months earlier and had celebrated his seventeenth birthday on the brig *Leo*, bound for Quebec from Wexford, and captained by one of his father's friends. Sailing up the St Lawrence, he had registered "the sublime genius of Catholicism among the pine woods of Canada, where the mountain tops are crowned with crosses, the landmarks of the first missionaries." From Quebec, he went south to join his aunt and uncle, Bella and Charles Morgan, in Providence, Rhode Island; a few weeks later, he moved with his cousin to Boston, in search of work. Staying with family friends, they trudged from newspaper office to newspaper office, only to find that "in general they want boys to do dirty work." But in the evenings he attended the city's Irish American temperance meetings, where his oratorical powers quickly attracted the attention of John W. James, who invited him to address the upcoming meeting on 4 July. With this Independence Day speech, McGee's North American political career was born.[2]

The listeners were left in no doubt about his nationalist sentiments. McGee spoke of the sufferings of Ireland "at the hands of a heartless, bigoted, despotic government," praised the Americans for throwing off "the galling yoke of British allegiance and oppression," and declared that "the same holy struggle could now be carried out in Ireland." "Many are the tales told me while at home by old men," he said, "themselves in many cases victims, of the harrowing sufferings endured by the people, from the tyranny of their upstart resident landlords, descendants of the adventurers brought over by Cromwell." But the days of "British allegiance and oppression" in Ireland were numbered. Thanks to Father Mathew's temperance movement, the Irish people were becoming sober, and Ireland sober would be Ireland free. Thanks to O'Connell's leadership, the Irish people were "learning to know their rights and feel their power" and would once again have their own parliament on College Green. The women of Irish America had their part to play. If they were single, they should form relationships only with nationalist men; if they were married, they should encourage their husbands to participate in the struggle for Irish liberty. And once Ireland was free, the country could return to its magnificent past. The Repeal Association, he declared, was trying "to make Ireland what she once was" – great, glorious, and free. "Such she was," he concluded, "and shall be again."[3]

McGee's speech fitted perfectly with a fifty-year tradition of Irish American nationalist rhetoric, in which the themes of British oppression, Cromwellian dispossession, and landlord tyranny were combined with the image of America as a model for Ireland, and with the belief that the quest for Irish independence was a sacred struggle. His emphasis on the political influence of women fitted equally well with broader American beliefs that republican wives and mothers must inculcate patriotic principles into their husbands and sons. His references to Father Mathew and O'Connell fed into a long-standing conviction that Irish independence was just a matter of time, and his approach to Irish history tapped into popular notions of "ancient splendour and present misery." McGee hit the resonant frequency with every phrase; it is no wonder that his speech was such a success.[4]

"My reception at the repeal meeting," he wrote to Aunt Bella, "was everything I could wish, even from my own countrymen." "If he were a sample of the Wexford boys," commented John W. James after the speech, "I hope we should soon have a cargo of them." McGee was asked to go on a speaking tour of New England "to arouse the repealers"; Patrick Donahoe, the proprietor of the *Boston Pilot*, appointed him the newspaper's agent for Connecticut and offered him a three-year contract. Within days of his speech, McGee was on the road, giving lectures in Hartford and New Haven on temperance and Repeal, and sending articles back to Donahoe. "You shall see occasional verses from me in his paper – all on National Subjects – whether Prose or Verse," he told his aunt. "By which I hope to make a better bargain with him, than a common apprentice would." Right from the start of his career, he combined patriotism with a shrewd sense of self-interest. By holding off on the contract, McGee was able to increase its value, and he was eventually offered $225 over three years. Although the final terms remain unclear (there was still no "lasting agreement" in November), Donahoe got his money's worth; McGee had hit the ground running and would keep up the pace for the rest of his career. Before long, he began to send articles back to Ireland under the pseudonym "One of the Macs"; his father, James McGee (or "McGhee," as he spelled it), reported that they were "read with much interest by your old friends," and commented with pride on the abilities and accomplishments of his sons.[5]

The "Macs" were a family on the move. McGee had been born in Carlingford, County Louth, on 13 April 1825, but he did not live there long. His father was a boatman in the Customs and Excise service and had been transferred the previous July to Rush, near Dublin. He stayed in Rush until 31 October 1825 and then moved to Garron Point, near Cushendall in County Antrim; this remained his home until

Point of Garron looking east, 1828. The site of McGee's upbringing on the Antrim Coast, between the ages of three and eight (1828–33). This was probably the house where his father worked for the Customs and Excise service. (Andrew Nichol, Ulter Museum, Belfast)

March 1833, when he was appointed tidewaiter at Wexford. His family stayed in Carlingford until 1827 or early 1828, when they joined him in Cushendall.[6]

The Macs could trace their ancestry back to Islandmagee, a peninsula on the northwest side of Belfast Lough. According to family tradition, they were descended from one of only three men who had survived a Protestant massacre of three thousand Islandmagee Catholics in 1641. "It is a source of pride to the present writer," McGee remarked in 1852, "that the blood of that martyred clan flows in his veins." The story of thousands of Catholics being driven to their death over the Gobbins Cliffs is still told today and occasionally surfaces in mainstream academic writings. It is, in fact, one of the many myths that run through Irish history. There were nowhere near three thousand people living on the peninsula, there is no evidence that anyone was pushed over the cliffs, and the death toll was actually around fifty.[7]

Redbay Castle, near Cushendall, 1828. Part of McGee's early world, and the setting of his first work of fiction, *Eva Macdonald* (Boston 1844). (Andrew Nichol, Ulster Museum, Belfast)

Nevertheless, the events of November 1641 were an ugly enough example of what today is euphemistically called "ethnic cleansing." The depositions of the survivors, taken at Carrickfergus twelve years later, tell of such men as Captain Alexander Adair from Ballymena bragging that he had "killed a number of the Irish not sparing man, woman nor child & specially named one Ever McGee an aged man whom they had killed & after they had killed him in his bed fired the house & so consumed him in that fire." Some Islandmagee inhabitants, such as Margaret Lowrye, tried to hide potential victims; others, such as William Gillis, participated in the slaughter of Catholic families. Many of the victims were indeed from the McGee clan. Brian Magee stated that he was the only survivor in his family; Turlogh Magee testified that his parents and three brothers were killed, along with his sister and her five children. After Turlogh Magee's evidence, he was beaten up outside the courtroom by William Gillis. A Truth and Reconciliation Commission this was not.[8]

Family "memories" of such events, distorted and exaggerated as they were, could only strengthen a sense of oppression; along with the tales told him "while at home by old men," they helped to form McGee's early political consciousness. Both his parents were firmly entrenched in the nationalist tradition, and they transmitted their attitudes and beliefs to their children. McGee's father supported O'Connell and looked forward to "the regeneration of our long misgoverned and oppressed Country, under the tyranny of the truculant [sic] Saxon yoke." In the evenings, McGee read articles to his father from the liberal-nationalist *Wexford Independent*, which he later described as "his primer in politics."[9]

Even more important was the influence of his mother, Dorcas Morgan. Her family had supported the rising of 1798, and McGee was proud of her "good rebel blood." "She instilled in my mind a love of poetry, and for the old legends of my native land," he recalled. "If I have any merit as a writer of verse, the poetic fire was inherited from her dear spirit, and was nurtured by the sweet Irish melodies she sang to me in childhood." She had high expectations of her son, as McGee's sister, also named Dorcas, wrote in 1841: "My Mother said when he was born he would be a great man yet with the help of God, and to the day of her death she lived in that belief." With this background, it was impossible for McGee to have been anything other than an Irish nationalist. Nor is it surprising that he spent most of his life trying to fulfill his mother's prophecy, albeit in ways that she could not have anticipated.[10]

It was, however, his mother's absence rather than her presence that had the greatest impact on McGee. During the spring of 1833, while the family was travelling from Garron Point to Wexford, his mother was thrown from her carriage, and she died of her injuries on 22 August. James McGee found himself in a new job in a new town as the single parent of eight children – five girls and three boys, the youngest of whom, James Edward, was three years old. The family was plunged into crisis; eight-year-old Thomas, the fourth child and second brother, had to cope with a shattering sense of loss and with the responsibility of looking after his younger siblings. Like his brothers and sisters, he came to idealize his mother – something that came into sharper focus when his father remarried in March 1840. James McGee's second wife, Margaret Dea, was three months pregnant at the time; their son, John Joseph, was born that August.[11]

Possibly because of the circumstances of the second marriage, deep tensions arose between the children and their stepmother. One of Thomas's sisters, Mary, had died in 1839; when a second sister, Betsy, died a few months after Margaret entered the house, the young Dorcas McGee immediately blamed her stepmother for Betsy's death. "From the day of my father's making a second choice," she wrote, "the shock was given [from] which she never recovered." If McGee's mother symbolized the warmth, affection, and security that had vanished on the road to Wexford, Margaret Dea was cast in the role of the intrusive outsider upon whom resentments were focused.[12]

Family tensions were exacerbated by precarious economic circumstances. As an excise officer, James McGee was part of an expanding Catholic middle class, whose ranks formed the backbone of O'Connell's campaigns for Catholic Emancipation and Repeal. By the standards of the day, he was relatively well off; the house he leased on Paradise Road was valued at a respectable three pounds fifteen shillings a year. But his ability to feed and clothe his family depended on the volume of trade coming into Wexford, and the town was suffering from an economic downturn in 1841. The family had also been hit with crippling medical bills, not only for Betsy but also for Thomas, who had been "very ill" with typhus for three months during the winter of 1840–41. Laurence, Thomas's older brother, could supplement the family income by working at sea, but they were still hard pressed to make ends meet.[13]

Despite such pressures, his father was able to send Thomas to a local "pay school," run by Michael Donnelly. The pay schools had evolved from the eighteenth-century hedge schools and were being replaced in the 1830s by a centralized government-funded system of education. But Donnelly had an excellent reputation as a teacher and continued to attract the sons of Wexford's Catholic middle class. If similar schools are any guide, McGee would have been taught the basics of reading, writing, and arithmetic, and then given a good grounding in history, literature, the classics, and the central tenets of Catholic doctrine. Don-

nelly was not only a devout Catholic but in all likelihood also a firm
nationalist. His father had been hanged at New Ross after one of the
bloodiest battles in the rising of 1798, and he himself had joined the
stream of refugees escaping to the rebel stronghold of Wexford, where
a makeshift revolutionary committee struggled to impose its authority
over an embattled community, where loyalist prisoners were piked to
death on the bridge, and where the triumphant forces of the Crown
stuck the decapitated heads of United Irishmen on the courthouse rail-
ings. Donnelly's stories formed part of an oral tradition that influenced
McGee at least as much as his formal education. Donnelly regarded
McGee as his star student, and many years later he talked with pride
about his "best-loved pupil and brightest scholar," the patriot and poet
who became a minister of the Crown in Canada.[14]

Among the lore about 1798 that McGee probably picked up in Wexford was the popular belief that the rising would have succeeded had
the rebels been able to abstain from alcohol. "Drunkenness, not British
valor defeated the Irish insurrection of 1798," he asserted in 1845; "the
spirit of malt, not the spirit of the Lion, prostrated the gallant rebels of
Kildare and Wexford." Such views had appeared sporadically in the
Irish nationalist press since the early nineteenth century and were given
much greater emphasis in the late 1830s and early 1840s during Father
Mathew's temperance campaign. Beginning in Limerick in 1839, when
more than 100,000 people took the pledge of total abstinence, Father
Mathew went on some 350 temperance missions over the next four
years; by May 1841, he claimed that more than five million people had
joined the movement. Speaking before immense audiences throughout Ireland, the "Apostle of Temperance" equated abstinence with self-
discipline, self-respect, and self-improvement, and insisted that sobriety would unite all creeds and classes in Christian harmony, thus eradicating the religious and social divisions that fractured Irish life.[15]

McGee was swept along in the current. His first published poem
was written in anticipation of Father Mathew's arrival in Wexford on
8 April 1840, when McGee was only fourteen years old:

> Rejoice, ye hearts, who love
> Your nation to be free,
> No more shall whiskey prove
> A source of slavery,
> He comes – the conquering hero comes,
> And with him brings us victory.[16]

Some 30,000 people took the pledge in Wexford, including McGee and his father. The first organization that D'Arcy McGee ever joined was the town's Juvenile Temperance Society; the first of his many published speeches was an address to the Wexford Temperance Union, delivered in January 1842 at the age of sixteen. He rejoiced that Father Mathew had saved six million Irish people from the "slavery of intemperance," but he warned that there had been too much backsliding and complained that the pledge breakers had been getting away with their "disgraceful conduct." They should be hooted with derision through the streets, he declared; such social ostracism would ensure that they never veered from the right path. A few days later, his second published poem, "Sobriety – An Ode," appeared in the *Wexford Independent*. Here, McGee praised the "Genius of Sobriety" for spreading peace, prosperity, industry, and liberty, and for "leaving behind crime, slavery, and shame." McGee later wrote that Father Mathew was "the moral regenerator of his people."[17]

Although Father Mathew insisted that the temperance movement should be non-political, O'Connell and his fellow Repealers attempted to harness teetotalism to the nationalist cause. There was a large degree of opportunism at work. O'Connell had been a strong supporter of the drink industry and had invested a large sum of money in his son's brewery. But he took the pledge in 1840 (later releasing himself on "medical grounds"), repeatedly identified temperance with Repeal, and reaped the political benefits. Temperance bands played at Repeal meetings, and temperance reading rooms became centres of Repeal activity; for tens of thousands of Irish people, the two causes were indistinguishable. McGee was no exception. In the summer of 1841, his sister wrote that "his heart burns within him" for the cause of Repeal and that he had "distinguished himself at Public assemblies for his eloquence."[18] McGee's instantaneous involvement in Boston's Irish Catholic temperance and Repeal organizations was simply a transatlantic extension of his earlier activities in Wexford.

This raises an obvious question. Why, if McGee was so devoted to the cause of Repeal, did he leave the country for the United States? In Boston, he spoke of "the weary manhood of my exile," but there was nothing remotely weary about him, and he was not an exile in any meaningful sense of the word. Like the overwhelming majority of the American Irish, he was a voluntary migrant; in his particular case, the decision to cross the Atlantic had more to do with personal factors than with politics.[19] Above all, he wanted to escape the tense family atmosphere that had arisen with the arrival of his stepmother. Towards the end of 1840, a way out presented itself. His mother's sister, Bella Morgan, wrote from Providence, Rhode Island, inviting Thomas and Dorcas to stay with her family. Although they were keen to join her, they needed both the transatlantic fare and their father's permission. In March 1841 Dorcas wrote to Bella asking for financial assistance, and that summer Thomas went on two voyages with his brother Laurence, probably to earn the money and to get away from their stepmother. After thinking it over, their father eventually agreed to let them go, and by the spring of 1842 they were ready to emigrate.[20]

Initially, Thomas and Dorcas planned to sail from Liverpool, but the emigration agents in the city did not return their letters, and they instead took advantage of a cut-rate price on the *Leo* from Wexford to Quebec. Laurence, who was beginning a career as a sailor, signed on as a deckhand, and the three of them prepared for the voyage. On 4 April, the day before the ship set sail, McGee attended the Wexford Temperance Festival, where five hundred people crammed into the Assembly Rooms under the banner "Let Brotherly Love Continue" while the "phil-harmonic band" played "several exquisite airs which would soften the most obdurate heart." Here, the chairman of the meeting, Charles Arthur Walker, presented McGee with "a book from the Juvenile Society, as a token of their esteem on his departure for America." In his farewell speech, McGee spoke of his work over the previous three years to spread "sobriety and self culture among the young hearts of Wexford," and emphasized the importance of maintaining the momentum. The "mothers of Wexford," he wrote, had a central role in preventing their husbands and sons from reneging on their pledges.[21]

The memory of his own mother and his two dead sisters weighed heavily on him. His early poems were full of farewells, with the compensatory hope of reunion in the next world or better days ahead. In the explanatory note to his poem "Farewell to My Friends," written just before he left Wexford, McGee described himself as an "emigrant, about to leave his native land for ever." His sadness at leaving friends who had helped him through the dark days was counterbalanced by the sense of possibility in the New World:

> Yet I go to a land, where the children of Erin
> Are welcomed to honour, to freedom and peace –
> Where the sons of Saint Patrick no tyranny fearing,
> Respected may live, and unenvied increase.

Three days into the voyage, he wrote "To Wexford in the Distance," which equated crossing the Atlantic with crossing the threshold into adulthood, with all its "care and sorrow's sense"; the brooding sense of responsibility proved difficult to shake off. But Aunt Bella awaited in Providence and might fill the gap left by his mother's death. Within weeks of their meeting, he began to describe himself as "your affectionate Son," and later he wished her "All the love I would give my mother if she were living." If McGee had left home in search of a substitute mother, in Bella Morgan he found one.[22]

And so Thomas and Dorcas McGee arrived in the United States via Canada in May 1842. The president, John Tyler, had been in office just over a year; he had encountered United Irish émigrés in his youth, and his son Robert was a leading American supporter of the Repeal movement.[23] Tyler presided over a rapidly expanding population that was thrusting westwards into the Oregon Territory, and into California and Texas, where pressure was building for annexation to the United

States. Methodist missionaries were moving into the Pacific Northwest, and the Mormons were on the trek that would eventually take
them to Salt Lake City. In upstate New York, the Millerites were preparing for the end of the world and the Second Coming, expected in
1843. In New England, the Transcendentalists combined romanticism
with Puritanical strains of mysticism to articulate new individualistic
spiritual values for a New World. In the northern cities, the Industrial
Revolution was increasing the general level of prosperity while accen-
tuating class divisions; in the south, cotton production generated western expansion, buttressing a planter elite above a broader population
of small farmers and a substratum of poor whites, and solidifying an
oppressive system of slavery. Throughout the country, but particularly
in the north, the railway boom was just beginning; railway mileage
would increase tenfold over the next two decades. Immigration was
accelerating to unprecedented levels, and Irish Catholics were becoming an increasingly important presence in American life, even before
the famine of 1846–51. These, then, were some of the central features of
the country to which the seventeen-year-old McGee emigrated – western expansion, religious experimentation, industrial growth, chattel
slavery, and rising immigration, all occurring within the framework
of a Protestant political, social, and religious culture.

Most people of Irish ethnicity in the United States were (and remain)
Protestant, and most Irish immigrants – Protestants and Catholics alike
– lived outside the major American cities; the view that Irish Catholics
were prepared to put up with urban squalor in return for the benefits
of communal solidarity is a recurrent myth in Irish American historiography. Equally exaggerated is the belief that the typical Irish Catholic experience in Protestant America was characterized by "No Irish
Need Apply" discrimination. The Irish American experience was far
too varied to be contained within such stereotypes of victimization,
and in many areas the Irish Catholics not only adjusted quickly to their
new environment but forced the environment to adjust to them. Nevertheless, the fact remains that Irish Catholics were much more likely
than other ethnic groups to settle in cities, with the points of greatest
concentration in New York, Philadelphia, and Boston. And in these
cities, many Irish Catholics did indeed face deep poverty and widespread prejudice.[24]

In McGee's Boston, with its population of about 94,000, the Irish Catholic presence had been growing over the previous two decades and probably constituted just over 15 percent of the population – a proportion that would rise significantly during the famine. Many of the immigrants worked as unskilled labourers in the city's booming construction industry, and crowded into increasingly unsanitary tenements in the North End and Fort Hill. Shopkeepers and publicans formed the next rung up the ladder, and above them stood a small but energetic professional middle class of lawyers, doctors, and teachers. Organizations such as the Repeal Association and the Young Catholics Friend Society, along with the *Boston Pilot* newspaper and a variety of temperance, literary, and musical societies, contributed to a distinct group consciousness, which was reinforced by the minority status of Irish Catholics in the city.[25]

Irish immigrants competed with Protestant Bostonians for jobs, triggering fears of Catholic incursions into the heartland of Protestant America. Conspiracy theories about Catholic plots to conquer the United States found a ready audience; lurid tales about nuns trapped in convents became instant bestsellers; and sermons about the Roman Antichrist echoed in Protestant ears. Anti-Catholic sentiments were translated into sporadic action with the burning of the Ursuline Convent in Charlestown in 1834, the Broad Street riot of 1837, and the public humiliation of the Irish Montgomery Guards by other militia companies later that year. Yet such events demonstrated the limits as well as the extent of anti-Catholicism in and around pre-famine Boston. The city's newspapers and leading politicians unequivocally condemned the outbreaks of violence and expressed support for the Montgomery Guards. No anti-Catholic political organizations grew out of the tensions during the 1830s, and the five years before McGee's arrival in 1842 were relatively quiet.[26]

In assessing his new environment, McGee viewed anti-Catholicism in Boston as an irritant rather than a threat. The Catholic Church in New England, he wrote, was "progressing rapidly"; thirty years ago there had only been one Catholic Church in the region, and now there were fifty. It was true, he continued, that a bewildering variety of Protestant cranks and fanatics fulminated against Rome, but they were very much on the margins. "We have a sect called mere 'Christians,'" he informed the folk back home, "all grades of Baptists, Pantheists or Infidels, Mormons, Transcendentalists, and Millerites, who have fixed the consummation of all flesh for the 23rd of April"; the anticipated all-consuming conflagration would have to be postponed, he added, if the snow still lay on the ground. "They disagree in all points," he noted, "save one, viz., to abuse the poor Papists, God help them." Such "brain-less Infidels" had little popular support, and public opinion had "long since condemned" such acts as the burning of the Ursuline Convent. In fact, he wrote, the legislature was planning to indemnify the convent, and there was a great deal of sympathy in Boston for the Catholic Irish and the cause of Repeal.[27]

McGee focused most of his attention on Irish rather than American affairs during his first two years in Boston. Moving among the city's Irish middle class and lodging with Patrick Donahoe, his central concern was the promotion of Irish nationalism in the United States. Travelling throughout New England and New York, gathering subscriptions for the *Boston Pilot*, and talking on "the good cause of Repeal," he was full of energy and optimism. From Hartford, he wrote about the city's new Catholic Church, and the good work of the St Patrick's Temperance Society. From Newport, he penned a wry account of the town's spa ("Like most watering-places," he remarked, it was "full of bustle, melancholy faces, hypocondriacs [sic], and extortion"). From New Haven he told Aunt Bella about his attraction to a "fair Georgian" who had attended his lectures, taken the pledge, and "subscribed handsomely" to the cause of Repeal. His personal letters had a strong streak of humorous self-deprecation, as if he could not quite believe his good fortune. He wrote of his involvement in "polly-tricks," described a talk he was about to give on the democratic principles of O'Connell and Andrew Jackson as "ahem! a very elaborate disquisition indeed," and warned his aunt not to praise him too much. "You know I'm proud enough already," he said, "and youl [sic] spoil me by making a practice of such things."[28]

By September 1842, he had launched his first literary project, a series of articles on "Irish Authors," later broadened to include "Authoresses." It ran through forty numbers up to February 1844 and was the first clear statement of his commitment to cultural nationalism. His articles were designed to demonstrate *that Ireland is a nation, at least, in intellect,"* and to assert a sense of dignity against the country's detractors. Viewing Irish literature through the lens of politics, he praised the "courage and great purity of intention" that informed the poetry of William Drennan and his fellow United Irishmen, and described Thomas Moore's *Irish Melodies* as a "masterly combination of sweet sounds, historic truths, and pure patriotism."[29]

Among Ireland's novelists, he singled out Charles Maturin and Lady Morgan for special praise. McGee commended Maturin for his "powerful and priceless national love," and described Lady Morgan as "the most eminent female writer of the age," who administered literary punishments to "orange butchers" and distinguished herself as "a firm advocate of the rights of woman." Her *Wild Irish Girl*, McGee wrote, was "a romance of the deepest and most impressive order." Taken together, he argued, the writings of Maturin and Lady Morgan "materially tended to revive the national hopes torn and broken on the wheel that bore native government downward and crushed Robert Emmet and his compatriots." Irish literature, he believed, boosted nationalist morale, instilled a sense of pride ("*The memory of Irish Genius shall not sleep*"), and provided a compelling argument for political independence. "At this time, when Ireland is striving for the right to govern herself," he concluded his series, "it cannot be superfluous to show that she possesses wisdom, learning, patriotism and ability sufficient to the task."[30]

A similar purpose lay behind McGee's writings on Irish mythology and music. Above all, he wanted to connect Irish culture to ancient Eastern civilizations and thus provide it with an eminently respectable pedigree. Like Charles Vallancey before him, McGee argued that Ireland's mythology constituted "the most convincing proofs of her eastern origin, and this parallel if fully developed would discover the closest affinity between the milesian aborigines of Ireland and the most celebrated nations of the eastern hemisphere." He compared Irish druidism with Persian fire worship and located Thomas Crofton Croker's fairy legends within a wider European and Asian context. Turning to the writings of early orientalist scholars such as Sir William Jones and William Marsden, McGee maintained that Eastern music, played on the harp, had come into Ireland from the Mediterranean before the birth of Christ.[31]

McGee believed that the greatest exponent of Irish music and poetry had been Ossian, "the Homer of the Celtic races of Ireland and Scotland," whose "majestic grandeur" had never been surpassed. After the "Invasion of the Saxons of the 12th century," McGee wrote, the tradition took on a sorrowful tone, out of which came such "beautiful and original" melodies as *The Coolin, Aileen Aroon, Molly Astore, Farewell to Lochabar,* [and] *Emun ac Knuc.*" But the Irish had more than the Saxons to worry about. The "Scotch" had tried to appropriate Ossian as one of themselves and had unscrupulously engrafted Irish compositions onto their own "barbarous and barren Minstrelsy" – pretty much what one would expect from a nation of plagiarists, in his view. There was clearly no sense of pan-Celtic solidarity here.[32]

In truth, McGee's "proofs" were far from convincing. Charles Vallancey was hardly a reliable source, and Ossian was a mythical figure rather than a real person. Nor did William Jones and William Marsden make the kind of claims that McGee attributed to them. Jones did write that "the wild, but charming melodies of the ancient highlanders" were based on one of the many scales that could be found in China and India, and the Wicklow-born Marsden noted in passing, "The Sumatran tunes very much resemble, to my ear, those of the native Irish." But neither man had set out to demonstrate the oriental basis of Irish music, and the differences were far more striking than the similarities. What McGee was doing, in effect, was to take fragments of disparate information, combine them with fanciful speculation, and fashion them into a serviceable myth to buttress the cause of Irish nationhood. He was not the first to adopt this approach and would be far from the last.[33]

Telling the Irish how great they were was a surefire passport to popularity; to do it at the age of seventeen, with such a broad range of knowledge and in such a confident tone, was guaranteed to pay dividends. The reactions to his "Irish Authors and Authoresses" were uniformly positive. "He has genius and talents of a high order," commented one reviewer. "The youthful author," wrote another, "is no common person, but one destined ere long to occupy a commanding position in the field of literature."

But McGee was not only writing about literature; he was also composing his own patriotic poems. His first poem for the *Boston Pilot* was a love song to Ireland: "And I love her the more that she is not free," it concluded, "For she will and must arise." In "To Ireland! – Written on the 4th of July," he wrote of the "fiercer passion" generated by the thought that the "earth's basest" had ground a nation of heroes into poverty. "Will none arise with sword or cross / To drive the fiend from your land?" he asked. When the sons of ancient men emulated the courage of their forefathers, he wrote, Ireland would recover its freedom and former glory. Variations on this theme would run through his poetry during the rest of the decade.[34]

Along with these public pursuits, McGee concerned himself with the health and well-being of his sister. Dorcas had been taken ill in Providence and had stayed with the Morgans while McGee moved to Boston. After he moved in with the Donahoes (where he was, he said, "as comfortable as I can be"), McGee set out to find accommodation and employment for her. Mrs Donahoe offered to take Dorcas in too, and McGee fixed her up with work as a dressmaker. In the fall of 1843 he told his aunt that Dorcas had arrived safely in Boston and was settling in well. He placed great value on family solidarity and success. Two years later he wrote to Aunt Bella, "I am not one to be thwarted in my sole ambition – the elevation of all my dear Mothers [sic] family and yours." Throughout his life, McGee made a point of looking after his relatives; his doors were always open, even though he spent long periods away from home.[35]

This was certainly the case in the summer of 1843, as he travelled through New England on his "Repeal mission," raising money for the cause. In Ireland, O'Connell had declared that 1843 would be the year of Repeal, and he organized a series of "monster meetings" to bring irresistible popular pressure to bear on Sir Robert Peel's government in London. O'Connell's strategy captured the imagination of Irish American nationalists, who redoubled their efforts to support the campaign. All things seemed possible. If the British government was rash enough to repress the Repeal movement, argued an editorial in the *Boston Pilot*, the result would be rebellion, and Irish Americans would rush money, men, arms, and ammunition to their compatriots. The task was to push the agitation to the point at which the government would be faced with the alternative of "Repeal or Rebellion," as well as assuring Irish Repealers that the "all-conquerable arm of America" was behind them.[36]

By the spring of 1843, McGee declared that the Repeal movement was making "glorious progress" in America, and pointed out that the Massachusetts legislature had given the Boston Friends of Ireland "the use of their Hall of Assembly for a special meeting" to publicize the cause, raise money, and win the support of Boston's leading politicians. In May, McGee became the Boston Repeal Association's first secretary. Addressing Repeal meetings throughout New England, he spoke in "burning language" about British oppression and asserted that the time had passed when Britain's "myriad robbers and cut throats" could "butcher a people daring to writhe beneath their chains." Working his county connection, he drummed up contributions from fifty-three Wexford men in Boston, and compared Wexford's role in the rising of 1798 with that of Massachusetts in the American Revolution. Britain was afraid of another Irish revolution, he argued, and the Irish would settle for nothing less than Repeal; with the backing of Irish America, O'Connell would prevail. The message hit home; by the end of July, he reported to a packed meeting of the Boston Repeal Association that his latest mission had raised $225. At the same time, he resigned as secretary so that he could spend still more time on the road.[37]

In September he attended the National Repeal Convention in New York, as the delegate from Connecticut. The pace of events in Ireland had quickened. At a "monster meeting" on the Hill of Tara the previous month, more than half a million people had gathered to hear O'Connell promise the impending liberation of Ireland; another mass meeting was being planned for October at Clontarf, and talk of revolution was in the air. Against this background, more than four hun-

Repeal meeting at Tara. The "monster meeting" at Tara in 1843, where the largest crowd in Ireland's history gathered to hear Daniel O'Connell espouse the cause of Repeal amid the display of nationalist symbols and the demonstration of popular power (*Illustrated London News*)

dred delegates converged on New York to discuss ways of helping the movement. At the convention, McGee mixed with such people as Edmund Bailey O'Callaghan, one of the leaders of the Canadian Rebellion of 1837, now living in New York and an advocate of moral rather than physical force. Also attending were some of the surviving United Irishmen in the United States, including the radical journalists John Binns and Thomas O'Connor. Amid such company, McGee gave "an eloquent and warm address" to the delegates and proposed a vote of thanks to O'Connell.[38]

All this was predictable enough, given the meteoric course of McGee's career. Less predictable, given his blood-and-thunder speeches of the summer, was his position on the Protestant aristocracy and Orangeism in Ireland. Unlike the majority of the delegates, McGee argued that Irish nationalists must bring the Irish gentry and at least "a portion of the Orangemen" into the Repeal movement – an early example of his inclusive idealism.[39] If this was a minority position in the United States, it corresponded with official nationalist thought in Ireland; both O'Connell and the younger generation of radical intellectuals grouped around the *Nation* newspaper in Dublin emphasized the importance of bringing Protestants into the fold.

But there was a massive discrepancy between aspiration and actuality, and McGee fell into the familiar nationalist pitfall of exaggerating Protestant support for Repeal. After he asserted that Orangemen were joining the Repeal movement and named prominent Protestants who supported O'Connell, he was taken to task by a Protestant Irish American writer for his "disingenuous and deceitful remarks." It was utterly misleading to imply that the Protestants who supported Repeal were typical of their community, argued the writer; one could just as easily list a number of Catholics who supported the Union and maintain that they represented majority Catholic opinion. The vast majority of Protestants, including himself, the writer said, rejected Repeal on the grounds that it was designed to destroy their religion. McGee replied that he had never meant to suggest that all Protestants supported Repeal, but merely to demonstrate that *"some* Protestants are for Repeal, because they love country better than sectarian prejudices." All his opponent had done, McGee added, was to prove that *"some* are opposed to it, and I know that it is because they love ascendancy more than liberty." In taking this position, he underestimated the depth and breadth of Protestant opposition to Repeal, and equated anti-Repeal sentiment with religious bigotry and Protestant privilege.[40]

Here, in miniature, was one of the central problems of nineteenth-century Irish nationalism. In theory, the Repeal movement was open to all Irish people, Protestants and Catholics alike; in practice, it was largely (but not totally) associated with Catholicism. Like other Irish Catholic nationalists, McGee latched onto the few Protestants who joined the movement as evidence of Irish nationalism's inherently non-sectarian character. But the other side of this position was the assumption that Protestant opposition to non-sectarian nationalism must be the product of "sectarian prejudice" and privilege. If – as was actually the case – almost all Irish Protestants rejected Repeal, the implications for Irish nationalism were dangerous at best, disastrous at worst. To view virtually an entire community as being bigoted could easily become a form of bigotry itself, made all the more insidious by the high moral ground from which the perspective was taken. And to argue that Irish nationalism should embrace a community that rejected its central premises was hardly a recipe for success. It is no wonder that McGee, in common with most of his compatriots, preferred to focus his attention on those Protestants who joined the Repeal movement, and chose not to think too deeply about the majority who did not.

If there was a major contradiction between the ideal and the real in McGee's approach to national unity, there were also deep tensions within his attitude to Anglo-Irish relations. "I believe I am not prejudiced towards England," he wrote in November 1843. "If you cast aside the multitude of the political crimes perpetrated by her rulers, I can look upon her literature, can admire her social institutions, and do homage to the genius of her many illustrious children with alacrity. But when I look upon her in connexion with Ireland my indignation outruns my judgment." The indignation pulsed through his writings; he believed that "the history of British rule in Ireland is one of the most inhuman compilations of cruelty with which the annals of the world abound," and noted with approval that native-born Americans and Irish "exiles" shared "a communion of hate for England" that was "restless and undying in its operation."[41]

Such language pointed in the direction of separatism, towards an Irish version of the American Declaration of Independence. Yet McGee believed that an independent Irish parliament should remain loyal to the Crown and cooperate closely with Westminster. He contended that the repeal of the Act of Union would mean the repeal of history – that centuries of hatred would dissolve and Anglo-Irish relations would become peaceful and harmonious. "We tell her we will forget the past," he wrote; "we will bury our many causes of hatred against her, (and God knows we have as many as there are hours in seven centuries!) We will stand by her in peril and prosperity – but on one condition, the Independence of our ancient parliament."[42] If his indignation ran one way, his judgment ran the other; McGee's long-term solution for Anglo-Irish relations was not an Irish republic but a partnership of equals under a common monarchy. At least some of his American readers, however, must have wondered why Ireland would want to remain connected to such a putatively malevolent state as Great Britain.

Then there was the question of how an independent Irish parliament could be achieved. Although he preferred moral to physical force, McGee's heroes consisted largely of men who took up arms against Britain, such as Patrick Sarsfield and Robert Emmet. He admired the American revolutionaries of 1776 and the Irish revolutionaries of 1798, and drew further inspiration from John Kells Ingram's recently composed (but anonymous) poem, "The Memory of the Dead." "If England must have blood," McGee declared, "Ireland must have justice." There was, in McGee's writing, a fine line between peaceful resistance and defensive violence, and between defensive violence and armed revolution. "The Irish in America," he added, "will not shrink in the trial hour."[43]

On all these issues – the place of Protestants within Irish nationalism, the Anglo-Irish relationship, and the relation between moral and physical force – McGee's attitude was characterized by ambivalence. "Good" Protestants supported Repeal, while "bad" Protestants clung to their sectarian prejudices and privileges; the fact that most Protestants were "bad" by his definition was conveniently overlooked. Britain was the incarnation of evil when it came to Ireland, but it contained much that was admirable and would become a good friend to Ireland once Repeal had been accomplished. Moral force was better than physical force, but the idea of defeating Britain in military conflict clearly had a strong emotional appeal.

McGee's ambivalence mirrored wider tensions within Irish nationalism during the "Repeal year of 1843." O'Connell wanted the cause of Repeal to transcend religious differences, but he privately assured Paul Cullen, the rector of the Irish College at Rome, that Protestantism would soon wither away under self-government.[44] (During the 1790s, the shoe had been on the other foot; leading Protestant United Irishmen such as William Drennan and Archibald Hamilton Rowan had argued that Irish independence would mean the demise of Catholicism.)[45] In speech after speech, O'Connell portrayed the Irish as being the "most moral, the most temperate, the most orderly, the most religious people in the world," and denigrated the "Saxons" as the most oppressive people on the face of the Earth. Yet he also promised that post-Repeal Ireland would remain loyal to the Crown and become a faithful ally of Britain; the name of his organization, it should be remembered, was the Loyal National Repeal Association.

Similarly, O'Connell sent out mixed messages about moral and physical force. In his famous "Mallow Defiance" of 11 June 1843 he declared, "We will keep within the law and commit no crime." But he also told his audience that they might "soon have the alternative to live as slaves or die as freemen." The government "may trample on me," he said, "but it will be my dead body they will trample on, not the living man." For many of his followers, including Gavan Duffy, "this declaration seemed to be the signal of pending revolution." As Richard Davis has argued, the Repeal movement in 1843 was characterized by "an ambivalence between the conscious objective of a strong and efficient passive resistance organisation, and an impulse to war and military victory."[46]

McGee appeared to take the revolutionary rhetoric seriously. What can be said with certainty, however, is that O'Connell did not. The monster meetings and the defiant speeches were designed to frighten Peel's government into backing down, just as the government had retreated over Catholic Emancipation in 1829; O'Connell was raising the stakes in a high-risk game of brinkmanship. But what if Peel's government did not back down? McGee believed that coercion would trigger an Irish revolution, but O'Connell had no desire to replay 1798 in 1843. The "trial hour" came in October, when the British government banned the monster meeting planned for Clontarf the day before it was to occur. O'Connell's bluff had been called; his climb-down and subsequent arrest came as an enormous shock to his more radical supporters. The determination never to repeat such a humiliating defeat was an important factor in propelling the Young Ireland movement – McGee included – towards revolution five years later.[47]

In Massachusetts, McGee put the best possible face on the situation and remained loyal to his leader. He insisted that O'Connell was a

man of integrity and honesty, whose decision had saved Ireland from
"avenging power screaming along the hill tops of the land, and pouring down rapine, treachery, and lust, into the hearts of the cities, and
upon the highways." Although war against England was fully justified
in theory, McGee argued, it should be avoided in practice, given the
power imbalance between the two countries; his judgment was getting the better of his indignation. Viewing Clontarf as a necessary tactical retreat in a long campaign, he said that it was now more important than ever that the Boston Repeal Association increase its fundraising efforts.[48]

But deflated hopes meant dwindling money, and in March 1844
McGee expressed considerable frustration over "the deplorable decrease
of the funds within the last four or five months." Members of the
Repeal Association, he complained, were spending too much time on
talk and not enough on action; they were also thinking of using their
money to support Irish manufactures when everything should be subordinated to the cause of "Parliamentary Independence." No matter
where he laid the blame, however, the root cause of the problem was
clear: more and more Irish Americans concluded after Clontarf that
Repeal was simply unattainable.[49]

This changing mood may have contributed to McGee's decision in
early 1844 to embark on a new career course. "Don't be startled," he
informed his aunt; "it isn't to marry or become a Methodist preacher –
but to study the law of the land." "To live by the pen alone is drudgery
of the darkest hue," he wrote, and he had no desire to "follow typesetting as a profession." Besides, he had been in Boston long enough,
and it was time to "shake off the dust of this puritanical City" from
his shoes. He had met an "excellent Irish Counsellor" from Cincinnati, who offered to take him as a student, and the opportunity was too
good to miss. "Why I prefer the West you may yourself guess," he told
Aunt Bella. "Less prejudice and more room for rising amongst others."
This was the first glimpse of his later view that the Irish had better
chances of prospering in the West than in the seaboard cities; it also
underlined his personal ambition. "I have made one discovery since
my residence in America," he wrote, "which I believe you must have
made also – that they who live by their wits live best. Now, amongst

my many good qualities heaven has blest me with a bold face, a fluent tongue and a love for Argument – in plain words with impudence, volubility and combativeness, the life, and soul and fortune of ten thousand lawyers."[50]

By March, all the plans were in place. The *Boston Pilot* announced that McGee would give his "FAREWELL LECTURE" on 1 April; the subject was "*Three Emmets*: Temple, Thomas Addis, and Robert Emmet." After that, he would leave for Cincinnati, start a two-year stint as a law student, and settle down in the American West.[51] Then Patrick Donahoe made him an offer he could not refuse. At the beginning of April, McGee was appointed editor of the *Boston Pilot* under the tutelage of Walter J. Walsh. His first issue came out on 13 April, his nineteenth birthday. McGee would continue to live by the pen alone, with the dust of Boston still under his feet.

CHAPTER THREE

Lessons of Democracy
April 1844 – May 1845

In his new editorial position, McGee intended to stay focused on Irish rather than American affairs. His aim was to make Ireland a "model nation in Europe," free from foreign rulers with their "slow-poison drugs of poverty and disease, their Bastile [sic] Poor Houses and their empty churches richly endowed." "For the abolishing these burdens," he wrote, "I have devoted all my energies, and shall continue to do so in future." Yet he would find it increasingly difficult to fix all his attention on Irish independence. The Repeal movement continued to languish after Clontarf, and Irish American heads were getting weary of brick walls. At the same time, growing tensions in the seaboard cities between Protestants and Irish Catholic immigrants became an urgent issue that demanded immediate attention. "It is no easy matter to suggest topics, in advance, for newspaper writing, since every week brings forth *its* own topic," McGee later told a friend who was about to become a newspaper editor; the comment came from experience. But if McGee could not control the agenda, he could respond to the topics that arose each week. In the process, he not only continued to write about Repeal but also became drawn into American affairs.[1]

On the question of Repeal, McGee continued to criticize the North American Irish for their inability to raise more money for the cause. Surveying the scene in the summer of 1844, he concluded that the previous September's Repeal Convention had been a failure, and he criticized the National Executive Committee for dereliction of duty, noting that after O'Connell's imprisonment in May 1844, some members of the committee had not even bothered to attend the protest meeting in Baltimore. What was needed, he argued, was more "nerve and sincerity." North of the border the verdict was mixed. Nova Scotia and New Brunswick had done "exceptionally well," and Toronto remained a Repeal stronghold. Elsewhere in Canada, however, the response was disappointing – something he found particularly surprising, given the need for Irish Catholics to stick together against the "Orange spirit" that pervaded the province.[2]

Turning to events in Ireland, McGee welcomed plans to establish Repeal reading rooms – a development that drew on the example of earlier temperance societies and anticipated the more radical Confederate clubs that McGee would help organize in 1847–48. The reading rooms, he argued, would carry the cause into the countryside, raise nationalist consciousness, and "strike at the very roots of Ribbonism, and Orangeism, and every other destructive *ism* from which Ireland's enemies could gain anything." The emphasis on education and the hostility to "illegal combinations and agrarian outrage" remained consistent features of his later career, with the important exception of his attempt to bring Ribbonmen into the revolutionary movement during the summer of 1848.

McGee also supported the Repeal proposal to form an Irish militia. Other colonies, such as Lower Canada and Jamaica, had militias, so why not Ireland as well? Militias were "not only a safeguard in war, but a wholesome fact in peace." His model was the Volunteer movement that had arisen in Ireland during the American Revolution and had secured a degree of legislative independence for Ireland in 1782. In practice, the reforms of 1782 had been limited; Britain had retained substantial control over Irish affairs, and the Irish parliament had remained the preserve of a Protestant elite. But what mattered to McGee was the inspirational myth of a national militia forcing a government to give the people their rights. It had supposedly happened in 1782, and it could happen again, only this time with a parliament open to both Catholics and Protestants. Other Irish radicals had the same idea and organized the Eighty-Two Club – closely connected to the Young Ireland movement – to bring about what McGee called "the full emancipation of their country."[3]

It is worth considering what McGee meant by "full emancipation" at this stage of his career. When in the fall of 1844 O'Connell flew the kite of federalism as an alternative to Repeal, McGee responded positively – in contrast to Duffy, who feared a sell-out. Although "entire nationality" was the ideal situation for Ireland, McGee wrote, it was "madness" to think that complete separation was possible, given the relative strength of Britain and Ireland. And if complete independence was unattainable, Irish nationalists were left with the choice of Repeal or federalism. By giving the Irish and British parliaments equality of status, he argued, "simple Repeal" would "place Ireland in a position to irritate England." (His earlier view that Repeal would result in Anglo-Irish harmony had been quietly dropped.) By contrast, under a federal arrangement, an Irish legislature would be responsible for domestic affairs, while Britain would have full control over imperial defence.[4] "Federalism," he wrote, "will give to Ireland all the advantages of self-legislation, without the tempting and dangerous prerogative of vetoing imperial projects." Ireland would secure the substance of freedom, British imperial interests would be protected, and Anglo-Irish relations would rest on foundations of friendship. As it became apparent, however, that Irish nationalists were divided over federalism, and as O'Connell himself began to backtrack, McGee let the issue slide. But the central point was clear: McGee had been willing to accept a new political arrangement that fell short not only of separatism but also of Repeal itself. Beneath all his rhetorical intensity, there was a remarkable degree of pragmatism and prudence.[5]

Gradually, the rhetoric was toned down too. In the spring of 1845, McGee continued to praise Irish and Irish American military heroes, but he noted that the times had changed and maintained that "a more pacific disposition" was preferable to military action. The Irish, he declared, should dwell "on the glories of an O'CONNELL, a MATHEW and a DUFFY," rather than on "the laurels of Sarsfield or Montgomery."[6] Peaceful agitation, education, and temperance would carry the day; it was also imperative to have the support of the Catholic bishops and clergy, without whom the cause of nationalism could not succeed.

Peel's government, McGee argued, was equally aware that the Catholic Church was the arbiter of politics in Ireland; that was why "the wily cabinet of England" had increased the grant to Maynooth College and obtained a papal rescript advising the Irish clergy not to become involved in politics. O'Connell had insisted that such English tactics must be resisted, and McGee fully agreed. Moral force with Catholic support, he wrote, would make the country "honourable, educated and prosperous," and would raise the reputation of the Irish throughout the world. The Irish in America would finally be treated with the respect and dignity that they deserved. "Your destiny and your character," he told them, "are inseparably connected, for good or evil, with the fortune and character of Ireland."[7] It was an argument that had become increasingly relevant after the Philadelphia riots of May 1844, in which conflicts between nativist Americans and Irish Catholics had escalated to unprecedented levels of violence.

———

"Nativism" is something of a misnomer. Tensions between Protestants and Catholics centred on what it meant to be American; place of birth was an important but secondary factor. Those people who regarded Catholicism as un-American included not only the American-born but also recently arrived British and Irish Protestant immigrants. In some respects, what passes for nativism in America was actually a continuation in the United States of ethnoreligious tensions in Ireland. Discussing manifestations of anti-Catholicism in New York, the special correspondent of the *Boston Pilot* reported that many nativists in the city were actually "the *spurious* offspring of some of our recreant countrymen from the North of Ireland" – a recurring variation on the "Orange bastards" theme.[8]

Of course, Irish Catholics in America had a vested interest in blaming nativism on Irish Protestant immigrants. Such a position retained the image of America as the land of liberty while blaming anti-Catholic prejudice on un-American outsiders. Nevertheless, it is clear that Irish Protestants (including their offspring, "spurious" or otherwise) joined native-born Americans in arguing that Irish Catholics were unfit for American citizenship. Irish Catholics were caricatured as an ignorant, illiterate, superstitious, and priest-ridden people, who were mired in poverty, crime, drink, and disease – as an alien people who con-

The Philadelphia riots, May 1844. McGee reacted by calling American natives
"cowards and sons of cowards" and by taking a hard anti-Protestant line that
anticipated his ultramontanism of the early 1850s. (H. Buoholzer, courtesy of
the Library of Congress)

tradicted the central values of American republicanism, and whose
increasing numbers were threatening the American way of life. With
the rapid growth of the Catholic Church, the increasing electoral power
of Irish Catholics, and Irish Catholic competition for jobs and houses,
many Protestants came to fear that they were becoming politically and
economically marginalized in their "own" country; it was time, they
believed, to take a stand.[9]

In Philadelphia, Protestant-Catholic tensions became focused on the
issue of religious teaching in the school system. Disputes over the use
of the King James Bible in the classroom flared into fears that Catholics were trying to undermine the Protestant basis of public education,
and the grassroots Protestant "American Republican" party began to
reap the political benefits in the local elections. When in May 1844 the
American Republicans held a meeting of three thousand supporters in
the heavily Irish ward of Kensington, it was broken up by gunfire from
the Hibernia Hose House. This triggered three days of rioting, characterized by a general rampage against Irish Catholic houses and stores

and the burning of two Catholic churches. By the time it was over, at least $250,000 worth of property had been destroyed, around forty people had been wounded, and fourteen more had been killed.[10]

The Philadelphia riots sent shock waves throughout the seaboard cities with large Irish Catholic populations. In New York, Bishop John Hughes called for Irish Catholics to keep away from nativist meetings, discouraged the formation of anti-nativist organizations that might increase ethnoreligious tensions, and told his flock that "the true course is to abstain from every thing that could give occasion to the least disturbance." "But," he added, "if, as has already appeared in Philadelphia, it should be a part of NATIVE AMERICANISM to attack their houses or their churches, then it behoves them, in case all other protection fail, to defend BOTH, *with their lives*." Hughes's militantly defensive stance eventually became magnified into the myth that he had publicly threatened to turn New York into a "second Moscow" if a single Catholic church was burned. Although there is no evidence that he ever made such a public declaration, the myth certainly caught his mood.[11]

Meanwhile, in Boston, Bishop Fenwick and his successor Bishop John Fitzpatrick (who was McGee's second cousin) adopted a much more low-key approach, on the assumption that confrontational language would backfire on the city's Catholic minority. McGee felt very differently. The Philadelphia riots shook him to the core, brought out a combative response, and marked a major shift in his political direction as he assumed the role of defender of Irish Catholics in the United States. It was "perfectly astounding," he wrote, that such things could happen in enlightened, democratic America; the riots revealed a fundamental contradiction between republican ideals and nativist realities. "If these things are countenanced," McGee declared, "... then it were far better for every Emigrant to return to the darkness of European despotism, where, at least, there will be a singleness and nobility about the tyrant, than to remain in a land mocked by the fruits of liberty." It was imperative, he argued, to reassert republican ideals, to show that nativism violated "the true American spirit, as we have felt it in social life, in our laws, and Institutions," and to pin the blame where it belonged – on "Calvinistic intolerance, Orange despotism and a prejudiced press."[12]

According to McGee, a handful of self-styled "Ministers of the Gospel" had joined with "a small number of Native bigots" to spread "enormous falsehoods" about Catholic idolatry and tyranny, the "Inquisition and its tortures," and the "adulterous abuses" of the confessional. Protestant newspapers had transmitted this propaganda to the "poorer classes of the population" and exploited their "low state of intelligence, and absence of all moral feeling." This would not be the last time that McGee wrote disparagingly about the working classes. Among the audience for such ideas, he argued, was a large contingent of Orangemen; they emigrated "in shoals," settled together "in certain localities," and were at the forefront of anti-Catholic activities. When the rioters were burning down St Augustine's Church, McGee claimed, a Protestant band celebrated by playing the Orange tune "Boyne Water." From his viewpoint, the Orangemen injected foreign prejudice into America, were loyal to a foreign monarch, and generally refused to take the oath of naturalization; as such, they were the very antithesis of Americanism.[13]

In effect, McGee had created a mirror-world of nativism, in which Orangemen rather than Irish Catholics were threatening American values, and in which the best way to prevent Old World bigotry from infecting New World institutions was to turn foreigners into naturalized citizens as soon as possible. It was, however, a distorted mirror; although Orangemen participated in the riots, they were almost certainly a minority presence. As Michael Feldberg has noted, "The crowds of nativists were too big, and too many persons voted for the American Republican ticket, to explain satisfactorily Philadelphia nativism simply as an Orange-based movement."[14]

Like the United Irish émigrés before him, McGee projected and externalized American nativism not only onto Orangeism but also onto the British government – familiar targets for Irish nationalists. The British government, he wrote, was strongly opposed to American expansion into Texas and the Oregon Territory, but dared not risk an outright declaration of war – especially since an American war would provide an opening for Irish nationalists, as had happened in 1782. As a result, Britain ("unscrupulous, corrupt, and liberty-hating as she is") was employing "all her machinery and some of her *secret service* money, in causing and promoting domestic *discord* in the United States." McGee was unable to provide any evidence to substantiate this argument, for the simple reason that he did not have any; it was the kind of thing that Britain was expected to do, and that was enough. Irish nationalists had long believed that Britain had employed a "divide and rule" strategy in Ireland; now McGee was applying the same argument to British policy towards America. If the "true spirit" of Ireland and the United States was one of harmony, then Britain provided a convenient scapegoat for the "false spirit" of discord.[15]

⋯

Nevertheless, the "native" component of American nativism proved too powerful to be ignored. When, in the aftermath of the Philadelphia riots, American nativists mocked the "physical inferiority" of the Irish, McGee was goaded into his notorious remark that the "*native* sons of America" were "cowards and sons of cowards." "It ill becomes any American to taunt Irishmen on the score of bravery," he declared; native Americans repeatedly ran from the battlefield, while Irish American patriots stood their ground. "As shopkeepers they are excellent," he wrote; "as merchants, enterprising and persevering; as usurers, they have no equals in the world; but as soldiers, every native ought to belong to the Peace Society." Irish Americans had frequently asserted that the Irish had played a crucial role in the War of Independence, but none had taken the argument to this length. Pushing his point even further, McGee claimed that because eight signers of the Declaration of Independence were Irish-born or of Irish descent, the Irish were entitled "to be a-sixth of the whole electoral body."[16]

McGee was reacting to extreme provocation – his indignation and his impassioned outburst are fully understandable – but in terms of judgment and reason, it is hard to imagine a worse response to nativism. His "cowards and sons of cowards" comments did nothing to improve the position of the Catholic Irish in America, and ran the risk of triggering an even stronger nativist backlash. As nativist anger mounted, the offices of the *Boston Pilot* were put under police protection; meanwhile, a storm of protest blew through American newspapers. The words would be repeatedly flung in McGee's face throughout his American career. In 1854 Boston nativists were still issuing handbills declaring, "These Irishmen have called us 'Cowards and Sons of Cowards!'" and denouncing the activities of "Vagabond Irishmen" in the United States. During the same period, Irish American revolutionaries also got in on the act, citing McGee's words as proof that he had always been fundamentally anti-republican and anti-American. McGee tried to undo the damage by insisting that he had been referring only to American nativists and not to Americans in general; it was not an entirely convincing effort. But he continued to insist that he was right to take a hard line against nativism. The *Boston Pilot*, he wrote in 1851, "was then the only one ... which dared to defend the church, or to stigmatize, as they deserved, the church-burglars and women-assaulters of Philadelphia."[17]

Just as McGee responded to taunts about Irish inferiority by arguing that the Irish were better republicans than the Americans, he reacted to anti-Catholic rhetoric by asserting that Catholicism was superior to Protestantism. Associating the Reformation with a satanic plot to sow dissension among the faithful, McGee regarded Protestantism as a dangerous heresy that placed private judgment ahead of "God's prerogative." If you began with "Private Judgment in matters of Eternal Concern," he wrote, you inevitably wound up with "poor mad Millerites" and myriad equally deluded denominations. The trouble with the United States was that "the humble" were "constantly dissatisfied and sliding from one sect to another"; this reflected not so much "a spirit of inquiry after truth" as "a state of nervous uncertainty easily acted upon." Protestantism produced "democracy without morality," which was "the most unbearable and ferocious form of tyranny." Only Catholicism, in his view, could save the country from sliding into mob rule.[18]

All these arguments would resurface during McGee's ultramontane period in the 1850s, as would his view that Protestantism had an inherent propensity for persecution. Even before the riots, he had published a short story entitled "The Priest Hunter," which pitted a villainous priest hunter against a virtuous and innocent people in the dark days of Elizabethan Ireland. In the end, the priest hunter was thrown over a cliff by a brave Irishman, who was himself killed, but who "wore a smile of triumph" in death.[19] After the events in Philadelphia, McGee reminded his readers that the Irish had "preserved the true faith in every misfortune and emergency"; he maintained that persecution only strengthened Catholicism. A revitalized Catholic Church, he wrote, would provide America with moral stability in place of licentiousness, a sense of authority in place of anarchy, and a consciousness of tradition in place of perpetual presentism. What was needed above all, he wrote, was "the *unprotestantizing* of the United States."[20]

Once again, McGee had inverted the arguments of his opponents. American Protestants were the villains who presented the greatest threat to republican values, while Irish American Catholics were the heroes who would defeat the latter-day priest hunters and protect the polity. Like his "cowards and sons of cowards" comment, McGee's religious remarks threw caution to the wind. His comments about the superiority of Catholicism and the "*unprotestantizing*" of America appeared to confirm the worst fears of the nativists that Irish Catholics were indeed plotting to take over the United States; here, it seemed, was a window into the conspiracy that Samuel Morse and others had been warning Americans about. It is no wonder that Bishop Fenwick cancelled his subscription to the *Boston Pilot*.[21]

McGee's assertions of Irish Catholic political and religious superiority were accompanied by an equally powerful sense of "racial" pride, which placed the Celts in the vanguard of liberty. Before the Philadelphia riots, McGee had focused on the Celtic heritage in Irish literature and music; now, in reaction to nativism, he constructed the republican Irish American Celt, who was contrasted to the aristocratic Anglo-Saxon. Although McGee demanded parity with the Saxons ("We must either be their equals or inferiors"), there is no doubt that he considered the Celts to be the superior race. After all, the Celts were originally from the East, the "cradle of population, letters, and arts," at a time when the Saxons were still skulking around German forests clubbing each other over the head. But the Saxons, with their lust for conquest, had invaded the Celtic countries of Europe, erected the British Empire, and colonized North America. The War of Independence, McGee wrote, was part of the Celtic counterattack. The "Celtic spirit," manifesting itself through patriots such as Patrick Henry and through the supposedly "unanimous rising of the Irish emigrants of the country," had been largely responsible for the success of the American Revolution. Thanks to the Irish, the "Celtic genius" was spreading throughout the United States. And with more Irish immigration, the country would remain true to its republican principles.[22]

—•••—

Central to the preservation and promotion of the "Celtic spirit" in the United States, in McGee's view, was immigrant education. By the winter of 1844–45, his attempts to establish adult education classes for the American Irish vied for column space with his articles on Repeal. McGee advocated the formation of mutual instruction clubs and emigrant reading rooms that would enable Irish Catholics to shake off their status as a "white slave class," inculcate a sense of self-respect, and help them become independent property owners – the people who constituted "the sole support of a real republic." Largely thanks to his efforts, in January 1845 his associates established the Friends of Adult Education, which opened its doors to all adults, irrespective of "creed or birth place." McGee had initially preferred an organization for Catholics only in order to resist the "sectarian narrowness" of New England and ensure that the immigrants remained true to their religion; he was, however, prepared to be flexible on the issue, and he gave the ecumenical initiative his "unqualified approval." He was impressed with the provisions for female education. Women would have a "teacher of their own sex," who would "cultivate their minds" and give occasional lectures on practical subjects such as "the simpler points of law, and the laws of digestion and health." "They might thus keep many men out of the hands of lawyers and doctors," stated the prospectus of the organization. By the time classes began in February, some two hundred people had enrolled.[23]

The classes focused on reading, writing, and arithmetic; from this foundation, McGee planned to transform Irish immigrants into true Celts and better American citizens while giving the lie to nativist stereotypes about the ignorant and drunken Paddy. By studying the "Rebel Literature of Ireland," particularly the writings of United Irish "Celts" such as William Drennan, Thomas Addis Emmet, and Arthur

O'Connor (strange bedfellows indeed), the American Irish would become inspired by men who were "poets in passion, and statesmen in political knowledge." And by studying Irish history, they would learn about the struggle for political and religious liberty, and acquire the knowledge to contradict the falsehoods and prejudice that dogged them in America. It was an urgent task; he complained of "our neglect, our wicked, suicidal, indifference to the country of our birth-land," and criticized his countrymen for their "disgraceful apathy" about their own history. "It is indeed a shame," he wrote, "that out of 20,000 of an Irish population in the city of Boston, you will not find *one thousand* conversant with our country's history." The study of Irish history was still in its infancy, he added; there was a great need for a "good *complete* history." Later, in Canada, he would make a serious and sustained effort to fill the gap by writing one himself.[24]

More immediately, McGee made his own contributions to the tradition with his first two books, an historical novella and a "narrative of Irish political biography" that focused on O'Connell and his fellow Repealers. The novella, *Eva MacDonald, A Tale of the United Irishmen, and Their Times*, was published in 1844. It was dedicated to Thomas Colley Grattan, the Irish-born British consul to Massachusetts, a brilliant conversationalist and prolific writer whom McGee greatly admired. "He is characterised by a sociable feeling and humorous disposition, and is a real Grattan," he wrote in 1843. (Had McGee known that Grattan was opposed to Repeal, he might not have been quite so impressed.)[25]

The book was set during the 1790s in Red Bay on the Antrim Coast, where McGee had lived as a boy. It featured a chivalrous Irish knight, Sir Cahir O'Doherty, a comely Irish maiden, Eva MacDonald, and a cruel and cunning English villain, Captain Sinclair. After a terrible storm, the shipwrecked Captain Sinclair is nursed back to health by the beautiful Eva; Cahir mistakenly believes that she is in love with Sinclair and leaves for Paris. Sinclair, having failed to seduce Eva, abducts her on a British ship bound for Dublin. Meanwhile, in Paris, Sir Cahir catches the revolutionary fever, changes his name to Citizen O'Doherty, meets Wolfe Tone, and joins the United Irishmen.

Learning about Eva's abduction, Cahir offers to become Tone's emissary to Ireland and sails to Dublin. Almost as soon as he steps off the boat, he encounters Sinclair and shoots him to death in a duel. Cahir then returns to France, joins Napper Tandy's invasion attempt in 1798, lands at Rathlin Island, and returns to Red Bay. The villain has been dispatched, and virtue is rewarded. Eva and Cahir get married and live happily ever after, and Cahir is universally regarded as "a perfect Gentleman of the Old School."

It was high melodrama, with some surprising howlers. One of the characters, Nanny of the Cave, was a young girl during the Battle of the Boyne but was still dispensing sweetmeats in the 1830s – which made her at least 150 years old. Throughout the book, there is a fixation on romantic heroes and benevolent aristocrats. It is not democratic republican principles that grip McGee's attention but the dashing figures of Wolfe Tone, Lord Edward FitzGerald, and Robert Emmet: "Where shall we find three so young – so brave – so gifted? Their memories shall ever remain like a trefoil of glory, to illuminate the path of men who would dare emerge from the darkness of slavery." In the end, Cahir was pardoned by a magnanimous Anglo-Irish landlord, on the grounds that his involvement with the United Irishmen was merely the result of his perceived romantic rejection. While the ending may signify a coming together of "good" Protestants with Irish Catholics, it trivializes the United Irish movement that McGee had treated with so much admiration earlier in the book. All in all, the requirements of romance overrode any kind of consistent political vision, just as they had dispensed with the realities of longevity. The book was not a success. McGee did not return to the genre of historical fiction until the winter of 1867–68, when he wrote the now-lost manuscript of his "Irish American tale."[26]

His second book, *Historical Sketches of O'Connell and His Friends* (1845), though a work of non-fiction, contained the same binary structure of thought that characterized his novella. On the one side stood O'Connell, the heroic Celt and personification of the Age of Reform, who taught that violence was counterproductive, that political actions must rest on Catholic morality, and that "the better way for men to recover lost rights, is by degrees." Alongside him were the priests, poets, and patriots – men such as Dr Doyle, who debated (and in McGee's view defeated) the best thinkers that Irish Protestantism could offer. The poet-patriots included Thomas Furlong, the Wexford poet who translated into English the lyrics of Turlough Carolan and took on the Tories and Orangemen. Greater still was Thomas Moore who, despite his "unhappy preference" for aristocratic habits, wrote the most moving patriotic songs ever heard in Ireland. On the other side stood the oppressors of Ireland, with the "criminal and destructive" Orangemen to the fore – a bunch of "adventurous Scots, bestial Hessians, and the promiscuous followers of the Prince of Orange" who had dispossessed the "legitimate proprietors" of the land, but whose power would soon be broken.[27]

In his treatment of recent history, McGee shared O'Connell's support for gradualist reform and maintained that the revolutionary strategy of the United Irishmen was morally and politically indefensible: "The evils attacked were only strengthened," he argued, "and driven more deeply into the ground." But where O'Connell had condemned the United Irishmen as "weak and wicked men who considered force and sanguinary violence as part of their resources for ameliorating our conditions," McGee continued to admire their courage and spirit. The United Irishmen may have been "ill-advised," he wrote, but their hearts were in the right place, their motives were pure, and their cause was just. In this way, McGee simultaneously reviled the revolution and revered the revolutionaries; his earlier ambivalence remained.[28]

McGee's book also provides an early glimpse into his approach to historical writing. He criticized earlier historians for one "radical defect" or another; Nicholas Taafe was "too declamatory," Geoffrey Keating was too credulous, and Thomas Moore too skeptical. McGee's historical writing, however, had defects of its own; he sometimes became carried away with his own rhetoric, and he slid into factual error, hagiography, and myth.[29] But his central purpose was to provide Irish Americans with a usable past that would strengthen their self-respect and nationalist consciousness, and in this he met with some success. *O'Connell and His Friends* received numerous glowing reviews and went into a second edition after only two weeks. Among the reviewers was Bishop John Hughes. "I have looked through it with great interest and pleasure," he wrote. "It may not be what you would wish, after some years from now; but it is intrinsically valuable, and, as a first essay, highly creditable."[30]

From the dominant Irish nationalist viewpoint, O'Connell was "the Liberator," the man who had accomplished Catholic Emancipation and was preparing the way for Repeal. But his Irish American admirers, including McGee, were faced with a problem: O'Connell was also an outspoken opponent of slavery who had signed an abolitionist address from the "People of Ireland" to "their Countrymen and Country-women in America," and refused to accept "blood-stained money" from anti-abolitionist American Repeal Associations. For the pro-slavery majority in the United States, O'Connell's address appeared an ignorant and dangerous foreign intrusion into American affairs; from there, it was a short step to accusing his Irish American followers of being anti-American. To counter such charges and to demonstrate that they were indeed good citizens, Irish American nationalists had to make a clear distinction between O'Connell's Irish and American politics, and put as much distance as possible between themselves and O'Connell's antislavery arguments.[31]

This is exactly what McGee did. *O'Connell and His Friends* contained no references whatsoever to O'Connell's antislavery arguments; the silence is deafening. McGee's first explicit reference to the subject came during the presidential election of 1844, in which he opposed the Whig party and attacked the vice-presidential candidate, Theodore Freling-huysen, for aligning himself with anti-Catholic Protestant evangelists. When the Whigs lost the election, nativists complained that Catholic priests and their Irish followers had brought the Democratic candidate, James Polk, into power. One Boston newspaper shouted that "ROME AND IRELAND ARE RULING AMERICA" and called for American employers not to hire the Irish. "They live like brutes," commented the *Boston Atlas*. "They underwork our mechanics and laborers, in the working months, and overflow our alms-houses during the winter season." In response, McGee insisted that Irish Catholics were as American as anyone else. The proof? They had "firmly and plainly" rejected O'Connell's antislavery address and had argued that the Papal

Bull condemning the slave trade did not apply to the United States – an interesting twist on American exceptionalism. "Are not these facts stronger than a thousand assertions?" he asked. Like many of his compatriots, McGee built his case for Irish Catholic membership in the American nation partly on the backs of black slaves.[32]

It was not that McGee actually approved of slavery; on the contrary, he argued that among the chief faults of the United States were "the evils of Negro slavery and Religious bigotry, both of which can be ameliorated only in time." But he believed that the Irish should focus on eradicating religious bigotry, and asserted that "we neither can nor ought to liberate the negro as he is." Afro-Americans were not yet ready for emancipation, he wrote; in any case, slavery was enshrined in the U.S. Constitution, to which Irish American citizens had pledged their "undivided allegiance." *We have sworn to support America's Flag and Cause*," he declared. The cause of America was still the cause of liberty, despite such temporary problems as nativism and slavery, and the United States remained the best hope for the "crushed and fettered" population of Europe. If this was the case, then the immediate task was to widen the arena of liberty; the attack on nativism came first, and emancipation would have to wait until the indeterminate future. Accordingly, McGee dropped the subject of slavery and focused instead on the annexation of Texas and the assertion of American power in the Oregon Territory.[33]

In supporting western expansion, McGee moved still further from O'Connell's position. "I regard with horror the annexation of another slave state to the American Union," said O'Connell in his famous "American Eagle" speech of March 1845. Denouncing slavery as "the greatest crime that can be committed by humanity against humanity," O'Connell argued that once Ireland had won Repeal, the country would willingly participate in a British war against the United States. "We tell them [the British] from this spot," he said at Conciliation Hall, "that they can have us – that the throne of Victoria can be made perfectly secure – the honor of the British empire maintained – and the American Eagle, in its highest pride be brought down. Let them but conciliate us and do us justice, and they will have us enlisted under the banner of Victoria – let them but give us the parliament in College-green, and Oregon shall be theirs and Texas shall be harmless." McGee must have choked when he read those words. His immediate instinct was to suppress the speech, but he reluctantly decided to publish it, "lest it should be represented worse than it is." Because they were good citizens, he wrote, the American Irish "cease to be accountable for the language of a foreign statesman"; for his part, there was no doubt about his "utter repudiation of Mr. O'Connell's sentiments."[34]

Like his fellow Irish American journalist John Louis O'Sullivan, who coined the term "manifest destiny" in 1845, McGee believed that the United States would take over the entire North American continent. "There will be, a couple of centuries hence, but two American nations, each covering a Continent," McGee wrote. "The United States must necessarily in course of time, absorb the Northern British Provinces ... One vast Federal Union, will stretch from Labrador to Panama." The Hudson's Bay Company could not block the western march of freedom; the "court-spawn" of Britain must be driven from the Pacific Northwest; "Indian natives" had no rights of prior possession and must be absorbed into the United States.[35]

If taking over Oregon meant war with Britain, so much the better. Ireland would seize the opportunity to push for freedom, while the United States would confirm its dominance of North America. Britain could not be allowed to control such an economically and strategically important river as the St Lawrence; either by purchase or conquest, Canada "must be yielded by Great Britain to this Republic." When that day came, the United States would dominate the New World, and "the New World will control the destinies of the whole earth." The Irish in America would play a crucial role in this process; if they educated themselves, they could "ascend to the dignity of arbitrators over two continents" and become "the most important portion of the New World's inhabitants." The Irish, then, had it in their ability to become the most influential people on the planet – not bad going for a Celtic race that defined itself against the Anglo-Saxon lust for power.[36]

—•••—

McGee's vision of an American empire with the Irish at its core ironically anticipates his later dream of a new northern Canadian nation that would stretch from the Atlantic to the Pacific and provide a model of good government for the rest of the world. At this stage of his career, however, both McGee and Canada were very different from what they would become. McGee still admired the principles of American republicanism, and Canada had yet to secure responsible government. In these circumstances, he was struck by the parallels between Canada and Ireland. In both countries, he wrote, an imported aristocracy and an Orange organization upheld bad laws, while a "bullying and well-bribed ministerial press" buttressed Tory rule and harassed reformers. It was not surprising, McGee noted, that there had been anti-Catholic Irish riots in Montreal. True, there had been similar outbreaks in Philadelphia, but they had occurred despite rather than because of the American system of government. In Canada, the blame lay with an unaccountable governor general and his Orange minions: "Yes, we repeat it – the ruling powers of Canada are answerable for the blood of those men who have fallen victim to the doctrines of irresponsibility in rulers." This was, of course, a very convenient argument for an Irish American Republican to make, and one that blithely ignored the evidence that the "ruling powers" in Montreal were no more – and no less – culpable than those in Philadelphia.[37]

Just as Canada and Ireland were common victims of British oppression, in McGee's view, they also shared similar forms of resistance. "'Repeal of the Union' is the Irish for 'Responsible Government,'" he argued; Canadian Reformers and Irish Repealers both believed that the people should be "fully represented in Parliament," that the governor should be responsible to the legislature, and that the state should fund educational institutions for all its subjects, regardless of religion. In connecting the causes of Canadian Reform and Irish Repeal, McGee was again demonstrating his willingness to accept a settlement within the British Empire, while leaving open the possibility of further change. After all, in the Canadian context he believed that responsible government would eventually lead to American annexation, and he saw no reason why Repeal could not give Ireland the freedom to win more freedom.[38]

McGee's moderatism was part of a more general trajectory within his first American career. One of the most interesting aspects of his final months in the United States was his increasing impatience with hyper-

nationalist orthodoxy. We have already seen this in his openness to a
federal arrangement between Britain and Ireland, and in his view that
moral-force nationalists were better role models than Ireland's military
heroes. But it manifested itself in other ways as well. In April 1845 a
rival editor remarked that McGee's "active, discerning mind seems
cramped by the Catholic religion," and suggested that he was torn
between his adherence to Catholic teaching and his belief in "the freedom and progress of the human mind, and of bodies politic." We know
from his later writings that he was indeed undergoing such a struggle,
and we know that other contemporaries made similar observations
about McGee.[39] Less obvious, but no less important, was the way in
which McGee's "active, discerning mind" was becoming cramped by
Irish American nationalist political culture. During the spring of 1845,
his writings registered a growing frustration with hyperbolic expres-
sions of patriotism, with a pervasive victim mentality, and with Irish
American resistance to rigorous self-criticism.

Particularly revealing in this respect was his attitude to St Patrick's
Day celebrations. Having calmed down after his initial reaction to the
Philadelphia riots, McGee now sought to depoliticize St Patrick's Day
and avoid a nativist backlash. "We are totally opposed to all public processions on next St. Patrick's day, or on any future recurrence of it," he
wrote. There should be no fighting, no drinking, no "frothy orations,"
no "vulgar triumph of party," and no "anniversary of any physical
victory." Instead, the day should be celebrated in a quiet, contempla-
tive, religious manner, in a spirit of Christian love and forgiveness.
In the evening, there should be a banquet with "song and sentiment,"
celebrating St Patrick, Father Mathew, and Daniel O'Connell. "For
heaven's sake though," he added, "let us have no humbug toasts. No
'shamrock wreaths' and 'sighing harps,' no comparisons between Mr.
O'Connell and Julius Caesar." Such self-congratulatory rodomontade
was suffocating; McGee needed more room to breathe. And his dismissive remarks about "drabbled processions" prefigured his later opposition to St Patrick's Day parades in Canada during the late 1850s.[40]

The critical tone that McGee took towards inflated nationalist rhetoric marked a significant departure from his first American speeches
and writings, which had threatened to bury the Irish in praise. Now

he was beginning to recoil against Irish exceptionalism – the view that the Irish were "the noblest yet the most unfortunate of men" – and to insist that healthy self-criticism was necessary to improve the condition of Irish immigrants. He attacked Irish American newspapers for treating the Irish as passive victims and for preaching up a "species of fatalism." "The 'Emigrant' Press," he wrote, "have foolishly concealed the faults of our people, and they have not sought out their weaknesses, nor attempted to cure their character of the strange solecisms which weaken and deprave it. This task yet remains to be accomplished, and before it can be the Irish in America must learn to listen to their own faults." It was time, he argued, to tell the Irish some hard truths about why they were "in some sort a marked and avoided class," and to stop them from blaming their condition on everyone but themselves. If his fellow editors shirked their responsibility, McGee would set out to accomplish the task himself.[41]

One of his main targets was the "evil" of internal divisions within the American Irish, caused in part by the transmission of local loyalties from Ireland to the United States: "Of all the low, narrow, and selfish follies of our race, this sort of parochial exclusiveness is the most detestable. Just imagine for an instant, men in their senses seeming to believe that there can be no good hearts, or honest souls out of their own parish, on the other side of a stream, or across a glebe boundary; what folly, what infamy! And others believing in the supremacy of their own county or province, in the higher order of mind in this or that locality, what madness!" Against such tendencies, McGee emphasized the importance of developing a broad, inclusive national consciousness. "The oppressor of all Ireland makes no distinction when he designs to enslave," he remarked, "why should we, when we intend to liberate?"[42]

The fight against "parochial exclusiveness" would continue throughout most of McGee's subsequent career, as would his criticism of another feature of Irish American life – the prevalence of ward bosses who built up a popular following for the sole purpose of acquiring money and power. The only way to "vindicate the national character from this accursed blotch upon its beauty," he wrote, was through education; the Irish must learn to think for themselves and to work for the greater good, rather than attaching themselves to local leaders and focusing on their immediate self-advantage. But the task of education was itself fraught with difficulties. McGee expressed considerable frustration about "our insensibility as a class to all improvements of the mind" and "our fierce and uncontrollable hostility to advice from any of *our own*." Giving people advice that they did not want to hear and trying to make them "listen to their own faults" was bound to rub many Irish Americans the wrong way; had McGee stayed in the United States beyond the spring of 1845, he would have had a major struggle on his hands.[43]

To a large extent, this was because any exercise in self-criticism could easily play into the hands of nativists. In effect, McGee had opened up a wide gap between his idealized version of the Irish "national character" and his sense of what was actually happening on the ground. According to his ideal, the Irish were a devout, spiritual, sober, broad-minded, and freedom-loving Celtic people; contradicting this image, he found much evidence of drunkenness, parochialism, ward-boss politics, and anti-intellectualism. The ideal seemed remote, abstract, and aspirational; the "faults" appeared immediate, concrete, and practical. There were so many "blotches" that the beauty threatened to disappear altogether. And these were the very "blotches" that nativists seized on to argue that the Irish national character was in fact ugly through and through. It is no wonder, then, that many Irish people were hypersensitive to criticism. "I'm afraid that, touch the Irish as you will, unless you tickle their vanity, you will stir a hornet's nest," commented Father John McCaffrey in 1848. "Their nationality is intense, touchy, suspicious, unreasoning, morbid, – as irritable & as easily hurt as a patient in inflammatory rheumatism."[44] Under conditions of external attack, internal criticism could easily appear as a species of betrayal; instead of closing ranks against the common enemy, McGee seemed to be supplying nativists with even more anti-Irish ammunition.

The full consequences of McGee's position would not work themselves out for several years; for the time being, he was saved by his departure for Ireland that May. His writings in America had impressed the Repealers in Ireland, and he was offered a position with the O'Connellite *Freeman's Journal*. The salary would provide him with a "large competence," the work would occupy only two or three days a week, and the location would put him at the heart of the campaign for Repeal; all in all, the opportunity was far too good to miss. On 13 May his "friends and admirers" gave him a farewell banquet at the Stackpole House; the guest list was a roll call of prominent Irish American Repealers, including some who came from Ohio, Virginia, and Nova Scotia. A series of speeches praised McGee for his contribution to the Repeal movement and his work on behalf of Irish Catholics in the United States. With his "practical experience" of the United States, observed one speaker, McGee would be able to teach the "lessons of democracy" to his benighted countrymen. In reply, McGee spoke of the need to "make for ourselves a name abroad, an independence at home, a flag, a literature, and a virtuous posterity." "Gentlemen," he said, "if ever, in after life temptation should try my sincerity, or any base suggestion be whispered in my ear by intrigue, I will remember this night, and its memory shall become the talisman of my rectitude." Three days later, on 16 May, he said goodbye to his friends and to Dorcas, and boarded the steamship *Hibernia*, bound for Liverpool.[45]

During the three years that had passed since he had first sailed into the St Lawrence, McGee had established a reputation as an orator, writer, and editor, as one of the most energetic supporters of Repeal, and as an outspoken and controversial defender of Catholic Irish Americans against nativist attacks. We need to remind ourselves that when he left the United States, he was only one month past his twentieth birthday; many of his contemporaries marked him out as a genius who was destined for still greater things.[46]

In the *Boston Pilot* and in his speeches and letters, McGee had articulated some of the major themes that would preoccupy him for the rest of his life. His views on the liberating potential of education and the importance of cultural nationalism were constant components of his later career. In contrast, the combative Catholicism that had arisen in reaction to the Philadelphia riots of 1844 faded away during his Young Ireland period, only to be reactivated and intensified by the resurgence of nativism during the early 1850s. McGee's attitude to the United States would change significantly, but signs of his later political conservatism were already visible by 1845. His attack on the "nervous uncertainty" of life in the United States, together with his denunciations of "parochial exclusiveness" and "place hunting" among the American Irish, reappeared during the 1850s and found their best-known expression in his Wexford speech of 1865. Other themes that were barely noticeable during his early American career acquired greater importance in the years to come. A passing remark that there was "less prejudice and more room"[47] for Irish Catholics in the American West foreshadowed his colonization schemes of the 1850s, just as a brief comment on the dangers of Ribbonism and Orangeism anticipated his later arguments against secret societies. There were all kinds of potentialities here, whose realization would depend on changing conditions and the pressures of circumstance.

Not only many of the central themes but also some of the inner tensions and contradictions in McGee's thought became apparent during his first years in America. He combined passionate anti-British speeches with the conviction that Ireland and Britain could cooperate as equals under the Crown, and a willingness to accept a federal Anglo-Irish settlement. He adopted an exclusive, ideologically based definition of the "Irish people" (Catholics plus Protestant Repealers) but also argued for an open and inclusive form of nationality. He admired revolutionary nationalists but rejected revolutionary nationalism; he believed that the route to Repeal lay through moral force, but his objection to physical force was based on practical rather than theoretical grounds. He allowed himself to be provoked into making rash, impassioned, and exaggerated remarks, only to backtrack and sidestep when his imprudence caught up with him; the McGee Shuffle became a regular feature of his career. He responded to criticism with knee-jerk reactions that simply inverted the arguments of his opponents; faced with nativist charges of Catholic Irish inferiority, he asserted the political, religious, and racial superiority of the Irish Celt over the American Anglo-Saxon. Yet he also demonstrated an awareness of the dangers of polarization, especially given the minority status of Irish Catholics in North America; this was the main reason why he objected to holding a St Patrick's Day parade in Boston in 1845, just as he did in Toronto thirteen years later. Much of his subsequent career was spent working through such tensions, trying to reconcile the contradictions, and attempting to find the centre between his passions and his intellect.

There was one thing, though, that McGee missed. Tucked away in one of the columns of the *Boston Pilot* in October 1844 was a short report on a "disease which seems to have infected the potatoe [sic] crop" in New England and New York.[48] The report wrote of the stench that filled the fields, the rotting tubers, and the speed with which the disease struck and spread. Nobody, not even the most perspicacious observers, realized the impending impact on Ireland of *phythophthora infestans*.

PART TWO

Ireland

Tell all my friends whom you may see in Providence that I am well
– right well. Tell them too that I am one of those who are called
"Young Ireland" – a body of men whose worth will be better known
ten years hence than it is now. Tell them we will not see Ireland sold
or swapped to any English faction for any boons, whatever.
Bid them watch us, and wait.

McGee to Bella Morgan, 3 October 1846

CHAPTER FOUR

The Double Curse of Famine and Dissension

May 1845 – December 1846

When McGee left Wexford for Quebec in 1842, he had travelled by sail on a journey that took over a month; when he returned from Boston to Liverpool three years later, he went by steamship on a trip that took two weeks, including a stopover at Halifax. The Atlantic was shrinking. "A voyage to America," he remarked, "is now no miracle." Steam power was also revolutionizing communications by land; although Ireland lagged far behind England in railway construction, with only sixty-five miles of track in 1845, there would soon be a rapid expansion of railway lines. Shortly after he arrived in Ireland, McGee included "railroad intercourse" among the factors that would "bring together the Catholic and the Protestant masses of the population." More generally, he argued that railways would "create an entirely new relation between the nations of the earth" and become "the bonds of a new state of society." If nostalgic images of a Celtic Golden Age informed McGee's sense of the past, a belief in the transformative and liberating potential of the new technology shaped his sense of the future. The central task, he believed, was to find the right balance between modernity and tradition, material progress and spiritual faith, intelligence and conscience.[1]

McGee's optimism was reinforced by the circumstances of his return; the promising but unknown youngster from Wexford had become a rising star in the American Repeal movement, and his reputation was opening up new opportunities and new friendships. During his brief visit to Halifax en route to Liverpool, McGee met Father Richard Baptist O'Brien, the president of St Mary's College, who later taught at the All Hallows Mission College in Dublin and became Dean of Limerick; the two men were impressed with one another and were still corresponding towards the end of McGee's life. After landing in Dublin (just missing the "greatest spectacle Dublin ever beheld," commemorating the anniversary of O'Connell's imprisonment on 30 May 1844), McGee returned to Wexford, where he was "munificently feasted" and welcomed home as the local boy made good. At a public dinner, the Very Reverend Dr John Sinnott, president of St Peter's College and a strong supporter of Repeal, congratulated him for his work as the "distinguished editor" of the *Boston Pilot*. "He was young in years," said Sinnott, "but he was a veteran in knowledge, in genius, in energy, and in the inestimable services he has rendered to the cause of Ireland." In response, McGee stated that Sinnott's praise was "the proudest laurel of his life." After three years in the United States, he said, it was good to be back in a country with a "stronger sense of religious duty" and a "wide and steady morality." True, Ireland was also "the poorest of nations," but this condition would soon by remedied by Repeal, the panacea for all of Ireland's problems.[2]

For the time being, however, family matters took precedence over politics. Back on Paradise Road, relations between his "father's family" and his stepmother had improved. "The step-mother [was] behaving herself very well," he wrote, "though more from policy than affection, of course." His brother had been rising through the ranks at sea. During the summer of 1843, Laurence had spent a month in a Quebec jail after getting into a fight with the ship's mate, Tom Codd, on the *Leo*. "I was satisfied for him to get a months incarceration," commented his father, "providing he beat the Scoundrel well for he is a horrid character." The captain agreed; Codd was discharged, and Laurence was promoted to chief mate. Having proved himself in that capacity, he had recently become captain of a Wexford ship, the *Dora*. Meanwhile, Dorcas was still in Boston, but McGee was making plans to bring her back to Ireland. "It would not be wise or just to let her stay alone there," he wrote. During his stay in Wexford, McGee also contemplated his own future. He decided to stay in Dublin for the next three or four years, keep working for the *Freeman's Journal*, and take a law degree at Trinity College; he would then either remain in Ireland or practise law in New York. "I see nothing to stop me in this career," he told his Aunt Bella.[3]

After spending the best part of a month in Wexford, McGee returned to Dublin, started work at the *Freeman's* office, and began attending meetings of the Repeal Association at Conciliation Hall, the "incipient senate of a Free Nation." Here, he listened to the speeches of Thomas Davis and William Smith O'Brien, and was transfixed by the oratory of Daniel O'Connell, who had been released from prison the previous September. As the seventy-year-old Liberator stepped onto the platform, McGee "felt a glow" going through him, as if, he said, "an electric wire were pouring in its flood at every pore of my body ... I had never seen a man with so great a load of history on his back, and the proximity of so much self-achieved greatness made the air hot about me, and immersed me in a kind of intoxicating delirium." And this was before O'Connell had even opened his mouth. The speech, when it came, more than lived up to McGee's expectations: "All the descriptions of it I have ever read," he wrote, "fall far short of the real magic of his manner, and the extraordinary inflections of his voice." What is most striking about these comments is not only their quasi-religious ecstasy but also their sense of immediacy; McGee was now at the centre of events and was meeting the men whose work he had admired from across the Atlantic.[4]

—•—

"From O'Connell, from Dr. McHale [sic], from 'Young Ireland' and all," he wrote, "my reception has been most cordial." Yet beneath the common cordiality, tensions were growing between O'Connell and Archbishop John MacHale on the one hand, and Young Ireland on the other. Although the Young Irelanders had reluctantly acquiesced in O'Connell's retreat at Clontarf, they felt that their leader had let them down, and worried that the Repeal movement was losing momentum. During the summer of 1844, the Young Ireland leaders feared that O'Connell was planning to abandon Repeal, move towards an alliance with the Whigs, and silence Young Ireland; O'Connell's flirtation with federalism later in the year appeared to confirm their suspicions.[5]

Daniel O'Connell speaking in Dublin in 1844, the year before McGee returned to Ireland (*Illustrated London News*)

Other differences were developing. O'Connell had refused to accept money from American Repeal associations that acquiesced in slavery; in response, Young Irelanders such as Charles Gavan Duffy, Thomas Davis, and John Dillon bristled with anger, insisting that Repeal must take priority over abolitionism. Dillon denounced O'Connell's "puerile folly" and complained that his position was "supremely disgusting to the Americans, and to every man of honour and spirit." When John O'Connell echoed his father's antislavery arguments, Dillon asserted that "public opinion is universally against him." The increasing prominence of John O'Connell in the Repeal Association was itself an issue for the Young Irelanders. John O'Connell not only let slavery get in the way of Repeal, they argued, but he also identified nationalism too closely with Catholicism, was lukewarm about Repeal, and was being groomed by his father for the succession.[6]

Matters came to a head in May 1845. As part of his strategy to detach the Catholic Church from the Repeal movement and to improve the quality of education in Ireland, Peel announced plans for three non-denominational universities: in Cork, Galway, and Belfast. The Catholic hierarchy was divided on the issue. Some were prepared to negotiate with the government, while Archbishop MacHale and his supporters came down unequivocally against anything that smacked of "mixed education." MacHale was also the leader of the Repeal faction within the hierarchy; to alienate him would undermine clerical support for the movement. Partly because of this, and partly through conviction, John O'Connell condemned the Colleges Bill at a committee meeting of the Repeal Association; shortly afterwards, his father joined the attack.

The Young Irelanders, in contrast, supported the non-denominational principle, believing that education, like nationality itself, should rise above religious differences. The division was so deep that it threatened to tear the Repeal Association apart; Daniel and John O'Connell fulminated against Peel's "Godless Colleges," while Davis regarded their position as nothing more than "blind bigotry." At a Repeal meeting on 26 May, Daniel O'Connell implied that Davis was anti-Catholic and denounced the "section of politicians styling themselves the Young Ireland Party." "I shall stand by Old Ireland," he said, "and I have some slight notion that Old Ireland will stand by me." Davis, taut with tension, professed his affection towards O'Connell and began to weep, whereupon O'Connell hugged Davis and expressed his love for him. A semblance of reconciliation had been achieved, but the underlying divisions remained, with most Repealers supporting O'Connell. "Exit Hibernia in tears," was the caustic comment of the Young Irelander Thomas MacNevin.[7]

McGee was four days out from Liverpool when this happened. Although he could not have known it, he was heading into a difficult situation. On the one hand, he was about to take up a position with O'Connell's *Freeman's Journal* and had great respect and admiration for O'Connell's achievements. On the other, he was closer in sympathy and spirit to the *Nation* newspaper, and his American writings were generally in tune with the Young Ireland movement. The one exception was the issue of federalism, where McGee had been closer to O'Connell than to Duffy – although even here it should be pointed out that other Young Irelanders, such as Davis, were prepared to be flexible about federalism. On the question of slavery, however, McGee was very much in the Young Ireland mainstream; he had also come round to the Young Ireland position on non-denominational education. From arguing in September 1844 that emigrant education should be "purely and truly Catholic," McGee had endorsed mixed education in early 1845, and had no qualms about planning to attend Trinity College, which he regarded as "an immense instrument of Protestant enlightenment" rather than a threat to Catholic souls.[8] Similarly, McGee's emphasis on cultural nationalism marked him out from O'Connell's utilitarianism and ensured that he would become part of Young Ireland's project to awaken the "spirit of the nation" through poetry, literature, music, language, history, archaeology, and antiquarian pursuits. When McGee returned to Ireland, the Repeal movement was still able to contain these differences, though the cracks were beginning to show. As the divisions between O'Connell and the Young Irelanders widened, there was little doubt about which side he would support.

Within weeks, McGee began to develop close connections with the leaders of Young Ireland. The summer of 1845 was the most important in his life in terms of the friendships he formed and the people he met. Wilson Gray of the *Freeman's Journal* introduced him to Duffy, whom McGee later described as the "father of my mind, fosterer of my principles." Over the next three years, McGee became one of Duffy's closest allies in the Young Ireland movement. As a republican exile in the United States, McGee aspired to follow Duffy's example and paid careful attention to his political advice. McGee's decision to move into Canadian politics was probably influenced by Duffy's emigration to Australia in 1855.[9]

For his part, Duffy had mixed opinions about his protégé. He was impressed by McGee's "fertile brains and great originality" as well as his "sweet and flexible voice," and informed Davis that McGee would be a "serviceable recruit." But he also found McGee's manner and appearance off-putting: "In the midst of a group of self-confident, somewhat dandified young men," wrote Duffy, "he looked ill-dressed and underbred, and till the exercise of authority much later gave him self-reliance, he seemed painfully deferential." "His dress," Duffy remarked, "was slovenly even for the careless class to which he belonged." If McGee's clothing was one "drawback," in Duffy's view, another was his "unaccountable Negro cast of features," which were "a constant source of jesting allusions." His enemies routinely referred to him as "Darky McGee."[10]

Writing towards the end of the nineteenth century about McGee's "decided African caste and woolly hair," Martin MacDermott speculated that this so-called "negro race-mark," which he had "noticed in two or three other instances," came from "one of those faithful countrymen of ours whom Cromwell or his son Henry sent as slaves to the West Indies, and who may be presumed to have married there women of African blood." One is tempted to dismiss this out of hand, except for the fact that similar speculations were made about Bishop John Fitzpatrick of Boston, McGee's second cousin on his mother's side. It is just possible that one of McGee's maternal great-grandparents was Afro-American, but in the absence of evidence skepticism is in order. At any (*facing page, left*) Charles Gavan Duffy (1816–1903). A co-founder of the *Nation* newspaper, a prominent Young Irelander, and a leading figure in the Irish Confederation of 1847–48, Duffy was arrested (and ultimately acquitted) for his revolutionary writings shortly before the rising of 1848. After his release, he formed the constitutional nationalist Irish Brigade, and became a member of Parliament for New Ross. In 1855, having come to the conclusion that there was "no more hope for the Irish Cause than for the corpse on the dissecting table," he emigrated to Australia, where he subsequently became the premier of Victoria. McGee in 1849 described Duffy as the "father of my mind, fosterer of my principles," and aspired in the United States to become "the Duffy of our Emigrants." (Charles Gavan Duffy, *Young Ireland* [1896], vol. 1)

(*facing page, right*) Thomas Davis (1814–45). A poet, songwriter, and romantic nationalist who believed that Protestants and Catholics could find common ground in Ireland's cultural heritage, Davis was the chief inspiration behind the Young Ireland movement. He played a leading role in the establishment of the *Nation* newspaper and in the attempt to express the "spirit of the nation" through the study of art, history, poetry, music, antiquarianism, and archaeology, and through the revival of the Gaelic language. McGee was deeply impressed by Davis, describing him as "an Apostle of Nationality." Davis, however, was less impressed by McGee: "He has read and thought a great deal," Davis remarked, "and I might have liked him better if he had not so obviously determined to *transact* an acquaintance with me." (Duffy, *Young Ireland*, vol. 1)

---

rate, McGee never publicly responded to any of the "Darky McGee" attacks, and there was nothing unusual about his views on slavery, which were virtually indistinguishable from those of his Young Ireland colleagues.[11]

Duffy provided McGee with an entry point into Young Ireland social circles and introduced him to Davis, "a man destined to largely influence his life." Describing Davis as "one of the most frank and pure-minded of men," McGee admired his prose and poetry, his view of nationality as a "spiritual essence," and his efforts to embrace "every

order and class in Ireland." Davis, like Duffy, was impressed with McGee's mind but had reservations about his personality. He found McGee too forward and felt that his "Irish nature" had been "spoiled ... by the Yankees" – another indication of the social gap that separated McGee from his Young Ireland contemporaries.[12]

The emerging image, then, is of a man who remained something of a social outsider but whose abilities were immediately recognized and respected. He was becoming a familiar figure among Dublin's intelligentsia, mixing with antiquarians, artists, and writers. Studying ancient manuscripts in the Royal Irish Academy, he met Eugene O'Curry, one of the foremost Celtic scholars in the country. Seventeen years later, when McGee had become a cabinet minister in Canada and was taking the waters near Rivière-du-Loup, he opened a newspaper and was shocked to learn of O'Curry's death: "Words cannot express my love and admiration for that rare old man," he told T.D. O'Sullivan.[13]

Another frequent visitor to the Royal Irish Academy whom McGee met was George Petrie, the landscape artist and founding father of

Irish archaeology. McGee was particularly impressed with Petrie's prize-winning work on the round towers of Ireland and his painting of Irish scenes, describing him as "the first who ever combined in so perfect a degree the antiquary and the artist." In McGee's view, O'Curry and Petrie, along with the antiquary John O'Donovan, formed a "third party" (the others being "Young and Old Ireland") that transformed the outlook of the "Irish educated class." "Instead of being ashamed of their country as their fathers were," he wrote, "they grew proud of it."[14]

McGee also met James Duffy, the publisher of the new Library of Ireland series, which disseminated Young Ireland writings on history and literature at cheap prices to a large audience, and which in McGee's view heralded the "intellectual emancipation of Ireland." At a party that James Duffy held in Bray, County Wicklow, McGee was introduced to Petrie's friend and fellow painter Frederick William Burton, whose *The Aran Fisherman's Drowned Child* (1841) remains one of the central works in Irish art. Also there was the writer William Carleton (not an admirer of Burton's famous painting), whom McGee described as "a sort of Meath farmer, who had just been at a cattle show, and *hadn't* got a prize." With them was virtually the entire cast and crew of Young Ireland, including Gavan Duffy and Davis. Walking along the Wicklow hills, McGee felt a deep sense of belonging. The day, he wrote, "passed over me like an enchantment, for I was among the fairest scenes of Ireland, with the men who had done most to raise her name in art and literature."[15]

Other excursions followed, replete with conversations about art, literature and politics. In August, McGee and Gavan Duffy went on a fortnight's walking tour in Wicklow, following directions that had been provided by Davis. They inspected the round tower of Glendalough, journeyed over mountains and through glens, visited the site of the battle of Arklow during the rising of 1798, "in company with an old man and woman, survivors of the fatal day," and walked along the coast road from Arklow to Bray. As they moved through the scenes of Irish history, they speculated about the "dead past and unborn future," and mused about time, fate, and destiny. The ideas of Thomas Carlyle were uppermost in Duffy's mind; he had met Carlyle in London

four months earlier, had imbibed his views on the interconnectedness
of the past, present, and future, and declared himself one of Carlyle's
"sworn disciples." Applying Carlylean concepts to Ireland's condition,
Duffy believed that Young Ireland was the present manifestation of
an eternal spirit of the nation, which lay behind the heroic battles of
the past and would inevitably culminate in Irish freedom. Such views
struck a responsive chord with McGee, whose earlier American poems
had spoken of Ireland's destiny. In some of his subsequent poems for
the *Nation*, the influence of Carlyle, mediated through Gavan Duffy,
is evident. In "Time's Teachings," for example, McGee wrote of Time
as the messenger of God, travelling along a path full of struggle and
sacrifice that led to liberty and prosperity while singing that "Reckoning delay'd will come at last." As Brian Lambkin has pointed out, such
ideas were a nineteenth-century forerunner of the Irish Republican
Army's slogan *Tiocfaidh ar lá* – "Our day will come."[16]

McGee and Duffy also spent much of their time discussing the political
and social situation in Ireland. The biggest obstacles to Irish justice and
freedom, McGee believed, were threefold – the landlords, the "vile
curse of sectarian animosity," and the "Orangemen of the North."
Within six weeks of his return to Ireland, he penned a scathing article
for the *Boston Pilot* on the Irish gentry. "The richest of them in posses-
sions are the poorest in spirit," he wrote, "and it is only on the con-
fines, where their class meets that of the commonalty, that we observe
any public character springing up." He characterized most landlords
as social parasites, enriching themselves through the sweat and toil of
their tenants. "You cannot imagine," he wrote, "the fierce hatred I feel
for that inhuman class." Although McGee did not condone agrarian
violence, he could understand and in some sense identify with what
he saw as its underlying motivation. The rapacity of landlords resulted
in "'murders in Tipperary,' and landlord shooting in general; summary ejectments were followed by as summary revenge; the landlord
was shot not for his religion but for his arbitrary harshness, and irresponsible tyranny." McGee was back in his binary mode of thinking
– oppressive landlords versus oppressed tenants, without a nuance in

sight. Given the degree of exploitation that did indeed characterize the Irish landholding system, with all its problems of subdivision and subletting, such anger is perfectly comprehensible. At the same time, it is difficult to see how McGee's view that the landlords were politically and socially oppressive could be reconciled with his conviction that an effective national movement must embrace all classes, including the gentry.[17]

Compounding the problem of landlordism was that of sectarianism. In Protestant Ulster, he wrote, tenants were given at least three months' notice before an eviction and were compensated for improvements they had made to the farm. But in the rest of the country, where the landlords were Protestant and the tenants were Catholic, the tenants were treated like "serfs to a Russian Lord." The landlords were motivated by sectarianism, whereas the "southern peasants" who fought and sometimes shot them were driven by desperation. At a more general level, the state itself was fundamentally sectarian, since "all the favors of England are showered down on one creed, and all her ill-humor on another." The problem lay not in rival Protestant and Catholic theological differences, but in the fact that the Anglican minority enjoyed the privileges of belonging to the established state church, while the Catholic majority did not. "The time is come I firmly believe when Ireland must either have two endowed churches," he wrote, "or each must be left to voluntary sustenance."[18]

The most extreme manifestation of sectarianism, in McGee's view, could be found in the Orange Order. Possibly under the influence of Duffy, who thought that Orangemen should be faced down rather than conciliated, and probably with recent memories in mind of the Orange-nativist alliance in Philadelphia, McGee took a hard line against the organization. He put little stock in the hope he had once expressed in America that Orangemen might be won over to Repeal; it was, after all, hard to see any of them switching sides. Ireland, he insisted, was a Catholic nation. Enlightened Protestants supported its struggle for freedom, while unenlightened Protestants attempted to perpetuate their religious, political, and economic privileges through Orangeism.

But if converting Orangemen to Repeal appeared to be a lost cause, McGee comforted himself with the belief that Orangeism in Ireland was on the point of collapse: "The Orangemen of the North are being broken into sections, disorganised, and effectually weakened." Fighting among themselves, and abandoned by the aristocracy, they had become "a strong and active, but headless body," with no sense of direction. A fundamental shift in the balance of power was occurring, he believed; the Orangemen were getting weaker at the very time that the cause of Repeal was gathering momentum. In fact, this was a major misreading of the situation. During the mid-1840s, the Orange Order was experiencing a revival and attracting conservative evangelical Presbyterians, while the Repeal movement was heading towards a split between Old and Young Ireland. But the history of nationalist images of Orangeism is full of premature obituaries, and McGee's views were no exception.[19]

Although he occasionally showed signs of pessimism – "I see no probability of a near remedy for the social grievances of Ireland," he had written in July – and although he recognized that the struggle for Repeal would be a long haul, McGee remained confident that the nationalist cause would ultimately prevail and that Young Ireland would be in the vanguard of change. But in September, Young Ireland suddenly lost its leading figure when Thomas Davis contracted scarlet fever and died within a week; he was only thirty years old. His death shook the movement to the core, and coincided with a wider crisis of personnel. John Dillon, one of the founders of the *Nation*, was himself seriously ill and recuperating in Madeira, while his colleague Thomas MacNevin was in the early stages of a brain disease that would take his life three years later. Two other prominent Young Irelanders, John Pigot and John O'Hagan, were leaving for London to take up their legal studies (O'Hagan would eventually become the first Catholic lord chancellor of Ireland since the reign of James II). Meanwhile, Duffy was reeling from a double blow: a few days after Davis's funeral, his wife had died from consumption. "Misfortune had not come single, but in troops," he wrote. Immediately after Davis's death, the entire movement seemed gripped by "discouragement and dismay," and "the men who had made the *Nation* a great power and a trusted counsellor of the people were stricken with sudden and unexpected paralysis."[20]

(*facing page, left*) John Mitchel (1815–75). From the Ulster Presbyterian radical tradition, Mitchel was on the ultranationalist wing of the Young Ireland movement and the Irish Confederation, and a militant writer first for the *Nation* and then for his own revolutionary newspaper, the *United Irishman*. In the spring of 1848 he was found guilty of treason-felony and sentenced to fourteen years' transportation in Australia. Escaping to the United States in 1853, he edited the New York *Citizen* in 1854 and then moved to Tennessee, supporting Irish freedom and Afro-American slavery with no consciousness of contradiction. In 1846–47 McGee and Mitchel were on good terms – so much so that McGee dedicated his *Memoir of the Life and Conquests of Art Mac Murrough* to Mitchel. By the winter of 1847–48, however, their political paths diverged sharply, and the two men became bitter political enemies – although each one, in his own way, came to share a common antipathy to the individualism and materialism they found in American life. (Duffy, *Young Ireland*, vol. 2)

(*facing page, right*) Thomas Devin Reilly (1824–54). An intense nationalist, who worked closely with Mitchel on the *Nation* and the *United Irishman*, Devin Reilly was on the revolutionary council that improvised the rising of 1848. After the failure of the rising, he escaped to the United States, where he immersed himself in revolutionary Irish American journalism, joined the Young America movement, and edited the *Democratic Review*. His political differences with McGee were exacerbated by personal antagonism; according to Duffy, Reilly had "a fierce jealousy" of McGee. The result was a series of personal attacks on McGee, in which Reilly had no compunction about hitting below the belt. (Michael Doheny, *The Felon's Track* [1849; 1951])

In these circumstances, Duffy set out to revive the movement and bring in new recruits – men whose careers would become closely connected to that of McGee. Among them was John Mitchel, who had been working as a solicitor in Banbridge. A brilliant polemicist, he was given a full-time job with the *Nation*, rapidly established himself as one of its most radical writers, and became the leading ideologue of revolutionary anglophobic Irish nationalism in the nineteenth century, diametrically opposed to the constitutional nationalism that Duffy came to exemplify. ("He would have lived and died a village attor-

ney," Duffy later remarked, "if I had not drawn him out of his obscurity and enlisted him in the national cause.") Working with Mitchel was Thomas Devin Reilly, a man with "red lightning in his blood" and a "constant sufferer from nervous headache," whose ultranationalist attitudes matched those of his mentor. Duffy was also joined by Thomas Francis Meagher, a "rather foppish" twenty-two-year-old from Waterford who had been educated in Ireland and England by the Jesuits, and who gave stirring nationalist speeches in an English accent. Another recruit was the nineteen-year-old Richard O'Gorman, a "young dandy" who had graduated from Trinity College three years earlier and became one of the movement's finest orators. Linking up with "veterans" such as Michael Doheny and Michael John Barry, and flanked by poets such as James Clarence Mangan and Denis Florence MacCarthy, these men formed what Duffy described as "the second Young Ireland party." They were determined to carry on the struggle and to resist any nationalist backsliding on the Repeal question.[21]

As yet, McGee was not part of this inner circle, even though he shared its dominant values and beliefs, and its hero-worship of Davis. "In him Ireland has lost a gifted poet, an ardent, single-purposed, (*facing page, left*) Thomas Francis Meagher (1823–67). An outstanding orator, popularly known as "Meagher of the Sword" after one of his speeches, Meagher was initially on the constitutional nationalist wing of the Young Ireland movement. But he became increasingly radical in the spring of 1848, joined the revolutionary council, and attempted to rally support for the rising that fizzled out in Ballingarry. His death sentence for high treason was commuted to transportation for life in Australia. Escaping to the United States in 1852, he became one of the most celebrated Irish American nationalists of his generation, fought with the Union Army during the Civil War, and died in mysterious circumstances after becoming the acting governor of Montana. Although McGee and Meagher were close during the Young Ireland years, their friendship could not withstand McGee's conversion to ultramontanism in 1851. (Duffy, *Young Ireland*, vol. 2)

(*facing page, right*) Richard O'Gorman (1826–95). One of the finest orators in the Young Ireland movement, O'Gorman moved from moderation to militancy in 1848, became part of the revolutionary council, and set out to organize the revolutionary movement in Limerick. He escaped to America in 1849, where he became a lawyer and judge, remained active in Irish American politics, and wound up as a cog in William "Boss" Tweed's corrupt political machine in New York. During his Young Ireland years, O'Gorman feared that Duffy and McGee were becoming dictatorial; in the United States, he responded with ironic detachment to McGee's ultramontanism: "Magee is now a pious Catholic and believes in Divine right as applied to all manner of respectable officials. I have long ceased to be Angry at him." McGee, in common with other Young Irelanders, respected O'Gorman's sharp mind, but added that he "thinks only when he is put to it." (Duffy, *Young Ireland*, vol. 2)

---

upright Repealer," he wrote, "a mind which was capable of the greatest achievements, whether of research or imagination, an Apostle of Nationality whose place it will be hard, almost impossible, to fill up." Almost impossible; it is entirely conceivable that McGee aspired to fill Davis's place himself. Duffy certainly believed that McGee had the abilities to do so, despite his reservations about McGee's moral standards. But in the autumn of 1845, McGee was unable to join the "second Young Ireland party." He was still working for the O'Connellite *Free-*

man's Journal, and there was no "honourable escape" from his contract. So he remained in the anomalous position of supporting the *Nation* while writing for its rival.[22]

It was probably in the *Freeman's* office that McGee first heard the news that would change the course of Irish history. The much-feared potato blight, which had crossed the Atlantic from the United States to continental Europe and spread to England, finally reached Ireland in September 1845. More than half Ireland's population depended largely on potatoes, and three million people subsisted entirely on a diet of potatoes and buttermilk; men on the lower rungs of the agrarian economy ate twelve to fourteen pounds of potatoes each day. The deindustrialization of Ireland outside the northeast meant that few employment possibilities were available apart from farming. While it was clear that a total crop failure would have catastrophic consequences, the extent of the potato blight remained uncertain between September and November. A government-appointed Scientific Commission reported that over half the crop had been lost. The actual figure was closer to a third, but the potential for disaster remained serious enough.[23]

Our understanding of the situation in late 1845 has been hindered by hindsight. We know that the potato was to fail almost completely in 1846–47, that the crop of 1847–48 would be too small to sustain the population, that the blight would return with a vengeance in 1848–49, and that around one million people would die and another million emigrate between 1846 and 1851. Contemporaries could not have anticipated this sequence of events. Most people recognized that urgent and immediate action was needed in the autumn of 1845 but had no idea how much worse things would get in the following years. McGee's first reaction to the "State of the Harvest," written on 17 October for the *Boston Pilot,* must be understood in this context. "Only those who personally know Ireland," he told his American readers, "can form a just opinion of the apprehension these tidings have created." At the same time, he cautioned them against alarmism: "On the whole, though we must expect some serious degree of scarcity, I think I may safely add there are as yet no sufficient grounds for apprehending anything like famine."[24]

If anything, his sense that Ireland could ride out the crisis increased towards the end of the year. "I certainly feel assured now," he wrote at the beginning of November, "from all I hear and see, that extraordinary exertions on the part of the Government and the wealthy, will be requisite to avert that fearful calamity." Public meetings in Dublin had called upon Peel's government to import duty-free food, to ban the export of oats, to establish public granaries, and to provide work and wages by encouraging railway construction. McGee endorsed all these demands, placing particular emphasis on the repeal of the Corn Laws, which prohibited the import of grain until domestic prices had risen to a fixed level.[25]

The idea behind the Corn Laws was to protect landed interests in the United Kingdom by guaranteeing farmers a minimum price; this meant that producers benefited at the expense of consumers, who had to pay more for their bread. Irish nationalists in general, and Young Ireland in particular, were divided over whether or not the Corn Laws should be repealed. O'Connell supported their repeal, on the grounds that free trade would bring more food into Ireland. In contrast, a significant section of Young Ireland argued that repeal was irrelevant for Ireland, on the assumption that there was already enough grain in the country to feed the entire population, and the point was to stop food from getting out rather than bringing it in. McGee aligned himself with O'Connell's position, arguing that repeal would reduce the price of food, and insisting that oats must be kept in the country – free trade for imports, in other words, coupled with selective protectionism for exports.[26]

In McGee's view, the repeal of the Corn Laws would not only alleviate the immediate economic crisis but also serve Ireland's long-term political interests. Once England became dependent on foreign countries for its food supply, he argued, its power would quickly wane: "England's arrogant *nationality* is gone. Give foreign nations the power of feeding her people, or stopping their supplies ... and their boastful reliance on the invincibility of their own roast beef and plum-pudding valor, is gone forever." Ireland, McGee asserted, produced more grain than it consumed. When grain from the Baltic and the United States flooded British markets, Irish grain would be consumed at home, and Ireland would become economically self-sufficient. Within six years, he predicted, the new economic situation would "loosen and destroy England's distinctive nationality" and "strengthen and hasten Ireland's nationality." His argument, which was very much in the United Irish tradition, could hardly have been more mistaken. It not only applied pre-industrial mercantilist assumptions to the new economic order, but it failed to grasp that even if all Irish grain were kept in the country, there would only have been enough to feed 40 percent of the population. The remaining 60 percent of Ireland's food needs came from the potato, and the potato crop had been hit by the blight.[27]

In one important respect, though, McGee got the story right. Although at first sight he appeared to underestimate the scale of the crisis, his view that there were "needless apprehensions of a *famine in Ireland*" in the season of 1845–46 was substantially correct. Partly because of Peel's relief policies, which included the purchase of 20,000 tons of American corn and oatmeal for distribution in Ireland, partly because the extent of the potato failure had been overstated, and partly because the rural economy had the capacity to withstand a one-year shock, there were few deaths at this stage. Scarcity had not yet turned into starvation.[28]

———

In this context, McGee insisted that relief measures should not include any offers of alms or charity for the Irish people. Charity, he believed, was fundamentally demeaning. "The Irish nation," he asserted, "will never consent to eat the bread of beggary." McGee shared the dominant Young Ireland view that charity would only demoralize and pauperize the people; in this respect, the Young Irelanders were closer than they realized to Charles Trevelyan, the head of the Treasury, who feared that prolonged government aid would foster a culture of dependence. But McGee also had strong ideological reasons for rejecting charity. In the United States, he had consistently argued that the Repeal of the Union must take preference over all other issues, such as slavery, or sending money to support Irish manufactures. Now he applied the same logic to the economic crisis that was engulfing the country; the failure of the potato crop, he believed, presented an opportunity to win independence for Ireland.[29]

What this meant in practice soon became apparent. When, in January 1846, McGee learned that his old boss at the *Boston Pilot*, Patrick Donahoe, was planning to raise money for famine relief in Ireland, he immediately attempted to pre-empt the proposal. "The opinion ... of the leading public men in Dublin – which I have personally obtained," he wrote, "is – that the project of alimentary relief to Ireland, from a foreign country, is up to this time, premature." Not only would it "force this disagreeable feeling of pauperism upon Ireland," but it would blunt the political struggle. "We are anxious to come to a point with our misrulers," he told his American audience. "*They, and they only*, must open the cornucopia of free trade upon our soil." Repeal of the Corn Laws would open the way for Repeal of the Union, but while American political aid was welcome, American economic assistance would be counterproductive.[30]

McGee's position created a storm of controversy in the United States. At a Repeal meeting in Philadelphia, Robert Tyler endorsed

McGee's argument, insisting that the only cure for Ireland's ills was independence, and that all other attempts at relief were "mere mockery." Against this, the Boston physician Robert White argued that the American Irish must take immediate practical measures to alleviate Irish suffering, rather than talking in abstract terms about free trade and Repeal of the Union; Ireland was too weak and divided to force through political change in the foreseeable future. "It is all very well," wrote White, "for the leading public men of Dublin, who have plenty to eat and drink and wherewithal to clothe themselves to talk so dogmatically ignorant of our noble movement." Such divisions seriously damaged American fundraising efforts, and they opened up a major rift between McGee and Donahoe.[31]

The issue resurfaced in Ireland in November 1846, when McGee's enemies in Old Ireland accused him of blocking American relief for the Irish poor and of falsely claiming that the leaders of the Repeal Association shared his views. By this time, the famine was in full force, and such criticisms had a correspondingly sharper edge. In reply, McGee attempted to clarify his position. He had merely stated, he wrote, that aid was premature in September 1845, when "there was no ground for anticipating a general famine"; what had been "premature" in September may have been "most judicious" in the spring of 1846; and he had never said that his views reflected those of O'Connell, Smith O'Brien, or other leaders of the Repeal Association. His defence was disingenuous at best; the McGee Shuffle was back at work. He had actually made his "premature" argument in January 1846, not September 1845, and had indeed implied that he was speaking for the leadership, though he had not given any names. Upon reading McGee's defence, Patrick Donahoe lost no time in exposing the contradictions. "Such conduct in a correspondent," he wrote, "was disrespectful to the public, to us, and to himself." He had a point.[32]

When McGee wrote his public letter to Donahoe in January 1846, he had left Ireland for London to become the parliamentary correspondent for the *Freeman's Journal*. His attention was focused on politics in Westminster rather than social conditions in Ireland, though he believed that both issues were closely connected. In typical fashion, he started with a bang. McGee's very first article, written on 9 December, scooped the London press with a report that Peel was about to resign. His editors were impressed. Thanks to the "zeal, and early and accurate information" of their London correspondent, commented the *Freeman's Journal*, "we are indebted for being the first journal in the empire to announce the intended resignation of the Peel Ministry." But, equally characteristically, his eagerness to scoop rival newspapers landed McGee in trouble the following week. "Lord John Russell is now Premier of England," he declared, and had promised the "TOTAL, AND IMMEDIATE REPEAL OF THE CORN LAWS!!!" As it turned out, Russell was unable to form a government, and Peel returned to power later in the month. Rushing into print had its hazards, and there was a fine line between glory and embarrassment.[33]

The parliamentary session that began in January 1846 was one of the great turning points in modern British history. Peel's decision to end the Corn Laws destroyed the old Tory party, paved the way for Lord John Russell's Whig government, and marked a decisive victory for laissez-faire policies over aristocratic protectionist interests; henceforth, Britain would be ruled on middle-class terms. McGee was a close observer of the debates, writing regular reports for his employers at the *Freeman's Journal*, while sending anonymous "Letters from London" to the *Nation*, its rival newspaper – a conflict of interest that reflected the tension between his employment obligations and his political sympathies.

Mitchel had urged him to show "a pretty thorough contempt for their damn'd Parliament," and McGee tried hard to follow his advice. Queen Victoria looked "pale, timid, and anxious" when she opened Parliament, he wrote, and the general quality of debate was deplorable: "If you wish to see fanatics, fools, or blusterers, you will not be disappointed; but if you look for philosophical politicians, and enunciators of great principles, you find them not." No matter how great Parliament may have been in the past, in its present form it was "a bad school for the future legislators of Ireland" and could not "teach them one wholesome lesson or supply one safe prototype." If Parliament was bad, London was little better. "It falls infinitely below my estimate of a great city," he wrote. Its inhabitants were even worse: "This people are eminently arrogant, possessing great powers of digestion, very loose principles, and very scanty religion."[34]

Despite his dismissive remarks about the debates, McGee actually learned a great deal about parliamentary oratory and political tactics during his time at Westminster, and he later drew on this experience during his political career in Canada. He critically evaluated the strengths and weaknesses of the debaters, and particularly enjoyed skewering speakers who stumbled and mumbled their way through their speeches. The speech of one protectionist, he wrote, was "prosy, ill-digested and worse-delivered"; those who followed were no better, "and the happy combination of long-winded men and stupidity was rapidly thinning the house." Another speaker droned on for forty-five minutes: "Had he continued much longer he would certainly have mesmerised, or, to speak more correctly, monotonized the 'house,' members, strangers, reporters, and all." Later in the session, he explained how an ultra-Tory ruined his case by adopting a loud and aggressive approach, which jarred with the dominant tone of the House of Commons, where "dignity and dullness are the universal characteristics."[35]

Among the speakers he admired, Robert Peel stood out – although McGee initially thought that Peel looked good only because those around him were so irredeemably awful. "With an intellectual House of Commons, he could not be Premier for a month," wrote McGee. But as the debate over the Corn Laws proceeded, his respect for Peel's speaking style increased; he was impressed with the prime minister's methodical reasoning, his flashes of humour, the modulation of his mood, and the "unequalled art" by which he could build his speech to a powerful conclusion. (On one occasion, McGee noted that Smith O'Brien – who had been the member of Parliament for Limerick since 1835 – made the mistake of beginning his speech in precisely the same tone that Peel had just used in his peroration, commenting that "this premature vehemence, of course, spoiled his speech.") McGee also praised the oratory of other free traders, such as Lord John Russell, Earl Grey, and the home secretary Sir James Graham: "Never will I forget the sudden change of tone and manner which took place in the Home Secretary ... Most men grow heated from passion, but he grew only more cool; the voices of most men are sharpened by embittered feelings; his seemed to grow more clear, emphatic, self-possessed." Parliament, it appeared, was not such a "bad school" after all.[36]

———•••———

Although McGee was a strong supporter of free trade, he was open minded enough to appreciate good speeches on both sides of the question, and found himself in sympathy with certain aspects of the protectionist critique of laissez-faire capitalism. The protectionist Stafford O'Brien, McGee commented, spoke with "great ability and power" and presented an "unanswerable" critique of "the new philosophy which, under the name of political economy, disregarding man in his moral character[,] would have him treated as a mere machine, created for the accumulation and distribution of wealth." After listening to Bushfield Ferrand's exposure of the "revolting secrets of factory life in England," McGee concluded that the "machine aristocracy" was even more oppressive than Irish landlords. He was appalled by some of the arguments that were used to support free trade, registering particular disgust at the "hard and repulsive Utilitarianism" of William Molesworth, who would "see the English people divided into two classes – the great capitalists and the labourers." Nothing could have been farther from McGee's organic vision of society, characterized by social, religious, and political cooperation, and balancing economic growth with moral improvement. Unregulated capitalism, buttressed by the "heartless theory" of political economists, he asserted, would culminate in class division, urban squalor, and moral degradation. The same conviction, and the same horror, lay behind his writings on the condition of the New York Irish during the early 1850s.[37]

As the debate on the Corn Laws continued, McGee also studied the parliamentary manoeuvring of the Tories, Whigs, Anti-Corn Law Leaguers, and "Ultra-protectionists"; there were lessons here that would prove important later in his life. He came to view Peel as not only "the first debater of his country" but also "the greatest tactician of his age," and he recognized that the art of forming alliances was at least as important as impressive oratory in steering controversial legislation through the House. When the decisive vote came in the House of Commons on 28 February, McGee left a memorable description of the scene, with the victorious Peel embracing Richard Cobden, leader of the Anti-Corn Law League, while the "doomed agricultural ascendancy" looked on. The protectionists, he wrote, contained "many most virtuous characters, and individuals of very great talent" who were "thoroughly sincere" in their opposition to free trade: "In the midst of Cobden's speech, a very old gentleman, tottering between crutches, with a most venerable head, and grey beard entered the house, and, assisted by two friends, proceeded to take a seat with the protectionists, amid profound and respectful silence ... I could not help imagining this gentleman, so feeble, so old, so valued by the earnest minority, must be the personified land monopoly now so crippled, obsolete, and yet so hugged to the hearts of the country gentlemen." One of the most revealing things about this description was McGee's capacity for sympathy and his generosity of spirit. There was not a trace of triumphalism, gloating, or vindictiveness in his account. Despite his best efforts, McGee found it impossible to sustain a contemptuous attitude towards "their damn'd Parliament."[38]

When it came to the treatment of Irish affairs at Westminster, McGee's tone was much harsher. As a result of the Act of Union, twenty-eight Irish peers and four Church of Ireland bishops sat in the House of Lords, and there were one hundred Irish MPs (including, of course, Catholics after emancipation in 1829) out of a total of 658 in the House of Commons. In McGee's view, the Irish Liberals were a bunch of mediocrities; the Irish Conservatives had "convictions of duty" but were racked with so much "hesitancy and incertitude, that instead of aiding the views they advocate, they do them the most serious damage." "What a sad sight," he declared, "to see a dozen men wasting their existence thus!" Taken together, the Irish Liberals and Conservatives failed to exert any influence over Parliament. When Irish bills came up for debate, McGee reported, most members of Parliament either talked through them or left the House. Ireland may have figured prominently in the debate over the Corn Laws, but it functioned more as a party political football than anything else. "The ministerial advocates found in the threatened

famine at once their shield and weapon," McGee commented, "while
the protectionists denied the existence of a scarcity, about which they ·
never took the trouble to inquire." All in all, he concluded, the situation underlined the necessity of establishing a coherent, independent,
and united Irish party at Westminster.[39]

In this sense, McGee argued, the example of Daniel O'Connell
and Smith O'Brien pointed the way. When O'Connell informed the
House about the "severe scarcity" and the spread of disease in Ireland,
he received the assurance of James Graham that *"Whatever might be the
extent of the calamity apprehended in Ireland, her Majesty's government would
not be taken by surprise."* "The tone of the Home Secretary throughout
was cautiously courteous to O'Connell," wrote McGee, "and (at least
affectedly) friendly to the Irish people"; his brackets spoke volumes.
McGee was also impressed with John O'Connell's argument that Irish
suffering was the product of "bad imperial laws" and that the Irish
people "did not come here seeking boons, but 'demanding' some small
restitution of the enormous sums by taxation and absenteeism, which
England annually continued to levy on Ireland." This kind of straight
talking, he believed, was exactly what was needed. McGee also praised
O'Brien's insistence that "the Irish people wanted work, not alms, that
they claimed justice, not benevolence." If there were more such voices
in Parliament, he wrote, British politicians could be persuaded to pay
more attention to Ireland's condition, to spend more money on relief
programs, and to back away from the "nefarious" and "despotic" Coercion Bill that was currently under debate.[40]

Beyond this, McGee's view from the reporters' gallery convinced
him that Irish parliamentary pressure could bring about Repeal of the
Union. When British politicians declared that Repeal was an "impossibility," McGee had his reply ready: "The emancipation of the Catholics
– the emancipation of the slaves – the abolition of tithes – the reform
bill – free trade – each had in its turn a refutation of an impossibility, yet each has been proved possible, and practicable, and beneficial."
And McGee knew, or thought he knew, the man who could pull it
off. While O'Connell was moving towards an alliance with Lord John
Russell and the Whigs, McGee thought that Ireland's best hope came
from none other than Peel himself: "If Ireland can expect from any

living British minister the legislative Repeal of the act of Union, this is the man ... I do not outstep the limits of probability, when I express the belief that the same statesman, who has given free bread and free trade to his own country, will yet give a free local legislature to ours." When McGee returned to Ireland in the summer of 1846, he was more committed than ever to constitutional nationalism and believed that the election of Repealers to the House of Commons was the key to Irish independence.[41]

McGee spent fourteen weeks working at Westminster. Then, on 11 April, two days before his twenty-first birthday, he was fired from the *Freeman's Journal*. It has sometimes been suggested that McGee incurred the displeasure of his employers because he was spending too much time reading ancient Irish manuscripts in the British Museum and not enough time recording debates in the House of Commons. McGee presented a rather different picture of the situation, telling Aunt Bella that he had left the *Freeman's Journal* because of political differences with one of the editors: "Doctor [John] Gray I found to be a trimmer, and rather than share that character with him, I would quit the Country."[42]

In fact, neither explanation is accurate. At the end of March, Gray had discovered that McGee was the author of the "Letters from London" in the *Nation*, and criticized him for violating the "etiquette of the Dublin Press." (Had he known that McGee had volunteered to become the parliamentary correspondent for the *Nation* while working for the *Freeman's Journal*, Gray would have been even more upset.) McGee replied that he had met all the terms of his engagement with the *Freeman's Journal* and was free to spend his leisure time as he pleased. When it became clear that he would not back down, Gray fired him. "I wish to know," McGee asked Duffy, "whether you think I acted as became an Irish writer of the Nineteenth Century?" Although he did not tell McGee, Duffy thought Gray was completely within his rights; the episode probably contributed to Duffy's doubts about McGee's integrity. Nevertheless, Duffy also recognized that the opportunity had arrived to bring McGee into the fold, and promptly offered him a job with the *Nation*. The underlying tension in McGee's position was suddenly released; from this point, he was unambiguously aligned with Duffy's "second Young Ireland party."[43]

In describing himself as an "Irish writer of the Nineteenth Century," McGee was making a wry allusion to his most recent book, *The Irish Writers of the Seventeenth Century*, which came out in January 1846 as part of James Duffy's Library of Ireland series. Contemporary Irish literature, McGee asserted, was reestablishing continuities with the early seventeenth century, after the dark period of Scottish and English Puritanism, the Protestant Ascendancy, and the Penal Laws – a time of "an overbearing and scoffing Protestant literature" and "an apologetic and hollow Catholic literature." During the early seventeenth century, Irish writers had been custodians of popular traditions: "True history," McGee wrote, "preserved in the tongue of the people, sung in their songs, painted on their walls, stored in their libraries, is worth more to that people than army, fleet, and revenue. While they retain it, all is theirs; when they lose it, all is lost." When the Irish took up the English language ("and improved it, and extended its vocabulary"), they cut themselves off from the traditions that had been articulated by the balladeers, antiquaries, and thinkers of the seventeenth century. But the new generation, growing up in the new era of Catholic Emancipation, was following in the footsteps of its early-seventeenth-century predecessors, and "from this fusion of poetry, research, philosophy, congeniality, and eloquence, a history of our Nation will be necessarily formed, which shall not pale beside the brilliant master pieces of modern France."[44]

As well as reconnecting the broken threads of Irish history, McGee believed that seventeenth-century Irish literature could provide models of political courage and lessons about sectarianism for the present generation. The writers whom McGee most admired were those who spoke truth to kings: "In no character does the man of letters appear to greater advantage, than when his pen is wielded as a defensive sword, between his country and her oppressors." At the same time, he recognized that the sectarian passions of the seventeenth century had warped and disfigured many of the country's greatest writers. The longer the religious conflict raged, he argued, "the more untrue and dogmatical became Irish writers on both sides." McGee tried to avoid "dogmatical" judgments himself and noted that at least some seventeenth-century writers had resisted the pull of prejudice. Sir James Ware was a case in point; he may have been a "placeman," but he rose above the "hell-broth of sectarian-war" and recognized the virtues of "an ancient Irish civilization." McGee's position revealed much about his own literary ideals. He viewed himself as a writer who challenged the abuse of power and who attempted to transcend the sectarian realities of his own day; in part, *The Irish Writers of the Seventeenth Century* can be read as a hidden autobiography.[45]

Moving farther back into Irish history, McGee retained the pre-lapsarian view of pre-conquest Ireland that he had expressed in the United States. He imagined a land of valorous soldiers, virtuous women, and mystical Druids; there were no human sacrifices on pagan altars in McGee's early Celtic Ireland. But then came the serpent, in the form of Henry II, who cheated, raped, and robbed his way through the country; hard on his heels came Gerald of Wales, who tried to justify the conquest by traducing the Irish people. Not the least of the achievements of seventeenth-century writers such as Bishop John Lynch of Killala was to refute such imperialist lies, declared McGee. The reviewer in the *Freeman's Journal* was impressed, admiring McGee's "concise and vigorous style," his "deep and sensible reflections," and his originality; he said that McGee was "the first to penetrate and explore the dark mine wherein were hidden from men's eyes and knowledge, much of valuable interest to the history of that period so generally unknown even to our more educated classes." The past was speaking to the present, the present would speak to the future, and the future would inevitably bring "nationality to Ireland."[46]

McGee's interest in Irish literature kept drawing him to the British Museum, whose Irish manuscripts had recently been catalogued by Eugene O'Curry. In March 1846, Gavan Duffy had advised McGee to drop the political commentary in the "Letters from London" and focus on cultural matters; in McGee's subsequent articles, the Corn Laws and Robert Peel gave way to Westminster Abbey and Duns Scotus. After McGee was fired from the *Freeman's Journal*, he stayed on in London, dining with his Young Ireland friends John Pigot and John O'Hagan, and continuing his studies at the British Museum. He kept his notes and later used them for his *History of the Attempts to Establish the Protestant Reformation in Ireland* (1852), one of the most widely read books in nineteenth-century Irish Catholic America.[47]

He also continued to visit the House of Commons, where he witnessed the emerging rift over parliamentary tactics within the Repeal movement. Smith O'Brien had embarked on a policy of obstructionism and refused to serve on any committee that was not directly connected with Irish interests. Found guilty of being in contempt of the House of Commons, he spent May in a makeshift parliamentary prison – a small ground-floor apartment, which in nationalist rhetoric was rapidly transformed into a "Saxon dungeon." While many Young Irelanders admired O'Brien's stand, O'Connell regarded it as an act of political foolishness and attempted to ensure that the Repeal Association did not become drawn into illegal activities. Relations between Young Ireland and O'Connell were further strained in early June, after rumours spread that O'Connell had told Lord John Russell that "all he ever desired was a *real union* with England, [with] equal rights and equal privileges." When Peel fell from power later in the month, the long-standing Young Ireland fear of an alliance between the Repealers and the Whigs assumed immediate political importance. Although McGee's specific writings for the *Nation* in this period cannot be identified, his position was clear: he admired O'Brien's "resoluteness" and believed that a Whig alliance would betray the cause of Repeal.[48]

McGee returned to Ireland in the summer of 1846 – the time he would later describe as the beginning of the famine. In July, he travelled to Donegal, visiting historical sites and going on a three-day pilgrimage to St Patrick's Purgatory at Loch Derg. He found it a deeply moving experience and wrote lyrically of the scenic beauty, the "freshness of Faith" that sustained the pilgrims, and the "wild, melodious" hymn sung by "a group of dark-haired, fine-featured young girls" as his boat left the island. Conspicuously absent was any discussion of the famine itself. This may have been because Donegal remained relatively unscathed during this period, because the new crop of potatoes had not yet failed, or because McGee preferred to focus on spiritual richness rather than material poverty.[49]

Nevertheless, the lack of attention to social conditions is striking, and it seemed to set a pattern for the next six months. Despite the approach of mass starvation towards the end of 1846, McGee appeared to be more preoccupied with internal nationalist political divisions than with the famine – so much so, that Robin Burns could remark that "he continued to write, speak, and act as if the famine did not exist." Appearances, however, can be deceptive. For one thing, McGee believed that the famine could only be prevented or ameliorated through political means and that self-rule was the key to effective relief policies. For another, the famine indirectly and directly intensified the stresses and strains that had already been building within the Repeal movement. In November, McGee lamented that "the famine which is fast making one wide graveyard of this island" was becoming "secondary in importance" to O'Connell's attacks on the Young Ireland movement.[50]

Without the famine, the Corn Laws would not have been repealed in 1846; without the repeal of the Corn Laws, Russell would not have become prime minister in June; without Russell's victory, the question of the Whig alliance would not have come to the forefront of Irish politics. We have already seen that there were significant differences between Young Ireland and O'Connell over federalism, slavery, Peel's Colleges Bill, cultural nationalism, and parliamentary tactics. Another major cause of tension had arisen the previous November, when Mitchel wrote an article in the *Nation* that linked the Repeal Association with possible guerrilla war against Britain. O'Connell was furious; Duffy and O'Brien, in contrast, defended Mitchel's position. Before the summer of 1846, the movement had been able to maintain a precarious unity. But the imminent prospect of an alliance between O'Connell and the Whigs pushed the divisions to breaking point.

From O'Connell's viewpoint, the Whigs offered the best chance of securing immediate reforms for Ireland, including denominational university education and a tax on absentee landlords. This meant that Repeal would be relegated to a rather vague long-term aspiration, and that Young Ireland would have to be brought under control. To assert his authority, and to ensure that the movement explicitly and exclusively committed itself to "peaceful, legal, and constitutional means," O'Connell in mid-July introduced a set of Peace Resolutions in the Repeal Association. All Repeal members were expected to renounce the use of physical force, in theory and in practice, in all circumstances, except for "necessary defence against unjust aggression."[51]

In practice, most Young Irelanders had no revolutionary intentions in 1846; like McGee, whose parliamentary experiences had reinforced his preference for moral force, they wanted to build an independent Irish party that would win Repeal through political means. But they generally agreed that there were circumstances in which armed revolution was justifiable, and balked at the idea of supporting such a general renunciation of political violence. By the end of July, after two days of intense debate, O'Brien walked out of Conciliation Hall, and the Young Irelanders followed him. Although the division was occasioned by the controversy over physical force, its underlying causes were the immediate issues of the Whig alliance and the watering down of Repeal; the denominational education question was also an important factor. The Repeal movement had split, and a clear majority had sided with O'Connell.[52]

McGee took no part in these debates; while the controversy was raging in Dublin, he was walking along the hills of Donegal. When he returned, Young Ireland was reeling and rudderless. O'Brien initially counselled patience, hoped for reconciliation, and escaped the "turmoil of agitation" in Dublin by leaving for his family home near Limerick. He did, however, suggest that individual Young Irelanders assert their right to attend Repeal Association meetings. One by one, they tried; one by one, they were rebuffed. In August, McGee informed the association's secretary that he had paid his subscription earlier in the summer and had not yet received his membership card. "I may add," he wrote, "that I fully concurred then, and do still concur, in the principle and policy of moral force, as that which is alone proper to the Association. Of physical force I will say nothing. I dislike meddling with abstract principles, and I think my brother members should avoid them as dangerous to the public cause." It was no use; the only response

William Smith O'Brien (1803–64). An aristocractic and radical member of Parliament for Limerick, 1835–48, William Smith O'Brien broke with Daniel O'Connell's Repeal Association in the summer of 1846 and co-founded the Irish Confederation in January 1847. After leading the rising of 1848, he was sentenced to death for high treason; along with the other leaders, he was reprieved and transported to Australia for life. In 1854 he was pardoned and returned to Ireland. Despite, or because of, the fact that he subsequently abstained from politics, he became a revered symbol of Irish nationalism during the mid-nineteenth century. O'Brien and McGee worked together in the Irish Confederation, and McGee was among those who campaigned for his release from Van Diemen's Land. The two men met each other when O'Brien visited Toronto in 1859, and they continued to correspond with each other about establishing a book exchange between Ireland and Canada. (Duffy, *Young Ireland*, vol. 2)

was a terse note declaring that he was "not and cannot be a member of the Association," followed by charges that he was a troublemaker. The rejection, he wrote, "altogether astonishes me"; not surprisingly, he asked for his money back.[53]

The Young Irelanders were in a state of political limbo. They did not want, at this stage, to establish a new political party, but they were comprehensively excluded from the Repeal Association. In September, McGee debated the issue at Wexford with the man who had welcomed him back to Ireland the previous year, John Sinnott. Speaking in a room "crowded to suffocation," McGee asserted the right of people "to think for themselves in politics," argued against the Whig alliance, and called for a united effort to send Repealers to Parliament and persuade Peel that their cause was just. Sinnott would have none of it; the people, he said, should put their trust in O'Connell and should give the Whig alliance a fair trial. If the Whigs failed to deliver "measures of justice to Ireland" within six months, he assured the audience, "they shall be met by an opposition as vigorous as ever the Tories had to encounter." Each man called for unity, but neither would give ground to the other. In the end, Sinnott's appeal to traditional Irish loyalty carried the day. "The people of Ireland have never been a people to reject authority," he declared, "and will not reject it now. They have acknowledged O'Connell as their leader in politics, and they will continue to acknowledge him." McGee, like his fellow Young Irelanders, remained very much in the minority.[54]

He responded to the situation with a mixture of frustration and wishful thinking. The momentum for Repeal had been growing, he wrote; the Irish Conservatives were coming round to the cause, Orangeism was dying out, and the Ulster Presbyterians were moving into the nationalist camp, with John Mitchel and John Martin taking the lead. None of this bore much resemblance to reality, but McGee felt the need to clutch at any available straws. With the Whig alliance, he argued, the Repeal Association had taken a large step backwards; O'Connell was allowing Repealers to take office under the very Union that they were supposed to break, and he had silenced his opponents by suppressing free speech within the organization. In the process, his son John had alienated the entire Young Ireland movement: "He has attempted to force the obedience of his superiors, to browbeat his equals, and to stifle remonstrance, and has thus damned forever his own prospects of leadership," wrote McGee. "He will be reduced in time to his proper mediocrity, and then we will have Union once more in our National Association." Despite all this, the Young Irelanders still commanded strong popular support, insisted McGee. And despite the "physical wretchedness" that was gripping the country, the "minds and the conduct of the people" continued to improve. The growth of literacy, the National School system, James Duffy's Library of Ireland series, and Father Mathew's temperance movement all pointed in the direction of emancipation, he maintained.[55]

McGee's reference to the temperance movement had personal significance. At some stage during his return to Ireland, he began to drink, and probably to drink heavily. In October 1846 he told his aunt that he had resumed the pledge, "or I would have been killed by hospitality here." His brother Laurence also had given up alcohol and had started to save money – "the first of the family, I imagine, who undertook such a feat as that." Wexford escaped relatively lightly during the famine, and "the Macs" were flourishing: "My father is wonderfully fresh and stout – his good woman thrives and is civil, and the little *half* " – six-year-old John Joseph, the future clerk of the Privy Council of Canada – "goes to school daily but pays more attention to his lunch than to the other contents of his satchell." McGee's brother James had "carried off two-thirds of the prizes" in his examinations at St Peter's College in Wexford, and his sisters Anna Maria and Rose were "well & at home." Dorcas had returned to Ireland and was once again living with Thomas; she was working as a silk milliner in Dublin and planned to start up a business in Wexford with her sisters. "Such is our family picture," he wrote, "in October 1846."[56]

Less than three months later it would change drastically. Shortly after McGee wrote that letter, Laurence went down with consumption (the same illness that had killed Duffy's wife). On 29 December he died; two days later he was buried at the St Skelsar cemetery, next to his mother and two sisters. "Sad faces and mournful thoughts followed the hearse which thus in the last lightsome hour of the last day of the year bore so young and so good a man to his sleep of ages," ran the obituary. "A good son, a good brother, a kind master, a sincere and practical Christian, he was in life a model for others of his own age and

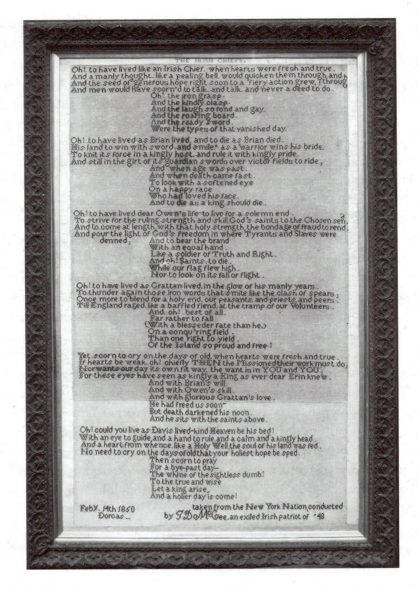

THE IRISH CHIEFS.

Oh! to have lived like an Irish Chief. when hearts were fresh and true.
And a manly thought. like a pealing bell. would quicken them through and h
And the seed of generous hope right soon to a 'fiery action grew. ſthroug
And men would have scorn'd to talk. and talk. and never a deed to do.
            Oh! the iron grasp.
            And the kindly clasp.
            And the laugh so fond and gay.
            And the roaring board.
            And the ready Sword.
            Were the types of that vanished day.

Oh! to have lived as Brian lived. and to die as Brian died.
His land to win with sword and smile. as a warrior wins his bride.
To knit its force in a kingly host. and rule it with kingly pride.
And still in the girt of its guardian swords over victor fields to ride,
            And when age was past.
            And when death came fast.
            To look with a softened eye
            On a happy race
            Who had loved his face
            And to die as a king should die.

Oh! to have lived dear Owen's life to live for a solemn end.
To strive for the ruling strength and skill God's saints to the Chosen sen.
And to come at length. with that holy strength. the bondage of fraud to rend.
And pour the light of God's freedom in where Tyrants and Slaves were
denned;   And to bear the brand
            With an equal hand.
            Like a soldier of Truth and Right.
            And oh! Saints. to die.
            While our flag flew high.
            Nor to look on its fall or flight.

Oh! to have lived as Grattan lived. in the glow of his manly years.
To thunder again those iron words that smite like the clash of spears.
Once more to blend for a holy end. our peasants. and priests. and peers.
Till England raged. like a baffled fiend. at the tramp of our Volunteers.
            And. oh! best of all.
            Far rather to fall
            (With a blesseder fate than he.)
            On a conqu'ring field.
            Than one right to yield.
            Of the Island so proud and free!

Yet. scorn to cry on the days of old. when hearts were fresh and true.
If hearts be weak. oh! chiefly THEN the Missioned their work must do.
Nor wants our day its own fit way. the want is in YOU and YOU.
For these eyes have seen as kingly a King as ever dear Erin knew.
            And with Brian's will.
            And with Owen's skill.
            And with glorious Grattan's love.
            He had freed us soon
            But death darkened his noon.
            And he sits with the saints above.

Oh! could you live as Davis lived-kind Heaven be his bed!
With an eye to guide. and a hand to rule. and a calm and a kingly head.
And a heart from whence. like a Holy Well the soul of his land was fed.
No need to cry on the days of old that your holiest hope be sped.
            Then scorn to pray
            For a bye-past day—
            The whine of the sightless dumb!
            To the true and wise
            Let a king arise,
            And a holier day is come!

Feby. 14th 1850   taken from the New York Nation. conducted
Dorcas ...   by T.D.McGee. an exiled Irish patriot of '48

"The Irish Chiefs." A needlework sample by Dorcas McGee, Thomas's sister. The poem was written by Charles Gavan Duffy after the shock of Thomas Davis's death, and was reproduced four years later in McGee's [New York] *Nation*. (Courtesy of Jenny and Brendan Meegan.)

condition. May his soul rest in everlasting peace." He was twenty-five years old.[57]

———

Meanwhile, the economic and political crisis deepened and widened. "We are smitten with the double curse of famine and dissension," McGee declared in November. In the absence of reconciliation between O'Connell and the Young Irelanders, O'Brien had suggested that the cause of Repeal should be kept alive by a "literary phalanx" in the *Nation*. McGee agreed to contribute a series of articles on Irish history, education, trade, and inspirational leaders, but quickly felt that this was a poor substitute for action. "It was evident enough to every observer," he wrote, "that so many sincere men could not continue among their books while the country was falling daily more deeply into corruption and ruin."[58]

The opportunity for a new political initiative arose during the autumn when a group of Dublin tradesmen began meeting to protest the Repeal Association's new policy. Sympathetic to British Chartism, and led by Patrick John Barry (who may actually have been a government spy), the movement constituted a working class, democratic, and republican challenge to O'Connell. McGee joined the organization in October, providing the crucial link between the protest movement and Young Ireland. Later that month he drafted a remonstrance for the tradesmen against O'Connell's Peace Resolutions and the Whig alliance; it was signed by almost one-third of Dublin's Repeal wardens. When the remonstrance was presented to the Repeal Association on 26 October, John O'Connell ordered it to be thrown in the gutter – an event that became deeply embedded in popular memories of the movement.[59]

At a crowded meeting in the Rotunda a week later, with "thousands outside, who were clamouring for admission," McGee gave his first public speech in Dublin. Speaking in a "calm, forcible and conclusive" manner, he condemned the Repeal Association for slandering the Young Irelanders and asserted that the cause of Repeal was greater than that of any single individual, even such "a great, an old, a reverend man" as O'Connell. And then came his key point: "If all hopes of reforming or remodelling the present Association were given up, the materials for the formation of a really national Association would not be wanting." The *Nation* reported that the speech was met with "tremendous cheering," Doheny recalled "the excitement it created," and McGee's brother James claimed (with considerable exaggeration) that "the awe, the spell, that still hung round the very name of O'Connell, was dissipated." McGee, who had himself once been under that spell, was pointing the way towards a new political party, which would adhere to what he conceived as the original principles of the Repeal Association.[60]

To provide the materials for a "really national Association," McGee published at the end of November his thoughts on the subjects needed "for the education and training of an Irish Party." Picking up one of the main themes from his American career, he stressed the importance of self-criticism: "To study our defects as a people, and to proclaim them, is the surest way to remedy them." Education was crucial; an Irish party should promote literature, art (including the establishment of a National Gallery), and a better understanding of Irish history. On the social and economic front, it should work to improve public health and housing conditions, and to promote Irish manufactures. Among other things, he suggested looking into ways to bring transatlantic trade into Irish ports such as Galway – an issue that would preoccupy him throughout much of the next decade. His political recommendations emphasized national unity; he wanted to break down "Provincial Prejudices" and encourage the "Intermarriage of Races," by which he meant the Celts, Saxons, Scots, Spaniards, Danes, and Germans of Ireland. One of his subjects for study was particularly striking in the light of later events: "Eminence of Irish Politicians in other Countries an argument for their fitness to govern their own." McGee was clearly thinking of the United States; ten years later, he would be applying it to Canada, and in some degree to himself.[61]

McGee's ideas contributed to an increasingly urgent debate about the formation of a new party. By the beginning of December, he had become secretary of the Dublin Remonstrants, as the tradesmen grouped around Patrick John Barry were now known, and in this capacity attended another packed meeting at the Rotunda. After making the usual arguments against the Whig alliance and for Repeal, they called for another meeting in January to "revive the struggle for Ireland's nationality," as McGee later put it. Unless O'Connell changed course, the Young Irelanders would stop seeking to reform the Repeal Association and would strike out on their own.[62]

O'Connell was now facing the prospect of a rival nationalist party, at the very time that the Whig alliance was manifestly failing to produce effective relief measures against the famine. As a result, he opened up discussions with Young Ireland, offering to limit the Peace Resolutions to Anglo-Irish relations, and agreeing to consider further reforms once the seceders were back in the fold. Some Young Irelanders thought that his proposals were worth pursuing, but most felt that it was a case of too little, too late. There had been no immediate movement on the key Young Ireland demands – an end to the Whig alliance, the stipulation that Repealers should not take government jobs, the accountability of Repeal Association funds, and the elimination of religious topics in political discussions. And there were deeper suspicions that O'Connell could not be trusted, along with bitter memories of the October remonstrance being thrown in the gutter.[63]

McGee had played a significant secondary role in the drive for a new Irish party. Over the next eighteen months, he would emerge as one of its principal organizers and most articulate advocates.

CHAPTER FIVE

An Incessant Defensive Struggle
January – July 1847

The winter of 1846–47 was one of the worst in Irish history in terms of sheer human suffering. In August 1846 the stench of rotting potato tubers filled the fields. Small tenant farmers, cottiers, and labourers who had been stretched to the limit by the partial potato failure of 1845 were now hit by the near total destruction of the crop. By the autumn, the first famine deaths were recorded; by December, horrific accounts of starvation in such places as Skibbereen reached the newspapers. Tenants who could no longer pay their rent faced eviction; homeless people were dying in ditches, and famine-related diseases were spreading throughout the country. With the failure of the potato, there was simply not enough food in Ireland to go round; three-fifths of the country's food supply had disappeared, leaving the three million people who depended entirely on potatoes in desperate circumstances. The sudden and savage food loss, along with the spread of contagious diseases and the prolonged nature of the crisis, meant that widespread loss of life was unavoidable during the late 1840s. Even had all the grain been kept in the country, there would have been an absolute food deficit. As it was, grain imports exceeded grain exports by three to one during the famine, and there was still not enough food to stave off starvation.[1]

But the situation was exacerbated by inadequate, inconsistent, and ideologically driven British relief policies. Mass death may have been inevitable; the scale of starvation was not. Senior bureaucrats and leading members of Russell's government sought to apply laissez-faire notions of political economy to Ireland's crisis, with the result that they often seemed more concerned about the long-term risks of creating a

Boy and girl at Cahera. Starving children in rags search for potatoes in west County Cork during the winter of 1847 (James Mahony, *Illustrated London News*)

culture of dependency than about the short-term need to save lives. They were also deeply influenced by the view that the famine was an act of providence, in which the Irish would move through what Chancellor of the Exchequer Charles Wood called "a purgatory of misery and starvation" into a stable, rational, and efficient economic order. Such presuppositions, along with the immense logistical difficulties of organizing famine relief, meant that government strategies to alleviate famine conditions were frequently ineffective and sometimes counter-productive.[2]

And so, during one of the coldest winters in living memory, poorly clothed and half-starved people were forced onto public works, where

Famine victim. One of the million people who died during the famine (A. Maclure, National Library of Ireland)

they built roads and broke stones for wages that lagged behind soaring food prices. The much-hated workhouses – "Bastilles," in popular parlance – were crammed to capacity, and many of them became breeding grounds for infectious diseases. Through the operation of the Gregory clause in the Temporary Relief Act of February 1847, anyone holding more than a quarter-acre of land was ineligible for relief; this meant that small tenant farmers could have only a fighting chance of immediate survival by sacrificing all hopes of long-term security. The situation was worst in the heavily potato-dependent west and southwest regions of the country, but no region was completely immune. Even in Dublin, which got off relatively lightly, tens of thousands of famine refugees brought disease and death with them, and the mortality rate spiked upwards in 1847.[3]

Against this background, the Young Irelanders formed their new party, the Irish Confederation, in January 1847, with Smith O'Brien at the head. McGee was among the forty men appointed to the Council

Ejectment of Irish tenantry. The "crowbar brigade" begin the work of level-
ling the cabin and removing its contents, while the tenants beg the landlord's
agent to stop. Up to 500,000 people were evicted during the clearances between 1846 and 1854. (*Illustrated London News*)

Village of Moveen. The evictions in the poor law union of Kilrush in west
County Clare were particularly severe. Entire villages, such as Moveen, were
cleared, leaving behind a landscape of desolation. (*Illustrated London Ne s*)

of the Irish Confederation, the core group of leaders who would organize monthly public meetings and adumbrate strategy. He was also one of the main speakers at the inaugural meeting, where he outlined the differences between the Confederation and the Repeal Association. The new party would allow freedom of discussion and dissent, rather than forcing its members into an O'Connellite straitjacket; it would be grounded on principles, rather than the cult of the leader. Above all, it would assert "Ireland's right to an Independent Legislature" and thus ensure effective relief measures to deal with the famine. The cries of Irish hunger, McGee argued, "are baffled and drowned in the winds and waves of the Channel" and failed to reach the legislators in the "modern Babylon" of London; but an Irish parliament would be forced to take action, if only for its own preservation. "So long as there was a sovereign in the Treasury, or a bill in the Exchequer," he asserted, "no Irishman then could die of want." McGee was quite right to argue that Irish calls for help sounded less urgent by the time they reached Whitehall and Westminster; it is extremely unlikely, however, that an independent Irish legislature could have commanded sufficient resources to deal with the magnitude of the crisis in 1847 and beyond.[4]

McGee's presence on the podium and his membership of the council reflected his organizational and intellectual role in the formation of the Irish Confederation. As secretary of the Dublin Remonstrants, he was admired not only for his "talented and patriotic labours" but also for his "kind, conciliating manners," which "allayed every approach to irritation, and converted antagonists into allies."[5] As a writer in the *Nation*, he helped to lay the intellectual groundwork for the new party by outlining the larger issues that it must address; it was precisely the combination of attention to detail and breadth of thought that made him such an important figure in the Irish Confederation.

Shortly before the formation of the new movement, he penned an article in the *Nation* entitled "Popular Fallacies about Irish History," in which he attempted to clear away the historical myths that impeded the growth of the Young Ireland movement. One of his "popular fallacies," for example, was the view that O'Connell had been the leader of the Irish people for half a century; in fact, McGee wrote, his leadership dated only from 1823. Another was the belief that Catholic Emancipation in 1829 was the "first great blow struck at the Irish penal code"; in fact, McGee countered, the first great blow had actually been struck in 1793, when O'Connell was still in his teens. All this was part of his continuing effort to break the reverence that many Irish Catholics still held for the Liberator.[6]

Moving beyond O'Connell, McGee identified other "popular fallacies" that threatened Young Ireland's campaign to build national unity and restore national pride. It was wrong, he said, to assume that the early Irish "were all of one race – all Milesians." Such thinking was "the prolific root of many of our modern dissensions, and of our indisposition to amalgamate with Normans, Britons, and Scots." Anticipating Estyn Evans's later comment that "we are all mongrels, and should be proud of it," McGee rejected narrow racial definitions of Irishness and advocated an inclusive form of nationalism that foreshadowed the "unity in diversity" approach he later adopted in Canada. He also set out to shatter the notion that there were no great heroes between the twelfth and seventeenth centuries. On the contrary, there were many great men who had challenged the English and who could serve as examples for the present generation – men such as Art Mac Murrough, whose biography McGee was currently writing. But perhaps the most insidious myth of all, in McGee's view, was "the common cry" in Ireland about "seven centuries of English oppression." In fact, he asserted, the period of oppression began in the seventeenth century, when James I assumed sovereign power over Ireland. "It is degrading, if it were not false," he wrote, "to be continually echoing that commonplace about the length of our bondage and our endurance." This kind of victim mentality, McGee believed, only reinforced a sense of political fatalism. By removing the shame of perpetual defeat, he hoped to prepare the way for political victory.[7]

McGee clearly believed that myths mattered. "These mistakes," he wrote, "may, and do often, lead us into very serious errors of conduct." Although his identification of myths shifted with his changing political perspectives, his conviction that popular beliefs shaped political, social, and religious behaviour remained constant, and it helps to explain the urgent, insistent character of his writing. But even as he challenged "popular fallacies" that impeded Irish progress, he perpetuated and even created myths that conformed to his own view of the world. In the context of the famine, for example, McGee contributed to the widespread nationalist view that Britain had caused mass starvation by allowing the export of "grain crops more than sufficient to support the whole population" – a fallacy that still has an apparently unshakable hold on popular perceptions. Debunking other people's myths was one thing; recognizing one's own was another altogether.[8]

———•————

More immediately, the task facing McGee and his fellow Confederates was to turn aspirations into action, and build an effective political party. The obstacles were immense. O'Connell remained popular, the Catholic Church generally supported the Repeal Association, and the Irish Confederation had low levels of support, with a correspondingly weak financial base. It was difficult to see how the party could bring together such disparate groups as Dublin artisans, Ulster Protestants, and the landed gentry, let alone win the support of the Catholic rural majority. But the aim was to unite all Irishmen behind a common nationalist program, and the leaders, including McGee, believed that the support of the gentry was crucial to their success. In early 1847, this was not quite as chimerical as it would later appear. On 14 January, the day after the formation of the Irish Confederation, nearly a thousand landlords met in Dublin to express their opposition to Whig relief policies, and talked about establishing an Irish party at Westminster "for the protection of Irish interests." The Confederation took some hope from this, though it remained unlikely that landlord anger with the Whigs could be translated into support for Repeal.[9]

In the face of these problems and uncertainties, the Confederation struggled to get off the ground. "For the first six months," McGee recalled, "it was an incessant defensive struggle with old and natural prejudices on the part of the people, and the power of the Whigs." Some of the Confederation's more radical contemporaries criticized it for being all talk and no action, and some of its historians have followed suit. "Confederates dissolved the famine in purple passages," commented Richard Davis, "and won Repeal by force of verbal imagery." This is, on balance, a rather harsh judgment. The Confederation contained an impressive array of intellectual talent, but as a minority nationalist group operating in the context of internal opposition, external hostility, and conditions of famine, its ability to act was severely constrained by circumstances.[10]

Besides, there was much more to the Confederation than fine speeches at their monthly meetings. The Council of the Confederation struck a variety of committees, addressing issues such as the famine, parliamentary elections, trade, and education. McGee proposed a committee on public instruction, "to diffuse the opinions of the Confederation, by lectures, meetings, publications, &c." As the chair of the committee, he prepared and presented its report to the Confederation in March. Drawing on the precedents of the temperance movement and the Repeal Association, he called for "a really national system of reading-rooms," in which the publications of the Confederation would be disseminated and discussed. The objective was "the creation of an Irish intelligence so irresistible that native disunion and foreign usurpation will vanish." While he recognized that other committees were more directly involved with the crisis of the famine and possible political remedies, McGee believed that education offered "the best way to raise a people to permanent prosperity and enduring freedom."[11]

He was under no illusions about the enormity of the task. As things stood, the Confederation faced the opposition of Protestant Unionists, the "indecision" of the landed gentry, the policies of the Whigs, and the "more dangerous" problem of English cultural hegemony. "Your public streets and squares," he declared, "are named with English names – your schools teach English history – your gentry servilely imitate English manners – your shopkeepers are salesmen for English manufacturers." The path to liberation lay through education: "To conquer these [influences], we require only truth, industry, and consistency." In taking this position, McGee contributed to the cultural nationalist tradition that found its most striking expression in Douglas Hyde's "The Necessity for De-Anglicising Ireland" (1892) and acquired institutional form in the Gaelic League.[12]

This was all very well in the long run; in the meantime, the famine demanded a more immediate response. As the crisis intensified, Confederates such as Michael Doheny, Thomas Devin Reilly, Father John

Kenyon, and John Mitchel adopted an increasingly radical stance. In March, Mitchel fulminated against "the deep & settled design of the English government to uproot the Irish from the soil & make them a nation of labourers working for wages from day to day." By April 1847, he was beginning to give up on the landlords, among whom he found a "very prevalent feeling" that Ireland was overpopulated and that it was "desirable to get rid of at least a couple of millions of them." It was pointless to work for change at Westminster, Mitchel argued; Parliament treated Ireland with contempt, and in any case the Confederation lacked sufficient resources to establish an independent Irish parliamentary party. The real battles had to be fought on Irish soil, where there was more than enough food for the entire population, and where the Irish people must have first claim on that food, "no matter what legal, social, or physical obstacles may now be in the way."[13]

The revolutionary potential of this position is obvious – Parliament treated Ireland with disdain, an independent Irish parliamentary party was neither possible nor desirable, action was needed at home, and the landlords were the enemy until proven otherwise. In the spring of 1847, however, Mitchel pulled back from the implications of his argument. "I have expressed myself with more revolutionary vehemence than I really feel," he told O'Brien, and clung to the hope that "it is still in the power of the aristocracy to save this nation & themselves at the same time." The longer the famine lasted, however, the stronger the revolutionary vehemence would become, in both expression and feeling.[14]

Central to Mitchel's outlook in 1847 was the conviction that Repeal must be connected to the struggle for the "material existence of the Irish People," that the Confederation would "excite no great enthusiasm" unless it embraced the urgent needs of tenant farmers who faced starvation, disease, and eviction in a land supposedly of plenty. In taking this view, he was strongly influenced by the writings of James Fintan Lalor, the reclusive son of an O'Connellite MP from Queen's County. Physically disabled and in poor health – Doheny described him as a "poor, distorted, ill-favoured, hunchbacked creature" – Lalor played a key role in linking nationalism with the land question. If McGee's cultural writings anticipated Hyde and the Gaelic League, Lalor's economic ideas anticipated Michael Davitt and the Land League. When

James Fintan Lalor (1807–49). An advocate of far-reaching land reform, Lalor aligned himself in 1848 with the physical-force republican wing of Irish nationalism, and spent several months in prison after the rising of 1848. Released in November 1848, and suffering from poor health, he attempted to revive the revolutionary movement. His efforts fizzled out in an unsuccessful raid on a police barracks at Cappoquin in County Waterford the following September. Three months later, in December 1849, he died of bronchitis; his ideas, however, continued to inspire revolutionary Irish nationalists on both sides of the Atlantic. (L. Fogarty, *James Fintan Lalor* [1918])

the Irish Confederation was being formed in January, Lalor wrote to Duffy arguing that the issue of landlord-tenant relations was more important than Repeal, and that the nationalist movement would be irrelevant without a program to bring justice and security to the tenant farmers.[15]

Duffy circulated the letter to his friends and invited Lalor to write a series of articles in the *Nation*; the first one appeared in April. Lalor's ideas not only influenced the radical coterie grouped around Mitchel but also made a "profound impression" on the Confederates in general, including McGee. After reading Lalor's initial letter to Duffy, McGee began to grapple with the land question, and he opened up a correspondence with Lalor to discuss the issue. Not surprisingly, given his history of putting Repeal above all other matters, McGee disagreed with Lalor's desire "to make Repeal subservient to land interests." But he now believed that the "tenure question" should become "the other rail of our road." "I will admit the Tenure agitation as of equal importance to the Repeal agitation," he told Lalor, "... but certainly not greater, and only *as great* in the circumstances of our condition."[16]

Lalor replied that he wanted to "combine and cement" the issues of land and Repeal, "to perfect and reinforce and strengthen and carry both." They could agree to differ on the relative importance of the two questions, he continued; the issue would only become divisive if the Confederation tried to win Repeal by an alliance with the landlords that sacrificed the interests of the tenants. ("But I am sure no such infamous arrangement will ever be offered, accepted, or entered into by the confederation," he added.) In his letter to McGee, Lalor outlined his position in a passage which he later published in the *Irish Felon* and which became one of the central texts in the history of Irish nationalism:

> My principle is this, that the entire ownership of Ireland, moral and material, up to the sun and down to the centre, is vested in the rights of the people of Ireland – that they and none but they, are the landowners and lawmakers of this island; that all laws not made by them are null and void, and all titles to land are invalid not conferred or confirmed by them; and that the full rights of ownership may and must be asserted and enforced by any and all means which God has put in the power of man.

These ideas, McGee informed Lalor the following week, had "spread in silence" among the Confederates. Mitchel had "always had some notion of such a policy" and "now thinks of it more than ever." McGee assured Lalor that his views were supported not only by Mitchel, Devin Reilly, and Michael Doheny, but also Richard O'Gorman, Thomas

Meagher, John Dillon, and Gavan Duffy. Smith O'Brien would probably be opposed, McGee said, but "even he would yield before the general voice which ... would be in its favor." If McGee's assessment of the "general voice" was correct – and his view was corroborated by Duffy's later writings – it appeared that the Young Irelanders were prepared to strike out in a much more radical direction.[17]

As McGee surmised, Lalor's principles were indeed too radical for O'Brien, who remained convinced that the landlords could be brought into the Confederation, provided that they did not associate Repeal with thoroughgoing land reform, confiscation, or democracy. Contrary to McGee's expectations, O'Brien did not yield on the issue; in fact, he would have retired from the Confederation sooner than accept Lalor's principles. It also transpired that many other leading Confederates were deeply ambivalent about Lalor's ideas. They might – and generally did – agree with Lalor in theory, but they had serious misgivings about the practicability of his policies, especially when he began to talk about agrarian agitation and a rent strike to force social change. They also came to share O'Brien's fears that Lalor's views would alienate the gentry and the "cultivated classes" – and any agitation that did not have significant gentry support, they believed, was bound to fail. "My opposition to Lalor's policy," Duffy recalled, "was based not on moral but strictly on political grounds. I believed it had not the slightest chance of success. His angry peasants straining to break their chains were creatures of the imagination." Among those who came to agree with Duffy were Dillon, Meagher, and McGee.[18]

Although McGee encouraged Lalor to participate in the Confederation, and although he believed that land reform and Repeal could reinforce one another, that was about as far their agreement went. McGee took national independence as his starting point and wanted to reform landlord-tenant relations; Lalor wanted to *repeal the Conquest, – not any particular part or portion but the whole and entire conquest of seven hundred years; – a thing much more easily done than to repeal the union.* In practice, Lalor did not seek the abolition of the landlord class and would have settled for landlord-tenant co-ownership of the land. For his part, McGee believed that tenants should be entitled to compensation for improvements they had made to their farms, but he stopped short of supporting co-ownership. In the end, the gap between the two men proved too large to bridge. Their correspondence dried up, and Lalor came to feel that he had been misled. McGee could not be trusted, he concluded, and the Confederation was frittering away its time with speeches and election campaigns when urgent action was needed. "Three-fourths of the tenant farmers of this County [Queen's] are served with ejectment notices," he told Mitchel. "I *now* understand *why* and *how* Ireland is a slave. Show this to Mr. Duffy, and to Mr. D'arcy McGee, or to any one else at your own discretion."[19]

———•·•———

Along with these growing tensions over the land question and strategies of resistance, the Confederation began to replicate earlier differences within the Repeal Association over the question of slavery. Most Young Irelanders continued to place nationalism over abolitionism, and had no qualms about accepting money from slaveholders in the United States. A minority, however, believed that the Confederation should have no complicity in slavery, and shared O'Connell's views on the subject. At the other end of the spectrum, Mitchel and Kenyon emerged as active supporters of slavery. The most militant nationalists were often the most vociferous racists; in Mitchel's case, this extended to anti-Semitism. The issue of slavery had been simmering right from the beginning of the Confederation, when Kenyon and the Quaker James Haughton debated the issue in the columns of the *Nation* in January and February. It reached boiling point in April, when Haughton chaired the Confederation's monthly meeting and urged the members to "shrink from any contamination with slaveholders, who may affect to sympathise with you in your efforts to secure your own freedom." "I am afraid," he declared, "we shall allow our hatred of man-stealing to be buried under the blood-stained dollars of slaveholders." There was an uproar in the crowd; Haughton was shouted down, amid "tremendous cheers" for America and calls of "Repeal! We want no slave lecturing here."[20]

McGee was very much with the majority, and was "received with loud applause" when he moved "the thanks of the Confederation to their friends in America." Agreeing that the question of slavery had no place in a Repeal meeting, he argued that the Americans and Irish were natural allies, and praised the Americans for their efforts to "relieve the overwhelming distress" in Ireland; his earlier opposition to American "charity" had evaporated under conditions of continuing famine. At the same time, McGee insisted that "there was nothing slavish or syco-phantic in the present relation of Ireland with America" – an insensi-tive choice of words, after Haughton's arguments. The Irish American relationship was celebrated the following week, when the American frigate *Jamestown* arrived in Cork, laden with food and provisions for the hungry. Amid the unfurling of "the green banner of Ireland" and the "starry flag of America," and against the background of "the inspiriting tones of American national music" and "Ireland's own anthems," McGee read the Confederation's address of thanks to the ship's officers. The banquet was sumptuous, and the subject of slavery was not mentioned.[21]

When he was not speaking at the monthly Confederation meetings, attending the weekly sessions of the council, and writing for the *Nation*, McGee was working on his third non-fiction book, *A Memoir of the Life and Conquests of Art Mac Murrough*, the Leinster king who fought and defeated Richard II's invasion forces during the late fourteenth cen-tury. Published in April, it was the last book in James Duffy's Library of Ireland series; McGee placed it within the general project of cre-ating "an Irish Literature in the English Language" and of reversing "the influence of the arrogant spirit and false philosophy of English-written books on Ireland." Rescuing Art Mac Murrough from English and Scottish historians who had treated him "most scurvily," McGee portrayed him as a paragon of virtue, the kind of great figure who could inspire Irishmen during the dark and divisive days of 1847. "In reading over annals of broils and discords," McGee wrote, "... the heart yearns for a hero, before whose figure, fixed on consistent principle as on granite, it can bow down, and do homage. May we not presume to say, lo! such a man is here."[22]

Combining cultural nationalism with the romantic myth of the hero, McGee's book inverted negative English stereotypes about Irish history, and assumed the melodramatic form of pitting virtue against vice. As we have seen, the same impulse to inversion had informed his earlier writings, such as "The Priest Hunter," and had intermittently manifested itself in his reactions against American nativism and British hegemony. Sharing such sensibilities, his reviewers praised McGee for restoring "another hero to the memory and imagination of our people" and for throwing "a romantic halo over dry and musty records." The *Kilkenny Recorder* declared that the book was "the most remarkable" one in the Library of Ireland series. There were, however, some interesting critical comments. One writer detected "traces of hasty composition," another felt that McGee exaggerated Art Mac Murrough's accomplishments, and a third expressed reservations about the book's "exclusive Milesian prejudices" – an ironic charge, given McGee's earlier attempt to break the "popular fallacy" that the Irish were synonymous with the Milesians. The reviewer in the *Nation* noted that Mac Murrough was "a provincial, not a national, hero" (a point that McGee had made himself), and warned readers against projecting modern notions of nationality too far back into the past. At the same time, the reviewer argued that McGee had brought specificity and clarity to vague and confused notions of "English conquest and oppression" that "floated in the popular mind, and got embodied in such dim phrases as 'seven centuries of wrong.'" In this sense, he concluded, McGee's historical writings were carrying on the great work of Thomas Davis.[23]

By the time that McGee's book came out, conditions in Ireland showed no signs of easing; on the contrary, some of the most graphic descriptions of starvation were recorded in March and April of 1847. The workhouses buckled under the pressure, the public works failed, and the government was turning to soup kitchens as an emergency measure; by the summer, three million people, more than a third of the population, were surviving on soup. While Lalor advocated agrarian agitation and McGee shared the Confederation's emphasis on political pressure, a group of prominent Irish political and religious figures concluded that the best way to save lives was through state-assisted emigration to British North America. The idea was the brainchild of John Robert Godley, a Poor Law commissioner who had travelled to North America in 1842 and later organized colonial settlement in New Zealand. He was joined by W.H. Gregory, best known for his amendment to the Temporary Relief Act, Richard Whately, the Protestant archbishop of Dublin and Ireland's most brilliant social scientist, and Morgan John O'Connell, Daniel's nephew. Ireland had too many people and too little land; British North America had too few people and too much land; voluntary migration seemed an obvious way to solve the problem and strengthen the British Empire. If they could persuade the government to invest seven million pounds in the project, and if they could involve the churches in the colonization scheme, it would be possible, they believed, to move one and a half million people from overcrowded Ireland to underpopulated Canada.[24]

The plan, for all its rationality and good intentions, was comprehensively denounced in the nationalist press. "To 'Hell or Connaught' – to Canada or the Grave," ran an editorial in the *Nation*, which argued that "an allied gang of coward landlords and knavish Whigs" was trying to depopulate Ireland for the benefit of Canada. The Catholic Church would never participate in such a plan, declared Bishop Edward Maginn, who described its proponents as "the hereditary oppressors of my race and my religion." In his view, the scheme was nothing less than a "wholesale system of extermination"; the only people who should be transported to Canada were the criminals who had "made the most beautiful island under the sun a land of skulls or of ghastly spectres." Instead of driving the Irish into North America, argued the *Nation*, the government should ban all grain exports and spend Godley's migration money on improving the Irish economy.[25]

McGee was equally scathing about Godley's plan, which he caricatured as a "swindling speculation" concocted by the "degenerate gentry of this kingdom" in a vain attempt to save their own skin. "Did ever human insolence go beyond this?" he asked. "In order that a few bankrupts may postpone their day of reckoning – in order that a few spendthrifts may destroy their wretched remnants of life and character – in order that a few usurers shall have their arrears of interest – 2,000,000 Irishmen are to be banished into the Canadian backwoods." The answer, he declared, was to drive famine, bigotry, and disunion out of Ireland, not its people. Similar sentiments appeared in his poems

"Life and Land" and "The Living and the Dead," which spoke of staying on the land and standing against tyranny.[26]

Ironically, McGee later advocated colonization schemes in Canada in order to move Irish immigrants out of American cities, and he faced the same kind of charges he had levelled against Godley. In 1847, however, he shared the nationalist assumption that there was more than enough food in Ireland to feed the entire population, and erroneously attributed malicious motives to Godley and his supporters. The colonization plan eventually failed, not as a result of nationalist opposition but because the government deemed it too expensive and because of resistance in Canada, where it was "condemned by the organs of all Parties."[27]

McGee's hostility to Godley's proposal was accompanied by a rising tide of anger towards the Whigs. Blaming the Whigs for the split in the Repeal movement, he accused them of bribing the O'Connellites into silence with the promise of government positions, in the old game of divide and rule. Having "destroyed the national organisation," the Whigs were then able to put the "Monied Interest of the empire" over and above the needs of the people. They sacrificed lives to the "avarice of the rich corn dealers in England, and their forestalling and extorting brethren in Ireland," and viewed the famine with a mixture of callousness and incompetence. "Of their relief works – their broken roads and tons of circulars – their cumbrous systems succeeding one another, with intervals of havoc in between – it is needless here to speak," McGee declared. "The memory of their perpetual blunders is as fresh in our minds as the graves they have made are fresh in every corner of the kingdom."

Impervious to cries for help and calls for change, McGee continued, the Whigs had opposed O'Brien's motion for a tax on absentee landlords and had rejected William Sharman Crawford's resolution to compensate tenants who had improved their farms. The result of Whig policies was "2,000,000 ministerial murders called 'deaths by starvation.'" "I do, in my soul, believe that we are now, at this very hour, in process of being exterminated as a people," McGee asserted in April. When John Mitchel made his famous statement in 1860 that "the Almighty, indeed, sent the potato blight, but the English created the famine," he was expressing in memorable form arguments that had been commonplace in the Confederation.[28]

In the terrible circumstances of 1847 and in his search for answers, McGee's sense of outrage had propelled him into the world of conspiracy theories. Like all good conspiracy theories, his contained an element of truth, along with severe exaggerations and distortions of reality. There had indeed been massive loss of life in 1846–47, but nothing like two million deaths; the figure seems to have gained credence by constant repetition in Confederate circles. The Whigs doubtless benefited from divisions within the Repeal movement, but the split was the result of internal tensions rather than external manipulation. It is true that corn dealers profited during the famine, but had the Whigs attempted to impose price controls, there would probably have been even less food in Ireland. Given the dimensions of the catastrophe, it is extremely unlikely that the land reforms suggested by O'Brien and Sharman Crawford would have made much difference. McGee's indictment of the Whigs' mean-spirited, inept, and ideological relief policies was well taken, but this is not the same thing as "murder." Charges of genocide – or, as McGee put it, "extermination" – cannot be sustained without evidence of intent. The Whigs were guilty of many things, but mass murder was not one of them.

Much of McGee's anger sprang from a sense of helplessness. There was no immediate prospect of Repeal, no effective Irish parliamentary opposition, and no groundswell of revolutionary sentiment in the country. Land reform, McGee believed, was central to preventing the evils of eviction and emigration, but the Whigs refused to budge on the issue. Industrial employment could alleviate the situation, but English competition had undermined Irish manufactures and choked off alternatives for farmers who had been hit by the famine.

What, then, could be done? Seeking room to manoeuvre, McGee saw an opening in the promotion of Irish trade and industry. Protectionism was out of the question, given the circumstances of British rule; it was not, in any case, a desirable option, in McGee's view. But it would be possible to develop a "protective public opinion" by organizing a "buy Irish" campaign to break Britain's economic stranglehold on Ireland, to revive Irish manufactures, and to provide work for a famine-stricken people. The Confederation might be on the political defensive in its struggle against the Whigs, but it could declare, fight, and win an "industrial war" with England. It was, McGee argued, a matter of life or death.[29]

In April he joined the Confederation's trade committee, which met twice a week to gather information about the development of industry in Ireland. At a speech to the Confederation the following month, he was cheered repeatedly when he argued that the Irish people were themselves partly responsible for famine deaths by buying English rather than Irish goods. There were still Irish cloths and hats being sold in Dublin, he said, and it was a simple matter of "practical patriotism" to seek them out and buy them; "and," he added, "if you will not patronise them, you have no business here – your nationality is a sham and a snare." He then addressed the women in the audience: "Ladies, which of your ribbons was made in Ireland? Indeed – I must even speak out – indeed you are not guiltless. Your silks are purple with the blood of the artisan, and your lawns and laces have been bleached in the tears of the female operative. There are still dresses manufactured in Ireland, and gloves, and lace, which any of you might shine in."[30]

McGee's speech prompted more women to become involved in the nationalist movement. Immediately after his speech, "Two Irish Girls" wrote an article for the *Nation* that called on Irishwomen to support their country by embracing "Irish thoughts and ways" and buying Irish goods. The following week, a Ladies' Irish National Association was formed with similar purposes in mind. "*Irish ladies would not consider it unwomanly to combine and protest, by speech and act,*" declared one of their supporters, "*against that social and political state which engendered such masses of moral and physical corruption.*" Maintaining the momentum, "An Irish Mother" argued that every woman in the country, "each in her own sphere," could promote nationalism, scorn treachery, and turn their children into patriots. "We women," she concluded, "can surely forge the weapons that shall overturn English rule in this island." Although

McGee must have welcomed this development, the fact that he did not pursue the subject in subsequent speeches indicates that it was not a high priority for him; like most Confederates, he viewed women as adjuncts in an essentially male campaign.[31]

His main focus, in the spring and summer of 1847, was on publicizing and implementing his economic program. As chair of the committee on manufactures, he planned to draw up "a list of such Irish articles as could be substituted for foreign"; he maintained that manufactures were the key to economic independence and set out to shatter the stereotype that the Irish were too "idle, inapt, and insubordinate" to succeed in industry. Had not the Irish demonstrated their skill and resourcefulness in the factories of Britain and America? With the right opportunities, they would do just as well at home. As McGee came to believe that Ireland must become a manufacturing state to survive, his earlier fears about a "machine aristocracy," class conflict, and the dehumanizing character of factory life faded into the background. When a fellow Confederate warned of the dangers of monopoly and of men becoming subservient to machines, McGee publicly replied that such a "dismal picture ... is a prospect so distant, that in 1847 I think we need hardly be afraid of it." Privately, he dismissed the argument as mere "twaddle."[32]

The centrepiece of his campaign was the "Report on Irish Manufactures" that he delivered to the Irish Confederation in July; the meeting, he told Smith O'Brien, promised to be "one of the greatest we have ever had." Gathering together the strands of his previous arguments, McGee showcased the Royal Dublin Society's exhibition of Irish manufactures as a practical illustration of Irish "mechanical genius." The Irish had long been renowned for wit, humour, poetry and eloquence, he argued, but "were not allowed to possess the character of persevering industry." With a strong home demand for Irish products, all this would change; he looked forward to the day when "the Irish name should be not only identified with intellectual gifts, but also celebrated for national industry and commercial enterprise."[33]

Although his "buy Irish" arguments commanded considerable support within the Confederation, they made little impact on the propertied classes in general. At a "Meeting of Peers and Commoners" held

in November, McGee wanted a stronger resolution on home manufactures, and he moved an amendment that from the middle of 1848
"we will not purchase nor allow to be purchased for us, any articles
whatever of foreign production, if the same articles can be produced as
cheaply in Ireland." The record shows that the amendment passed by
a vote of 47 to 37; the reality was rather different. As Duffy recalled,
O'Gorman Mahon, one of the tellers, "reckoned the ayes in this fashion
– 'Twenty seven, twenty-eight, twenty-nine; forty, forty-one,' and so
on. 'By G——, sir,' he whispered to M'Gee, 'I have added ten to your
score.'" Upon learning this, Duffy continued, McGee decided to drop
the scheme, on the grounds that such a majority was worthless; thus,
Duffy remarked, McGee's project was "entirely ruined by a dishon-
est stroke apparently intended to promote it." This was something of
an oversimplification; McGee was still pushing his plan in early 1848,
until it was overtaken by revolutionary events. But the "protective
public opinion" that he sought remained elusive, and his plan could not
work without widespread support.[34]

Despite all its efforts, the Irish Confederation had failed to become
a dominant political force, and the nationalist movement remained
deeply divided during the famine. There were sporadic discussions
about reconciliation with the Repeal Association, and McGee was part
of an eight-man negotiating team that met the Old Irelanders in May.
But the two sides were too entrenched in their previous positions for the
differences to be overcome, and the Confederation continued to fight
the Repeal Association as well as the Whigs. Then, later in the month,
news reached Ireland that Daniel O'Connell had died in Genoa, en
route to Rome. Given the Liberator's immense popularity and the fact
that the Confederation had broken with his leadership, O'Connell's
death served to isolate the Young Irelanders further; Duffy would
later write of the "startling revulsion of opinion" against the Confederation. Supporters of the Repeal Association declared that the Young
Ireland secession had broken O'Connell's will to live. From Wexford,
John Sinnott denounced the Young Irelanders as the "murderers" of

The obsequies in Marlborough Street Chapel. Although Daniel O'Connell died in May 1847, he was not buried until August – which just happened to coincide with a general election, when the Repeal Association vied with the Irish Confederation for the nationalist vote. Pilloried as the "murderers" of O'Connell and caricatured as anti-Catholic, the Confederates were kept very much on the defensive. (*Illustrated London News*)

O'Connell. Charges of murder, it seems, were common political currency in the Ireland of 1847.[35]

Along with this, the Confederation faced the continuing hostility of the Catholic Church; Young Irelanders were routinely criticized for their supposedly dangerous secularist tendencies and even for kowtowing to Orangeism in their quest for Protestant support. In response, McGee asserted both his Catholicism and his right to free speech on political matters. "I never learned," he said, "that religion was an engine with which to gag a troublesome speaker." Nor did he respect the kind of layman "who seems to think the whole duty of a Christian in the church to be, to ding out his orthodoxy from the steeple." In fact, he became precisely such a layman only four years later. In the summer of 1847, though, he tried to convince himself and others that clerical attacks on Young Ireland did not reflect the feelings of "the Catholic priesthood generally." "The clergy of Ireland," he told the Irish Confederation in July, "would not be found arrayed on the side of corruption" – at which point an O'Connellite in the crowd shouted and swore at him. The man was ejected from the meeting, "not in the gentlest manner," and was almost certainly a minority of one within the Confederation. Outside the hall, however, his protest probably reflected majority opinion. For the most part, McGee and his fellow Confederates tried to avoid a fight with the Catholic Church by simply ignoring its criticisms. On the few occasions the Confederates did respond, it was clear that they were very much on the defensive.[36]

"What has Young Ireland done for Ireland?" became a common taunt of their enemies, who answered that the Confederates had accomplished precisely nothing, apart from dividing the Repeal movement. It was true, McGee replied, that they had failed to repeal the Union and that there was no immediate prospect of success. But they had given Ireland its first national library, they had restored "the ancient landmarks of an ancient nation," and they had provided a sense of pride and self-worth to a downtrodden people by showing that "heroes had been born of their blood, and scholars renowned through the earth begotten of their race." "It was no despicable task," he declared, "... to give Nationality a retrospect as well as a prospect." And even if Repeal remained on the distant horizon, the Confederation had at least pointed out the only way to get there – by working for religious cooperation and insisting on independent political action.[37]

Yet the message kept falling on deaf ears. In preparation for the upcoming general election in August, the Confederates declared that they would only support Repeal candidates who pledged to refuse government appointments. It cut little ice with the electorate. The backlash against the "murderers" of O'Connell was intensified by

John O'Connell's decision to delay the burial of his father until early August, almost three months after his death, and immediately before the election; the importance of Ireland's funerary culture was not lost on the Repeal Association. Excluded from the funeral service, attacked (sometimes physically) as "the men who had killed the Liberator," and opposed by the Catholic Church, the Confederates suffered a steep drop in morale. "Some talked of retiring," wrote Duffy, "as if such a people were not worth an honest man's labour." Many Young Irelanders felt that the people had let down the People.[38]

After six months of "setting our principles before the Irish people," Richard O'Gorman wrote, the Protestants and the gentry had manifestly not supported the Confederation, and Young Ireland's principles had been rejected by most Irish Catholics. "In fact," he added, "we have been abandoned by all, except the Dublin Remonstrants and a few here and there in the Province." His assessment was borne out by the election results, which were disastrous for Young Ireland. Only O'Brien won a seat; the other Young Irelanders did not run for election and would have been defeated if they had. If the movement was to survive, let alone flourish, a stronger organizational base and new political strategies were imperative. In both areas, McGee was to play a crucial and highly contested role.[39]

CHAPTER SIX

The Golden Link
July – December 1847

McGee was well positioned to initiate and implement the changes that would enable the Confederation to move from defence to attack. At the end of June, he was unanimously elected secretary of the party at a salary of £126 a year, and threw himself into the work with his customary energy. "I believe firmly in making the Confederation powerful," he told Smith O'Brien, "and I will not spare myself." His colleagues were enthusiastic about the choice. Meagher was convinced that McGee would "give *great strength, character and effort* to the Confederation," and John Pigot argued that having "a man of such past and prospective reputation and achievements" in the post of secretary would raise the reputation of the party and ensure that the Confederation's business was "rightly done."[1]

Before getting down to business, however, McGee celebrated the most important personal turning point in his life. On Tuesday, 13 July, he married Mary Teresa Caffrey, whom he had met at an art exhibition in Dublin. He celebrated their love in romantic poems, and her remaining letters show that she cared deeply about him. They appeared well suited to one another; among their friends in Young Ireland, Meagher believed that their marriage would turn out "very happily." In fact, it suffered many stresses and fluctuating fortunes; being married to McGee was no sinecure. They were torn apart by exile and continually uprooted as McGee moved from Dublin to New York, Boston, Buffalo, back to New York, and then to Montreal. When McGee was on the road, as he often was, and when they lived in Buffalo, Mary experienced periods of intense loneliness; when he was at home, she

often had to deal with his heavy drinking. There were personal tragedies as well; of their five children, only two survived into adulthood.
Yet there was also great affection and tenderness within the family, as
McGee's letters to his children attest. For her part, Mary continued
to write of "my darling Thomas" until the end of her days. Still, one
suspects that she could easily have echoed the words of Nora Barnacle
about James Joyce: "You can't imagine what it was like for me to be
thrown into the life of this man."[2]

- - - - -

All this, of course, lay far in the unforeseeable future during their
brief honeymoon in the Wicklow hills. In his capacity as secretary
of the Confederation, McGee was faced with the immediate tasks of
strengthening the party's finances and recruiting more members. Since
its formation in January, the Confederation had relied on voluntary
contributions, on the grounds that it was unreasonable to insist on
membership fees during the "distress and destitution" of the famine.
But, argued McGee in July 1847, "these things had happily passed away
in a great measure, and thus was removed a very great obstacle to the
organization of their friends." Henceforth all members of the Confederation would be required to pay fees; by September he could report
that "we are now completely out of debt – and about £30 in pocket."
While this made organizational sense, the premise behind the change
was revealing: like Lord John Russell and Charles Trevelyan, McGee
assumed that the famine was over in the summer of 1847. They would
all be proved very wrong.[3]

While McGee was looking at ways to improve the Confederation's
financial situation, Duffy came up with a much more far-reaching
initiative – the formation of a network of Confederate clubs, which
would spread Young Ireland principles throughout the country. In
contrast to ethnically based secret societies, the clubs were to be open
and non-sectarian; through classes on Ireland's history, literature, and
economic development, they were intended to establish the educational
foundations for a new citizenry. As someone who had pioneered adult

education classes in Boston, had chaired the Confederation's committee on public instruction, and had committed himself to broadening
the party's base of support, McGee warmly embraced Duffy's plan and
became one of its most enthusiastic supporters.[4]

In early July, McGee became president of the newly formed Davis
Club, which organized classes in English grammar, arithmetic, and
accounting, along with lectures on history and literature. At its first
meeting, he donated his now lost edition of *The Works of Thomas
Davis* to the club, delivered a lecture on Davis's life and character, and
declared that the clubs were the key to Ireland's liberation. "They
had first to organize Dublin," he said, "then Ireland, then England,
and then America, and their freedom would assuredly be won." The
Confederation's goal, he told the Davis Club in August, was to create
five hundred associations in Ireland; this would make the movement
impossible to suppress, and make it equally impossible for a latter-day
O'Connell to assume quasi-dictatorial power over the cause of Repeal.
McGee then cut short his presence at the meeting, explaining that "he
had to attend elsewhere at the formation of a club." Once McGee had
committed himself to a project, there was no stopping him.[5]

The clubs would demonstrate that "the famine had not broken the
heart in the patriotism of the people," McGee asserted. By September,
the Davis Club was thriving, with 110 members and a working committee of 10. Among the works that McGee presented to the club was
Bishop John Hughes's "Lecture on the Antecedent Causes of the Irish
Famine," which had been delivered in New York in March. "I may
be told," Hughes had said, "that the famine in Ireland is a mysterious
visitation of God's providence, but I do not admit any such plea. I fear
there is blasphemy in charging on the Almighty what is the result of
man's own doings ... No! no! God's famine is known by general scarcity – there has been no general scarcity of food in Ireland either the
present or the last year except in one species of vegetable." The real
causes of the famine, according to Hughes, were "bad government"
and "a defective or vicious system of social economy." In this way,
McGee transmitted an early Irish American genocidal interpretation
of the famine to a receptive audience of nationalists in Dublin, as part
of his program of educating the Irish people.[6]

McGee was also active outside Dublin. In September, he travelled through County Wexford on an organizational drive, establishing clubs in Wexford, Enniscorthy, Taghmon, and New Ross. "On the whole I think I may safely say the County Wexford is more with us, *socially*, than with the others," he informed O'Brien. "A little more success in other quarters ... & it will break out as suddenly & as strongly as it did in '98." In his capacity as secretary of the Confederation, he reported that clubs were being formed in Cappoquin, Waterford, Newry, and Galway, and were spreading to northern England. By November, he wrote, there were twenty-three clubs in Ireland and Britain, and more were being established. This was still well short of the five hundred clubs he hoped for, but things were moving in the right direction.[7]

One of the great advantages of the clubs, in McGee's view, was that they were "founded on a federal, as distinguished from an imperial or centralised system," and would engage people at the local level. In taking this position, he was strongly influenced by David Urquhart, the charismatic leader of a small band of British pro-Repeal MPs in the House of Commons. A political maverick, Urquhart combined support for free trade with a Tory-radical outlook that reached back to Bolingbroke and had been carried into the early nineteenth century in populist form by Cobbett.[8]

Among other things, Urquhart wanted to roll back the centralizing power of Parliament and to restore the primacy of local government. Centralization, he argued, not only produced "mental confusion" but also resulted in "the powerlessness of laws, the extinction of the knowledge of affairs and of citizenship"; unless it was reversed, its consequences would be fatal to Britain. Urquhart's nostalgia for the imagined Ancient Constitution also led him to support a revival of the royal prerogative and a reduction in the franchise; a Patriot King together with his informed and intelligent subjects would restore honour and justice to a country that was being undermined by corruption, greed, and hypocrisy.[9]

Urquhart had visited Dublin in the summer of 1847, shortly before his election to Parliament in August, and met the leaders of the Con-

David Urquhart (1805–77). Born in Scotland and educated in Europe, Urquhart was best known for his warnings about Russian expansionism and for
his fascination with Turkish culture. But McGee was captivated by Urquhart's charisma and influenced by his Tory-Radicalism; McGee's views on
the "golden link of the crown" owed a great deal to his correspondence with
Urquhart. (Gertrude Robinson, *David Urquhart* [1920])

federation. Duffy later wrote a humorous account of his encounter
with Urquhart, who "looked like an Oriental Pasha condescending to
mate for a moment with the dullards of the West," and whose egotism
reached staggering proportions. But McGee was susceptible to charismatic figures. In the United States, he had fallen briefly under the spell
of Thomas Colley Grattan, and a hunger for heroes ran through all his

early books. So it was with Urquhart. McGee found him a compelling individual, described him as "one of the most remarkable men of the age," and was deeply struck by his ideas. "It is strange what magic there is in personal exertion," he wrote to Urquhart. "If all your writings had been coming for an age, I think they could not have made such an impression, as your few days conversation." After Urquhart returned to England, McGee spent two days reading his *Portfolio* and his pamphlets in a "fever" of excitement; his subsequent letters to Urquhart read like those of a convert to the master.[10]

Urquhart's views influenced McGee in three main ways. First, McGee now located his support for the Confederate clubs within a theoretical framework that emphasized the importance of local initiatives as a means of producing an educated, enlightened, and politically aware populace. Second, McGee had a major change of heart about England as he came to accept Urquhart's quasi-apocalyptic belief that the country was being destroyed by corruption. As he told Urquhart, "I have lost all vindictiveness towards England, & now regard her with deep sympathy not unmixed with awe. This awe arises from an uncertainty of her final fate for though I see plainly her danger I do not as plainly see her escaping. My former prejudice & hatred against her was sustained by envy & jealousy. I thought her safe & sound while we were crumbled like dry turf but now that I see she too has her powerful enemies, her internal traitors, her blindness & her pitfalls – a fellow feeling lightened by the reverse in my own mind is the result." It was "not *England* but 'Ministers'" who were the enemies of England, McGee concluded. The conviction that the Irish and English people shared a common enemy in the Cabinet fitted very well with the drive to organize Confederate clubs in England; there were apparently opportunities there for an alliance between the Confederation and English radicals. And third, Urquhart's concept of the Crown as both a symbol and a guardian of liberty opened the way for a significant reappraisal of the Anglo-Irish relationship – and this was the area in which Urquhart had his most important influence on McGee.[11]

In Urquhart's view, an overweening Parliament had encroached on both the prerogatives of the Crown and the liberties of the English people; McGee extended the argument to include Ireland and found a historical warrant for his views in the half-remembered events of 1541. In that year, he told Urquhart, the Celtic and Norman chiefs of Ireland had assembled in Dublin and elected Henry VIII as King of Ireland; it was this compact, and not conquest, that formed the basis of the "Crown Connexion." But since the Act of Union, Ireland had been subjected to the same kind of "ministerial aggression" that Urquhart had identified in England. Had it not been for the "odious innovations" of power-hungry English ministers, along with their "heartless & false conduct" during the famine, Ireland would have been the most "loyal Nation on the Earth." Even now, he informed Urquhart, there was no support for complete Irish independence: "I know not & never heard of one Repealer of our Party who was for separation." If the original compact was restored, and was given the same force as an international treaty, the days of British parliamentary tyranny over Ireland would end, and traditional Irish loyalty would reassert itself.[12]

From this perspective, McGee described himself as both a loyal subject of Queen Victoria and an implacable enemy of Parliament. The British Parliament, he wrote, "outrageously burst through legal limitations, and declared the [Irish] Parliament at an end, and the People, no longer capable of governing themselves." "For this Parliament," he continued, "& the bloated monster into whose bowels the wretched thing has crept, I have no respect, & to its ordinances I am not, and please God, never will be loyal."[13]

Through the medium of Urquhart's Tory-radicalism, McGee was able to bring together the different components of his political thought and action. His work with the Confederate clubs fitted into Urquhart's emphasis on decentralization; the extension of these clubs into Britain corresponded with Urquhart's view that the British people were the victims of parliamentary tyranny. At the same time, the glorification of the Crown supplied a conservative justification for political radicalism; it was the Unionists who were the dangerous innovators and the Confederates who were the guardians of tradition. And the myth of 1541 – for myth it was – appeared to provide a historical foundation for McGee's pre-existing position that equal but distinct Irish and British legislatures should share a common allegiance to the Crown.

McGee's next task was to persuade his colleagues and the public at large to accept his argument about the difference between a benign Crown and an aggressive Parliament. "All Ireland does not feel so satisfied with this distinction as I do, and those to whom I have personally explained it" he told Urquhart, "but before twelve months all Ireland will understand it & hold by it." It seems that some of Urquhart's megalomania was rubbing off on him. The day after he outlined his ideas to Urquhart, McGee tentatively broached the subject with Smith O'Brien: "You have always recieved [sic] so well any of my suggestions, however wild, that I venture to put in one here – namely, that we should fall back on the old Crown Connexion of the two Countries, and show that 'the golden link' is no metaphor, but an useful bond, established honorably." Such an approach, McGee argued, would "show that it is not a new species of arrangement we want, only a restoration of the old & only constitutional one." "It would also," he added, "silence the bleating about separation" – a statement which reveals that McGee had misled Urquhart about separatist sentiment in the Confederation, and intended to employ the "golden link of the crown" as a weapon against the separatists in the organization.[14]

His first public statement on the issue came three days later, at a speech he delivered to the Confederates in Liverpool. McGee had been invited to Liverpool by Terence Bellew MacManus, who had informed him that "the iron is hot" in the city. Before an audience of five hundred people, McGee asserted that the Act of Union violated the compact of 1541, and maintained that the Union had been responsible for the famine. He also addressed the argument that an independent Ireland would produce a "Catholic Ascendancy" that discriminated against Protestants. This would never happen, he said; any such attempt would constitute an act of rebellion against both the Crown and the new Irish parliament. Again, McGee was following Urquhart, who had made exactly the same argument in a letter he had sent to McGee the previous week.[15]

After visiting Liverpool, McGee travelled to Manchester. Here, he met Bernard Treanor, a Dubliner who had organized a Confederate

Club in Stalybridge and who would resurface in McGee's subsequent American career. Speaking to the Manchester Confederates, McGee continued to push Urquhart's ideas, repudiated separatism, and came out unequivocally against physical-force nationalism. Echoing one of O'Connnell's best-known phrases, he declared that Ireland would rely on the "never-failing power of truth and justice to dissolve the unnatural union of 1800, and without the shedding of a single drop of blood." On his English tour, McGee was positioning himself on the conservative wing of the Confederation, in anticipation of political battles to come.[16]

Having tested his constitutional theory on the road, McGee brought it directly to an Irish audience. At a lecture to the St Patrick's Club, with his friend Father Charles Meehan in the chair, McGee expounded his views on 1541 and "the golden link of the crown." "The crown has done us no wrong," he said; "but the London cabals, called ministries, have utterly beggared us both in fortune and allegiance." The Unionists had shattered the Ancient Constitution, and the Federalists wanted "to destroy all past wisdom that they make a mosaic of the pieces to please their own fancies"; federalism was now part of the problem rather than a possible solution. McGee's lecture was published in the *Nation*, and he sent a copy to Urquhart, who strongly approved. This was not altogether surprising, since most of the ideas were his. "I was no less startled than gratified ... to find in it the stiches [sic] taken up from our former work on the Portfolio," he told McGee, "not only as confirmatory of the course which we had adopted, but as an evidence to me, of the faculty in you to select & adapt." McGee was delighted by Urquhart's positive response. "Your note," he wrote, "has made me happier than anything that has occurred to me since my wedding day."[17]

McGee was much less happy at the reactions he received in Ireland. His compact theory triggered considerable controversy and alienated a significant section of the Confederation. In some respects, it was the Burke-Paine debate revisited. McGee stressed custom, precedent, and the ancient constitution; his opponents asserted the primacy of the present against the accumulated rubbish of ages. "'Tis better to leave those time-worn constitutions to moulder amid the dust of ages, than waste our time in search of them," wrote Michael Kerney; "for were we to discover them, they would be as little suited to the customs and manners of the present day, as the mailed armour of the 14th century would be for our modern warriors." There was not "a scintilla of proof," he argued, that such a compact had ever existed. Another writer, William J. Byrne, added that the Irish chiefs who submitted to English authority in 1541 were merely a bunch of "hypocritical swindlers" and "renegades to their country's cause." Kerney was equally unimpressed by McGee's distinction between the Crown and the ministers. The Crown appointed the ministers, he pointed out. If the Crown did not have sufficient power to control them, then it was politically superfluous. "Is this writer," he asked, "the Mr. M'Gee who is our secretary – this legitimist, loyalist, the principal officer in our essentially democratic institution? Are those the doctrines he learned in free America, whose majestic mountains inspired him with the thoughts of liberty which I had the pleasure of hearing him descant upon in fervid eloquence? *Coming from Mr. M'Gee, they have the appearance of insincerity.*"[18]

Faced with these criticisms, McGee put up a strong rearguard action. He emphasized the "natural connexion" between Britain and Ireland, and insisted that separatism was neither possible nor desirable: "Whatever Confederate intends to act, or does act, hostile to that connexion, is not a Repealer, but a Separatist. I conceive the sooner we attain to clear views and deep convictions on this topic the better." There was nothing incompatible between his views and the policy of the Confederation, he argued; the party was national, rather than republican or democratic, and embraced different classes, religious beliefs, and political attitudes. He did not directly tackle the charge of insincerity. But McGee's compact theory was not so much an "about face" (as Robin Burns argued) as an elaboration and extension of his earlier conviction that Britain and Ireland should have a common connection to the Crown. The argument he took had changed, but the objective remained the same.[19]

For all his efforts, McGee's compact theory failed to capture the popular imagination. The Confederation had initially intended to publish his "golden link" lecture. But as the controversy continued and the divisive character of the compact theory became clear, McGee in December requested that the lecture be withdrawn from the party's list of publications. The prospect of converting "all Ireland" within twelve months was receding, and the republicans in the Confederation were regarding McGee with increasing suspicion. He had "sneered at the Republicans of Ireland," they claimed, was "an enthusiast in the cause of our 'lovely QUEEN,'" and was motivated by "the advancement of his own selfish views." The republican image of McGee as an ambitious adventurer dates from the debate over the "golden link of the crown."[20]

• ┅ •

Among the many accusations of selfishness levelled at McGee over the years, one of the most striking appeared in the *Irish Canadian* in 1865. Reviewing McGee's career, the paper stated that the central defect in his character was an "overwhelming desire to aggrandise himself and his family." He had supported Young Ireland only because it was his best route to power and fame. Similarly, in America he had given "speeches in favour of democracy, and thought 'If I gain but sufficient footing in this strange land what may I, D'Arcy McGee, not become?'" And in Canada, "we find him the execrator of Democracies, the champion of monarchial rule, thinking 'If I play *this* game well what may I not become?'"[21]

Had the paper's editor, Patrick Boyle, seen some of McGee's private letters during the Young Ireland years, he might well have concluded that they clinched his case. We have already seen that in 1845 McGee informed his aunt that his "sole ambition" was "the elevation of all my dear Mothers [sic] family and yours." In his correspondence with Urquhart, McGee explicitly connected his personal political ambitions with the success of the Irish Confederation. After reading the "golden link" lecture, Urquhart asked McGee if there was any possibility that he would become a member of Parliament. "At present, none," he replied. "In the first place I have not the qualification, in the next my name for usefulness & work is irretrievably bound up in the success of the Confederation. To succeed myself, I must make it succeed. I may say too, that though such a sphere of action seems to be utterly inaccessible, there is none I wd rather reach."[22]

The key question, though, is not whether McGee was ambitious – that is indisputable – but whether he sacrificed his principles for his ambitions. And on this one, Patrick Boyle got it wrong. He was certainly mistaken about McGee's American career. After 1851, most of McGee's speeches were highly critical of American democracy – something that would hardly have been the case had he been interested only in self-advancement. In 1847, McGee did not see any conflict between his personal ambition and his public cause, so the issue simply did not arise. "I do not know much," he told Urquhart, "but I wish to know all things. I love labor for its own sake & Irelands [sic] deeply & I desire to have an honest fame that I may with others share it, & my thoughts as a legacy to my country." As far as McGee was concerned, his quest for "honest fame" was inseparable from his commitment to the Irish Confederation in particular and the betterment of Ireland in general. It was a case of "both and," not "either or"; he equated his personal advancement with the advancement of Irish nationalism.[23]

As part of his attempt to ensure the success of the Confederation, McGee joined O'Brien, Mitchel, and Meagher in a Repeal "mission" to Belfast in November. The idea was to proselytize the non-sectarian principles of the Confederation in the heartland of unionism, despite concerns that the city's Orangemen would attempt to break up the meeting. In the event, the opposition came not from Protestant Unionists but from an O'Connellite crowd, which was determined to prevent the deputation from speaking. The previous year, Young Irelanders in Belfast had disrupted a pro-O'Connell demonstration in the city; now it was time for payback. Throughout the country, tensions between Young and Old Ireland showed no sign of abating. There had been fist-fights in Dublin, Cork, and Limerick; Belfast fitted into a larger pattern. The divisions within Irish nationalism, it was clear, were at least as important as the divisions between nationalism and unionism.[24]

The Confederates planned to speak at the Music Hall, with McGee giving the opening speech. As he tried to speak, the O'Connellites in the building lit up "squibs of gunpowder," and the crowd outside began to shatter the windows with stones. When Meagher followed him to the podium, some forty or fifty people armed with poles rushed onto the stage and "proceeded to deal furious blows at the heads of Mr. Meagher, Mr. M'Gee, and others." The police intervened and cleared out the protesters. When McGee made a second attempt to speak, someone set off a stink bomb, and a full-scale fight ensued, with Mitchel shouting "that he would not be removed, unless he were made a corpse." Once again, the police ejected the demonstrators, and Meagher made himself heard through the constant barracking and heckling.

McGee was eventually able to deliver part of his speech, in which he addressed "the fear of Catholic ascendancy which many Protestants honestly entertain," and insisted that an Irish constitution would enshrine "complete religious freedom." In the immediate context of the Music Hall, his argument missed its mark: words that were designed to reassure Protestants were actually delivered to deeply divided Catholics. As far as many Protestant Unionists were concerned, the Belfast meeting was anything but reassuring. It appeared to confirm their stereotypes about the inability of the Catholic Irish to govern themselves, and to demonstrate that the Confederates were in no position to make good on any promises they might make about civil and religious liberty.[25]

Matters got worse a few days later, when the Confederates tried to hold a second meeting and were stopped in their tracks by the "Hercules Street butchers." An attempt to hold another meeting the following day was drowned out by a cacophony of rattles and shouts. At a dinner that night for the "Young and Old Ireland Repealers," McGee finally had a second chance to speak. This time, his speech was classic Urquhart. He not only talked about "the advantage of local government over centralization" and the "golden link" of the Crown, but he echoed Urquhart's views on the evils of empires, "the greatest enemies of the happiness of nations." At the same time, he invoked the inspirational ecumenicalism of Davis as an antidote to the disturbances earlier in the week. When McGee returned to Dublin, he found that his colleagues were "highly pleased" with the conduct of the Belfast deputation and were all in "capital spirits." The *Nation* declared that the

"Mission to the North" had been "a complete moral success." A few more moral victories like that, and the Confederation would have been wiped out completely.[26]

—•••—

The presence of McGee and Mitchel at the Music Hall in Belfast concealed the growing division within the Confederation over strategies and objectives. In April, McGee had dedicated his *Life of Art Mac Murrough* to Mitchel; towards the end of the year, however, the two men were moving farther and farther apart. McGee's constitutional arguments put him on the conservative wing of Young Ireland, while Mitchel's trajectory towards revolutionary republicanism placed him firmly on the left. McGee had gravitated towards Urquhart and pulled back from Lalor's agrarian radicalism; Mitchel had gravitated towards Lalor and came to dismiss the "golden link of the crown" as mere "humbug."[27]

Their differences had already become clear before the trip to Belfast. The occasion was a meeting of the Irish Council in early November, when the question of "tenant right" was discussed. Following Lalor's principle of co-ownership, Mitchel argued that any tenant who was evicted should receive compensation from his landlord. Such compensation, he maintained, should be based not on any improvements that had been made but on the fact of prior occupancy. McGee strongly disagreed, on the grounds that Mitchel's position violated the rights of private property and would have disastrous political consequences. Compensation should be given only for improvements, McGee argued; occupancy in itself was not a "saleable commodity," and "where it had not been purchased, it should not be permitted to be sold." Mitchel's proposal, in McGee's view, amounted to an illegal and immoral confiscation of private property and would effectively kill off potential landlord support for Young Ireland. After a protracted debate, Mitchel lost by two votes; the fact that his opponents included not only McGee but also Duffy and O'Brien contributed to his growing sense of disillusionment with the Confederation.[28]

The emerging split between McGee and the more radical Confederates was exacerbated by personal tensions. There is no evidence that

McGee and Mitchel were on bad personal terms towards the end of 1847, but things were very different between McGee and Devin Reilly, whose militancy at times outpaced that of Mitchel. According to Duffy, Reilly "cherished a fierce jealousy of McGee, whom he believed to be more favoured." As McGee's stock rose within the Confederation, Reilly felt that his own contributions were being undervalued; in Duffy's view, Reilly "avenged his wrong like a boy by quarrelling with McGee and neglecting his own duty." The personality clash proved difficult to contain; there had been several attempts to patch things up, none of which was successful. When these personal differences were combined with divergent political views, the conflict between McGee and Reilly became even more intense.[29]

What brought these tensions to a head was the Whigs' Coercion Bill, which was being debated in the House of Commons in November and December. As the number of evictions rose, so did the level of popular resistance. Amid reports of increasing violence in south-central Ireland, Lord Clarendon, the lord lieutenant, pressed the government for the suspension of *habeas corpus*. The Whigs, who had come to power by opposing the Tories' Coercion Bill for Ireland, now decided to introduce one of their own. It did not go as far as Clarendon would have liked and was criticized in Parliament for being too weak; among other things, it provided for disarmament measures and an increased police presence in proclaimed counties. But it went much too far for the Confederates.[30]

At a meeting of the Confederation on 1 December, Mitchel launched an all-out attack on the Coercion Bill. Emphasizing that he was speaking for himself rather than the Confederation, he urged the formation of "local militia, for their mutual defence against aggression." "Farmers everywhere should not pile their arms at the nearest police station," he declared, "but keep them safe and in good order, wear them and use them." The following day, McGee sent an urgent note to O'Brien: "Mr Mitchel I am sorry to say made a very indiscreet speech – so indiscreet that the Council is to meet tomorrow to counteract its effects by at once determining on a Parliamentary policy." O'Brien had already presented a report to the Confederation, committing the movement to moral force, parliamentary pressure, and an Irish legislature under the Crown. Duffy was currently working on a strategy document on the "ways and means by which it [the Confederation] intends to win Repeal"; the idea was to supplement O'Brien's generalities with a specific plan of action. They all agreed that the Confederation must immediately and unequivocally repudiate Mitchel's position.[31]

In consequence, McGee and Duffy did everything they could to isolate the revolutionary faction that was cohering around Mitchel, Devin Reilly, Michael Doheny, and John Martin. To Richard O'Gorman, who supported Mitchel's "bold stand" against the government, it seemed that Duffy and McGee were more exercised about Mitchel's arguments than about the Coercion Bill itself. In fact, complained O'Gorman, Duffy and McGee "seem rather in favour of letting the Bill pass without any opposition from us." This was unfair. McGee argued that an independent Irish parliamentary party would have put up a far more vigorous fight against coercion than the current crop of Irish MPs did, and he wanted to channel the opposition through constitutional means rather than popular resistance. This was all very well as a long-term strategy; in the immediate context of the Coercion Bill, however, it appeared utterly inadequate to Mitchel and his supporters.[32]

While walking home with Mitchel immediately after his "indiscreet speech," Duffy informed him that his ideas contradicted Confederation policy and could not be countenanced in the Nation; two days later, Mitchel and Reilly resigned from the paper. "We have been all going very wrong here this some time past," O'Gorman wrote to O'Brien. "Indeed it seems as [if] some wicked demon were lurking unseen to set us by the ears ... I see or think I see symptoms of intended dictatorship on the part of Duffy and McGee – and that I for one won't stand." A special meeting of the Confederation council was called for 31 December to discuss Duffy's "Report on the Ways and Means of Repealing the Union" and to hammer out "the future policy of the Confederation." Both factions geared up for what was expected to be a decisive confrontation.[33]

Writing to O'Brien the day before the meeting, McGee estimated that half a dozen members would probably support "extreme and revolutionary tactics." The majority were moderates, he observed, but might be swayed by Mitchel's oratory. All in all, he viewed the situation with acute anxiety. He knew that Mitchel was planning to start his own newspaper that would present a radical alternative to the *Nation*. Meanwhile, he wrote, "Duffy is hot *& seems* dictatorial, Meagher is not a student of ways and means, and O'Gorman thinks only when he is put to it." If the Confederation split – as seemed likely – it would "lead to the formation of two parties within a weak Confederacy, to favouritism *&* bitterness, *&* perhaps, ultimately destruction."[34]

Precisely because the consequences of a split were so serious, the moderates tried to play for time. After Duffy delivered his report and Reilly read "a paper of Objections" to it, John Pigot moved that the issue be referred to a subcommittee of nine members, including McGee. The day of reckoning had been delayed, but it could not be postponed indefinitely. As Duffy put it, the prospect of "a secession from the secession" threatened to ruin the Confederation. It was with good reason that McGee expressed his "deep concern" about the future.[35]

CHAPTER SEVEN

A General European Explosion
January – May 1848

Underlying the divisions that threatened to tear the Confederation apart was a fundamental discrepancy between the ideal and the real, between what its members wanted and what they could achieve. As its first anniversary approached, the Confederation had made little or no practical progress and was faced with a Whig government that had effectively turned its back on the country by arguing that Irish property should pay for Irish poverty. Only by securing control over its own affairs, argued the Young Irelanders, could Ireland be saved from starvation and subjection. But this objective appeared utterly unattainable in the short run – and during the famine it was the short run that counted.

The moderates, including McGee, believed that Repeal could only be achieved through an alliance with the gentry, the support of a significant section of the Protestants, and sustained constitutional pressure at Westminster. But most of the gentry and the vast majority of Protestants wanted nothing to do with Repeal, and constitutional means were manifestly failing. For militants such as Mitchel, the way out of the dilemma was to push forward without the gentry and the Protestants, and to win independence through the threat or reality of physical force. But the Mitchelites were a minority of a minority, and there was little revolutionary sentiment in the country; the radical alternative appeared as futile as the constitutional strategy.

To understand subsequent events, and McGee's role in them, it is important to realize that the divisions between the moderates and militants were not quite as stark as they seemed. Smith O'Brien, Duffy, and McGee did not rule out physical force under all conditions. McGee never – not even in his later career as a Liberal-Conservative politician in Canada – repudiated the notion that Ireland, like any other nation, had the theoretical right to fight for its freedom. What was at issue was the practical application of that right. And in the circumstances of early 1848, he was convinced that physical force would be disastrous for the cause of Repeal. For his part, Mitchel was not advocating an immediate insurrection: "I have nowhere recommended the Irish nation to attain legislative independence by force of arms in their present and broken condition," he declared in February. But he wanted to provoke the government into repressive policies that would radicalize and revolutionize an armed population, which would then fight to overthrow British rule in Ireland.[1]

The difficulties facing the Confederation were enough to drive some of its members to despair. "I ... think all *agitation* for Repeal *useless*, if not *mischievous*," wrote Michael John Barry, "and I am disposed to think that it is *both*." O'Gorman was "wearied and disgusted with our squabbles" and would rather have dissolved the Confederation than allow it to become "the organ for the dissemination of the mischievous and foolish doctrines of the Infant Ireland," as he called the Mitchelites. Torn between his heart and his head, Meagher feared that a policy of gradualism would lead to "*despair and utter subjection*," and was tempted to risk everything in "one desperate effort" for emancipation. But he believed that such an effort was bound to fail, and reluctantly concluded that "the constitutional policy advised by Duffy" was the only available option. "I support his constitutional strategy, not from choice, but from necessity," he said. "My strongest feelings are in favour of the policy advised by Mr. Mitchel. I wish to God I could defend that policy."[2]

Against this background, Duffy's "Report on the Ways and Means of Repealing the Union" was debated, clause by clause, over five meetings of the Confederation council in January. The way ahead, Duffy argued, was to build an organized and disciplined parliamentary party of around twenty MPs, backed up by massive popular support in Ireland. Given the factionalism of the House of Commons, such a group would possess a degree of power out of all proportion to its numbers, and would set out "to stop the entire business of parliament, till the constitution of Ireland be restored." The government would then be faced with the choice of repealing the Act of Union or expelling the Irish MPs from Parliament. If they were ejected, the parliamentary party would summon a "Council of the Nation" to resist British tyranny. "Against the will of the Irish nation," Duffy wrote, "the minister would be powerless. Of necessity, he would capitulate, as the Peel ministry capitulated in Canada in 1842." And if the British government still refused to capitulate, the "Council of the Nation" would take over the country. "If there be any shorter road to independence open to a people so divided and broken as ours," he concluded, "I do not know it."[3]

McGee agreed with every word, as did a substantial majority of the Confederation council. It remained to be seen, however, whether the Confederation as a whole would endorse Duffy's strategy over Mitchel's more radical program. The division became public on 8 January, when the two men aired their differences in the *Nation*. Mitchel maintained that the aristocracy had taken sides against the people; while the Confederates were arguing against class war, he believed, the gentry were actually waging one. One of the gentry's main weapons was the Coercion Bill, which enabled landlords to eject and "exterminate" their tenants with impunity. Equally oppressive was the Poor Law, which was designed to make the "land of Ireland pass, unencumbered by excessive population, into the hands of English capitalists, and under the more absolute sway of the English government." Urgent action was needed: "The stupid 'legal and constitutional' shouting, voting, and 'agitating' that have made our country an abomination to the whole earth should be changed into a deliberate study of the theory and practice of guerilla warfare."[4]

Four days later, on 12 January, the Confederation held its anniversary meeting. There were no explicit references to the emerging split, but McGee's speech implicitly supported Duffy's position. It was true, McGee said, that some of the landlords were indifferent to the suffering and destruction that surrounded them; nevertheless, there were many patriots within the gentry, and national unity was a prerequisite for national independence. "I never joined in the savage howl against them [the gentry]," he declared, "and I never will." While the Confederation's public meeting preserved the façade of unity, the moderates and militants battled it out in private. On the same day that McGee delivered his anniversary speech, he also read an ultimatum from O'Brien to the Confederation council proposing that in the light of Mitchel's "guerilla warfare" letter to the *Nation*, Mitchel should be removed from the council.[5]

To force the issue, O'Brien drew up "Ten Resolutions," which would commit the party to the "force of opinion," rather than to the rent or rate strikes favoured by Lalor and Mitchel, and which reasserted the Confederation's principles of constitutional action and class unity. Ironically, O'Brien's Ten Resolutions had much in common with O'Connell's Peace Resolutions, which had precipitated the split within the Repeal Association eighteen months earlier. History appeared to be repeating itself, with O'Brien playing the role of O'Connell and the Mitchelites cast as the secessionists. As secretary, McGee was expected to take a neutral position in the impending debate. "I am obliged now to be tongue tied & hand tied while nonsense & mischief are saying and doing all around me," he told O'Brien. To release himself from these constraints, he resigned his position on 24 January; henceforth, O'Brien and Duffy would have one of the Confederation's greatest orators on their side.[6]

O'Brien's resolutions passed in the council a week later by a vote of eighteen to ten; the next step was to debate them in the Confederation. For three days, from 2 February until the early hours of 5 February, O'Brien, Mitchel, and their respective supporters thrashed out the issues at the Rotunda. On 3 February, McGee stood up "amid loud cheers" to challenge Mitchel's position on armed resistance and class conflict; his words still rang in Duffy's ears more than thirty years later. "I dislike and oppose these principles," McGee declared, "not because they are bold, but because they are mad – not because they are treason against the law of the land, but high treason to the common sense of the kingdom." Far from advancing the cause of Irish nationalism, the radicals would in fact be serving "the English interest in Ireland," he said; the result of their actions would not be national liberation but national suicide.[7]

Speaking again the following day, McGee defended Duffy's constitutional strategy on the grounds that Parliament was "the weakest point in England" and that twenty distinguished and disciplined Irish MPs could "turn the flank of the British power in Ireland." His analysis of the House of Commons came straight from Urquhart. "Every new power it usurps is a new step to its dissolution," he argued. "If I hated England, I would wish her, as the worst calamity that could happen [to] her, a perpetuity of such a House of Commons." He had made the same point in a letter to Urquhart the previous September. Having asserted the viability of constitutional action, McGee challenged Mitchel's views on the use of force. Mitchel had maintained that "armed opinion" was perfectly compatible with the Confederation's rule that its members must work for legislative independence through the "force of opinion." This was sheer nonsense, in McGee's view. If you begin with the premise that "force of arms is force of opinion," you wind up with absurd conclusions: "A line-of-battle ship is a world of opinion in itself; the police are opinion; Sir Edward Blakeney [the commander-in-chief] is opinion; a bombardier's lintstock, a powder monkey, and a gunner's match are all opinion."[8]

McGee then switched to a serious tone as he addressed Mitchel's argument that the Confederation should abandon its attempt to unite all classes behind Repeal. "For the first time for two hundred years," he said, "the monstrous doctrine of class warfare had been openly avowed in Ireland ... I think we have had all too much of hatred, and should now try a little of love, if it were but for an experiment." It was all too easy to criticize every class in the country for putting its own self-interest above the public good, McGee argued; it was more important to work for harmony and friendship than to engage in the politics of denunciation. Apart from anything else, he noted, "whatever class you assail is thereby driven at once to rely on England." Only if the Confederation remained true to its original principles could it win over the hearts and minds of the Irish people and break British power in Ireland. With that, he sat down to "loud cheers." The moderates, recognizing his oratorical power, had chosen McGee to make the closing speech against Mitchel's position, and their expectations were not disappointed.[9]

Predictably, Mitchel was unimpressed, and he replied with his own brand of sarcasm and anger: "But beware, says Mr. M'Gee, beware of exasperating class against class; once disturb the ethereal calm – the sweet confidence and affection that reigns between classes in Ireland, and you know not where it may end. I answer, Skibbereen! Bantry! Schull! Westport! I point to the exterminations, the murders, the hangings, the coercion act!" Mitchel's speech was greeted with "loud and continuing cheering"; it was clear that he commanded considerable support, and the outcome of the debate remained uncertain. With the time approaching one o'clock in the morning, O'Brien made some final remarks and called for a division. The result: 314 for O'Brien's resolutions, and 188 for Mitchel. Later that day, Mitchel announced that he would resign from the Council of the Confederation; Devin Reilly and John Martin left with him. The moderates, it seemed, had won a resounding victory.[10]

But success came at a price; the much-feared "secession from the secession" had materialized, and the nationalist movement was now split into three groups, with the Confederation sandwiched between the Repeal Association and the Mitchelites. To counter the Confederation, Mitchel began to build up a power base in the clubs, which he viewed as the vehicle for radical change. He also launched his own newspaper, the *United Irishman*, to disseminate his ideas as widely as possible. The *United Irishman* was to the *Nation* what the *Nation* was to the *Freeman's Journal*; it became an instant publishing success, selling five thousand copies a week.[11]

Meanwhile, the Confederation had little to show for its success, and constitutional methods continued to fail. At Westminster, the government ignored the attempt of Irish MPs to inquire into the workings of the Irish Poor Law. At a by-election in Waterford, Meagher came a distant third at the polls, despite the appearance of widespread artisan support. For all the talk about "Meagher's Triumph," and all the claims that he was really "the Representative of the People," the hard fact was that he had lost. Mitchel offered the prospect of action; the Confederation's gradualism required patience and a willingness to substitute moral victories for actual defeats. Beneath the surface, the tensions and frustrations that Meagher, O'Gorman, and Michael John Barry had privately expressed in January still permeated the Confederation.[12]

And then suddenly, unexpectedly, the news came through from France: after two days of demonstrations and street fighting, Louis-Philippe had abdicated, a provisional government had been formed, and a republic had been proclaimed on 24 February. The events in Paris detonated what McGee later called "a general European explosion" – a chain reaction of liberal and nationalist revolutions that spread through Germany, the Habsburg Empire and Italy, shaking the traditional order to the core. What particularly impressed the Irish nationalists was that it all seemed so easy; after a show of strength by the people, their rulers had either capitulated or fled. The Confederates were not only inspired by the example of France; they were also convinced that European events would provide Ireland with the opportunity to strike for independence.[13]

Right from its eighteenth-century inception, it had been an axiom of Irish nationalism that emancipation would be hastened by Britain's involvement in a European war. During his debate with Mitchel in January, Duffy had commented on "the great difficulty of Ireland, which is to have Europe at peace." "Whatever accidents in the evermore complicating relations of Europe may open us a road to our rights cannot be calculated," he had written; it was precisely because Ireland could not rely on external events that he justified his constitutional gradualism. But now everything had changed. "A Republic means war with Europe," he declared; "and war means Irish liberty." Like many Irish nationalists before and since, Duffy welcomed the destruction and carnage of a general war on the assumption that an independent Ireland would emerge from the ashes.[14]

News of the French revolution reached Ireland just before the Confederation's meeting of 2 March. McGee was laid up with illness and could not attend. There is no doubt, however, that he shared the general mood of euphoria that swept through the crowd. Duffy declared,

"All over the world – from the frozen swamps of Canada, to the rich corn fields of Sicily – in Italy, in Denmark, in Prussia, and in glorious France, men are up for their rights." After what had happened in France, said George Duggan, "revolutions are to be expected; they have become subjects of universal conversation, and may be considered as the order of the day"; the language of Thomas Paine reverberated through the Rotunda. And if any country was ripe for revolution, it was Ireland, the country that had "suffered more than any other in Europe," in O'Brien's words.[15]

Immediately after the 2 March meeting, Meagher told Duffy that he was "in raptures" about the revolution in France and its reception in Ireland. "We *must* have it – *bold strokes*, and nothing else!" he wrote. "I, for one, do think that the time for talk, *&c*, is gone bye, and the time for *new* and *decisive* action has arrived." At one stroke, France had wiped away the dilemma of the necessary but impossible revolution; all the pent-up frustration and anguish of the previous months was suddenly released. In a series of meetings throughout the country, feelings of intense anger and bitterness about the famine exploded to the surface, in conjunction with celebrations about the events in France.[16]

The French revolution also enabled the moderates in the Confederation to exonerate themselves from the charges of cowardice that the Mitchelites had levelled at them. "Whoever voted as I did at the last meeting against rash words and rash courses," said Duffy, "are doubly bound when the opportunity which we promised has arrived to prove that wise caution, not slavish cowardice, was our motive." McGee shared these sentiments and later argued that it was "the fear of being thought afraid" that kept the moderates in the Confederation on the path to an Irish revolution. The Mitchelites, after all, could and did present themselves as more "advanced" nationalists than the moderates – "advanced" in the sense that they had been more prepared to fight, kill, and die for a republic, while the moderates supposedly did nothing but talk. This meant that the moderates were constantly at a psychological disadvantage as they were pushed into the defensive stance of arguing that they were just as brave and just as patriotic as the militants. Now, with the revolution in France, they were in a position to compensate – or overcompensate – by demonstrating their own courage and nationalist credentials.[17]

What, then, of the moderates' earlier insistence that Repeal must be based on a "combination of classes" and that the rules of the Confederation committed its members to the "force of opinion"? Given the general enthusiasm in Ireland for the French revolution, the Confederates believed that a common front could be formed with the Repeal Association and the Mitchelites, and that the liberal gentry and enlightened Protestants would join the movement. External events, in this view, would be the catalyst for internal unity. In these new conditions, the "force of opinion" rule was simply ignored; the Confederates who had applied it so vigorously against the militants only three weeks earlier now behaved as if it had never existed. Instead, they planned to establish a national guard that would play the same role in 1848 that the Irish Volunteers had played in 1782 – putting pressure on the government for legislative independence while imposing order in the countryside. They also intended to elect a national council, which would form the nucleus of an independent Irish parliament. Once the inevitable European war broke out, Ireland would be ready, and France would provide the necessary support.

This, at least, was the theory. To back it up, the Confederates pointed out that Alexandre Ledru-Rollin, France's minister of the interior, had attended O'Connell's "monster meeting" at Tara in 1843, and that Alphonse Lamartine, the foreign minister and *de facto* leader of the provisional government, had issued a circular expressing sympathy for "nationalities long oppressed in Europe." There was a considerable degree of wishful thinking and deliberate distortion at work here. In his speech to the Confederation about Lamartine's circular, John Dillon omitted the awkward fact that Lamartine had referred specifically to Switzerland and Italy, but had not placed Ireland on the list of oppressed nationalities. Equally unrealistic hopes were pinned on the British Chartists; despite their doubts and fears about democracy, Duffy and O'Brien believed that the Chartists could be valuable allies in the struggle for Irish independence.[18]

In this conjunction of events, McGee moved in tandem with Duffy; their views remained very close, although not quite identical, in the spring and summer of 1848. After he recovered from his illness, McGee planned to attend a demonstration of Repealers and Chartists at Manchester on St Patrick's Day. "It is not against the English people but against the so-called English Government, we entertain hostility," he wrote, "and ... no earthly power shall ever influence us to regard our English allies with other than friendliest feelings." Seeking a historical warrant for his views, he created an Irish version of the English "Norman Yoke" myth: "It was the Norman knights not the Saxon commons that originated the quarrel between this country and England; it is the chiefs of parties and not the people who keep it up." At the last moment, though, McGee cancelled the trip. The Confederation was organizing a demonstration in Dublin, originally planned for 17 March, and there were rumours that the government would prevent it from occurring. With a possible showdown looming, most of the Confederate leaders decided that they should stay at their posts.[19]

So McGee was in Dublin for both the next scheduled Confederation meeting on 15 March and the demonstration that was to follow. The Confederation meeting was one of the most remarkable in its history; more than three thousand people crowded into the Music Hall, which was so packed that several of the leaders could only get in through the windows. In what was clearly a seditious speech, O'Brien recommended that Irishmen should study guerrilla warfare – the very point for which he had condemned Mitchel the previous month. Evoking memories of the battle of Fontenoy, when Irish soldiers in the French army triumphed over British troops, O'Brien spoke in favour of the proposed "Address of the Irish Confederation to the Citizens of the French Republic." Tapping into Irish American nationalism, he called for "an Irish brigade in America, composed of Irish emigrants, which might, hereafter, serve as the basis of an Irish army." He reiterated earlier calls for the formation of a national guard, and proposed that a national council of three hundred should meet in May. Echoing O'Connell's "Mallow Defiance" of 1843, O'Brien argued that if the government used force to prevent the upcoming Repeal demonstration, he would "take the front place at that meeting and allow them to shoot me if they please." Not that it would come to that, he added; troops who were ordered to fire on the crowd would shoot the man who gave the order. More generally, he encouraged Irish patriots to fraternize with the police and the British army, one-third of whose soldiers he believed to be Irish; in this way, the forces of oppression would be undermined from within.[20]

It was brinkmanship without the bluff, O'Connell without Clontarf. The strategy was to use the threat of force to make the government back down, but to turn the threat into reality if the government did not. Speaking shortly after O'Brien, McGee invoked Hobbes and Locke to argue that the British system of government was based on a contract between the governors and the governed. If the government abused its power, if peaceful demands for redress were rejected, and if the people were "unanimous, or nearly so," then armed resistance was fully justified.[21]

All these conditions, McGee claimed, were being met. Lord Clarendon and "the pack that yelp and echo at the heels of power" were tyrannizing the country: "Have they not scourged, and swindled, and spat upon, and crucified that majesty of the people, by whose authority they are here, by whose election the Irish crown is on her Majesty's head? I tell Lord Clarendon from this place, to beware of the ground on which he stands; treason against the people will justify rebellion against the crown." Nor could there be any doubt that peaceful demands for Repeal had been repeatedly rejected, he said. That left the crucial question of unity. The earlier controversies within the Confederation had been "decided in the streets of Paris," and discussions were currently under way to reunite Young and Old Ireland. A few hard-line Orange Lodges might support the government, but the voices of "fifteen hundred or fifty thousand slaves" counted for nothing next to the "majesty of the people." In this way, Irish loyalists were simply conjured out of existence; they were only a tiny percentage of the population and had effectively excluded themselves from "the people."

Towards the end of his speech, McGee connected the right of resistance with the condition of his country. In language that articulated common feelings of anger and helplessness about the famine, he offered the prospect of hope where there had been despair, liberty where there had been oppression. A sense of rage ran through it — rage at the devastation of the famine, the guilt of the government, the horrors of the transatlantic voyage, and the psychological numbing that came from the inability to alleviate the suffering. The speech concluded with a quasi-apocalyptic sense of release, of struggle and sacrifice and redemption, in which Ireland would take its place among the free nations of the Earth:

As one Irishman, I declare here to-night that I would rather perish by rope or steel than survive this opportunity. My heart is sick at daily scenes of misery. I have seen human beings driven like foxes to earth themselves in holes and fastnesses; I have heard the voice of mendicancy hourly wringing [sic] in my ears, until my heart has turned to stone, and my brain to flint, from inability to help them. I cannot endure this state of society longer. Nothing green, nothing noble will grow in it. The towns have become one universal poorhouse and fever shed, the country one great grave-yard. The survivors of the famine and pestilence have fled to the sea-coast and embarked for America, with disease festering in their blood. They have lost sight of Ireland, and the ships that bore them have become sailing coffins, and carried them to a new world, indeed; not to America, but to eternity! Alas! that we could recall them. At least, let us try to save the living. Yes, I feel we shall save them, for I see here visibly to-night the ancient spirit of Ireland's freedom ... Fear not for Ireland – she wakes – she lives – she must be free! The spirit of God walks the earth, blasting tyrants, their fortresses, and chain forges; liberating states and peoples. Nothing but our own folly and discord can keep Him from our shores.

In its fusion of form and content, its rhythm, its Ossianic peroration, and its striking imagery, this was one of McGee's most powerful speeches. It also helped to bring a new expression into Irish history. His reference to "sailing coffins" created a sensation in the Confederation, and before long the boats that carried famine migrants across the Atlantic became known as "coffin ships."[22]

As the meeting in the Music Hall drew to a close, there were reports that "additional forces of cavalry and infantry" were being drafted into Dublin in anticipation of the demonstration that had been planned for St Patrick's Day. The Confederates postponed the mass meeting until 20 March, in the hope that continuing negotiations with John O'Connell would bring the Repeal Association into the fold. Although the negotiations failed, some ten to fifteen thousand people congregated near the North Wall in Dublin. While the military kept their distance, the meeting unanimously approved an address of support to "the Citizens of the French Republic," along with an address to Queen Victoria calling for Irish self-government. The address to the Queen dispensed with the customary deferential tone. "The freedom of our country and the welfare of its people," it asserted, "are of more importance in our estimation than the security of the throne." In his speech, McGee described the impending conflict as one of "life or death." "Everywhere the flood tide of democracy is out," he said, "and tyrants are flying before it, or are borne along its deep and rapid current. Ireland alone is unmoved by the mighty events of the age – Ireland, too confiding, too sanguine, leader-ridden Ireland. My friends, this must end." And the best way to end this situation was to present the government with a united front, expressed through a national council and backed up by a national guard. "Your time is coming at last," he told the crowd, "if you be wise to use it."[23]

A remarkable thing had happened between the beginning of February and the middle of March. After the French revolution, it seemed that McGee and the moderate majority in the Confederation had come round completely to the position of Mitchel and the militants. "The last time I had the honor of addressing you," said Devin Reilly at the Confederation meeting of 15 March, "I did not feel at home. I did not feel that my sentiments, and wishes, and opinions, were yours. But all this is changed now ... I have heard Mr. O'Brien speak of guerilla warfare, and arming the people in a national guard. I have heard Mr. Meagher flinging 'combination of classes' to the winds, and getting at once to the barricades. I am, therefore, quite at home, and at my ease once more among you." Reilly could also have pointed to the fact that O'Brien and Duffy had recently warned counterrevolutionary landlords that their estates would be confiscated, and that Duffy had issued his last appeal to the gentry in the *Nation*. Mitchel felt equally at home; he and Reilly had been welcomed back into the Council of the Confederation, and their popularity was growing by the day. According to Duffy, Mitchel was a changed man, who "demeaned himself as if the French Revolution and the new opportunities it furnished were his personal achievements." Mitchel, it appeared, had been vindicated by events, and he was now in the best position to shape them.[24]

Behind the scenes, however, significant differences persisted between the moderates and the militants, and a major power struggle was being conducted in the clubs and the Confederation council. McGee played a central part in this battle, and this helps explain why the Mitchelites attacked him with such venom even during his republican phase from the summer of 1848 to the spring of 1849. One of the main differences concerned the question of timing. Anxious to avoid a premature rising, McGee insisted in March that the Confederates should "wait till England is engaged in a foreign war." Mitchel, in contrast, felt that this would hold Ireland hostage to events over which it had no control, and argued that the revolution should begin when the government tried to disarm the people. By April, Mitchel was pushing for "immediate action," while the moderates were arguing that they should wait until the autumn, when the harvest had been gathered. It was, O'Gorman recalled, one of the strangest debates he had ever heard, since it took place at a time when Dublin was "fully garrisoned by British troops" and the Confederates had, "with the exception of some incompletely armed clubs, no organization whatever of a military kind."[25]

A second area of contention focused on the familiar question of national unity. While Mitchel wanted to press ahead with a revolutionary alliance of artisans and peasants, the moderates feared that his strategy would reproduce the French revolutionary Reign of Terror of 1793–94. In a letter to O'Brien, written immediately after the "French news" of February 1848 reached Ireland, Duffy argued that a "mere democratic" revolution in Ireland would either be crushed by Britain or bring "death and exile to the middle, as well as the upper classes." Without middle-class leadership, wrote Duffy, the moderates in the Confederation would suffer the same fate as the Girondins in France: "You and I will meet on a Jacobin scaffold, ordered for execution as enemies of some new Marat or Robespierre; Mr Jas Lalor or Mr somebody else." He then imagined the situation after such a revolution: "Mr Meagher was ordered for execution, Richard O'Gorman died of starvation in trying to escape the guillotine; M.J. Barry had his own hymn of freedom chanted by his poisoners; T.D. McGee was piked, and John Pigot killed himself in horror and despair." The only way to avoid these scenes, he argued, was to effect an alliance with Old Ireland; the model for a "peaceful and happy revolution" must be a new and improved 1782, rather than a replay of 1789 or 1798.[26]

Sharing these views, McGee seconded Duffy's motion at the Confederation meeting of 9 March that Young and Old Ireland should reunite; he emphasized the importance of union in every speech, and supported the national council as a means of ensuring class unity. "If a class conquers, a class must govern," he warned. "After fighting the foreigner we will have to fight our countrymen, and the freedom we win will be lost in the feuds that always follow a sectarian victory." Significantly, McGee did not join Duffy and O'Brien in threatening recalcitrant landlords with confiscation; he clearly felt that such statements would only alienate potential allies, and he continued to hope that the gentry could be drawn into the movement. The greater the degree of unity, he believed, the more likely it was that Ireland could break the external power of Britain and contain the internal forces of social and religious conflict.[27]

As well as differing on the questions of timing and national unity, the Mitchelites and the moderates also disagreed about the objectives of an Irish revolution. Mitchel wanted a separate republic; it was no coincidence that he named his newspaper the *United Irishman*. McGee, in contrast, demanded "full legislative independence" under the Crown, with a national army, a national navy, and a national flag. An armed and united people, he said, should present their ultimatum to the "Queen of Ireland," and lay down their alternative – "legislative independence or separation, Repeal or a Republic." McGee was using republicanism as a threat to scare the government into settling for "unconditional Repeal." For Mitchel, republicanism was the first choice; for McGee, it was a last resort. In taking this position, McGee anticipated Duffy's famous "Creed of the Nation," issued three weeks later, which stated that "a settlement made by negotiation" was preferable to "a republic won by insurrection," but he added that if negotiations failed, the Irish would opt for insurrection and republicanism rather than give way.[28]

While the moderates and the militants jockeyed for position, plans were underway to organize a national guard and elect a national council. McGee and Duffy were both on the subcommittee for the national council, which was to "speak on behalf of the *entire people*; and to negociate [sic] our liberties with England, if the example of European events has yet awakened her to the necessity of concession – and if not to put the country in an attitude to enforce our rights." As part of the attempt to influence European events, the Confederation sent a deputation to Paris at the end of March. O'Brien, Meagher, and O'Gorman presented addresses of support and solidarity to the French Republic and hoped for reciprocal statements of French sympathy for Irish nationalism. They were to be deeply disappointed. As O'Gorman recalled, Lamartine's response was "careful, cold and uncompromising. It was very evident that the French Provisional Government were unwilling to do or say anything which might hazard a rupture with Great Britain."[29]

Back in Dublin, McGee tried to put the best possible light on the situation. "Lamartine's reply is not much liked here," he told O'Brien, "but it is beginning to be understood as an official matter of course." The assumption was that Lamartine had made a public announcement to please the British but secretly supported the Confederation. Duffy even announced that France was prepared to send fifty thousand men to "support the Irish nation in a struggle for her freedom." Nothing could have been further from the truth; Lamartine's official position was also his actual one. The prospect of a European war was fading, and there was no prospect of French support for an Irish revolution. For the Mitchelites, who had not wanted to wait on external events, this did not present a problem; for the moderates, however, it was a huge blow.[30]

Other difficulties were developing. The Confederates had believed that the Chartists posed a significant internal revolutionary threat to the British government and that any attempt to repress the Repeal movement would trigger "desperate retribution" in England. But on 10 April, the limitations of Chartism were revealed when its leader, Feargus O'Connor, called off a march from Kennington Common to

Westminster; from then on, the Chartist movement was in retreat, and more British troops would be available for service in Ireland. Later that day, O'Brien made his last appearance in Parliament, where he was shouted down and denounced as a traitor. It was becoming clear that the government had no intention of negotiating with the Confederates, and that it was preparing to confront the Repealers and republicans in Ireland. In March, O'Brien, Meagher, and Mitchel had been charged with sedition, and the government was now introducing a Treason-Felony Bill that broadened the definition of treason while reducing the sentence from execution to deportation. This would, as Lord Campbell put it, provide the government with "the effectual means of sending Messrs. Mitchell [sic], Meagher and Smith O'Brien to Botany Bay."[31]

To make matters worse, the radicalization of the Mitchelites was alienating the Old Irelanders with whom McGee and Duffy wished to unite. In the *United Irishman*, Mitchel denounced Daniel O'Connell as an "aider of English plunderers"; this was hardly the language of conciliation. Tensions came to a head on 29 April, when the Sarsfield Club of Limerick invited Mitchel to share a platform with O'Brien. Mitchel accepted, apparently in breach of an earlier understanding with O'Brien that they would not speak at the same meetings, given their deep political differences. When the O'Connellites learned that Mitchel was coming to Limerick, they decided to launch a protest, organized by Father Richard Baptist O'Brien, the former president of St Mary's College in Halifax, Nova Scotia, whom McGee had met three years earlier. Things quickly got out of hand. Unable to find Mitchel, the crowd vented its anger on Smith O'Brien; he was badly beaten up, and he remained in pain for several weeks with a broken rib.

McGee shared the general nationalist revulsion about the assault on Smith O'Brien but did not join the vociferous condemnations of his "old and valued friend," Father Richard O'Brien. On the contrary, McGee publicly praised Richard O'Brien's character, dissociated him from the violence of the "misguided or corrupt crowd," and published his comments about "the abominable conduct of the mob" in Limerick. Personal loyalties counted; McGee was quite prepared to risk the unpopularity of his colleagues in the Confederation by defending an old friend from what he saw as unfair attacks.[32]

After the Limerick riot, Smith O'Brien briefly considered retiring from politics; in the event, he decided that he would stay in the Confederation only if Mitchel left. Already feeling that the Confederation had reacted too slowly to revolutionary events in Europe, Mitchel and Reilly resigned on 5 May. At the same time, the conservative Confederate Dr Charles West resigned from the Confederation council on the grounds that it had "been going too fast lately." Others, including David Ross of Bladensburg (a disciple of David Urquhart) and Michael John Barry, protested privately that the Confederation was becoming too radical and withdrew from the organization. Political unity remained chimerical; McGee's repeated emphasis on the need for national unity was a good index of its absence.[33]

Despite these difficulties, the Confederation continued to make plans for a national council and national guard; the revolutions in Europe kept Confederate hopes up, while the charges of sedition against O'Brien, Meagher, and Mitchel intensified popular anti-government feeling. The Confederation decided to organize the national council and national guard through the Confederate clubs, which according to McGee had "more than doubled their numbers" by early April. Later in the month, McGee and Duffy went on an organizing drive in Leinster. McGee was also active in Dublin, where he became president of the newly formed Mercantile Assistants Club. At a Confederation council meeting in early May, he moved "the formation of a Club in each ward in the City in consequence of the increase of the Confederates," and took steps to collect the names of those who had "signified their willingness to become members of a national guard."[34]

By this time, the number of Confederate clubs in the country had increased to forty, and their members were starting to arm themselves and conduct rifle practices. The *Nation* began to publish articles on guerrilla war tactics and provided practical advice on the use of rifles and pikes: "To talk of pulling a dragoon from his horse, or of cutting his bridle *with a hook*, is fully as absurd and puerile as to talk of catching birds by putting salt on their tails," ran one such primer. "The simplest and most obvious operation is to put your pike into his body."

McGee and Mitchel may not have agreed on much, but they both welcomed these developments; the more that the people armed themselves, they believed, the less would Ireland have to rely on external support. After the Confederation's mission to France, McGee began to move away from his earlier view that the Irish should wait for a European war, although he continued to argue that an Irish revolution should not be attempted until the preparations were in place and the people were united.[35]

Believing that "the Confederation alone cannot liberate Ireland," McGee sought reconciliation between Young and Old Ireland, and looked for common ground between Protestants and Catholics. While Mitchel was making scathing comments about the Old Irelanders, McGee argued that the Confederates should avoid "verbal violence," and attempted to lower the political temperature within the nationalist movement. He also maintained that Protestants and Catholics were more alike than they realized. "They [Protestants] desire to retain the monarchy," he said; "so do many Catholics. They desire religious equality, so do we all. They seek national prosperity, so do we. I say then there are no walls between us, though there may be cobwebs of great antiquity." As part of his effort to "suppress all attempts to excite religious feuds and dissensions," McGee called on the people "not to allow themselves to be entrapped into secret societies," and insisted that the struggle against British rule must be conducted through the open strategy of the national council and national guard.[36]

While McGee wanted to avoid "verbal violence" within nationalism, he had no such reservations when it came to denouncing the government and its agents in Ireland. Upon hearing rumours that spies had infiltrated the Confederation, he accused the government of "despotism," and had harsh words for the "wretched men who live by secret service money in this city." I do not so much denounce them – their profession is their punishment," he said. "They live on the earth, not so much as men among men, but as fiends, whose element is falsehood and whose trade is perjury." The rumours were accurate; from the middle of April, McGee himself began to feature in government spy reports, which among other things noted that "*Detectives, and Spies &c*, came in for a good share of abuse from McGee."[37]

Along with the use of spies and the charges of sedition against O'Brien, Meagher, and Mitchel, the government presented the Confederation with another challenge in early May, when it issued a proclamation banning the formation of a national council and national guard. At the Confederation meeting of 3 May, Duffy ostentatiously tore up the proclamation and flung it into the crowd "amid loud and enthusiastic applause"; the Confederates would ignore the ban, and carry on with their plans. In a supporting speech, McGee once again called for unity, arguing that "glorious success" would be inevitable once "all classes of Irishmen" combined for their liberty. What was not reported in the *Nation* – but featured in the spy reports – were McGee's comments that the Irish should prevent the next harvest from leaving the country and that the Confederation was planning a run on the Irish banks. "*Such proceedings would eventually destroy England*," he argued. What they might have done to the Irish economy was not considered.[38]

In common with other Confederate leaders, McGee believed that government repression was likely to strengthen national unity. "The Country is almost thoroughly roused – the Trials will do the rest," he told O'Brien in April. O'Brien's trial was held on 15 May. Despite the overwhelming evidence that he had delivered a seditious speech to the Confederation two months earlier, he was acquitted, thanks to a split jury. The same thing happened with Meagher the following day. Next up was Mitchel; the original charge of seditious libel had been dropped, and he was being prosecuted under the new Treason-Felony Act. With the acquittal of O'Brien and Meagher fresh in his memory, the sheriff ensured that there were hardly any Catholics on the panel of jurors. The tactic worked; Mitchel was found guilty and sentenced to fourteen years' transportation.[39]

As McGee had anticipated, there was an enormous nationalist backlash. The packed jury, the verdict, and the severe sentence provoked angry demonstrations throughout Ireland and among Irish communities in Britain. Not only the Confederates but also the Old Irelanders in the Repeal Association were outraged; John O'Connell, who had attended a protest meeting just before the trial, had correctly predicted that Mitchel, if convicted, would become a martyr to Irish nationalism. But in other respects, Mitchel's sentence both exposed and exacerbated the deep divisions within the Confederation. The militants wanted much more than indignant speeches; they wanted to spring Mitchel from jail and in the process launch the Irish revolution.[40]

The pressure from the militants had been building before Mitchel's trial. Joseph Brenan, a revolutionary firebrand from Cork who would come to view McGee as a traitor, told the St Patrick's Club in mid-May that Mitchel must be freed by force, and declared, "We will die to a man before a hair of his head is injured." He then rounded on the moderates: "But there are some men amongst you – 'leaders' – God bless the mark! who desire to hold you back, to put an extinguisher on your patriotism, to file dilatory pleas to the revolution – who tell you that you are unprepared, undisciplined, and disunited, and should, therefore, on this great occasion, this splendid 'opportunity,' do exactly – nothing. Listen to them not, if they lecture you; if they oppose you, walk over them!" Similar sentiments were expressed in the Swift Club, where the Council of the Confederation was charged with cowardice, and where John Rea from Belfast ("*a very warlike man*," according to a spy) promised that fifteen thousand armed men would rise in the north. Before Mitchel's trial, it was reported, "warlike men were looked upon with suspicion, the contrary is now the case, and *the man who recommends* anything bordering on *Peace is considered a Government man*."[41]

For their part, the leaders in the Council of the Confederation were convinced that any attempt to free Mitchel and start the rising would have been a "fatal error." "I went through the clubs," recalled O'Gorman, "sought information from all sources accessible to me, and satisfied myself that the people were, for all purposes of insurrection, unprepared, unorganized, unarmed, and incapable of being even roughly disciplined for any military attempt, and that the idea of rescuing John Mitchell [sic] in the way proposed, was utterly hopeless." In the *Nation*, Duffy made the same point, adding that all the food in the country was "laid up in store-houses under the guns of the English garrison," and that the government could easily destroy or withhold the supplies. "Men cannot fight without food," he wrote. "Hunger would turn an army into a mob in four and twenty hours."[42]

Jane Verner Mitchel, John's wife, was not convinced. "The leaders have a great deal to answer for," she told John Martin. "Now I do think if there is another conviction no matter in whos [sic] case the moment the Judge passes sentence he should be shot, next the Attorney General then the Sheriff and lastly the whole Jury that is what ought to have been done in John's case and if the Men are not wholly slaves they will do it." Among the leaders who had let her husband down, she listed John O'Connell, Gavan Duffy, and D'Arcy McGee.[43]

The Confederation had reached the crisis point. The French were not interested in Irish nationalism, the eagerly awaited European war was not materializing, and the British government was in no mood for concessions. Although revolutionary sentiment was growing in the clubs, there was no real revolutionary organization, and the leaders had failed to establish a national council and national guard. Unless something was done, and done quickly, the Confederation would go the way of Clontarf. The people, wrote Duffy, "will demand of us if *this* be the end of all the threats and promises uttered in thunder to the Irish people, and echoed from pole to pole. They will ask if '48 was only another '43, a thousand times more boastful and more false." There was only one way that such questions could be answered; revolutionary practice must be brought into line with revolutionary theory.[44]

CHAPTER EIGHT

A False Sense of Honour
June – September 1848

The prospect of success was remote. In the absence of European war and French aid, the Confederates would have to rely on their own resources. But they were confronted with immense obstacles; there were divisions within the Repeal movement, the Catholic hierarchy remained deeply suspicious of the Young Irelanders, most Protestants rejected Repeal, and the gentry were hostile. And even if all these difficulties could be overcome, it was extremely unlikely that the Confederates could defeat the superior military power of Britain.

But they had gone so far that they could not turn back, and the consequences of not starting a rising appeared even worse than the consequences of defeat. "The success of a revolutionary movement, as far as the actual fighting was concerned, seemed to me more than doubtful," recalled O'Gorman, "but the attempt, if made on a grand scale, could scarcely fail, even in its defeat, to raise the character of the Irish people in the eyes of Europe, and win for them a more respectful sympathy, than had theretofore been accorded to them."[1] What O'Gorman, O'Brien, Duffy, and McGee had in mind, it seemed, was a grand revolutionary gesture that would restore dignity and pride to a people broken by famine. To have done nothing would not only have been an act of cowardice; it would also have allowed the initiative to pass to the clubs and might have culminated in the very kind of Jacobin revolution that the leadership feared.

Looking back on these events nineteen years later, McGee argued that the Confederates had been driven to ruin by "a false sense of honour." "It must be recorded," he wrote, "that the moderate men among the Young Irelanders, after the French revolution of '48, failed in moral courage, and thereby threw the reins into the hands of the MITCHELLITE sect, who had a definite object, though a mad one, set steadily before them." The truly courageous course of action, he came to believe, would have been to recognize that the revolution was doomed to defeat and to have opposed the radicals on this ground. It is entirely possible that such thoughts crossed his mind during the summer of 1848. When writing his book *O'Connell and His Friends* three years earlier, McGee had criticized the United Irishmen for launching a premature rebellion. "Rashness," he had written, "was mistaken for zeal – deliberation for cowardice; and victory was lost." Any doubts he may have had, however, were immediately suppressed. Instead, he shared Duffy's view that the Confederates had failed to achieve any "practical results" after six weeks of speechmaking and that they needed to reorganize themselves if they were to control or influence the revolutionary movement.[2]

Central to the reorganization was the relationship between the Council of the Confederation and the clubs. As popular anger mounted after Mitchel's sentence and the Confederation's refusal to make a rescue attempt, the clubs proliferated at a rapid rate. At the beginning of May there were about forty; by mid-July there were more than two hundred, with a total membership of around forty-five thousand. According to Lord Clarendon, the clubs were "the real nucleus of armed resistance" and posed a more serious threat to British rule than the Confederation or its council. Mitchel agreed with this assessment. Not only was the existing council excessively cautious, he believed, but it had expanded to more than a hundred members, could easily be infiltrated by government spies, and was far too unwieldy for the purpose of planning a revolution. Writing from Newgate Prison on the day of his sentence, 26 May, he asserted that "the Confederates, the Clubs, the *people* in some form should actually elect the members of the Council." His supporters in the Dublin clubs were coming to the same conclusion, and Father Kenyon, who quickly became Mitchel's successor, opened up discussions with Duffy on the subject.[3]

Partly in response to popular pressure and partly because the Confederate leaders agreed that reform was necessary, the Council reduced its number to twenty-one and held new elections at the end of May. Surprisingly, McGee was not elected; it may be that his "golden link" views had alienated too many people. Nevertheless, he continued to focus his energies on editing the *Nation*, organizing the clubs, and working for union with John O'Connell and the Repeal Association.

A few days after the council was restructured, a core group of moderates and militants formed a secret committee of six to plan the revolution. Duffy and Dillon were among the former moderates; Father Kenyon, John Martin, and Devin Reilly represented the radicals. Together, they "commenced a formal conspiracy," as Duffy put it; this involved getting "money, arms, and officers" from Europe and America, organizing a diversion among physical-force Chartists and Repealers in England, and preparing "particular local men to expect the event." Although McGee must have known what was going on, he was not, at this stage, one of the revolutionary leaders.[4]

The task of raising revolutionary consciousness throughout the country was facilitated by the emergence of two new radical nationalist newspapers, which took over from Mitchel's *United Irishman*. Dalton Williams and Kevin O'Doherty edited the *Irish Tribune*, and John Martin edited the *Irish Felon*, which became the principal medium for the views of Reilly and Lalor. The Confederation, complained Lalor, had only succeeded in turning Irish nationalism into a laughing stock, and it had been the same story during O'Connell's day: "What was Tara? A million men stood there. What did they do? Speculated, spouted, cheered, resolved, declared, petitioned, and adjourned." All this must change, he said; it was time to establish a military organization of Felon clubs that would turn ideas into action.[5]

Among the people who heeded the call was a schoolteacher from Clonakilty, County Cork, who told Joseph Brenan: "I did not join the Confederation for I did not think it went far enough. I had grown sick of moral force and tired of a useless and *degrading* agitation. I now offer myself to you as a member of the Felon Club ... I have devoted myself to the propagandism of republican principles and, to the endeavour to render those principles general in my neighbourhood when I was looked upon as a wild theorist." A year after he wrote this letter, he emigrated to British North America, became the leading Irish Canadian journalist in New Brunswick, fought McGee over Confederation, and eventually wound up as Speaker of the Canadian House of Commons. Also, he succeeded in concealing all traces of his revolutionary past. His name was Timothy Warren Anglin.[6]

Meanwhile, the *Nation* spoke with a stronger revolutionary accent in June and July. All talk of a cross-class alliance with the aristocracy was abandoned, especially after the country's leading lords declared that Repeal would "entail incalculable misery on Ireland" and announced their "solemn determination to maintain the Union between Great Britain and Ireland." When McGee now spoke of national unity, he meant unity with Old Ireland, not with landlords. As it became clear that the aristocracy was rejecting the revolution, he began to move towards Lalor's position. "I believe it is possible," he wrote in early June, "... to change the whole face and being of Irish society." Among the "Social Results of Independence," he listed the abolition of the landlord system, explaining that a new Irish government would "give the land to its own inhabitants."[7]

By July, he was advocating a "social revolution" in Ireland. There was, he argued, £80 million worth of produce in the country – enough food, he believed, to last for two years. The Confederate clubs, under the direction of the council, should initiate a "war for the possession of the soil" and forcibly redistribute the food to "preserve the survivors" of the famine: "If any man said nay, and put forth his hand upon the people's food, their answer should be the pike point or the bullet."[8] His earlier opposition to peasant proprietorship and universal manhood suffrage had stemmed from the conviction that the nationalist movement required the support of a "patriot aristocracy." Now, in an article entitled "What if We *Don't* Fail?" he declared that he was "undeceived" and that a combined social and political revolution was the only way of preventing the country from "lapsing into barbarism."[9] In a career with many turns and sharp angles, this was as far to the left as McGee ever came.

From his base in the Mercantile Assistants Club (for reasons unknown, he had resigned as president of the Davis Club), McGee continued to organize the revolutionary movement. On 18 June he helped
to form the Tallaght Club; it had over a hundred members, who immediately began to "*purchase* their *arms wholesale* by subscribing weekly
and *then draw lots for them*." His speeches became increasingly radical.
At the Confederation's final meeting, on 21 June, he insisted that it was
time to "*drive the English altogether out of this Country*," and "*spoke in the
most provoking ... manner of the Government*," according to government
spy reports.[10]

The same mood permeated his poetry. Among his pieces was "A
Harvest Hymn," which pushed the Confederation's "hold the harvest"
line:

> Look on this harvest of plenty and promise –
> Shall we sleep while the enemy snatches it from us? ...
> Swear by the bright streams abundantly flowing,
> Swear by the hearths where wet weeds are growing –
> By the Stars and the Earth, and the four winds of Heaven,
> That the Land shall be saved, and its Tyrants outdriven.
> Do it! and blessings will shelter your grave,
> God has been Bountiful – will ye be brave?

Duffy would later include this piece in his account of the revolutionary poetry of 1848. By far McGee's most popular revolutionary poem,
however, was "The Reaper's Song," which he set to the tune of "The
Jolly Shearers":

> "How will we go a-shearing,
>   Dear friends and neighbours all?"
> "Oh! we will go with pike and gun,
>   To keep our own or fall;
>   We'll stack our arms and stack our corn
>   Upon the same wide plain;
>   We'll mount a guard on barn and yard,
>   And give them grape for grain."

> Then a shearing we will go —
> Oh! a-shearing we will go;
> On our soil 'twill be no toil
> To cut the corn low.

When Bernard Treanor, the organizer of the Confederate club in Stalybridge, returned to Dublin in 1848, he "caused 15 thousand copies of that song to be printed and he himself circulated some of them for the purpose of sowing Treason." Such poems, Treanor contended, made McGee "equal if not superior to Thos Moore."[11]

———•••———

While the Confederation became increasingly revolutionary in temper and tone, it also moved towards a political accommodation with the Repeal Association — something that had always been a high priority for McGee. In the aftermath of Mitchel's trial, John O'Connell opened up negotiations with the Confederation, and in early June a tentative agreement was made to amalgamate the two parties in a new Irish League. O'Connell's Repeal Association was in deep financial difficulty, and he hoped that union with the Confederation would provide a political alternative to the increasingly radical clubs. Duffy and McGee, in contrast, hoped to bring the Old Irelanders into the revolutionary camp. As McGee pointed out, the Confederates were strongest in the towns, while the Repeal Association commanded "the passes that lead to the rural districts"; if the Confederates could absorb the Repeal Association, they would have the time and opportunity to extend their influence into the countryside — and the countryside was crucial to a successful revolution.[12]

Because the Repeal Association had close connections with the Catholic Church, McGee also hoped that unity would "bring together Young Ireland and the Priesthood — the two vital elements of Irish politics." As he realized, the Catholic Church was the arbiter of Irish nationalist politics. If the church threw its weight behind the revolutionary movement, the chances of success would be much greater; without widespread clerical support, the revolution would almost certainly collapse. By the middle of June, McGee thought that the church could go either way. Many priests and some bishops – including Bishop Maginn, who was apparently talking about buying rifles – appeared to be moving in a revolutionary direction. But Archbishop Daniel Murray, most bishops, and many other priests distrusted Young Ireland and feared that the clubs were becoming hotbeds of irreligion and socialism. Recalling his experience of the rising of 1798, Murray warned his countrymen about the horrific consequences of violent revolution. Among the Old Irelanders, John O'Connell refused to become the linkman between the Confederation and the Catholic Church. When he discovered that the Confederation viewed the Irish League as a means of advancing the revolutionary cause – a discovery that he could not fail to make, thanks to Duffy's and McGee's speeches on the subject – he withdrew from politics. And as O'Connell pulled back, his clerical supporters pulled back with him.[13]

Meanwhile, the French revolution had lurched into violent conflict between its middle-class leaders and the artisans and workers of Paris; during the insurrection of the "June Days," the archbishop of Paris, Denys-Auguste Affre, was shot to death while attempting to mediate at the barricades. The Catholic Church in Ireland, as elsewhere in Europe, was outraged, and Lord Clarendon milked the event for all it was worth, commenting that Affre "never did a better thing in his life than getting himself murdered." From that point, any prospect of a clerical-Confederate alliance disappeared; even Father Kenyon cracked under the pressure of his bishop and dropped out of the movement, much to the disgust of Duffy. On the other hand, the Confederation claimed to have the continuing support of Bishop Maginn, whom McGee described as "a believer in the right of nations to resort to arms for the defence or assertion of their just claims." "If banners had appeared last year in the summer over the fields of Ireland," wrote McGee in 1849, "his benediction would have hailed them as they rose." Even if this assessment was accurate – and the evidence is ambivalent – Maginn was very much the exception by the summer of 1848.[14]

The revolution, however, would not be postponed. On the contrary, it was brought forward to the first week of August, before the harvest. The strategy was to organize diversionary risings in the countryside, draw the troops out of Dublin, and take over the city. McGee later explained that they were planning a guerrilla war, modelled on the Spanish resistance to the French during and after 1808 – the resistance from which the word "guerrilla" entered the revolutionary vocabulary. The Confederates, wrote McGee, intended to lure British forces into "districts where only infantry could act with ease," and fight them on equal terms. He also spoke of a scorched earth policy in Ireland's towns and cities, based on the Russian campaign against Napoleon in 1812. But for all this to work, there had to be significant support in the countryside. The leaders sounded out the state of opinion, the supply of arms, and the general level of preparation in the south and west. "The information we received was quite encouraging," recalled O'Gorman. "It turned out, when put to the test, to have been wholly untrue."[15]

At this point, the Confederates were hit by another wave of government repression. The first had been the arrest of O'Brien, Mitchel, and Meagher in March; the second had been the ban on the national council and national guard in June; now, in early July, the government decided to round up all the radical newspaper editors in Dublin and to move against other leading Confederates. On Saturday, 8 July, Duffy was intercepted on his way to McGee's house at Ranelagh. McGee accompanied him to the police station and later helped avert a riot when Duffy was committed for trial. The two men would not meet again for seven years. Other arrests swiftly followed – Martin, Williams, O'Doherty, Doheny, and again Meagher. On 12 July it was McGee's turn. Charged with sedition, he was released on £200 bail; the next day, he was brought before the Wicklow grand jury, who decided that "there was *not* on the face of the indictment sufficient grounds for a prosecution for sedition." Along with Doheny and Meagher, who also were released, McGee was free to continue the work of organizing the revolution.[16]

With Duffy in jail, McGee took over as editor of the *Nation* and helped to organize the first full meeting of the Irish League, which was held on 19 July. The previous day, Lord Clarendon had applied the coercion law to Dublin, Drogheda, Cork, and Waterford, empowering the government to disarm people in these areas. Against this background, the *Nation* claimed that five thousand people crammed themselves into Dublin's Music Hall, where O'Brien and McGee gave speeches that wrapped revolutionary intentions in the cloak of constitutional agitation. McGee's definition of constitutionalism proved to be somewhat flexible. The Irish League, he said, "has chosen to define its policy to-night as 'constitutional,' and I presume it uses that phrase in its largest signification ... The word 'constitutional' means the right to have, to use, and to keep arms. It means the right in a people to recall their allegiance from an unjust government." By the time he had finished, McGee had turned constitutionalism into an argument to defy the government. "I, for one," he declared, "distinctly desire that the people of Dublin should not throw down their arms."[17]

His editorial in the *Nation* that week went still further. Claiming that a hundred thousand men had turned out for the Irish League and that another quarter million were on the verge of joining, he argued that the clubs "must be strengthened, increased, and extended," and maintained that armed conflict was inevitable. "The League does well to take a constitutional position at first," he wrote, "but can it keep it? No, the Government will not suffer it ... The League must know when it is beaten from the halls of argument to the fields of force, and that, I foresee, is not a distant event." In the classic revolutionary manner, McGee shifted the responsibility for violence onto the shoulders of the government. And with Duffy in Newgate Prison awaiting trial on 8 August under the Treason-Felony Act, the next three weeks would be critically important. "The next Jury packed in Ireland," McGee declared, "will be the signal of a revolution." He was beginning to sound a lot like John and Jane Mitchel.[18]

But who, exactly, would give the signal? Duffy and Martin were in jail, and Kenyon had left the Confederation; of the leaders whom Duffy named in the "formal conspiracy" to plan the revolution, only Dillon and Reilly were still at large. In these circumstances, delegates from the clubs met on 21 July to elect a new revolutionary council. Along with Dillon, Meagher, O'Gorman, and Reilly, they chose McGee, who was now at the heart of the revolution. Almost immediately, however, they were knocked off balance. On 22 July news reached Ireland that the government was about to suspend habeas corpus. The members of the revolutionary council suspected that the government knew their names, and they were right: within hours of their election, the information had landed on Lord Clarendon's desk. If they stayed in Dublin, they would all join Duffy in Newgate Prison.[19]

O'Gorman had already left for Limerick to organize the south and west; Dillon, Meagher, and McGee hurriedly met to consider their options. They knew that their preparations were incomplete and realized that the chances of success were minimal. But they felt that they could not retreat — they believed that their personal honour and the honour of Ireland were at stake, and they hoped that an initial victory might trigger a wider revolution. Submission was out of the question; the only choice left was rebellion. And the only way to start the revolution, they agreed, was to rally their supporters in the countryside. Dillon and Meagher decided to leave for Wexford, where O'Brien was staying; from there, they planned to head for Kilkenny, "the very best place in which the insurrection could break out," in Meagher's view.[20]

While they went south, McGee went north. On the previous day, when the revolutionary council had been elected, a delegate from the Confederate Club of Glasgow had told McGee that the revolutionary movement was well organized in and around the city. They had four or five hundred well-armed men, he said, who were eager to participate in the Irish revolution; if one of the Dublin leaders would rally them, they would volunteer for an expedition to Ireland. On Meagher's and Dillon's advice, McGee undertook the mission. The secrecy was so tight that, for once, the government had no idea what was happening; spies erroneously reported that he had travelled with John Drumm or James Fintan Lalor to Manchester, and the authorities in the city were put on the alert.[21]

Arriving in Scotland on 25 July, McGee immediately linked up with Peter McCabe, one of the leading Confederates in Glasgow. McCabe seems to have been on the moderate wing of the movement; the more militant figures in Glasgow included James Adams and John Daly, who had close connections with physical-force Chartists, and who strongly supported armed revolution in Ireland. The initial plan was, in Meagher's words, to "seize two or three of the largest merchant steamers lying in the Clyde" and "with pistols to their heads, compel the engineers and sailors to ... steer round the north coast of Ireland." In today's world, this would be called terrorism. The proposed landing place was Killala, in County Mayo, the site of the French invasion of 1798 – not exactly an auspicious precedent. The army would then gather support in Sligo, Leitrim, Roscommon, and Mayo, and take the authorities by surprise. "It would," McGee wrote, "be like hitting the enemy in the back of the head." They intended to draw British troops out of Munster and conduct a guerrilla war in the bogs and mountains of the Upper Shannon, which was "difficult ground for the movements of a regular army."[22]

Over the next four days – from Tuesday, 25 July, to Friday, 28 July – McGee travelled around the Clyde and into Edinburgh seeking recruits. Buoyed by exaggerated reports saying that "O'Brien and his friends had been received with open arms in the South," nearly four hundred men promised to fight in Ireland. The idea of hijacking a ship was dropped when the officers and crew of an Irish steamer agreed to take them from Greenock to Sligo. Meanwhile, the authorities were looking for him; McGee was delighted to read that the *Times* had described him and Meagher as "the two most dangerous men now abroad." On Friday, while he was in Edinburgh, he learned that someone had tipped off the police about his presence and that he would be arrested if he returned to Glasgow. His friends assured him that they would organize the expedition from Greenock, and they advised him to return to Ireland and make the necessary preparations in Sligo.[23]

It was a highly risky endeavour. His description had been posted in the "Hue and Cry," and his face was well known in Ireland. On Saturday, 29 July, he travelled by train from Edinburgh to Carlisle. At Newcastle, one of the last people he expected to encounter boarded the train and sat opposite him – Thresham Gregg, a fundamentalist Irish preacher and Grand Chaplain of the Orange Order, who "was on a lecturing excursion against the Pope in the North of England." They had met before, and, as McGee put it, he "looked very hard at me from under his traveling-cap with his half-shut cunning eye" and "kept constantly inquiring the distance to Carlisle." McGee was convinced that the game was up. But although Gregg must have recognized him, he did not alert the authorities.[24]

In Carlisle, McGee met two priests from Dublin who were heading to Scotland for a walking tour. They informed him that a warrant for his arrest had been issued the previous day. He was accused of forming a "Traitorous Conspiracy to Levy War Against Her Majesty and depose her from the Throne of these realms," and was charged with "Treasonable practices and of being guilty of high Treason against Her Majesty." It was no wonder that the priests "seemed surprised" by McGee's plan to return to Ireland; the penalty for high treason was death.[25]

On Monday, 31 July, he took the steamer from Whitehaven to Belfast, arriving early on Tuesday morning. This was dangerous territory. He had been in Belfast with O'Brien, Mitchel, and Meagher the previous November, when the police had been called out to protect them from an O'Connellite crowd, and there was a good chance that he would be spotted. As he left his cabin, he passed two policemen who had boarded the boat; much to his relief, they did not recognize him. So he walked through the city, took the train to Armagh, and travelled on to Enniskillen, where he spent the night. The next day, 2 August, he took the back roads to Sligo, where he checked in at the Hibernia Hotel under the name of Mr Kelly. Here, he "read with surprise and bitter indignation, the list of the places where, and clergymen by whom, the Southern movement had been '*denounced*,'" and realized that the revolution was in deep trouble.[26]

In fact, the situation in the south was even worse than he thought. When the members of the revolutionary council had fled Dublin, they had instructed Thomas Halpin, the secretary of the Confederation, to communicate their plans to the clubs. But the detectives were on Halpin's trail, and he was either unable or unwilling to contact the club leaders. As a result, the clubs had been thrown into "complete confusion" and were in no position to respond when the government proclaimed them illegal on 26 July. The chances of a rising in heavily garrisoned Dublin, never great to begin with, virtually disappeared. This meant that everything now depended on the countryside.[27]

But the revolutionaries were experiencing serious difficulties in Kilkenny. The Confederates lacked the arms and organization to attack the garrison, so O'Brien decided to gather an army in Tipperary that would return to the city and begin the revolution. Near Carrick they met John O'Mahony, who told them that the area was teeming with support for the Confederates – a view that appeared to be borne out when up to five thousand people enthusiastically welcomed O'Brien in the town. But popular enthusiasm was one thing; revolution was quite another. Knowing that O'Brien and Dillon had failed to rally supporters elsewhere, the local Confederates were torn between revolutionary sympathies and practical realities. "Why should Carrick be selected?" they asked; the thought of fighting and dying for a lost cause was not particularly appealing. Still more dispiriting for the leaders was the situation in Cashel; instead of being a revolutionary stronghold, it appeared more "like a city of the dead."[28]

Disappointed in the towns, the leaders fell back on the rural areas, and established their base in the village of Ballingarry on 26 July. Here, there assembled a veritable roll call of mid-nineteenth-century Irish nationalism – the former moderate Young Irelanders O'Brien and Dillon; the militants Michael Doheny and Devin Reilly; the future Fenian leaders John O'Mahony and James Stephens; Terence Bellew MacManus, whose funeral in 1861 would galvanize revolutionary Irish nationalists from San Francisco to Dublin; and the republican journalist and author Charles Kickham, whose novel *Knocknagow* would fix an ideal of Irish rural life in the popular imagination. Their immediate prospects were bleak. An attempt to march to Slievenamon failed dismally, and popular morale was collapsing rapidly. With few weapons, inadequate provisions, and the opposition of priests who insisted that "O'Brien *must be mad*," their ranks were becoming thinner and thinner. In desperation, some of the leaders were sent to assess the situation in other parts of the country; O'Brien, Stephens, and MacManus were among those who stayed in the village.[29]

On 29 July, the same day that McGee was sitting across from Thresham Gregg on the train from Newcastle to Carlisle, a contingent of forty-seven policemen marched on Ballingarry and ensconced themselves in Mrs McCormack's farmhouse. An attempt to dislodge

The affray at the Widow M'Cormack's House. This was the end of the line for the Irish revolution of 1848. The attempt to make a grand revolutionary gesture that would win "respectful sympathy" for the Irish people culminated in a humiliating failure and dismissive comments about the "cabbage-patch revolution." For moderate nationalists, the lesson was to focus on constitutional politics; for the revolutionaries, the lesson was to get it right the next time. (*Illustrated London News*)

them was repulsed by superior firepower, leaving two of O'Brien's men dead and several more wounded. With news that police reinforcements were on the way, the leaders went on the run; there were hardly any followers left. As troops blanketed the region over the next few days, the rising was effectively suffocated, amid loyalist jeers about the "cabbage-patch revolt" in "Widow McCormack's garden." The revolutionaries had not only failed to defeat a force of fewer than fifty men; they had also failed in their larger quest to boost the international reputation and honour of Irish nationalism.[30]

After all the impassioned speeches, intense arguments, fine words, and the proliferation of the clubs, it had come down to this. "We had all been woefully deceived – wholly misinformed as to the condition of the people in the remote Counties," recalled O'Gorman. Ironically, McGee had sounded the warning only six weeks earlier: "You must never forget this," he had declared in June, "Dublin is not Ireland." If the militants' image of an indignant people bursting for national liberation was a mirage, the moderates were guilty of ignoring their own advice. Like disappointed revolutionaries all over the world, they blamed the people for failing to live up to their high expectations. The people were too ignorant and too parochial to understand the idea of nationalism, wrote O'Gorman: "Their Political education had taught them only the virtue of meetings and Processions and eloquent harangues. They had heard Revolution and Civil War so often threatened without any result, that they looked with a kind of astonishment at men who invited them to face the desperate ordeal of Cival [sic] war then and there." Similarly, O'Brien wrote: "It matters little whether the blame of failure lies justly upon me or upon others; but the fact is recorded in our annals – that the people preferred to die of starvation at home, or to flee as voluntary exiles to other lands, rather than to fight for their lives and liberties." It did not cross their minds that the Young Irelanders might have deceived themselves or that the "people" of Kilkenny and Tipperary were actually responding in a prudent and rational way to idealistic and unreasonable revolutionary demands.[31]

McGee would have known none of this at the beginning of August. While O'Brien was on the run, he was reconnoitring the barracks at Sligo. Things looked promising; there were only ninety men, inadequately protected by an eight-foot wall, and the local authorities were "completely lulled to sleep." On the other hand, there was no Confederate organization in the town. "The only local societies," he wrote, "were secret – Molly Maguires and Ribbonmen." As recently as April, McGee had warned his countrymen to shun secret societies; in the United States, he had described Ribbonism as a destructive force in Irish life. But now, under the pressure of circumstances, he did something that had previously seemed unthinkable: He attempted to form an alliance with the Molly Maguires and Ribbonmen. Nor was he alone. Unknown to him, his fellow Confederates had done exactly the same thing in south Tipperary, where the clubs became virtually coterminous with agrarian secret societies.[32]

Just south of Sligo town, McGee met one of the local leaders, whom he found to be "wary, resolute, and intelligent." "Bring us by this day week assurances that the south is going to rise or has risen," he told McGee, "and we will raise two thousand before the week is out." A messenger was sent south to assess the situation; the leader went to meet his district chiefs, and McGee set out to contact Confederate sympathizers in Sligo and Donegal. Having been in the area during his pilgrimage to Loch Derg two years earlier, he had already encountered some of them; now he travelled to Bundoran to discuss plans with his friends. Here, he had yet another close escape. One of the guests in his lodging house was Thomas Blake, the resident magistrate who was responsible for security in the region; McGee actually had to go through Blake's bedroom to get to his own. "We met quite frequently," McGee recalled, "but he was quite unsuspicious." No one expected that McGee would be in the northwest. Besides, as Blake later learned, the description of McGee in the "Hue and Cry" made him three inches shorter than he actually was, at five foot three rather than five foot six.[33]

Before long, he met an emissary from Scotland, who had come to find out what was happening; the newspaper reports from Ireland during the first week of August had discouraged the Scottish Confederates, who did not want to sail into an already defeated revolution. McGee sent him straight back, with instructions to bring the men to Sligo as soon as possible. With two thousand Ribbonmen and Molly Maguires, along with another five hundred armed volunteers from Scotland, they could seize and hold the Sligo garrison, build on their success, and double their numbers. An army of five thousand men, he believed, could hold Sligo for up to three months, by which time more aid from the United States would start flowing in. Memories of Owen Roe O'Neill danced through his mind. Was this not the area in which O'Neill had arrived from Spain and gradually built up his forces until they won their famous victory at Benburb in 1646? Could not history repeat itself and a new Benburb pave the way for a new nation?[34]

Then came the devastating news that O'Brien had been arrested on 6 August. In desperation, McGee arranged a meeting with the leaders of the Ribbonmen and Molly Maguires, and pleaded with them to take up arms. "The proposals I then made ... I will not repent," he wrote a year later, "for now, even to myself, I confess they look wild and extravagant. But I felt the whole futurity of shame that awaited us, for abandoning the country without a blow." For two nights they argued it out "with great animation," McGee aligning himself with the most extreme faction. The leaders were deeply divided, but eventually the opponents of a rising prevailed, "on the argument that, unless it would be general, it would be fruitless."[35]

Even then he did not give up. For the next "ten dismal days" he travelled through the area, trying to persuade the local chiefs to change their minds. In Ballyshannon he stayed with Dr O'Donnell, the postmaster, and his two sons, James and Joseph. Posing as John Kelly, a student at Maynooth, he went with James to Loch Derg and to Donegal town; according to one man who recognized him, he was "greatly emaciated" – not surprising, given the famine conditions through which he moved. (Interestingly, his "Personal Narrative" of these events makes no mention of the famine; neither, for that matter, did O'Gorman's account of his own activities in Limerick.) It was all to no avail: the secret societies would not turn out, and the Irish volunteers in Scotland had gone back home. News of more arrests followed. Meagher had been caught near Cashel; MacManus had made it as far as a ship bound from Cove to America when he was recognized and brought back in handcuffs; the other leaders were on the run. "Then, indeed," wrote McGee, "I knew 'all was up!'" The question was no longer how to organize a revolution; it was how to evade the authorities and get on a ship to the United States.[36]

———•·••·•———

From his headquarters in Donegal town, the resident magistrate Thomas Blake conducted the search for McGee and gradually pieced the information together. He learned that McGee had been "quite Public" in the town, that he had been seen with James O'Donnell, and that he was using the alias of John Kelly. On 16 September, Blake travelled to Ballyshannon, where he sent one of his constables to the O'Donnell family home to investigate. There was no sign of McGee. Dr O'Donnell insisted that his son "attended this Mr John Kelly at Bundoran for 3 or 4 days as an Apothecary, that he never met Kelly before or knew any thing of him and that his son believed him to be a student from Maynooth." Immediately afterwards, O'Donnell stormed over to Blake's hotel, vehemently denied sheltering McGee, and, as Blake put it, "held up his fist in a threatening way to my face." It was a bravura performance, but it fooled nobody. Other sources had identified Kelly as McGee, and it was well known that McGee had stayed with the O'Donnells two years earlier. "I am convinced," wrote Blake, "that the father aided and assisted with his Sons in the disguise & escape of Thos D'Arcy Magee, & I respectfully suggest that an example ought to be made of this family."[37]

Further inquiries were equally unsuccessful. On 15 October, Blake reported rumours that McGee had been spotted "about Killybegs watching an opportunity to embark for America," and recommended that there be "a closer watch upon the many foreign in and out bound vessels coming and leaving Derry." He was six weeks too late; McGee had left the country on 1 September. Not only had Blake failed to recognize McGee in Bundoran; he was acting on hopelessly out-of-date information. It was not exactly one of the greatest episodes in the history of counterintelligence. Not surprisingly, Blake was subsequently relieved of his position.[38]

The O'Donnells were not the only people who helped McGee to leave Ireland; he also received critically important support from Bishop Maginn of Derry. Although it is unclear whether or not Maginn supported the rising, there is no doubt that he sympathized with the revolutionaries and wanted to keep them out of the clutches of the authorities. Maginn did not personally make the arrangements for the escape, McGee later wrote, but "some of his kind and courageous clergy were the chief promoters of it." According to local lore, they took McGee to Tremone Bay, to the west of Inishowen Head, where he was rowed by one Robert McCann to a waiting ship, the *Shamrock*, bound for Philadelphia. The story got around that McGee had been disguised as a priest; in some versions, he was even asked to marry a couple on board the ship. It makes for a romantic tale, but it is inherently implausible. As McGee's sister Dorcas pointed out, he had pretended to be a Maynooth student, not a priest; all the rest, she wrote, was make-believe. Because Maynooth students trained for the priesthood, and since Maginn's priests facilitated McGee's escape, it is easy to see how the story grew. Nevertheless, the key point remained: McGee had successfully eluded the authorities and was heading as an exile to America, rather than as a prisoner to Australia.[39]

During his three years in the Young Ireland movement, McGee's nationalism had mutated from a constitutional to a revolutionary form. Before February 1848, the constitutional strain had been dominant. Through a combination of parliamentary pressure, political education, and popular support, he wanted to win an independent legislature while retaining "the golden link" of the Crown. Such an arrangement, he believed, would harmonize Irish interests with British security requirements, and would reflect both the separate and interdependent characteristics of the Anglo-Irish relationship. Like Thomas Davis, he stood for a pluralistic form of nationalism, which would embrace all regions, religions, "races," and classes. Central to this vision was the belief that nationality was a "spiritual essence" that could be discovered and expressed through literature, music, and history. Once the Irish people reconnected with their roots, they would simultaneously break with English cultural hegemony and develop a sense of their own pride and dignity.

This process would be facilitated by a greater degree of Irish economic independence; a "buy Irish" campaign would promote domestic manufactures, encourage technical skills, shatter the stereotype of the feckless Paddy, and stem the flow of emigration. Railways promised to play a pivotal role in the political, cultural, and economic development of Ireland; they were forces of unity, progress, and improvement, which would break down parochialism, open up communications, and bring Protestants and Catholics closer together. Although Ireland was suffering terribly through the famine, McGee remained convinced that the "spirit of the nation" would ultimately prevail and that a great destiny awaited his country.

Considering McGee's career in its entirety, there are striking parallels between the nationalism he articulated in Young Ireland and the nationalism he subsequently adopted in Canada. Legislative autonomy within the British Empire, pluralism and minority rights, cultural and economic nationalism, railway development, and an overarching sense of destiny – all were central components of both his early Irish and his later Canadian views. In Canada, McGee applied and adapted old principles to new circumstances. There was a direct but invisible line connecting McGee and Young Ireland with Canadian Confederation; in this sense, Thomas Davis, Gavan Duffy, and Smith O'Brien should be counted alongside McGee as the Fathers of Canadian Confederation.

But there is another side to the story. Before the spring of 1848, the revolutionary strain of McGee's thought had been recessive. The major themes had been clear enough: an alliance with the gentry, an abhorrence of agrarian secret societies, and an advocacy of moral force. Yet every so often there were glimpses of a more militant mindset: the expression of "fierce hatred" towards exploitative, parasitic landlords; the impression that he could empathize with the motivation, though not the murders, of agrarian secret societies; the sense that only the superior power of Britain held him back from a physical-force position. On the eve of the French revolution, his principles appeared to be increasingly detached from reality, for the gentry were overwhelmingly opposed to Young Ireland, and the vast majority of Protestants rejected Irish nationalism in both its militant and moderate forms.

The "general European explosion" seemed to offer a way out of the contradiction; in the process, the recessive revolutionary nationalism gradually became dominant. There remained a considerable degree of commonality between the two strains; McGee did not simply abandon all his earlier principles. But the differences between the two strains became increasingly pronounced. At first, it was largely a question of means; the earlier emphasis on moral force gave way to a strategy in which a show of physical force would extract legislative independence from the British government. As it became clear that the government intended to break the incipient Irish revolution, he believed that the only honourable course of action was to resist; the threat of physical force, he believed, must now become a reality. The man who had attacked Mitchel in January for advocating guerrilla war began to plan guerrilla war in June and July, denounced spies as "fiends," and supported a run on the banks to bring Britain down.

As the means changed, so did the ends. McGee had once said that he would never join the "savage howl" against the gentry; he now argued that landlords were the enemies of the people and that landlordism must be abolished. He had previously argued that to be an Irish Confederate was not necessarily to be a democrat; now he supported universal manhood suffrage. After warning his countrymen to avoid secret societies, he not only worked with the Molly Maguires and Ribbonmen but aligned himself with their most extreme elements. And under the pressure of all these events, he severed the "golden link" and became a separatist republican.

Now, none of this could be enlisted in the service of an argument connecting McGee with Canadian Confederation. It points in a different direction altogether – in the direction of Fenianism. A fierce hatred of tyrannical landlords, together with the desire to destroy landlordism; viewing the famine as an act of British genocide (or "2,000,000 ministerial murders," to use his own words); adopting physical-force nationalism in the service of a separate republic; supporting guerrilla war and allying with secret societies; calling for a run on the banks and denouncing spies – there is nothing here that would be out of place in the most militant of Fenian circles. There was a direct but invisible line connecting McGee and Young Ireland with the Irish Republican Brotherhood; in this sense, McGee should be counted alongside James Stephens and John O'Mahony as a Father of Fenianism.

To view McGee as a Father of Confederation seems natural, normal, and safe; to view him as a Father of Fenianism appears outrageous and shocking. Yet the point is that in the summer of 1848, on board the *Shamrock* and heading for Philadelphia, McGee's mind contained the seeds for both Canadian Confederation and Irish American Fenianism. The question, then, becomes: Why and how did McGee wind up as a ferociously anti-Fenian Father of Confederation and not as a ferociously anti-Canadian revolutionary republican? Part of the answer lies in his reassessment of Irish politics under the influence of Duffy. But most of it lies in his experience of the United States over the next eight years.

PART THREE

The United States

Consistency, while circumstances are consistent, is a duty;
but when circumstances change, consistency to the past
is a crime against the present.

McGee, *Nation* (New York), 29 September 1849

CHAPTER NINE

A Traitor to the British Government
October 1848 – May 1849

While the revolutionary movement in Ireland was gathering momentum in the spring and summer of 1848, Irish American sympathizers had been mobilizing to provide money, men, and moral support for the Confederates. When McGee had learned in April that the Friends of Ireland in the United States were planning to hold a convention in July, he urged them to speed up the proceedings and send money to Ireland as soon as possible. After Mitchel's arrest in May and the emergence of Duffy's "formal conspiracy" for revolution, the Confederation sent two agents – one of whom was William Mitchel, John's brother – to the United States to promote the cause. They found a receptive audience, which included Robert Tyler, recent Irish immigrants, and veteran United Irish émigrés such as John Binns. Speaking in support of an "Address from America to the Confederation," Binns described the history of Ireland as "a detail of merciless cruelties, broken treaties, repeated confiscations, and the infliction of sufferings of every kind," and invoked the valour of "the men of '98" to inspire the new generation of Irish revolutionaries.[1]

By August, it seemed that Young Ireland was completing the unfinished business of the men of '98. When news reached America that the British government had suspended habeas corpus, the directory of the Friends of Ireland held an "immense mass meeting" at Vauxhall Garden in New York to express solidarity with the Confederates and raise funds for the revolution. "Precious hours are being wasted," the directors proclaimed; "precious blood is flowing. The Dying call for Vengeance – the Living Hope of Ireland implore your aid. Let us promptly answer the call. Awake to instant action!"

Among the speakers was Bishop John Hughes, who declared that "the oppressor and his victim stand face to face," that "the Government of England is justly responsible for the death by starvation of one million of Irishmen," and that the Irish people were entitled to "throw off their allegiance and resume their national independence." The Irish nation had suffered terribly, and no one could say that it had "rushed rashly into this contest," he told the crowd. "I am a man of peace, not a man of war. I believe in the efficiency of other means. But be that as it may, all that is now passed ... My contribution shall be for a shield, not for a sword – but *you* can contribute for what you choose." Although the future was uncertain, Hughes added, there was no doubt that the Irish would "fight like men, brave as the lion in the battle and gentle and human as the dove after the battle is over." And with that, he donated $500 to the movement.[2]

A week later, reports of Ballingarry reached New York. The news was so shocking that most Irish American nationalists simply refused to believe it; the English newspapers, they insisted, had "always distorted the Irish news," and this was no exception. "It is really ludicrous," commented Horace Greeley's *New York Tribune*, "to observe the attempts of the English press to prove that the long gathering storm of the Revolution and Resistance in Ireland had begun and blown over in an insignificant collision with a few score of Police Constables." Far more credible was the report from a "confidential correspondent in Dublin," who had smuggled a ciphered letter to the *Tribune* to "evade the vigilance of the British Post Office." Here was the truth: at Slievenamon, O'Brien's forces had killed and wounded six thousand British troops; a woman who arrived in Dublin reported that "for three miles the stench arising from the dead men and horses was almost suffocating"; there were reports of mutinies throughout the British army, and of sixty thousand men who had joined O'Brien's armies.[3]

This was more like it. The following day, the Friends of Ireland held a mass meeting that attracted twenty thousand Irishmen; they dismissed the reports of Ballingarry as "a delusion, a mockery, and a snare," and cheered for ten minutes when Bartholomew O'Connor announced that the Irish had battered the British at Slievenamon. "Let them garble, let them conceal the truth if they can!" he said of the British government. "They cannot entirely conceal it." Then came the call for money – "and no sooner was the word given," reported the *Tribune*, than contributions began to pour in, and were kept up, for some time, in one uninterrupted flow." Up to the podium came William Mitchel. He poured ridicule on the Ballingarry story, spoke scornfully about the "policy of the English to distort the real facts," and confirmed the authenticity of the secret letter from Dublin. Shortly afterwards, Bernard Devlin from Montreal spoke about "striking in Canada" to distract the attention of the British government from Ireland. The Irish had already spiked a number of military guns in Quebec, he said; in Canada East they were ready to rise, and "if 10,000 men invaded Canada they would walk through it in a week."[4]

The only trouble with all this, of course, was that the British reports were accurate, and the Battle of Slievenamon had never occurred. Paranoia about British "propaganda," together with a deep-seated desire to compensate for years of disappointment, meant that the myth spread like wildfire; inevitably, it burnt itself out just as quickly. As more news came in from Ireland, including the account of O'Brien's arrest, the *Tribune* and the Friends of Ireland were left with a lot of explaining to do. The report of the "confidential correspondent in Dublin" was actually an Irish American forgery, insisted the rival newspapers, which claimed that Horace Greeley and the Friends of Ireland had perpetuated a political fraud to obtain "money under false pretences" from the dupes who were unfortunate enough to believe their rhetoric. For Irish American nationalists, the hard truth of Ballingarry and the lies about Slievenamon created feelings of acute embarrassment and shame. And these feelings were compounded by a gnawing sense of their own gullibility, which was continually reinforced by the mocking jibes of their enemies.[5]

As the shock waves from Ballingarry pulsed across the Atlantic, McGee clambered aboard the *Shamrock*, still seething with anger about the "ulcer-giving Devils" who possessed his country, and furious about the failure of the rising. With the Derryveagh Mountains and Bloody Foreland receding into the distance, he wrote "A Vow and Prayer," the poem that O'Donovan Rossa later turned against him:

> Ireland of the Holy Islands,
> Circled round by misty highlands
> Highlands of the valleys verdant,
> Valleys of the torrents argent,
>   If I ever cease to love ye,
>   If I ever fail to serve ye –
> May I fall, and foulness cover
> All my hopes and homestead over;
> Die, a dog's death, outcast, hurried
> Into earth as dog's are buried![6]

But how could Ireland best be served in America? Landing in Philadelphia, and talking to his fellow countrymen, McGee ran straight into the atmosphere of disgrace and demoralization that was suffocating the movement. "When I arrived in the United States," he recalled, "I saw every Irishman's head hanging down with shame, a sneer on every Saxon's lip, a pitying, cold contempt in every free Republican's manner." There could be only one antidote – a public letter clarifying what had happened in Ireland, and why the rising had been defeated. Only in this way, he believed, would it be possible to save the Irish name from "utter scorn" and restore "some degree of American sympathy" for the cause.[7]

So on 12 October McGee published in the Philadelphia *Spirit of the Times* his account of the "Rebellion in Ireland." He discussed the organization and the arming of the Confederate clubs, and described the secret cells that operated within the clubs – sections of ten men, each with its own "master," who trained them in the use of arms. These sections, he wrote, had survived the repression and would be reactivated when the time was right. He explained that the clubs were strongest in the towns and that the Confederates had intended to use the Irish League as a conduit to the countryside: "It is not fair to assume that there was no system of operations agreed on among the confederates. There was

a feasible and well understood path." This path involved urban guerrilla warfare, along with diversionary operations in rural areas.[8]

What ruined their plans, McGee claimed, was the opposition of the
Catholic Church. "I am satisfied," he declared, "that if the Church had
been involved even ever so little in 1848, we would have beaten the
English." It was true that the Irish clergy had made a strong case against
rebellion, but the point remained that "they made the revolution fail
by preaching that it would fail." It was also true that revolution meant
bloodshed: "I know there would be slaughter," he admitted, "but
Fever and Famine, now under the protection of the British flag in Ireland, will destroy more lives and with worse weapons, than the sixty
thousand armed men could have killed. And then compare the two
results!" The revolutionaries may have suffered a serious setback, but
the sections remained intact, and important lessons had been learned.
"Next time," he concluded, "they must trust in local leaders, like the
Rapparees and the Catalonian chiefs, fierce men and blunt, without
too many ties binding them to the Peace. They must choose, too, the
favorable concurrence of a foreign war, an event which is likely to pre-
cede the settlement of the newly awakened races of the Continent."
Having delivered the message, he identified the messenger: "THOMAS
D'ARCY MCGEE. A Traitor to the British Government."[9]

McGee's letter was clearly intended to salvage the reputation and
honour of the Irish in America; nevertheless, it was a stunning act of
indiscretion. While he was writing, many of his colleagues were on
trial in Ireland for high treason, and the government was arguing that
repressive policies were necessary to counter a revolutionary conspiracy in the country. McGee had just handed them a smoking gun. The
first person to recognize this in print was Robert White, with whom
McGee had crossed swords three years earlier on the issue of American
relief for Irish hunger. Such "premature and imprudent disclosures,"
wrote White, were acts of "madness"; if leaders such as McGee lacked
the common sense to realize that they were "innocently and unwittingly supplying the place of the informer," it was no wonder that their
rebellion ended so ignominiously.[10]

In Ireland, the initial nationalist reaction was one of disbelief.
Although O'Brien, Meagher, and MacManus had already been tried,

Prisoners of 1848. William Smith O'Brien (seated) and Thomas Francis Meagher (standing next to guard) in Kilmainham gaol, and looking remarkably relaxed (Kilmainham Gaol Museum)

found guilty, and sentenced to death (later commuted to transportation for life) when McGee's letter arrived, more trials were in progress. Commenting on the "utter recklessness which the letter exhibits for the lives, liberties, and fortunes of Mr. M'GEE's recent associates, still within the grasp of the British Government," the *Limerick Reporter* expressed "grave doubts" about McGee's authorship. "If its statements be accepted as true," it stated, the letter "forms a complete justification of the Executive in the eyes of the world." Indeed, the letter fitted the government case for repression so well that many people were convinced that it had been concocted in Dublin Castle.[11]

Not surprisingly, the conservative newspapers and the government pressed home their advantage. The "Traitor's Letter," maintained the *Dublin Evening Post*, was a "complete vindication" of Lord Clarendon's policies. Had not McGee written that the sections were still ready to act? Did he not insist that the next revolution would incorporate the Rapparees and other secret societies? All this served to confirm the government's position that repressive measures should be sustained.[12] When, in February 1849, George Grey introduced a bill to continue the suspension of habeas corpus, he quoted extensively from McGee's letter to buttress his case. "After a letter of this kind from such a man as this," he said, "I confess I am astonished that any hon. gentleman should get up and say this was a mock insurrection."

By this time, McGee's authorship was not in question, and the opponents of Grey's bill were forced onto the defensive. McGee was writing sensationalist articles to boost his newspaper sales, argued John O'Connell; McGee was a poet who let his imagination run away with him, said James Fagan, the MP for Wexford. No one was convinced by such arguments, least of all O'Connell and Fagan themselves. The bill would almost certainly have passed even without McGee's letter, but there is no doubt that he had made things easier for the Whigs and correspondingly harder for their opponents.[13]

McGee remained unrepentant. It was not true, he wrote, that he had endangered the lives of his friends, since there was nothing in his letter that the government did not already know. Besides, it was self-demeaning for the Irish to pretend that "there was no intention of rebellion." Instead, they should publicly declare that they had made a stand against "forty years of insult and robbery, and three years of famine and extermination." Far from damaging the cause, he asserted, his letter had demonstrated that the Irish were men, not slaves. And far from harming the prisoners, the existence of a powerful Irish American lobby had prompted the British government to commute the death sentences to transportation.[14]

It was a spirited defence, but it was not enough to undo the damage. McGee had handed a weapon not only to the government but also to his enemies within the nationalist movement. For the Mitchelites, who already distrusted McGee, the letter confirmed their worst suspicions, proving that he had no compunction about sacrificing the lives of his fellow Confederates to advance his own self-interest.[15] The charge of betrayal resurfaced during McGee's attack on Irish American revolutionary societies in the mid-1850s and became a staple of anti-McGee Fenian invective.[16] It followed him to Canada, where his political opponents quickly got in on the act; the Conservatives used it against him when he was a Liberal, and the Liberals used it against him when he was a Conservative.[17] Even some of his closest allies in the Young Ireland movement had serious problems with the letter. Smith O'Brien, for example, exonerated McGee from the charge of treachery but nevertheless felt he had been inadvertently "*indiscreet*."[18]

———

A product of his passion, frustration, and anger about the failure of 1848, this indiscretion was closely connected to his conviction that the immediate requirements of courage and confrontation overrode any considerations of prudence and compromise. In this sense, McGee was reproducing in a new context the same reactive patterns of thought and feeling that had characterized his response to the Philadelphia riots of 1844 and to British assertions of cultural superiority during his Young Ireland years. Now, in the face of British repression and American ridicule, with his closest friend and mentor Gavan Duffy in Newgate Prison, McGee was in no mood for the middle ground. Combining feelings of rage and revenge with the ideology of republicanism, he committed himself to the cause of breaking the British Empire.

Moving from Philadelphia to New York, and working at a feverish pace, McGee launched an Irish American newspaper within three weeks of his arrival in the United States. Significantly, he called it the *Nation*; it was to be a revival in America of its suppressed prototype in Ireland. The tone was struck in the first issue, which opened with his poem "To Duffy, in Prison." McGee described the Union Jack as a "bloody rag," and swore on his mother's grave

That my days are dedicated to the ruin of the power
That holds you fast and libels you in your defenceless hour;
Like an Indian of the wild woods I'll dog their track of slime,
And I'll shake the Gaza-pillars yet, of their godless mammon
    shrine.

The Empire "must be dragged to pieces"; Ireland must have no part of such an oppressive system. "*Ireland,*" he insisted, "*can only be free as a Republic.*"[19] If this was pure Mitchel, his attitude to the land question was pure Lalor; he called for a rent strike and a social revolution that would turn occupiers into owners.

The Irish in America, he believed, had a crucial role to play in the revolutionary struggle. Because they had actually experienced republicanism, they could provide much-needed direction to their countrymen in Ireland. The failure of the rising was not only the result of counterrevolutionary clerics; the Irish people themselves had let their country down and were "not pure enough, disciplined enough, courageous enough or tolerant enough to conquer."[20] But if Irish Americans could disseminate their republican principles in Ireland, all this would change. If each of the hundred thousand letters that went annually from America to Ireland contained a copy of the Declaration of Independence, "Ireland would be a Republic before our generation passed away."[21] It was not, perhaps, one of his more astute ideas; sheer desperation had warped his sense of political reality.

Along with his scheme of flooding Ireland with copies of the Declaration of Independence, McGee attempted to use the New York *Nation* as a focal point for the underground revolutionary movement that had persisted into the autumn and winter of 1848–49. In Dublin, the remnants of the Confederate clubs circulated his newspaper, amid plans to establish a distribution agent in every town.[22] One of these agents, a man named Fannan, was part of the post-1848 revolutionary conspiracy being formed by Fintan Lalor and Joseph Brenan.[23]

But the difficulties were enormous. The demand for McGee's papers far exceeded the supply, the government intercepted the mail, there were rumours that anyone selling the paper would be fined fifty pounds, and at least some of the agents were scared off.[24] In this climate of fear and defeat, revolutionary exaggeration compensated for political weakness. McGee's comments about a hundred thousand letters became magnified into stories that the Irish Americans "intend organizing one Million of Men and if another Million here responded to them they will invade this Country." Similarly, an account in the New York *Nation* of an Irish American lecture series was transformed into reports that "they expect to have an army ready drilled in three years which will invade England."[25]

It was not enough to send letters and newspapers back across the Atlantic, McGee argued; the American Irish must also lead by example. In December, he laid out the fundamental principles behind his new political position: "*Ireland can only be free as a Republic; the Irish in America can make her a Republic; but they need to elevate each other, before they can lift her. Let us begin, therefore, with ourselves, and widen our intelligence that we may extend our influence.*" Central to this task was the same kind of Celtic consciousness-raising mission that he had conducted during his earlier years in the United States, pointing out that the history of the Celts was "a grand struggle for liberty against all central tyranny." They had resisted the Romans, the Goths, and the Normans; now they must make America sufficiently powerful to destroy the "fourth Despotism" of Britain.[26]

To fulfill their historic mission, the Irish on both sides of the Atlantic must bridge the gap between their proud past and their shameful present. In the United States, members of the same race that had once spread Christianity to Europe, and had once excelled in arms, arts, and oratory, were now reduced to "waiters at Hotels ... shovellers of earth-works – carriers of mortar – spades and axes, tools and tackle, for other mens [sic] uses." They must face the unpleasant realities: "We tell them ... that they are an inferior class, as a class, in America; we tell them they are an ignorant class; we tell them they are foolish and easily misled; more dangerous to their friends than terrible to their enemies." Once they recognized how far they had fallen, the American Irish could begin to recover their self-respect and enter a "new era of education, of combination, of brotherhood." "Our cure for all this is – Educate! Educate!" he insisted.[27]

In Ireland, the fall from grace had taken a different form, McGee said. There, the ancient Celtic heroism had given way to timidity and fear. His poem "The Flight of Human Deer (Suggested by Accounts of Ireland in December 1848)" contrasted the "cowed and cold" people of contemporary Ireland with the "spirits of our brave fathers" such as Brian Boru and Owen Roe O'Neill:

They fly, yet they have not fought, nay, never a blow struck they;
'Tis altered times in Ireland since you led your brave array,
And Priestly preachers of cowardice are chiefs in Ireland now,
Oh, well may every spirit hand smite every spirit bow.[28]

The reference to "Priestly preachers of cowardice" was pivotal; the Catholic Church, in McGee's view, had transformed heroic Celtic warriors into abject slaves. "The present generation of Irish Priests," he wrote, "have systematically squeezed the spirit of resistance out of the hearts of the people."[29] Unless and until the political influence of the Catholic Church over its flock was broken, the Irish people would never be free.

———

As he read these words, Bishop John Hughes's patience – such as it was – finally snapped. On 13 January 1849, writing as "An Irish Catholic," he countered McGee's criticisms of the church with a series of blistering letters in the New York *Freeman's Journal*.[30] In the process, he propelled McGee into one of the major controversies of his life and opened up a fundamental debate on the relationship between Catholicism and nationalism. To understand Hughes's position and the intensity of his arguments, it is necessary to consider briefly both his own background and the immediate political context in which he wrote.

Born in Monaghan in 1797, Hughes had moved to the United States in 1817, and quickly rose through the ranks of the Catholic Church. Ambitious, authoritarian, and aggressive, he was not a man to be crossed; he knocked his opponents to the ground and kicked them when they were down. "I will suffer no man in my diocese that I cannot

John Hughes, bishop (and later archbishop) of New York (1797–1864). McGee and Hughes locked horns in early 1849, were reconciled after McGee's conversion to ultramontanism two years later, and fell out once again in 1856–57 over McGee's plan to establish Catholic Irish colonies in Canada and the American West. They were never fully reconciled, although each man retained a grudging respect for the other's abilities. (John R.G. Hassard, *Life of the Most Reverend John Hughes* [1866])

control," he once wrote. "I will either put him down, or he shall put me down."[31] As a young man in Ireland, he had exhibited strong anticlerical tendencies. "I had a kind of spite against priests and bishops," he recalled – a spite that was "based on the false impression that they stood between our people and their liberties – that but for them Ireland would be free."[32] In attacking McGee, Hughes was attacking something he had once felt within himself.

Although Hughes had long since abandoned his anticlericalism, he remained a strong Irish nationalist. Applying Catholic "just war" criteria to Ireland, he argued that the people had the "right of revolution," provided that three conditions were fulfilled: the country must be "borne down by a grievous weight of tyranny"; the "cause and object" must be just; and the revolutionaries must have sufficient strength to realize their aims.[33] Since he already believed that the famine constituted clear proof of tyranny and that the cause of Repeal was just, the key question was whether Irish nationalists had a good chance of defeating their oppressors. During the summer of 1848 he became convinced that they were indeed strong enough to succeed. This belief was not altogether surprising. Anyone whose information about Ireland came primarily from the *Nation* and other nationalist newspapers would have had a severely distorted view of revolutionary consciousness and preparedness in the country. In effect, Hughes had fallen for Young Ireland propaganda. Hence his speech at the Vauxhall Garden in August, when he argued that the revolutionary leaders were not behaving rashly and that their followers would fight like lions; hence also his $500 donation to the cause.

But all these "high hopes" had come crashing down at Ballingarry. It now appeared that the leaders had been "rash, improvident, short-sighted, and altogether unfit to discharge the duties of the office which they had arrogated to themselves." "One thing appears to be certain," he said, "that there was no organization, no plans matured, no scheme of combination and concert – and this alone would be sufficient to destroy confidence in the capacity of those who urged on the crisis, but were unfit to meet it when it came." Responsibility for the humiliation of 1848 lay not with the Catholic Church but with the incompetent men who had launched a premature rising. Far from taking the blame, the Catholic Church should be praised for recognizing the reality on the ground and preventing the people from being led "as a defenceless herd to the slaughter."[34]

And now here was McGee, blaming everyone but himself and his fellow Confederates for the failure of the rising, and making scapegoats out of the very priests and bishops whose actions had prevented the revolution from becoming a bloodbath. On top of this, news had recently arrived from Europe that Pope Pius IX had fled from the revolutionary government in Rome and had condemned the radicals who were establishing a democratic republic. As far as Hughes was concerned, McGee was no better than "the cut-throats who have expelled the Pope from his capital."[35] Such a man should be comprehensively denounced and defeated; the letters of "An Irish Catholic" set out to do precisely that.

The attack moved along three lines – the personal, the political, and the religious. As part of his attempt to discredit McGee's character, Hughes accused him of being all talk and no action. "His cry in the *Pilot*," he wrote of McGee's earlier American career, "was 'organise, organise, organise: – educate, educate, educate'; – and yet he himself neither organised nor educated." The same syndrome had been carried over to Ireland, where McGee blustered about revolution yet was nowhere to be seen when O'Brien was at Ballingarry. Not only was McGee a coward, asserted Hughes, but he had insulted the Irish people by describing them as "a mean, craven, and degenerate race."[36] Much of this attack was false or misleading: McGee had in fact helped to organize adult education classes in Boston; his mission to Scotland and Sligo accounted for his absence at Ballingarry; and his criticisms of the Irish people were intended to stimulate self-regeneration. But the charges stuck and were brought up again and again in subsequent years – mainly, however, by the republican left rather than the religious right.

Hughes's political case against McGee can be summed up in a single sentence: "Talents he undoubtedly has; – but, as hitherto directed, they are talents of DESTRUCTION ALONE."[37] There was no shortage of examples, in Hughes's view. McGee's comments in 1844 about American natives being "cowards and sons of cowards," together with his remarks about the necessity of "*unprotestantizing*" the United States, had inflamed the "demagogues of 'Nativism.'" Just as McGee had inadvertently encouraged nativism in America, he had strengthened unionism in Ireland by "pulling down" O'Connell's Repeal organization and "building up nothing substantial in its stead." Furthermore, McGee and his colleagues had been "doing the Prime Minister's work, when they were abolishing the Repeal Association." Even more disastrous, declared Hughes, was McGee's support for the rising of 1848; after all their "warlike manifestoes," the Young Irelanders had presided over a rebellion that had been put down by a "squad of Policemen." As a result, the Irish people were now "*prostrate* under the iron heel of their oppressor." They were "disheartened at home," and their countrymen abroad were "mortified and humiliated." Hughes's point about the disastrous consequences of the rising was indisputable, but his other arguments were hardly fair. He was wrong to argue that the Confederates had "abolished" the Repeal Association, and he conveniently ignored the fact that he himself had taken a hard line against American nativism in 1844, albeit without McGee's obvious indiscretions.[38]

But the part of Hughes's attack that stung most was the argument that McGee had turned against the Catholic faith and joined the ranks of its enemies. The effect of McGee's writings, according to Hughes, had been to transfer the "odium of oppression" from the British government to the Catholic clergy.[39] McGee's position that the Catholic Church had somehow let the people down, wrote Hughes, ignored the fact that the vast majority of Catholic clergymen had never supported the Confederation in the first place. And why should they have supported the Confederation? Had not the Confederates themselves repudiated clerical influence in the "silly hope" that this would enable them to win over the Protestants and Orangemen of the north?

Not only had McGee falsely blamed the clergy for the failure of the rising, argued Hughes; he had also maintained that the "great question of the age" was "to reconcile Religion and Liberty," thus implying that the Catholic Church was the enemy of freedom. In spreading such ideas, with their "subtle mixture of Infidel poison and pretended Irish patriotism," McGee was corrupting "the young and inexperienced Catholics of this country." McGee indeed had the right to publish his "infidel sentiments" in the United States, Hughes conceded. "But I will tell you what he has *no* right to do: He has no right to call himself a Catholic, if in reality he is an infidel ... His writings are anti-Catholic, directly in some instances, indirectly in all."[40]

All true Catholics, Hughes concluded, must be protected from this poison. "Unless the *Nation* shall purify its tone," he declared, "let every Diocese, every parish, every Catholic door be shut against it."[41] Before long, reports of doors shutting reached the columns of the *Freeman's Journal*. In New Jersey, a priest agreed that the *Nation* was "unfit reading for a Catholic who wishes to save his soul," and a reader from Springfield, Massachusetts, wrote that he was taking "immediate steps to discontinue the *Nation's* visit to this town."[42] From Baltimore, Father John McCaffrey applauded Hughes's hard line against McGee's *Nation* and other Irish American republican newspapers. "The fault in dealing with them is this," he told Orestes Brownson. "We say they have done harm *& if they do not amend*, they must be put down. If they do not amend? But they will not – cannot amend. Their Editors & Contributors are men of wrong principles and bad principles. Therefore never hereafter mention or even allude to them, except as things to be condemned for the evil they have done & to be avoided for the evils they will do."[43]

McGee claimed not to know the identity of "An Irish Catholic," complaining that he had been attacked by an "anonymous slanderer," and expressing shock when he learned his opponent's identity.[44] This should not be taken at face value; Hughes was probably correct when he remarked that "it was a mere *stage trick* in him to affect ignorance."[45] Whether or not this was the case, McGee denied that he had become an "infidel" and insisted that his political views were not subject to clerical control. He would obey the Catholic Church in matters spiritual, but its authority ended where politics began. This did not mean that religion and liberty were incompatible; liberty meant "leave to do good," and religion was "the source and teacher of all goodness." The implications of his argument were clear: McGee had committed no "theological error," while the Catholic clergy in Ireland had committed a serious political error by opposing the "Revolution for Liberty."[46]

There was, however, a curious coda to the Hughes-McGee controversy. On 10 February, McGee publicly professed his "sincere desire that this argument should end" and signalled his intention to drop the debate.[47] Around the same time, he contacted James A. McMaster, editor of the *Freeman's Journal*, and possibly Hughes himself, to discuss ways of defusing the situation. McGee was motivated, he said,

by "my own spiritual interest and the success of my paper"; Hughes
wanted to ensure that McGee would stop criticizing the church. On 15
February, McGee drew up a series of "Resolutions and Promises," in
which he described himself as "a sincere Catholic in my religious faith
& convictions," admitted that he had inadvertently "uttered and published propositions" that were at variance with Catholic doctrine, and
acknowledged that he had not considered the "possible effect on the
minds of my Catholic Readers." He promised Hughes that he would
not repeat these mistakes, agreed to learn more about "the doctrinal
and moral principles of my religion," and undertook to "frequent the
sacraments of my religion." In return for these pledges, he asked the
bishop to stop denouncing the *Nation*.[48]

It seemed a complete capitulation, though one that avoided public
humiliation and held out the prospect of easing clerical pressure on his
newspaper. Over the next few months, criticisms of the Irish clergy
disappeared from his editorials, and he rarely wrote about the relationship between Catholicism and nationalism. He had not, however,
changed his mind on the subject; he had simply made a tactical retreat
in the interests of political and economic survival. It may even have
worked. Far from being broken by the controversy with Hughes, the
Nation actually increased its readership, size, and advertising revenues
in the spring and summer of 1849.[49]

But McGee found it difficult to censor his own beliefs, and the Catholic Church remained generally hostile to his newspaper. In March,
he printed an article that criticized the Canadian clergy for holding
back the rebels of 1837.[50] Meanwhile, Catholic clergymen continued
to denounce the *Nation* from the altar and attempted to prevent its cir-
culation; one of McGee's subscribers was even refused confession. By
July, McGee decided that there was no longer any point in suppressing
his own views. "The Irish clergy behaved badly, very badly, last year,"
he wrote, "and they behaved still worse in denying it." In August, he
called for "the destruction of the slavish dependence of our race on
the dictates of clerical politicians." The Irish hierarchy, he argued, had
"strengthened the chains of the English in Ireland, more than all the
Beresfords and all the Clarendons." Priests had no business meddling
in politics, just as politicians had no business meddling in religion.

His verdict on the Irish clergy, like his advice to the Irish people, was unequivocal: "As priests, none are better; as politicians, none are worse; confine them to their mission as priests; keep them out of politics, if you would keep yourselves, as a people, any longer on the earth."[51]

Although Hughes had silenced McGee only temporarily, the letters of "An Irish Catholic" served as a warning to all subsequent Young Ireland exiles: Challenge the church at your own risk. The intention – and, to some extent, the effect – was to create a chill among the revolutionaries. When Michael Doheny reached America in January, his fellow Irish nationalist Charles Hart commented, "He was at first red hot about the priests but from the tone we took, and when he heard of the sort of fix in which McGee then was owing to his contest with the bishop, changed his tune." This did not prevent Doheny from getting drunk before having dinner with Hughes and behaving in "a very disgusting manner ... treating the Bishop with a rude and vulgar familiarity."[52] But it did mean that Doheny trod carefully around the question of religion and nationalism. Although his *Felon's Track*, published later that year, criticized individual priests in Tipperary, there was nothing "red hot" about it, and he assiduously avoided any general condemnation of the church.[53] Indeed, the absence of conflict between the church and the republicans was usually a function of nationalist self-censorship; McGee was the exception who proved the rule. And even then, McGee's insistence on the separate spheres between priests and politicians must be treated with skepticism. On the few occasions when priests or bishops agreed or appeared to agree with his politics, McGee had been more than willing to welcome their support.

While McGee had briefly been forced onto the defensive in his conflict with the church, there was no let up in his revolutionary republicanism. On the contrary, he located himself within an international struggle between liberty and tyranny, and believed that the United States was destined to play a central role in the outcome. His poem "Hail to the Land" described America as the "vanguard of the human race" and a model for all those who believed in truth and justice.[54] He worried, however, about the growing gap between the rich and poor in the United States, just as he had expressed similar concerns about class differences in Britain during his period as a parliamentary reporter. "The creation of classes in this Commonwealth," he wrote, "would be the first step to a social, anti-republican, revolution." To counter this development, it was essential to "protect labor against capital, by limiting the hours of toil, and by establishing the principle that wages should be regulated by the value of labor expended in production." His support for protective legislation and his acceptance of the labour-value theory of production were not quite as progressive as they might appear. If the abuses of employers could be prevented, he argued, there would be no reason for trade unions and strikes. Traditional notions of republican harmony would then prevail over the divisive and danger-ous forces of modern industrial society.[55]

Even more troubling, in McGee's view, was the notion that the United States was an Anglo-Saxon country with close "racial" ties to England. The Saxon, commented one American newspaper, was "the most intellectual, most moral, most considerate, and mightiest being on the globe," and provided the driving force behind both Brit-ish imperialism and American "manifest destiny." Such a position not only allied the United States with the greatest enemy of liberty in the world, McGee argued, but it reduced the Spanish, French, Germans, and above all the Irish to a subordinate status within America. "We have small patience," he wrote, "with this criminal, canting, flippant, puffed-up ignorance, which puts such theories and thoughts into the minds of men."[56]

The Anglo-Saxon argument was wrong on three counts, he wrote. It glossed over the fact that there were many "races" in England, includ-ing the Celts, Danes, and Normans. It forgot that only half the Ameri-can population was Anglo-Saxon and that the whole point of the War of Independence had been to get rid of Anglo-Saxon power in Amer-ica. And it ignored the critically important role of the Celts and other "races" in "elevating this Republic to its present enviable position."[57] As the Anglo-Saxon racial myth became increasingly powerful over the coming years, McGee redoubled his efforts to debunk it. In 1849 he remained convinced that Anglo-Saxonism contradicted true American republican values, just as he had previously argued that nativism was anti-American. During the 1850s, as we shall see, this position became harder and harder to sustain.

All this meant that the Irish must keep the United States on the right track, just as the United States must inspire the Irish and provide a base from which the Young Irelanders could support the struggle back home. This is why he founded the American-Irish Society in the spring of 1849, with its motto "Ourselves alone," and its aim to regenerate the Irish on both sides of the Atlantic. Essentially an educational organization, it held a series of lectures in New York; the speakers included Henry Giles, Michael Doheny, Horace Greeley, and McGee himself. But it was hard to attract much popular support in the aftermath of 1848; attendance was irregular, and McGee was putting the best possible face on things when he described the series as "tolerably successful."[58]

His poetry also attempted to raise the morale of the Irish revolutionary movement — or what was left of it. In February he published his "Song for 'The Sections,'" which spoke directly to the revolutionary underground in Ireland:

> What though we failed in 'forty-eight
> To form th' embattled line,
> The more our need to compensate
> Our friends in 'forty-nine ...
> For Ireland and for vengeance, then,
> Arise and be prepar'd,
> And strike the Tyrant to the heart,
> The while his breast is bared.[59]

Still more popular was his "Ossian's Celts and Ours," which drew on an imagined past to inspire a new future, and which invoked images of a glorious heritage:

> Long, long ago, beyond the misty space
> Of twice a thousand years,

> In Erin old, there dwelt a mighty race,
> Taller than Roman spears.

Their deities included Manannán Mac Lir, god of the sea; their heroes were Finn Mac Chumaill and, above all, Ossian, the "inspir'd giant" who towered over the Celtic world. From the memory of such men, revolutions could be made:

> Ask not for Ossian! Ask a hero age:
> Ask power and skill!
> Ask wisdom from the Seer and the Sage!
> Breast wave and hill!
> Do these! and, like your fathers, warfare wage;
> The world to fill!
> And write your name on a new Ossian's page
> Forever, if ye will.[60]

At the same time, McGee supplied his American readers with a running commentary on Irish news. When he learned that Queen Victoria was planning to visit Ireland, for example, he recommended that the Irish people greet her with "dogged, sullen, systematic silence" and place human skulls rather than "evergreens and flowers" on her route. "Is she not embodied England ...?" he asked. "Is not that the hand that waved the accursed scepter over Skibbereen and Skull [sic], before whose sweep whole villages were depopulated and submerged?"[61] In fact, she was greeted by cheering crowds in Cork and Dublin; the Irish people, it seemed, required much more education.[62]

McGee had moved as far from the "golden link of the crown" as it was possible to get. But he retained one crucial component of David Urquhart's outlook – the view that Russian ambitions in Turkey would trigger a general European war. And such a war, McGee claimed, would precipitate an Irish revolution, in which the "damned spot of '48 would be wiped from our souls, forever."[63] Employing the very kind of Mitchelite rhetoric he had once caustically rejected, McGee maintained that armed opinion would carry the day. "Nothing," he asserted, "is so practical as a bullet."[64]

As a good revolutionary republican, McGee believed that the British Empire should be fought wherever possible – including in Canada, which he viewed as a standing affront to republicanism. He had, of course, favoured the annexation of Canada to the United States during his previous stay in America. Since then, both Canada and Nova Scotia had secured responsible government, which the Young Irelanders believed would culminate in complete independence for all the British North American colonies, and which was sometimes seen as a model for Ireland. During the debate between the moderates and Mitchelites in the winter of 1847–48, Gavan Duffy had employed the Canadian example to show that constitutional methods worked, and had used the failed Rebellions of 1837 to illustrate the consequences of premature revolution. After the French revolution, however, the wheel turned again, and Louis-Joseph Papineau, who had led the rebellion in Lower Canada, was magnified into a revolutionary Canadian folk hero.[65] In the Confederate clubs, it had been expected that the revolution in Ireland would be accompanied by an Irish American attack on Canada; McGee himself believed that the United States government would invade Canada as soon as Britain became involved in a European war.[66]

During the summer and autumn of 1848, there had been much talk in New York of an Irish American expedition to "liberate" Canada. In a pattern that reached back to the War of 1812 – and anticipated the Fenian invasions of Canada in 1866 and 1870 – Irish veterans of the Mexican war formed the Irish Republican Union, linked up with the "Friends of Ireland" in Montreal, and dreamed of wiping the British Empire off the North American map; hence the presence of Bernard Devlin at the Vauxhall Garden meeting in August.[67] After the failure of the rising of 1848, the Young Irelanders who escaped to New York continued to discuss the feasibility of a Canadian invasion; in October, William Mitchel was sent to Canada to sound out the situation. There was much speculation and little military organization; Charles Hart called it a "harum-scarum" scheme, and this view eventually prevailed.[68]

Although McGee did not advocate an Irish American invasion of Canada, he encouraged Canadian revolutionaries who sought either Canada's annexation to the United States or its transformation into an independent republic. His "Song for 'The Sections'" had urged action "for Ireland and for vengeance." An Irish-supported revolution in Canada might not help Ireland, but it would certainly provide a measure of revenge for the famine and Ballingarry. In March 1849, McGee drew up an address from "the Irishmen in New York, to the Irishmen in Canada," calling on Irish Canadians to "avenge the famines of '46, '47, and '48, on their heartless authors," and to "redeem the character of our race, deeply wounded by late events at home." Recognizing that the Irish Canadians were not powerful enough in themselves to start a revolution, he argued that they must be prepared to act with their French Canadian allies when the time came. "Never had men holier cause," he wrote. "You strike at the empire in the name of all its victims. Strike but a blow for each of them, and that empire will plunder round the globe no more."[69]

His attitude to the Canadian polity in this period was one of complete contempt. The Tories, he wrote, were a bunch of irrational, bigoted monarchists, backed up by a "formidable colony of Irish Orangemen"; the Reformers were a corrupt crew of "place beggars"; and the government had displayed an "utter disregard of human life" at Grosse-Île, Quebec, and Montreal during Black '47. Against them stood the "Revolutionists," led by Papineau and followed by "the great mass of the inhabitants, both French and Irish" – or so he convinced himself.[70]

Before long, a flurry of letters from Irish Canadians arrived in the Nation's office, pointing out that the reality was a little more complicated. From London in Canada West, Peter Murtagh wrote that Protestant prejudice against Irish Catholics was neither as deep nor as wide as McGee suggested. He said that in his district there were many Protestants from the north of Ireland who supported radical reform. The real bigots in Canada were "the officials of Dublin Castle," who had been "rewarded with Canadian land," the pensioners who had served in the wars, and the "besottedly, ignorant portion of Irish Orangemen – a great many of them from the South of Ireland."[71] In Toronto, "A Celt" reported that the Canadian Irish were not a homogeneous group;

along with the split between the Orange and the Green, there were major divisions within the city's Irish Catholic community, particularly over the handling of funds that had been raised for the Repeal Association and the Young Ireland prisoners.[72]

More generally, an "Irish-Canadian Democrat" in Montreal set McGee straight about the character of Canadian politics. Although the Catholic Irish and the French shared a common religion and a common hostility to Britain, he explained, they eyed each other with jealousy and suspicion. Far from commanding widespread popular support, Papineau had "little or no influence"; most French Canadians followed the lead of their church in opposing republicanism and annexation, which were seen as threats to the faith. "Here, then, is the difficulty," wrote the correspondent. "By supporting the French Canadians, Canada will remain connected to the British crown, and Irish revenge will remain unsatiated." Ironically, he observed, the main source of support for annexation actually came from the Tories, who were furious with the government for its supposedly soft line on French Canadians. But it was unthinkable for Irish democrats to form an alliance with Canadian Tories.[73]

A few days after this letter was written, Lord Elgin, Canada's governor general, gave his assent to the Rebellion Losses Bill, which compensated French Canadians for property they had lost during the 1837 rebellion. For Montreal's Tories, this was the last straw. They were already angry with the British government for its free trade policies, which they blamed for their economic problems; now they complained that their own legislative assembly was rewarding the French Canadian rebels of 1837. On 25 April, when Lord Elgin signed the bill, Tory protests quickly escalated into one of the worst riots in Canadian history; the crowd set fire to the Parliament Buildings, took possession of the streets, and destroyed the property of prominent Reformers. Among the places the crowd "battered" was the tavern owned by Francis Bernard McNamee, who later emerged as the chief Fenian organizer in the city.[74]

Viewing these events from New York, McGee reminded his readers that this was a riot, not a revolution. But the great advantage of such riots, he said, was that "they teach disloyalty." The initial reports from Montreal indicated that the forces of authority had capitulated to the rioters; in an elemental struggle for power, the Tories had demonstrated that it paid to use force. There was a lesson here for the Irish and the French Canadians, McGee noted. The French Canadians were already prepared to take on the Tories; it was time for the Irish to follow suit. "We urge upon them the necessity of organizing and arming," he wrote; if Canadian independence could be achieved only by force, the Irish would be ready.[75]

It might, after all, be possible to avenge Ireland on Canadian soil, he believed. In this respect, as in his intense republicanism, his outspoken attacks on the British government, and his insistence that the Catholic Church should keep out of politics, McGee was in the vanguard of revolutionary nationalism. "Every one knows," commented the *Montreal Herald* in 1867, "that except in that particular phase of Fenianism which consists in an attack upon Canada, Mr. McGee was in 1849 a Fenian, though that name had not been invented."[76]

CHAPTER TEN

Modified Moral Force
May 1849 – July 1850

McGee was driven by deep passions during his time as a republican exile in New York. His "hatred to the crown and government of England" was intensified by the famine, the humiliation of 1848, and the trials and imprisonment of his fellow Confederates. His conviction that the Catholic Church had betrayed the Irish people was so strong that he could not contain his anger; when he learned that the Irish bishops were welcoming Queen Victoria to Ireland and declaring their loyalty, he denounced them as "vermin engendered by bad blood and beggary." His desire for a "day of vengeance" against Britain fuelled his efforts to create and sustain "an anti-British influence" throughout North America. In the issues of the New York *Nation*, a sense of rage beats off almost every page.[1]

Beneath the surface, however, countercurrents were stirring. Although his attitudes appeared to anticipate Fenianism, McGee had been experiencing a deep inner conflict during the spring of 1849 between his militant and moderate impulses. On the one hand, he wanted to continue the fight against British rule in Ireland; on the other, he had a growing sense that the time for revolutionary politics had passed. Central to this changing outlook was the influence of Duffy, who started writing to McGee from Newgate Prison in February 1849.

After some complimentary remarks about McGee's poetry and lectures, Duffy sharply criticized his plans to revitalize the Irish revolutionary movement by distributing the New York *Nation* throughout Ireland and flooding Ireland with copies of the Declaration of Independence:

The notion of turning Ireland into a Republic by force of pre-paid letters is mere midsummer madness. To run a career of usefulness and honour you must base yourself on quite a different foundation from this. Consider for a moment to what we are come here – and consider if this fragment of a people, cowed and deserted, are likely to be stimulated to revolutionary achievements ... And, if not, ought you waste an hour on vain and incredible hopes? If I were a free man, I would strive to nurse the sick and poverty-stricken people into comfort and confidence before I attempted any political operations.

In the changed circumstances of the famine and after the collapse of revolutionary nationalism at Ballingarry, the task was to rebuild from the bottom up – a task that could be undertaken only in Ireland itself, wrote Duffy. Rather than pursuing the impossible dream of an Irish revolution, McGee should focus his energies on strengthening the political influence of the "new Irish nation that is growing up in the States."[2]

As we have seen, McGee valued Duffy's opinions and friendship highly; indeed, Duffy's imprisonment had been a major source of McGee's feelings of anger and vengeance, as expressed in his poem "To Duffy, in Prison." During the winter of 1848–49, McGee had written an adulatory biography of his friend, describing him as "the greatest Irish production of this century," admiring his literary accomplishments, and praising his political beliefs. In it, he had quoted Duffy's declaration: "I am a nationalist – Nationality is broad, comprehensive, and universal; inspiring generous emotions, and compassing noble ends. I, for one, will never consent to dwarf it down to the selfish schemes of a class in society, or the pedantic theories of a sect in politics." Duffy's definition of "nationality" was indistinguishable from McGee's own position.[3]

All this meant that when Duffy spoke, McGee listened. Duffy's letter reached McGee towards the end of March. Although it made no discernible difference to his editorials in the New York *Nation*, he was mulling over its contents. When the news reached America in May that

Duffy had eventually been released – after five indictments, ten months in prison, and three trials – McGee's letter of congratulation indicated that he had absorbed and accepted Duffy's ideas. The real struggle must take place in Ireland, he agreed, and revolutionary nationalism was no longer a viable option. "Assume that Mitchelism is dead," he told Duffy. "It is dead ... Mitchel's policy was driftless and reckless as O'Connell's – the one was mad, the other a cheat. Between them lies your course, and in the very same quarter lies victory." McGee had also taken to heart Duffy's suggestion that he focus on Irish American concerns. "I have thrown myself on the race in America," he declared. "I aspire to be the Duffy of our Emigrants."[4]

A few days later he went public with his new position. The hard reality, he wrote, was that an Irish revolution, however desirable in theory, was impossible in practice: "Morally and materially Ireland has sunk, within our own memory, lower than, perhaps, she ever was ... To talk to a people so circumstanced – a people, without arms, or chiefs, or ideas, of a military revolution – is to talk moonshine ... For God's sake, let us have no more loud threatenings, which are to end in nothing." Given that revolution was out of the question, the only alternative left was "to return boldly and at once to a modified moral-force argument."

Moral-force principles should be adapted to Ireland's new conditions: "Let it be remembered that it is not a choice between a revolution or not – between a Republican, or a constitutional home government." "That choice might have been offered last year, but will not, perhaps, be presented again for years to come. The alternative is simply between doing something and doing nothing – between a struggle and a suicide." And "doing something" meant working for specific practical improvements, such as a more just taxation policy, the completion of public works, reforms to the land system, a more efficient public service, and closer trade connections between Ireland and America. Only through such efforts would it be possible to "save the survivors from the wreck."[5]

Rather than confronting the "is" with the "ought," McGee had chosen to work within the politics of possibility. This approach affected not only his approach to revolutionary nationalism but also his attitude towards republicanism. Although he continued to argue that he was "personally" a republican, McGee came to view republicanism as a distant aspiration rather than an immediate goal. Ireland could become a republic only by defeating Britain in a military campaign, and that was inconceivable in the context of 1849.[6] In the present circumstances, he would accept "a national constitution under the British Crown" in the extremely unlikely event that it would be put on offer. Such a constitution could then be used to "hasten and secure separation within half a century." But any attempt to speed things up would be disastrous.[7]

From this perspective, McGee combined his "personal" republicanism with a growing conviction that any attempt to fight for an Irish republic in the foreseeable future must be strongly resisted. By September 1849, he could write that it was "rank nonsense to talk of a Republic" in Ireland, and he endorsed Duffy's argument in the newly revived Dublin *Nation* that "we cannot win our rights at a blow, but *we must win them in detail.*" As McGee put it,

> The great fact in the present condition of Ireland is the new
> era made by the famine. Within three years every class in that
> country has experienced change. The peasantry, the priesthood,
> the aristocracy, stand no longer where they did. Starvation,
> alienation, experiment, defeat, bankruptcy, have gone forward;
> habits, traditions, interests, have perished. We speak the literal
> truth when we assert that the Irish of 1850 are a quite different
> people from the Irish of 1840 and '45. Mr. Duffy fully perceives
> this change. He bases himself on the new order of things. He
> does not strive to bend the facts to him, which would be in
> vain; he recognizes and scrutinizes them ... We confess we like
> this courageous avowal of change of tactics. Consistency, while
> circumstances are consistent, is a duty; but when circumstances
> change, consistency to the past is a crime against the present.

Duffy's "slower and more plodding plan" would prove much more effective than the mad schemes of the Mitchelites. As in the days of the Irish Confederation, Duffy and McGee were working closely together, with Duffy very much in the leading role.[8]

In repudiating revolutionary republicanism, McGee was bound to encounter the enmity of Mitchel's supporters in the United States. But the initial attack on his new position came from an unexpected quarter – his former colleague and fellow Confederate John Dillon, who had escaped from Ireland to New York the previous October. Dillon had long suspected that McGee had secretly opposed Smith O'Brien's strategy in 1848, and he reacted angrily when the New York *Nation* published a letter from its Dublin correspondent criticizing O'Brien's actions at Ballingarry. McGee immediately disassociated himself from the article, but the damage had been done.[9] It was against this background that Dillon read McGee's "modified moral-force argument" of May 1849, in which McGee described Duffy as "the head and front of the Confederacy," endorsed his gradualism, and criticized the attempt "to *improvise* an Irish revolution" in 1848.[10]

As far as Dillon was concerned, this constituted clear proof that McGee viewed O'Brien and Meagher as "the intemperate and unmanageable subordinates of Mr Duffy," as men whose headstrong behaviour had resulted in the fiasco of 1848. In a blistering letter to McGee, Dillon accused him of "deliberately and systematically endeavouring to damage, and to derogate from, the reputations both of Mr O'Brien and Mr Meagher, with a view, as it would appear, to exalt that of Mr Duffy and (with *it* I presume) your own." "It is my wish," he concluded, "that we should stand in the relation of strangers to each other."[11]

In retrospect, it is difficult to understand Dillon's logic, since McGee was writing about the lessons to be learned from 1848 and had nowhere attacked O'Brien and Meagher. On at least two other occasions, Dillon displayed a similar propensity to believe the worst of McGee. The first concerned the Young Ireland attack on Portlaw Barracks in Kilkenny the previous September; according to Dillon, McGee had pretended to have participated in the action. While it is true that the New York *Nation*'s Dublin correspondent reported rumours that McGee had fought at Portlaw, McGee himself had never claimed to have been there and would soon write openly about his activities in Sligo and Scotland.[12]

The second occasion was in a letter that Dillon wrote to Duffy, complaining that McGee had made a "scandalous" attempt to present himself as "a sort of agent of yours in America." Shortly afterwards, Dillon predicted to his wife that McGee would tell "*the grossest lies* to Duffy to *counteract* the impression which my letter may have made."[13] When Duffy wrote back in defence of McGee, Dillon was convinced that his prediction had come true.[14] He could not have known, of course, that McGee was actually writing under Duffy's influence. Although Dillon's criticisms appear unfounded, there is no mistaking their intensity. It is clear that Dillon could not stand McGee, and this hostility continued right through into the 1860s. In contrast, McGee seems to have remained unaware of just how much Dillon disliked him.[15]

If Dillon's position was surprising, the reaction of the Mitchelites was entirely predictable. They had not forgotten McGee's earlier position on the "golden link of the crown," his alignment with Duffy against Mitchel and Devin Reilly before the French revolution, and his refusal to support the plan to spring Mitchel from prison in May 1848. As a result, many of them had treated his subsequent conversion to revolutionary republicanism with deep skepticism; Joseph Brenan, who had become co-editor of the Mitchelite *Irishman*, never believed for a moment that McGee had been sincere. Even during McGee's most militant period in the winter and spring of 1848–49, Brenan had accused him of cowardice during the rising of 1848 ("*he* was not there") and had described the New York *Nation* as "a vile rag, full of paradoxes, exaggerations and lies."[16] When McGee's supporters, including his brother James, wrote letters of protest to the *Irishman*, Brenan had refused to publish them.[17]

All this was *before* McGee announced his "modified moral-force" position; afterwards, the vituperation reached new levels of viciousness. Devin Reilly, who had arrived in New York in December, wrote that McGee was "innately and irreclaimably treacherous," "perseveringly mean and vengeful," and "repulsive to truth." "There are some men who would make money of the honor of their mother," Reilly declared, "... and of such men one is Mr. McGee."[18] Duffy later described Reilly's words as "a disgrace to Irish-American journalism by their foulness and mendacity."[19]

Meanwhile, in Dublin, Brenan not only dusted off the usual list of charges against McGee – that he was a coward, a liar, and an all-round "despicable character" – but added that McGee had absconded with £200 of the Confederation's money and used it to start up the New York *Nation*.[20] He did not provide any evidence, probably because he was lying through his teeth. When Duffy read Brenan's article, he was livid; far from cheating the Confederation, Duffy pointed out, McGee had offered to donate his profits from the New York *Nation* to cover the costs of Duffy's trial. Duffy sent two letters to the *Irishman* to defend McGee from such "open, debauched and shameless lying"; neither was published. "I am not acquainted in the blurred and chequered history of the press," he wrote, "with any transaction baser than this false charge against an absent man, persisted in without a particle of evidence, and sheltering itself from refutation, by suppressing the testimony of the very part cited as a witness for the prosecution."[21]

While McGee's alignment with Duffy alienated Dillon and angered the militants, it produced an increasing preoccupation with Irish American affairs; the man who aspired to become "the Duffy of our Emigrants" began to devote more and more column space to Irish American issues. Right from the start, one thing was clear: moral force in Ireland did not rule out physical force in Canada. If anything, McGee's relative moderation about Ireland actually heightened his feelings about Canada; the revolutionary anger that he had focused on Ireland was now being directed north. In the same issue of the New York *Nation* that applauded Duffy's gradualism, McGee began a series of articles about military campaigns in Canada, for the benefit of "our Canadian and boundary readers."[22]

A month later, McGee argued that the war against the British Empire must take different forms in different places, according to circumstances. In Ireland it required "an honest united movement" that combined words with actions but stopped short of physical force. In Britain it involved an alliance between Irish nationalists and the working classes. And in the British Colonies it necessitated "arms, secrecy, incessant vigilance, social association" – all of which anticipated Fenian activities in Canada.[23] When one of his correspondents wrote that Irish Canadians would resist British oppression with a "war to the knife," McGee cheered him on: "If all men in Canada were of his mind, the freedom of Ireland and of other Colonies, might be won by the St. Lawrence before many days."[24]

Most of the letters McGee received from Canada supported his views on annexation by the United States, though some pointed out that Irish Canadians were divided on the issue. In general, his Irish Canadian correspondents viewed annexation as a means both of avenging Britain and of destroying Orangeism in British North America; it was also expected to deliver Irish Canadians from "the advertisements which stare us in the face with the motto, 'No Irish need apply.'"[25]

At least one letter, though, bucked the republican trend. Writing from Montreal, an "Observer" commented that Canada was "now in the free enjoyment of a constitution which she had been long demanding" and which "for all practical purposes ... allows absolute self-government." There was no church ascendancy and no starvation in Canada, he wrote. By demonstrating their loyalty to the Canadian constitution, Irish Canadians could provide a "practical lesson" to England – "that the right of directing her own affairs demanded by Ireland is one which her sons can exercise wisely, and which, seeing the result of its free concession to Canada, there can be no good reason to refuse."[26] At the time, McGee ignored these arguments; within a few years, however, he would make them his own.

———•··•———

More compelling to McGee in 1849 was the fact that Canada was in the British Empire, and the British Empire was Ireland's greatest enemy. "I proclaim to-night the British Empire, as presently constructed, a vast conspiracy against human rights," he told an Irish American audience in Philadelphia: "In your presence I proclaim its literature a lie and its journalism a fraud. In your presence I proclaim its constitution a fiction, and its religion a trade. In your presence I declare its sovereign a bauble, and its statesmen the tools of the monopolists. In your presence I declare its subjects slaves to a gigantic debt contracted in great part for their own oppression, and augmented by the cost of innumerably unjust wars."[27] The notion that monopoly finance was the driving force behind the empire – that the national debt was enriching a parasitic elite of speculators and impoverishing the rest of the country – was commonplace among British radicals, and had found its most forceful and sustained expression in the writings of Cobbett. A central component of this critique of empire – and one that historians have sometimes glossed over – was the belief that Jewish financiers were among its most powerful controllers and principal beneficiaries. Anti-imperialism and anti-Semitism could be very close cousins. And in 1849 something of this outlook rubbed off on McGee.

In his Philadelphia speech, McGee explicitly identified "landlords and money lenders ... and Jews" as the people who had created the famine in Ireland. Elsewhere, he listed "Jews, Lords, Landlords, Lawyers" as the oppressors of the British and Irish people, and attacked what he called "Jew-Bank" laws.[28] But this position sat uneasily with his liberalism; as chairman of the Davis Club in Dublin, for example, he had supported a resolution in favour of the emancipation of the Jews.[29] His anti-Semitic comments were compressed into a period between the summer of 1849 and the spring of 1850, and even then they coexisted with the contrary conviction that the Irish and the Jews were common victims of famine, failure, and flight. Just as God had delivered the Jews at Hebron, McGee argued, he would deliver the Irish, "a nation like their own."[30] Ultimately, this was the view that triumphed; on the few subsequent occasions that he referred to the Jews, he regarded them as fellow sufferers, as nationalists without a nation, rather than as part of the enemy.[31]

—————

If the British Empire, with or without the Jews, was the source of all evil in McGee's world, the United States remained the bastion of liberty. But that liberty could not be taken for granted. McGee had already identified an emergent financial aristocracy and Anglo-Saxonism as dangers to American democracy; in the summer of 1849 he argued that the republic was also threatened by socialism on the one hand, and conservative Catholic sectarianism on the other. He did not spend much time on socialism, summarily dismissing its adherents as "Laputian philosophers."[32] But the Catholic Church received much more attention. The Pope, in his view, was an avowed enemy of republicanism; the church had sided with tyranny in Italy and with imperialism in Ireland; and Catholic American bishops regarded political dissent as religious heresy.[33]

Irish Catholics must resist such conservatism, he insisted; such a stance would have the added benefit of undercutting nativist arguments that Catholics blindly followed the political instructions of their priests.[34] They must also fight the church's attempt to establish a segregated educational system; this meant, among other things, supporting the Queen's Colleges which Peel had established in 1845 and which had been rejected by Rome. The great advantage of the colleges, McGee wrote, was that "Protestant and Catholic youth will grow up together, and sectarian feuds be forgotten in early friendship."[35] It was essential that Irish Catholics examine and expunge their own sectarian tendencies, even as they criticized sectarianism in others: "It takes two factions to keep each other alive," he wrote in response to reports about Orange attacks on Catholics at Dolly's Brae in Ireland and at St Catharines in Canada West. "The only cure for bigotry in others, is to get rid of it in ourselves."[36] Although his views on education would soon change dramatically, his sense of the mutually reinforcing and mutually destructive dynamic of ethnic conflict, together with his belief that Catholics could not shift all the blame onto the other side, anticipated his anti-Fenian writings during the 1860s.

McGee's attitude to Catholic sectarianism fitted well with his emphasis on self-criticism as a necessary prerequisite for self-improvement. This had, of course, been a staple feature of his writings, but in 1849 it began to assume a different form. While he continued to believe that Irish Catholics must celebrate their Celtic heritage, he increasingly felt that they were in danger of becoming mired in tradition. "We are a primitive people," he declared, "wandering wildly in a strange land, the Nineteenth Century."[37] To make the strange become familiar, the Irish must divest themselves of cultural characteristics that had become handicaps to progress. The Gaelic language was a case in point. Although he "grieved over the extinction of the Gaelic," McGee was glad that "the Irish people are soon to have the Anglican for their national language, because it is a living language – because it is the language of America, of our own great orators, novelists, and poets, of Shakespeare and Scott."[38] The English language would widen opportunities for the Irish on both sides of the Atlantic, and it was already being turned against the very oppressors who had used it as a "weapon of subjection" in their attempt to conquer Ireland.[39] As such, it was an essential element in the Irish struggle for economic prosperity and political liberty.

McGee applied similar logic to the Irish sense of history. It was one thing to take pride in the past, but quite another to become stuck there. Instead of continually going on about their heroic forebears in the American Revolution, Irish Americans should think more about their current contribution to American life: "We are bored to death with Montgomery and Commodore Barry," McGee declared. "What have all the rest been doing ever since these two men died?" Not enough, clearly – and an important reason for this lay in their traditional world view. If the Irish were to succeed in America, they must jettison "many of the local habits and hereditary customs" that they had brought with them from Ireland. The same attitude informed his approach to St Patrick's Day celebrations in 1850: "Metaphorical trash about 'days of old,' and 'unstrung harps,' and 'British lions' are as odious to the taste as a vomit to the palate."[40] Irishmen must stand up and think for themselves, manage their money carefully, and stop "*living on each other*," he insisted; only by embracing liberal individualist values could Irishmen make it in the New World.[41]

McGee was not arguing that the Irish should forget their language, history, and culture. He believed, for example, that Irish scholars should continue to study Gaelic, along with the languages of Greece and Rome – "and no dead language," he added, "can hope for more."[42] And he continued to insist that the Irish learn more about their heritage and their literature. But love of the past must be balanced with the needs of the future. As he wrote in December 1849, "A new age and a new order of things surround the Irish of to-day. Art has invaded their island. A railway-bridge is being constructed across the Shannon. A steamer's funnel smokes the wall-flowers on the ruins of Cong, and the lichens on the rocks of Loch Corrib. Ceim-an-eigh is a natural cutting, and the Giant's Causeway will soon be a depot. The low-backed cars, the wooden ploughs, the fairies, the Celtic speech, are passing or have passed. The people themselves, whether they will or not, *must* change."[43] If McGee was a Romantic, there was no sign of it here. The point, though, was to blend the best of the traditional with the best of the modern so that the American Irish could retain their "distinct existence" while working towards "an harmonious amalgamation" with American society. "By amalgamation," he wrote, "we do not understand swallowing up; we mean the union of relative natures, fit and proper to be united, in the fruits of which each constituent is represented by the good qualities he brings to the common stock."[44] Eight years later, this vision would become completely Canadianized.

Bringing out the best in the Irish necessarily involved getting rid of the worst. Writing in the first issue of Duffy's revived *Nation*, McGee continued his criticism of Irish American demagogues and the rodomontade that surrounded the reports of revolution at Slievenamon in 1848. But his sharpest comments were directed at the "crisis of character" that he perceived within the Irish in America. "Here, as at home," he wrote, "the social training of our people has been sadly neglected. They were not taught (at least till of late) punctuality, cleanliness, sobriety, caution, perseverance, or the other 'minor morals.'"[45] Such words were a deliberate attempt to shock Irish people into their senses. ("When one faints," he later explained, "you never ask pardon before dashing water in her or his face.")[46] And shock it certainly did; as far as McGee's growing list of enemies was concerned, he had played straight into the hands of those who derided the Irish as being irresponsible, dirty, drunk, impetuous, and irresolute.

Earlier in the year, Bishop Hughes had attacked McGee for supposedly denigrating the Irish people; now it was the Irish American republicans who went for the jugular. A newly established Mitchelite newspaper, Patrick Lynch's *Irish American*, described McGee's letter to the *Nation* as "the vilest, most calumnious, most lying, most insulting,

Michael Doheny (1805–63). On the physical-force wing of the Irish Confederation, Doheny was among the revolutionaries who attacked the police at Widow McCormack's house in July 1848. He evaded the authorities and in January 1849 reached New York, where he continued to publicize the separatist republican cause, became the colonel of an Irish militia company, and a cofounder of the Fenian Brotherhood in 1858. Described by one contemporary as "warlike and choleric," Doheny despised McGee's "modified moral force" position and put his own preference for physical force into practice when he assaulted McGee on a New York street in 1849. (Duffy, *Young Ireland*, vol. 2)

document ever published against the Irish race, in America."[47] Doheny and Reilly spread word that McGee despised the Irish in America; according to Doheny, McGee had "denied them every manly attribute, accused them of meanness, falsehood, stupidity, dishonesty, and cowardice, and insinuated away every trait of heroism in which the poor country ever took pride." McGee initially ignored these attacks, but by November he had been provoked beyond endurance. There was hardly a barroom in New York, he wrote, in which Doheny and Reilly had not accused him of "cowardice, drunkenness, envy (of themselves), and all the other deadly sins."[48]

Doheny was so incensed by McGee's remarks that he confronted him on the street and demanded a retraction. When McGee refused, Doheny punched him down a flight of stairs into a cellar. Rather than fighting back, McGee decided to prosecute Doheny for assault, "as he would any ordinary bar-room bully."[49] The case came to court the following February; Doheny pleaded guilty and was fined ten dollars. "There is not as much charged for beating an Irishman as an American, in some of our courts here," commented the *Boston Pilot*.[50] Within transatlantic Irish republican circles, Doheny was widely celebrated for his assault, and McGee was mocked for going to the law – a course of action that was seen as confirmation of his cowardice. Over the years, the story grew that Doheny had "horse-whipped" or "cow-hided" McGee, along with comments that McGee had received exactly what he deserved for his "ruffianly" behaviour.[51]

Doheny's physical attack was accompanied by a continuing barrage of verbal violence. Unlike the republican editors of the *Irishman*, who refused to print letters that criticized their position, McGee offered to open up his columns to his opponents while retaining the right of reply. In December he published, with much "personal disgust," a vitriolic letter in which Reilly claimed that McGee had conspired with the government in 1848 to create the Treason-Felony Act, as a means of removing Mitchel from the political scene. It was, responded McGee, "the most audacious thing of its kind in the entire annals of journalism"; the charge was so absurd that he had no difficulty in refuting it point by point.[52]

Reilly's letter tapped into long-standing rumours that Duffy and McGee had been "delighted to have Mitchel transported" in 1848, because Mitchel's *United Irishman* was outselling Duffy's *Nation*.[53] These accusations were boosted in December 1849 when Joseph Brenan arrived in New York. Having learned nothing from the rising of 1848, Brenan had attempted to trigger a revolution in September 1849 by launching an attack on the police barracks at Cappoquin in County Waterford. It was a complete disaster – notable mostly for the fact that its leaders later played a central role in transatlantic Fenianism.[54] After Brenan escaped to New York, McGee denounced him as "a man who asserts as truth, what he knows not to be true" – an entirely reasonable statement, given Brenan's writings in the *Irishman*. Brenan, however, did not see it this way and immediately challenged McGee to a duel; the invitation was declined.[55]

In the conflict between the Mitchelites and McGee, a pattern was developing. As editor of the *Irishman*, Brenan had censored the arguments of his enemies; in the United States, Brenan, Doheny, and Reilly spread malicious rumours about McGee and were prepared to use the threat and sometimes the actual use of physical force against him. In contrast, McGee believed that the truth would triumph in open debate; he generally (but not always) eschewed scurrilous journalism, and he maintained that personal conflicts should be settled through the rule of law rather than through duels or fights in the street. Nevertheless, after Doheny's assault, there were reports that McGee began to carry a brace of pistols to protect himself against assassination.[56]

Meanwhile, in Ireland, Duffy was fighting the same battle and was attempting to provide institutional expression for his gradualist strategy through a new political party, the Irish Alliance. In some respects, the Irish Alliance revived the pre-revolutionary position of the Irish Confederation; there would be no "place begging," no "sectarian discussions," and no partnership with the Whigs.[57] But there was an increased emphasis on securing major reforms within the Union; among other things, the Irish Alliance stood for tenant right, the disestablishment of the Church of Ireland, and a wider suffrage. In McGee's view, this strategy was the "only course left for Ireland's present redemption or future salvation."[58] To provide transatlantic support for Duffy's party, he organized the American Irish Alliance; the first meeting was scheduled for the Coliseum Rooms in New York on St Patrick's Eve, 1850.[59]

Given the failure of 1848, the embarrassment of Slievenamon, and the endemic infighting among the exiled Confederates in New York, McGee's plan was greeted with a combination of indifference, skepticism, and opposition. Dillon dismissed it as a waste of time, and other prominent Irish American leaders stayed away. The revolutionary republicans, however, showed up. Amid shouts that the meeting had been called by "the enemies of John Mitchel," Brenan and his allies in New York's Irish Regiment rushed the stage and tried to take over the proceedings. They were met with a hail of hoots and hisses, but refused to budge. McGee, confident that he could defeat his opponents in open debate, tried to secure a hearing for Brenan; the majority, however, were in no mood to let Brenan speak. One of New York's leading Irish American populist radicals, Mike Walsh, forced his way to the front and declared that such behaviour only played into the hands of those who argued that the Irish were unfit for liberty. Walsh's call for unity was greeted with loud cheers, but changed nothing. The American Irish Alliance supporters literally pulled the stage from underneath Brenan's feet, and the meeting broke up in disarray.

A second meeting was arranged for the following week, by invitation only. But Brenan and his men broke into that one as well, and the organizers were forced to reconvene at a private house. McGee tried to downplay the events and blamed the newspapers for magnifying a scuffle into a riot. Nevertheless, it was clear that the American Irish Alliance had a major struggle on its hands, and that Walsh had been correct – the conflict had indeed further damaged the reputation of the Irish in America. The whole affair, commented the *Boston Pilot*, was "a scandalous exhibition of Irish irascibility."[60]

The fracas at the Coliseum Rooms, the hostility of the *Irish American*, and intimidation on the streets only served to strengthen McGee's anti-revolutionary position. Irish liberation, he concluded, meant much more than throwing off English rule; it also meant breaking the power of unscrupulous ideologues, on the one hand, and Catholic authoritarianism, on the other: "To beat England would not be to save Ireland. Ireland in 1849, might have had need to be saved from herself, had she succeeded. If Dr. MacHale could still govern Connaught; if rowdies, such as we see here, could embroil the towns; if base dissimulating journalists and low local bigots were to lord it over Ireland – better far that she should remain ungoverned."[61] In McGee's view, Brenan, Doheny, and Reilly were Irish Jacobins who threatened liberty from below, while Catholic bishops such as MacHale with their "dictatorship and censorship" threatened liberty from above. "I am a Catholic from conviction," he wrote in 1849. "But the reign of the horsewhip and the denunciation – the reign of unreasoning, blind, obedience must end."[62]

As he searched for a middle path, McGee found himself on very narrow ground. "In this country," the Fenian John O'Leary later advised William Butler Yeats, "a man must have either the Church or the Fenians on his side."[63] During his exile in New York, McGee had alienated both the church and the forerunners of the Fenians; not surprisingly, the city's American Irish Alliance floundered and failed. "I regret to say," he told General James Shields in May 1850, "that body has not received as yet, from the Irish community, such support as all men admit it deserves."[64] McGee began to re-evaluate his position in New York and to think seriously about going back to Ireland, where he believed the real work had to be done.

————

His thoughts of returning were not only a product of political frustration; there were also changing family circumstances to take into consideration. When McGee escaped from Sligo in August 1848, Mary had remained in Dublin, partly because she was pregnant and partly because she was a defence witness in Duffy's trial. During the winter, she had made one of her few interventions in politics, defending McGee against the *Irishman*'s accusations that he had denigrated O'Brien's leadership at Ballingarry. "My husband's character is dearer to him than his life," she wrote; "and I could not be at ease while any one might suppose that he would publish a slander on the great and good man who is suffering for his country."[65]

After the birth of their first child, Martha Dorcas (named after both their mothers), Mary was "rather ill with sore breast," and McGee learned from a friend that she was looking "thin and anxious." "I begin to be rather uneasy about her," he told Aunt Bella.[66] Mary and Martha Dorcas arrived safely in New York in August 1849, accompanied by McGee's nineteen-year-old brother James, who came to help with the New York *Nation*.[67] But the move to New York did not improve Mary's condition. She may also have suffered from homesickness. According to McGee's friend John Byrne, "the state of Mrs. M'Gee's health" convinced him that he should move back home.[68] At the same time, Duffy was stretched to the limit editing the Dublin *Nation* and urged McGee to come home and help him. "If you come you had best come quickly," he wrote in April 1850. "I would expect you to commence operations here on the 1st September with the second year of the *Nation*. Thomas O'Hagan assures me you would not run the smallest risk of prosecution ... On that score there is no difficulty."[69]

So in early June 1850, to the "astonishment" of his friends, McGee announced that he was closing the New York *Nation* and returning to Ireland.[70] He planned to go on a farewell tour of New England, to visit Canada East, and to spend Independence Day in Boston, after which he would sail to Dublin and resume his work with Duffy. The days of his exile, it seemed, were finally over.

———

From the spring of 1849, McGee had been reaching towards some kind of balance between his heart and his head, his passion and his reason. Although his hostility to the British government remained undiminished, much of his anger had been directed at the politics of the Catholic Church. Britain, after all, was expected to behave like an oppressor; but the Catholic Church had betrayed the very people it was supposed to protect. "On the question of the priests you are angry, and therefore unreasonable," Duffy told him in October 1849. McGee's attacks on the church, Duffy said, were both unfair and futile; most priests had never supported the Confederation to begin with, and writing against them would only intensify their hostility. "A wise navigator," wrote Duffy, "does not preach against rocks ahead, but takes entirely different precautions."[71]

If McGee's passions pushed him into familiar patterns of reactive anger, his judgment kept pulling him back towards the centre. The attempt to navigate between extremes informed his approach on a whole range of religious, cultural, and social issues. It can be found in his warnings about the dangers of self-validating sectarian conflict, and in his insistence that Catholics should root out their own sectarian tendencies rather than simply casting all the blame on the other side. It lay behind his changing views on the relationship between tradition and modernity; the cultural legacy of the Celtic past, he believed, must be balanced with the needs of the future in the same way that a balance had to be struck between Irish ethnicity and assimilation in the United States. And it informed his new attitude to teetotalism, his first cause; rather than supporting total abstinence, McGee argued that "teetotallers, like all new-light moralists, insist on their theory beyond its bounds," and he now stressed the importance of moderation.[72]

Above all, though, the quest for balance brought him into the nationalist middle ground, between O'Connellism on one side and revolutionary republicanism on the other. As we have seen, the Mitchelites – who had never trusted McGee to begin with – responded with a storm of criticism. Ironically, the intensity of the republican attack triggered in McGee the very kind of extreme reaction that he had been trying to escape, as he passionately defended the pragmatic centre against revolutionary purism. Significantly, McGee's major battles during the winter of 1849–50 were fought with the republican left rather than the religious right. As he took on the Mitchelites, he began to tone down his attacks on the politics of the Catholic Church. This was partly because Duffy's message, twice repeated, was finally getting through to him, and partly because McGee was coming to believe that republicanism was a more serious threat to the Irish nation than Catholicism.

By June 1850, McGee was even arguing that in certain circumstances – a great national crisis, for example, or "invasions from without or within" – priests not only could but should "interfere in politics," provided that the civil power approved.[73] McGee had not, at this stage, fully thought through the possible implications of supporting clerical intervention against "invasions from within," and he had failed to define what he meant by a "great national crisis." But if, in the summer of 1850, he had been forced to choose between revolutionary nationalism and the Catholic Church, between Mitchel and MacHale, there is little doubt which way he would have turned.

CHAPTER ELEVEN

An Unequivocal Catholic Spirit
August 1850 – June 1852

In the event, McGee did not go back home. He received word from Dublin that he would be prosecuted for high treason if he returned to Ireland, and decided not to take the risk.[1] Meanwhile, at the end of June, a group of his Irish American admirers in Boston invited him to start a newspaper in the city, with their financial support.[2] He accepted the offer and arrived during the summer. While he was preparing for his new position, he became the foreign news editor of the *Boston Daily Times*, writing a regular column for the paper during the late summer and fall. Aiming to counter the prejudices of British newspapers with "real facts," the column focused on "Irish, Scotch, and German news," and combined foreign reports with pen portraits of British and Irish radicals, ranging from William Cobbett to Gavan Duffy.[3] But most of his energy was directed towards his own newspaper, whose first issue appeared in late August. "I desire to begin anew – to commence on a clean tablet, with fresh pencils," he wrote, "and to avoid in the next newspaper, the errors and omissions of the past."[4]

His decision to stay in the United States has sometimes been seen as the beginning of his transition from exile to immigrant.[5] Although there is some truth in this, McGee still saw himself primarily as an Irishman who was living in America and, *pari passu*, as part of an international Celtic community. This was reflected in the name of his newspaper, the *American Celt*, and in its opening poem, "Salutation to the Celts": "One in name, and in fame, / Are the world-divided Gaels." The paper's masthead depicted a proud Hibernia holding a harp and saluting across the Atlantic, above the words of William Drennan's

well-known poem "Erin": "Her back turn'd to Britain, her face to
the west."[6]

The name of the paper was also chosen with immediate American circumstances in mind, as a riposte to those who believed that
Anglo-Saxonism was the secret of America's success. The *American Celt*
intended to "adopt the opposite side of a popular theory, namely: that
all modern civilization and intelligence — whatever is best and most
vital in modern society, came in with the Saxons or Anglo-Saxons."
The Celts, McGee argued, were "a People brave, zealous for liberty,
jealous of religious rites, capable of the highest discipline, and wielding
the divinest powers of mind."[7]

As a self-styled Celt in the United States, McGee looked for practical ways to improve the condition of Ireland. Among other things, he
revived a theme that he had first raised during his Young Ireland days
— the establishment of a commercial union between the United States
and Ireland, with Galway as the focal point for American exports to
Europe.[8] In the short run, he believed, this would inject prosperity into
the poverty stricken west of Ireland, and in the long run it would eman-
cipate Ireland from British economic domination: "It would assuredly,
proclaim a new age and herald in a new existence for old Ireland."[9]

This was more than a vague aspiration. In the summer of 1850,
McGee attended the Portland Railway Convention, where politicians
from the Maritimes and Maine planned a railway line from Portland
to Halifax, along with a shipping route from Halifax to Galway; the
new Galway-Dublin railway would also be integrated into the system.
The idea was to cut the transatlantic crossing to five days.[10] To secure
a loan for the project, the Nova Scotia government sent Joseph Howe
to London; meanwhile, McGee vigorously promoted the project in the
American Celt.[11]

But the British government refused to support the plan. Powerful
Liverpool business interests opposed anything that would weaken their
city's transatlantic trade, while imperial politicians preferred an east-
west rail link in British North America to north-south connections
with the United States. By the time Howe returned to Nova Scotia, he

had switched sides and accepted the British position. This did nothing to improve McGee's image of the British Empire. Ireland's needs had been sacrificed to imperial interests, he declared, and Howe was nothing more than a "pimp" and a "place beggar."[12]

As well as bringing Irish American support to bear on the Galway project, McGee backed the Tenant League that Gavan Duffy and Charles Lucas established in August 1850, with the objective of securing fixity of tenure and rent reductions for Irish farmers. The land question was fundamental to Ireland's post-famine reconstruction, McGee argued, and could be settled only by replacing the old aristocracy with a new class of owner-occupiers – something that he thought was already happening. He pointed out that the famine had bankrupted many landlords, and believed that the Encumbered Estates Act of 1849 – which could compel indebted landlords to sell their land – was paving the way for a massive transfer of land to Irish farmers.[13] Convinced that Catholic and Protestant farmers were uniting to build a "new society," McGee set about raising money for the movement.[14] Most Irish Americans, he told Duffy, had left Ireland to escape excessive rents and had a deeply ingrained hostility to landlordism; if this potential was tapped, funds would quickly flow across the Atlantic.[15]

In his support for the Galway project and the Tenant League, McGee was attempting to fill the post-1848 political vacuum with economic and social initiatives that supposedly promised "the salvation of Ireland."[16] Yet as with his political writings in Young Ireland, wishful thinking triumphed over objective reality. The Encumbered Estates Act did not in fact undermine Irish landlordism, and there was no movement towards peasant proprietorship; similarly, the Tenant League failed to establish a durable Catholic-Protestant alliance or to change the system of tenure.[17] During the early 1850s, the prospect of reform in Ireland seemed only slightly less remote than that of republican revolution.

Meanwhile, the failure of 1848 presented McGee and his fellow émigrés in America with a more specific problem – the fate of the Confederate leaders who had been transported to Australia for their role in the rising. In the summer and fall of 1850, McGee participated in the Irish American campaign for their release, sometimes in the teeth of deep divisions between physical- and moral-force nationalists.[18] As the campaign continued, he gathered signatures for a petition to President Millard Fillmore, requesting him to exert diplomatic pressure on the British government for the release of the prisoners.[19] In January 1852, McGee joined the Irish American delegation that presented the petition to Fillmore at the White House. The president gave them a sympathetic hearing while telling them that the United States could not interfere in the internal affairs of another state. In reply, McGee explained that they sought "mediation" rather than "intervention," and gently urged the American government to do all it could "for our dear friends in exile." The meeting was harmonious, but the results were disappointing.[20]

Throughout all these campaigns, McGee sought to strengthen Irish American political power by encouraging immigrants to become citizens, with full voting rights. The issue was so important to him that in January 1851 he changed the name of his newspaper to the *American Celt and Adopted Citizen*.[21] Half a million Irish voters in the United States, he maintained, could form a powerful Irish American lobby group in support of the Galway project, the Tenant League, and the release of Young Ireland prisoners. At the same time, and somewhat contradictorily, American citizenship would prevent the Irish from being regarded as "aliens" in the United States. Here was the perfect way to challenge anti-Catholic organizations such as the United American Mechanics, to combat the emerging "British Party" in the seaboard cities, and to create a Celtic counterweight to American Anglo-Saxonism. Once they found their collective political voice, the Irish could transform the social character of the United States. Within ten years, he predicted, "America will be no longer Anglo-Saxon, in tone and temper, but semi-Celtic, in heart and purpose."[22]

These ideas were encapsulated in McGee's *History of the Irish Settlers in North America*, which he completed on St Patrick's Day, 1851. The first book to be written on the Irish in America, it pioneered a long historiographical tradition and proved to be immensely popular, running into six editions by 1855. It was a masterpiece of myth making, which could easily have been entitled "How the Irish Saved North American Civilization." Presenting the illusion of Irish unity, McGee asserted that the "whole Irish race" supported the American Revolution, and portrayed the "proto-martyr" Montgomery (with whom he had been "bored to death" only the previous year) and the "soldier-statesman" Andrew Jackson as exemplars of the true Irish spirit.[23] Irish American heroes were contrasted with a variety of villains, ranging from Indian "savages" and British oppressors to American nativists. All these enemies had been overcome, he declared, even though nativism was still alive and kicking in the eastern seaboard cities. The overall image of the Irish in the United States was one of remarkable success; they had spread democracy and Catholicism throughout North America, they were prominent in business, politics, and the military, and they helped to keep the continent "anti-British in temper and policy."[24]

McGee's book was not only a classic example of ethnic filiopietism; it also helped to fix the "famine as genocide" myth within Irish American nationalism. He had, of course, already made this argument during his Young Ireland years; now, in one of the most widely read Irish American books of the nineteenth century, he pressed home the point: "There were grain crops more than sufficient to support the entire population. But to all remonstrances, petitions, and proposals, the imperial economists had but one answer, 'they could not interfere with the ordinary currents of trade.'"[25]

The dominant emotions in McGee's book were anger at Britain and pride in the accomplishments of the Irish in America. Along with the anger there was the possibility of revenge; pondering Edmund Spenser's remark that Ireland might one day stand as a judgment on England, McGee suggested that the Irish in America were well placed to fulfill the prophecy. And along with the pride there was the possibility of still greater achievements. The purpose of his book, he wrote, was not to "gratify vanity" but to encourage Irish Americans to emulate the example of their illustrious predecessors and seize the unprecedented opportunities that were opening up in the American Northwest. Through education, energy, sobriety, and hard work, they could become successful farmers and model American citizens: "No people – not even the natives of New England – have a greater interest in the preservation of the Union, than the Celts in America. What we never got from England, we have here, – equal laws and equal justice."[26]

———•••———

This portrait of the Irish as a proud, principled, and patriotic people permeated the columns of the *American Celt,* where he continually attacked any manifestations of the traditional Paddy stereotype. ("Paddy," he later wrote, was "a New-England coined term of general reproach"; in Britain and Ireland, the abbreviation was simply "Pat.")[27] Particularly demeaning were the "stage Irish" routines that characterized American theatre: "Some adventurer and his trull picks up a few points of Irish mis-pronunciation, furnishes himself with a commodity of dilapidated hats and cloths, a cudgel and a 'cutty,' and bounces, in on the stage, singing a doggerel ballad, or blaspheming the sacred name of our Saviour. With an idiotic 'whoop!' he comes on, presents his mistress with a present of potatoes he has brought her in his pocket, and with a leer and a low grimace bounces off, loudly applauded." What was especially galling about this "vile trash" was that the loud applause came largely from "Irish men, women and families" in the audience. "If a Race are so lost to the keen sense of national character as to keep their own worst libellants in cash and countenance," he wrote, "of a certainty they deserve to be the pitied and scorn'd, fag-end of all Humanity." They should hoot the actors off the stage or, better still, stay away from the theatre altogether, "unless when some approved piece is presented."[28]

The actual Irish people, unlike the ideal, had a nagging habit of letting McGee down. They had failed to join the rising of 1848, they were deficient in matters of cleanliness, sobriety, and honesty, and they relished their image as whooping, blaspheming, happy-go-lucky potato eaters.[29] All the more reason, then, for "social training" in the virtues of respectability and self-help, until they earned the middle-class stamp of approval.

A similar concern with establishing Irish credentials as respectable patriots lay behind McGee's assertion that the "Celts in America" were the strongest supporters of the American Union. He attacked both the "angry agitators in the South" who spoke of secession and the "absurd theorists in the North" whose antislavery arguments, he was convinced, threatened to plunge the country into civil war.[30] McGee welcomed the Compromise of 1850 as the best way to preserve national unity, and argued that all Americans were duty bound to support the new Fugitive Slave Law. Those who counselled resistance to it, he wrote, were nothing less than traitors.[31] Like many of his United Irish predecessors, McGee pushed the argument further and maintained that the Irish were actually more oppressed than the Afro-Americans. The New England abolitionists, he declared, "would rouse the community to treason, for some score colored fugitives, yet they look on mute and insensible – nay satisfied and in admiration of England, while tens of thousands of her white fugitives land upon these shores, more ill-abused in body, and more darkened in intellect, even than the Negro."[32]

Accordingly, McGee was outraged when a group of Afro-Americans rescued the fugitive slave Shadrach Minkins from a Boston courtroom in February 1851. Their action, he wrote, portended "danger to the Union, civil war, separation, weakness, partial legislation, and the general depression of liberty everywhere." For Minkins, however, it meant freedom in Montreal, where he and his fellow Afro-Americans subsequently described themselves as "loyal and dutiful subjects" of the Crown, with "rights and privileges as Free Citizens."[33] Six years after condemning Minkins's rescue, McGee himself moved to Montreal and wrote in similar terms about his loyalty to British North America. It is not known whether the two men ever encountered each other on the city's streets.

More immediately, McGee's abolitionist opponents were quick to point out that a man who had fled from an "arbitrary sedition law" in Ireland was now supporting an even more draconian law in America. As one rival newspaper asked, "How would this Thomas D'Arcy McGee like to be delivered up to the tender mercies of Lord Clarendon under a treaty with Great Britain? What would he say to a law delivering up fugitive Irishmen on claim of owing service or labor? If there ever was a reptile that deserved to be spit upon and spurned from the footstool with loathing, scorn and everlasting contempt, it is the fugitive Irishman, who swaggers and plays the bloodhound against the fugitive negro."[34] McGee denied that there was anything inconsistent about his position: in Ireland, he had been fighting against a government that violated the national will; in the United States, he was upholding laws that reflected the national will.[35]

Central to his position was the assumption that political actions should be assessed by potential consequences rather than first principles. He occasionally reminded his readers that he did not approve of slavery in principle, but he more frequently insisted that the abolitionist ideas of the "ultra theorists of New England" would have disastrous results in practice.[36] The most likely outcome, he believed, would be a war that would cost countless lives and break up the country; the "Empire of Liberty" would be shattered, and Britain would reassert its influence on the continent.

The same pragmatic outlook lay behind his attitude to Irish revolutionary republican nationalism; although separatist republicanism was all well and good in theory, any attempt to implement it in the circumstances of post-1848 and post-famine Ireland would culminate in bloodshed, failure, and a loyalist backlash. Like Edmund Burke – whom he had been reading in the winter of 1850–51 – McGee believed that the "rights of men in governments are their advantages; and these are often in balances between differences of good; in compromises sometimes between good and evil, and sometimes, between evil and evil."[37] In the case of Ireland, this political reasoning led him to his "modified moral force" position; in the case of America, it led him to support the slave catchers who tried to return Shadrach Minkins to Virginia.

Up to this point, in the spring of 1851, McGee was very much in the mainstream of transatlantic constitutional nationalism. His support for the Galway project and the Tenant League, his agitation on behalf of the Young Ireland prisoners, his attempt to increase Irish American political power, and his efforts to turn his countrymen into respectable and prosperous middle-class citizens all fitted neatly with his ambition to become "the Duffy of our Emigrants." But running through these endeavours, and occasionally glimpsed in his subordinate clauses, lay a growing conviction that the world was changing in fundamental ways, and that Europe and America were in the first throes of a major and decisive conflict between Catholic Celts and Protestant Anglo-Saxons.

During the winter of 1850–51, he sensed that the walls were closing in on Catholics in general, and on Irish Catholics in particular. And the more he came to think and feel this way, the more he gravitated towards the kind of defensive and aggressive Catholicism that had character-ized his reaction to the Philadelphia riots of 1844. The man who had moved from revolutionary republicanism to constitutional nationalism was about to shift still further to the right, to jettison his moderate liberalism and to embrace an extreme form of Catholic conservatism. It was a trajectory that surprised and shocked his former Young Ire-land allies, none of whom had any knowledge of his earlier American writings. Had it been otherwise, they might have guessed that similar circumstances would push McGee in a similar direction.

McGee's conversion to ultramontanism must be located in the con-text of changing Protestant-Catholic relations on both sides of the Atlantic. In England, a resurgent Catholic Church, its numbers boosted by pre-famine and famine Irish migrants, decided to place itself on a firmer organizational foundation; for the first time since the Reforma-tion, it took steps to establish a diocesan structure with bishops and an archbishop. Such "papal aggression," as the *Times* called it, produced an immediate and intense Protestant reaction, which found political expression in Lord John Russell's Ecclesiastical Titles Bill. The new legislation not only prohibited the diocesan organization of the Catho-lic Church in Britain but was extended to Ireland, where the structure was already an accepted fact of life.[38]

Irish Catholics were outraged, and McGee was no exception. Rus-sell, he wrote, was a "new Cromwell"; England was little more than a slave state, characterized by "No-Popery frenzy" and controlled by a hereditary Protestant caste; the Ecclesiastical Titles Bill was a new Penal Law, which would suffer the same ignominious fate as its pre-decessors. In response, the Irish must form a Catholic party in Britain and work with the "Friends of Religious Liberty" to defeat the legisla-tion. And defeat it they surely would: "The whole policy of 'the Ref-ormation,' will go down, in the next conflict," he declared. "Root and branch, Tithes and Peerage, will be utterly extinguished."[39]

McGee's position, it should be noted, implicitly accepted the framework of the Union, at least in the short run; his answer to the Ecclesiastical Titles Bill was an Irish-led Catholic party to protect Catholic interests in Ireland and Britain. In taking this position, McGee was moving with majority opinion in Catholic Ireland and Irish America. But he was also moving farther away from his earlier ecumenicalism. It was difficult, after all, to be ecumenical when mainstream Protestants were denouncing Catholicism and when the British prime minister was publicly associating the Catholic religion with "the mummeries of superstition."[40]

The Protestant attack on Catholicism in Britain and Ireland not only prompted McGee to call for a Catholic political party; it also made him rethink his earlier position on non-denominational education. If Irish Catholics were under threat – and he had no doubt that they were – it was imperative that they protect their children from Protestant proselytizers. Thus he fully supported the position taken by a narrow majority of the Synod of Thurles that Catholics must reject Peel's secular colleges and form their own university. "If the Queen's Colleges are unworthy of the confidence of Catholic parents," he wrote in 1850, "then the sooner, the new University is established, the better for Ireland and Religion." This was a complete reversal of the position he had taken the previous year, when he argued that secular university education would diminish sectarian prejudices in Ireland.[41]

If McGee's sense that Catholicism was under siege had been formed by events in Britain and Ireland, it was strengthened by his own immediate experiences in Boston. He subsequently wrote that his political and religious views began to change after he moved to the city from New York in the summer of 1850.[42] In New York, he observed, Irish Catholics were confident and assertive; but in Boston, the "Unitarian city" where Cromwell was "considered as Washington's counterpart," they were a beleaguered minority.[43] "There is much bigotry exhibited about Boston," he remarked in February 1851.[44]

In Boston, it became increasingly difficult for McGee to combine liberalism and Catholicism. He had arrived in the city with a reputation as a liberal who had taken on Bishop Hughes and had asserted that priests and bishops had no right to interfere in politics. One of the most attractive features of his liberalism, for his Boston supporters, was its emphasis on intellectual independence; people who were attacking the Catholic Church as a threat to American liberty found much to admire in McGee's earlier New York writings. But this put McGee in an increasingly uncomfortable position. Although he had rejected the church's involvement in politics, he remained part of the Catholic community, and had always identified with the church's moral and religious (as opposed to political) teachings. The longer he stayed in the city, the greater grew the tension between his liberalism and his Catholicism.

What brought this tension close to the breaking point was the Treanor libel case of early 1851, a forgotten but important episode in McGee's American career. As we have seen, Bernard Treanor was a former member of the Stalybridge Confederate Club in England and had met McGee in Manchester in 1847; during the following year, he supported the revolutionary movement in Dublin.[45] After the failure of the rising, Treanor moved to Boston, where he became a trade union organizer, and he was among those who invited McGee to the city in the summer of 1850. The *Boston Pilot*, now under clerical influence and edited by Father John Roddan, opposed the invitation. An article in the newspaper commented that McGee's backers were "as disgusting a set of brawlers as ever pandered to the anti-Catholic – no-Popery – priest-hating prejudices of the enemies of God and His Church." The article went on to claim that Treanor had been fired from one labour organization, and implied that he was currently swindling another.[46] Not surprisingly, Treanor demanded a public apology. When one was not forthcoming, he decided to sue Patrick Donahoe, the paper's proprietor, for libel.

The case came to court on 7 February 1851. Donahoe was found guilty, which seemed only reasonable in the circumstances. But the jury went farther and awarded Treanor $1,800 damages, plus costs – a staggering sum by the standards of the day.[47] During the subsequent appeal, the judges agreed that the damages were "much larger" than they would have given, but nevertheless upheld the jury's verdict.[48] In the trial, Treanor's lawyer had portrayed the *Boston Pilot* as an intolerant Catholic newspaper, and noted that Donahoe had supported the suppression of the American Protestant chapel in Rome.[49] Convinced that the heavy damages stemmed from the anti-Catholic prejudices of an all-Protestant jury, the *Boston Pilot* argued that the libel suit was an attempt by McGee and his supporters to destroy their principal rival. In the *Boston Pilot*'s view, McGee was merely the latest in a long line of "young, vain and self-willed agitators who have, in every age, lifted up their hands against the church."[50]

The charge hit home; the inner contradictions in McGee's position were becoming intolerable. On the one hand, he believed that Catholicism was everywhere under attack. Across the Atlantic, he could point to the Ecclesiastical Titles Bill, Russell's contemptuous remark about the mummeries of superstition, and the continuing power of the Protestant Ascendancy in Ireland. In the United States, prominent politicians were boasting about their Protestant heritage and talking about a transatlantic Anglo-Saxon alliance. Abbott Lawrence, the Boston businessman who served as the American minister to Britain, declared that the United States was a second England in laws, religion, and policy, and described the Americans as a Protestant Anglo-Saxon people.[51]

On the other hand, McGee was identified with what appeared to be a Protestant backlash against Boston's leading Catholic newspaper, and he was being cheered on by those who feared Catholic power in America. He later described the libel case as the only unpleasant part of his time in Boston – and no wonder.[52] "I may have misled others, since I so misguided myself," he said in 1853. "What excited my apprehension was, that those whom I knew to be the social enemies of our religion and race, applauded my career. I hesitated – I reflected – I repented."[53]

Although the debate between the *American Celt* and the *Boston Pilot* over the libel case remained vigorous, there were some indications that reconciliation could be reached. McGee dissociated himself from the Protestant press in the city and maintained that the libel action had occurred without his knowledge or approval. For its part, the *Boston Pilot* argued that McGee was sincere but tragically mistaken, and trusted that "the time will come when he will have other ideas, and other associates." He was intelligent but immature, the paper added: "Talented boys always make this mistake, and when they become greyheaded, they say, – what fools we were, in our young days."[54] If the comment was patronizing, it also turned out to be prescient; McGee would indeed look back on his youth in this way, using the very words that Roddan, the paper's editor, had predicted.

***

While the Treanor libel case embroiled McGee in what appeared to be a broader Protestant assault on Catholicism, the Henry Lytton Bulwer controversy of April 1851 strengthened his belief that there was an equally aggressive Saxon campaign against the Celts. The controversy began when McGee published what he described as an "intercepted dispatch" between Bulwer, who was the British minister to the United States, and Lord Palmerston, Britain's foreign secretary. By a remarkable coincidence, the "dispatch" confirmed in detail McGee's long-standing arguments that Britain was fomenting American political divisions over slavery, and that the American Irish, if they ever acted as a unified force, constituted the greatest threat to British machinations. It was all too good to be true: either McGee was gullible enough to believe that he had received a genuine document or, much more likely, he wrote it himself.[55]

Had Bulwer simply denied writing the letter, that would probably have been the end of the matter. Instead, he delivered a speech to the St George's Society of New York that brought down the house:

> Although *it is natural to conjecture from the semi-barbarous, semi-clad, and Celtic origin of my Boston friend* – (laughter) – that he had been guilty of the crime of which he boasted, namely, theft – he has in reality been guilty of an offence which more appropriately belongs to a farther advanced stage of pantaloons and refinement – (laughter) – I mean forgery; another example, by the way, of the general maxim, *that all savages, whether Celtic, or otherwise,* when they take to inhabiting cities, even such moral cities as Boston, adopt the vices, without acquiring the virtues or graces of civilized life. – (Cheers and laughter.)[56]

It is not clear what incensed McGee more – Bulwer's "insolent phraseology," as he put it, or the fact that the audience lapped it up. The issue of forgery faded into the background; many Irish Americans were insulted by the speech and demanded Bulwer's recall. Bulwer backtracked as fast as he could, explaining that it had all been in "good humour" and that of course he had never intended to suggest that the Irishman or Welshman of today was a savage.[57] Neither McGee nor his former Confederate colleagues saw the joke; for McGee, Bulwer's comments, along with the cheers and laughter, were further proof of Saxon prejudice. Just as Protestants were hammering Catholicism, the Saxons were hammering the Celts. Enough was enough; it was time to take a stand.

And take a stand he did. On 17 May 1851 he made an announcement that stunned his liberal and Protestant readers, and gladdened the hearts of conservative Catholics. "After much reflection," he wrote, "it is made plain to us that a state of social hostility exists between citizens of Saxon and Celtic origin in the old Atlantic States. – There is a war without the forms of war – a struggle to exclude one race from power, reputation, and wealth, and to secure all these to another race. – There are no proclamations, banners, or bugle-calls, but there is conspiracy, contempt and a most insatiable avarice of all authority." It was a religious as well as racial war, he declared. Celts were Catholics, Anglo-Saxons were Protestants, and religious reconciliation was impossible: "Our first great difference with the Anglo-Saxons is, we have a creed and they have none." And it was a war in which one side or the other must prevail: "We must, in one word, beat down the Anglo-Saxon aristocracy, or they will continue to force us down, lower and lower."[58]

Neutrality was out of the question, and moderation was misguided. McGee had moved into a black-and-white world of conspiracy and conflict, in which compromise was unconscionable. With Protestant readers accusing him of bigotry and cancelling their subscriptions in droves, McGee dug himself in more deeply. His "A Catechism and a Confession," published on 31 May, asserted that Catholicism was the One True Faith and that Protestants were simply wrong; they were heretics who had persecuted the faithful and whose liberalism (or "selfish rationalism") was just as anti-Catholic as their religion. He declared that "Protestantism was no religion; that it had no apostolicity, no unity, no authority; that what was blooming in its gardens was gone before the winter; that sect begat sect, as crackers ignite and explode each other; that in short it might be a Philosophy, or a rule, of living, more or less complete, but that, it had no creed, no Theology, no inspiration."

As devious as they were heretical, Anglo-Saxon Protestants were employing a range of literary, historical, and educational weapons to destroy Catholic Celts, he maintained. Popular English writings were poisoning American minds with negative images of the Celts as lazy, incompetent, superstitious savages. Protestant history books glorified tyrants such as Queen Elizabeth and Oliver Cromwell while denigrating the brave Celts who fought for their faith and nation. But most insidious of all, the Protestants tried "to steal our children, so that they make them apostates to our Faith, and scorners of our history." "The tactique of Anglo-Saxon Protestantism here is to catch the second generation," he wrote. "To snare the souls of our children. To leave our emigrants heirless in faith, in this land of their adoption."[59]

If his Protestant readers were offended by all this, too bad. From now on, the *American Celt* was going to be conducted along Catholic lines and would devote more space to Catholic news. Henceforth, McGee wrote, he would adopt "an unequivocal Catholic spirit." When his original backers recoiled in horror, McGee replaced them with Thomas Sweeney, a Catholic bookseller, and eventually took over the paper himself, with the help of his brother James. "If we mistake not, he is already beginning to know who his friends are," commented the *Boston Pilot* in June. And those friends were ultramontanist to a man.[60]

McGee's new friends were part of a conservative Catholic intellectual world that spoke to his condition. External circumstances and the internal tensions they generated propelled him towards an intensely emotional conversion experience, and made him highly receptive to writings that he had previously denounced as "slavish ultramontane dogmas."[61] The conversion experience appears to have been as sudden as it was profound, and took him back into the imagined security of an idealized childhood. "When I saw the beautiful but terrible brow of our august Mother and Mistress unbend," he recalled, "and heard

John Fitzpatrick, bishop of Boston (1812–66). McGee's second cousin on his mother's side, Fitzpatrick became bishop of Boston, his native city, in 1846. During the mid-1850s, he noted with satisfaction that McGee had repudiated his Young Ireland politics and was "now truly converted and labouring with sincerity and success for the cause of religion." Fitzpatrick might have added that he played a large part in McGee's conversion in the spring of 1851.

accents sweeter than an Angel's, coming from lips that I knew had power to bid the lightnings strike wheresoever her finger pointed, I felt my childhood come back upon me ... I think the charity of every true Catholic, whether so born, or by conversion, will enable him to feel what I felt then."[62] His intellectual rebirth, in contrast, had a much longer gestation, and was deeply influenced by both his immediate environment and his wider reading.

A pivotal figure in Boston was his second cousin, Bishop John Fitz-patrick, who had become an ultramontane during his education in Paris, and who insisted on a strict adherence to orthodox Catholic theology and doctrine; rather than making the teachings of the church adapt to society, Fitzpatrick believed, Catholics must ensure that society adapted to the teachings of the church.[63] Equally important was Father John Roddan, who had undergone his own transition from liberalism to conservatism over the previous year, and who taught McGee his "first satisfactory lessons as to the real designs of radicalism."[64] But the men who played the greatest role in his intellectual and religious transformation – the "three masters," as he put it – were Edmund Burke, Jaime Luciano Balmez, and Orestes A. Brownson.[65]

Having been engaged in a series of politically ferocious and personally unpleasant battles with Mitchelite republicans, it is not surprising that McGee increasingly identified with Burke's attacks on British and Irish Jacobins during the 1790s. Burke had characterized the French Revolution as *a Revolution of doctrine and theoretick dogma*," and had denounced its supporters as men who would sacrifice living individuals for utopian abstractions. In Burke's view, Jacobinism inexorably culminated in terror, the tyranny of the majority, and the destruction of religion. There was much here that McGee recognized. He believed that the Mitchelites were latter-day Jacobins – ideologically intransigent and irreligious demagogues who believed that the ends justified the means, and who must be fought in the same manner, with the same weapons and same intensity that Burke had employed against their eighteenth-century prototypes.[66]

In combating Mitchelism, McGee asserted Burkean values – respect for tradition, the concept of society as a compact between "those who are living, those who are dead, and those who are to be born," and the belief that reason could not in itself control passions and restructure society.[67] Like Burke, McGee emphasized the importance of complexity, circumstances, and caution in political matters, and argued that the greatest threat to "real liberty" came from below rather than above. Order, authority, social cohesiveness, and religious morality were all needed to counter the disruptive forces of democratic individualism. Perhaps most significantly, McGee also came to share Burke's view that the French Revolution was comparable to the Reformation, and that the best bulwark against revolutionary ideology was the Roman Catholic religion.[68]

Although this helps to explain McGee's conservatism, it does not account for its ultramontane content. For that, we have to turn to the second figure in McGee's "triumvirate of authority,"[69] Jaime Luciano Balmez. A Catalonian priest with a brain "like a boiling cauldron,"[70] Balmez was one of the most influential Catholic writers of the nineteenth century. His best-known work, *Protestantism and Catholicity Compared in their Effects on the Civilization of Europe*, was translated into English in 1849; the first American edition came out the following year, and McGee read it in early 1851. For the next three years, McGee's writings on religion were virtually indistinguishable from those of Balmez.

The key questions in life, stated Balmez, were both simple and profound: "What am I? whence do I come? what is my destination?"[71] Only the Catholic Church had the right answers; the tragedy of the modern world was the heresy of Protestantism, which had got the answers terribly wrong. "Before Protestantism," Balmez wrote, "European civilization had reached all the development that was possible for it; Protestantism perverted the course of civilization, and produced immense evils in modern society; the progress which has been made since Protestantism, had been made not by it, but in spite of it."[72] The fundamental problem with Protestantism, argued Balmez, was that it substituted "private judgment for public and lawful authority."[73] Although it pretended to be about freedom of thought and the spirit of liberty, the Reformation was actually the work of proud, ambitious, self-seeking, and intolerant men, who shattered European unity and disrupted the social order.

On one side was the true Christian religion; on the other was a "whirlwind of Protestant sects."[74] Rejecting all authority but its own, Protestantism was inherently fissiparous, a breeding ground for all kinds of fanaticism, and a pathway to deism and atheism. Not only that, but Protestants had misrepresented Catholicism as a religion that was hostile to liberty and civilization. Yet the opposite was true, argued Balmez: the Catholic church had *"civilized the nations who embraced her, and civilization is true liberty."*[75] Catholicism had spread the morality of Jesus Christ throughout Europe, brought order and knowledge into a world of chaos and ignorance, abolished slavery, improved the condition of women, fostered "gentleness of manners," and checked arbitrary power.[76]

In fact, it was actually Protestantism that fostered tyrannical governments, asserted Balmez. Once the moral authority of Catholicism had been undermined, governments increasingly relied on physical force to control their populations. Protestantism was simply incapable of imposing religious morality on society. "Catholicity," in contrast, "having constantly maintained the principle of authority which Protestantism rejects, has given to moral ideas a force and influence which Protestantism could not."[77] The Catholic Church watched over public morality with "extreme vigilance," and fought error whenever and wherever it appeared; tolerating human frailties was one thing, but tolerating heresy was out of the question. Catholics, wrote Balmez, "consider error in regard to great moral and religious truths, as one of the greatest offences which man can commit against God."[78] The Spanish Inquisition had to be understood in this context. Despite a few local difficulties about its "excessive severities," Balmez viewed the Inquisition as a necessary defensive measure against threats to the faith emanating from Jews, Moors, and Protestants.[79]

All these ideas resonated with McGee's experiences and resurfaced in his writings. Balmez's analysis of revolutionaries in the Reformation echoed Burke's analysis of Jacobins in the French Revolution, and corresponded with McGee's attitude to the Mitchelites. Balmez's argument that Protestantism fuelled sectarian fanaticism fitted with McGee's belief that there was too much licentious individualism in the United States and too little order, authority, and morality. And Balmez's defence of the church was perfectly suited to McGee's situation in Boston, where anti-Catholicism appeared to be increasing at an alarming rate. Thus, McGee absorbed Balmez's ideas, including his defence of the Spanish Inquisition, and transmitted them to a wider audience through the *American Celt*, applying them to the specific issues that arose each week.[80]

McGee's third "master" was Orestes Brownson, the Boston-based editor of the *Quarterly Review*. One of nineteenth-century America's most brilliant intellectuals, Brownson had travelled through the religious spectrum in much the same way that McGee had moved through the political. Initially a Presbyterian, Brownson had become a Universalist, a Unitarian, and a Transcendentalist before converting to Catholicism in 1844, partly under the influence of Bishop Fitzpatrick.

Orestes Brownson (1803–76). Along with Bishop Fitzpatrick, Brownson was a pivotal figure in McGee's conversion to ultramontanism and a major influence on McGee's new conservative philosophy. In 1854 Brownson and McGee fell out when Brownson argued that immigrants should be permanently excluded from the franchise. Their differences deepened the following year, when McGee visited Ireland and publicly criticized the American way of life, and when Brownson opposed McGee's project to establish Irish Catholic colonies in Canada and the American West. (*Magazine and Democratic Review*, April 1843)

At last, he had seen the light: The Catholic Church, with its spiritual authority emanating from Rome, was the embodiment of God's eternal truth.

Like Bishop Fitzpatrick, Brownson argued that this God-given truth must be rigorously applied to changing social and individual circumstances, and that it provided a powerful antidote to the twin American evils of individualism and indifferentism. And like Balmez, he viewed Protestantism as a destructive social and political force. "The

Protestant, as such," Brownson wrote, "has, in the ordinary sense, no principles to maintain, no character to support, no consistency to preserve; and we are aware of no authority, no law, no usage, by which he will consent to be bound." When it came to the salvation of souls and the religious character of society, there could be no compromise with such heretics.[81]

In 1852 McGee's close friend James Sadlier told Brownson, "McGee owes his present course to the Bishop of Boston and yourself, and in bringing him back to the right track you have done a good work."[82] McGee praised Brownson's theological articles as being "full of profound distinction and exposition."[83] Before long, they were working together – and, behind the scenes, with Bishop Fitzpatrick – in the Massachusetts Central Society for the Promotion of Naturalization, which encouraged Irish immigrants to become citizens and to throw their political weight against abolitionists and Free Soil Democrats.[84]

Through his connections in Boston and his reading of Burke and Balmez, McGee was drawn to the intellectuals who towered over the European conservative Catholic tradition – the seventeenth-century French bishop, Jacques Bossuet, whose theological attacks on Protestantism were a source of inspiration for subsequent generations, and the anti-Enlightenment thinker, Joseph de Maistre, whose work *Du Pape* became a foundation text of ultramontanism. "We now hold to the general system of Bossuet, Burke, de Maistre, and Balmez," McGee wrote, "instead of the system of Paine, Priestley, and Fourier." His politics, as he put it, had "undergone a fundamental change." He had moved as far as it was possible to get from his revolutionary republicanism of 1848–49.[85]

⁕

With his Catholic conservatism and his conviction that he was living through an undeclared war of religion, McGee viewed Britain as the greatest enemy to the Catholic faith, the Irish nation, and the American republic; his ultramontanism was inseparable from his anglophobia. McGee's anger reached its peak when he learned of the census of 1851, which revealed that Ireland's population had fallen from eight to six million people over the previous decade. Here was stark and shocking statistical proof of the magnitude of the famine. Exaggerating an already terrible situation, and ignoring the role of emigration in the statistics, McGee exploded with rage. The British government, he declared, had "destroyed THREE MILLIONS of human beings, and procured abortions to the extent of ONE MILLION MORE." "Gloss it over as ye will, statesmen and journalists of Great Britain," he continued, "it is the foulest murder since the time of Christ. Explain it, escape it as you will, for this year or the next, the world is not to be so cheated by pretexts – the dead millions were foully murdered, and by you."[86]

Lord John Russell, in this reading of recent history, was the man "upon whose soul rests this awful load of guilt," the man who had "in cold blood destroyed two millions of our race."[87] The famine and the Ecclesiastical Titles Bill were part of an Anglo-Saxon Protestant conspiracy to crush Catholicism; Russell's government had begun by attacking the people's lives and was now attacking their religion. And the Queen, who should have tried to protect the people, had been sublimely indifferent to the fate of her Irish subjects – a point McGee made in one of his most powerful poems, "Midsummer, 1851." It opened with a series of questions:

Why standeth the labourer in the way, with sunken eyes and dim?
Is there no work – is there no hope – is there no help for him?
Why rusteth his swift, bright sickle, that swept down Saxon grain,
Stuck in the patch of rugged thatch that keepeth not out the rain?

The peasants, the priests, and the writers for the *Nation* knew the truth, McGee wrote, while the Queen remained cloistered in her palace:

The Lady of Windsor little thinks how you have racked and
   wrought
Your bones and brains to foster all that thus has gone to naught.
Little she knows that round her stand a gang of thievish Earls,
Whose founts are fed, whose wines are cooled, with tears of
   humble churls;
Little she knows that to their Gods of Rank and Fashion rise
Daily a litany of groans, and a human sacrifice!

Significantly, in the light of his conflict with the Mitchelites, the poem called not for revolution but for justice:

> The robber knights are all around; from every castle-top
> They stretch their necks, a-hungering after the poor man's crop;
> We ask that Justice have her seat amid the up-stacked corn,
> That all he sowed and nursed may not from Labour's grasp be torn.

The poem ended on the same note that McGee had struck in his famous "sailing coffins" speech of March 1847: it was imperative to save the living and to ensure that such a catastrophe would never happen again.[88]

Irish resistance to British misrule, McGee now believed, must be steeped in ultramontane principles. A new "Catholic organization," becoming "aggressive by degrees," must fight the "heretical church" and "heathen state" that were destroying Ireland.[89] "The new Catholic movement," he wrote, "should aim at nothing less than to reverse the entire policy of 'the Reformation' in both islands."[90] Irish Catholicism and nationalism were coterminous; the Catholic hierarchy, reeling from the Ecclesiastical Titles Bill, was in the vanguard of the national struggle, and its leadership would pave the way for independence. Everything, including the Tenant League, must be subordinated to the struggle for Irish Catholicism. While McGee had initially seen the Tenant League as a force for religious cooperation, he now viewed it as part of the Catholic counterattack against Anglo-Saxon Protestantism. Agrarian issues were not in themselves sufficient to produce a nationalist consciousness, he argued, but all good Irish Catholics would rally behind their bishops and priests.[91]

Once again, McGee was being carried away by his passions; the Catholic hierarchy did indeed resist the Ecclesiastical Titles Bill, but it had no intention of leading a movement for Irish independence. On the other hand, McGee's attitude to education and literature fitted perfectly with Irish ultramontanism. He continued to condemn secular colleges as a threat to the Catholic faith and argued that without a Catholic university "three-fourths of the eager students of Ireland will have to choose between Apostasy and Ignorance – between mental darkness and moral death!"[92] And in the best ultramontane tradition, McGee now renounced the secular writings of Young Ireland, insisting that all literature should be suffused with Catholicism. Anti-Catholic writers such as Milton and Hume would all be "buried from sight when the British empire caves in," he claimed. Meanwhile, all Irish writers had a duty to deepen the Catholic faith: "If they would make a poem, a picture, a book, or a proverb live, let it be conceived in a Catholic spirit, and guided by a Catholic judgment."[93] McGee had previously believed that literature should serve nationalism; now he believed that it should serve Catholicism.

The religious conflict in Britain and Ireland, according to McGee, was part of a wider struggle for the soul of civilization. In an appendix to the 1852 edition of the *History of the Irish Settlers*, he wrote that the world was dividing into "two universal parties." On one side were the modernists, who rejected religion and authority, who attempted to build new institutions on the shifting sands of private judgment, and who sought to "confiscate and distribute property." On the other side stood the "christianized Celts of Italy, Spain, France, Ireland and America," who were "working for the law of God and the deliverance of men."[94] The Irish, straddling the Atlantic, had a critically important role in this conflict. "Once more," he declared, "the Irish race are summoned to save the Ark of God, and to defend the outworks of civilization. Christendom and Socialism are about to grapple, and our part is plain – our duty is imperative. Let us draw closer and closer our bonds of unity – let us frown down every dividing demagogue – let us clothe ourselves in suffrages, and calmly await the issue. Even to the end of time God is pledged to his people!"[95]

On the American front, the fight for Catholicism was direct and immediate; in Boston, McGee was encamped at the heart of enemy territory. The city's mayor believed in the unity of the Anglo-Saxon peoples; the Whigs and Democrats were "equally sectarian"; and Irish Catholics were in danger of becoming "white slaves."[96] To preserve and promote Catholicism in this environment required vigorous and sustained political pressure; his earlier campaign for naturalization now became harnessed to his ultramontanism, and the need for separate Catholic educational institutions became more pressing than ever.

While the first edition of his *History of the Irish Settlers* had painted a positive picture of life in the United States, his 1852 post-ultramontane appendix presented a very different image. The second generation of Irish Catholics, he wrote, was succumbing to American "smartness" – "a certain impertinent self-assurance, in swearing, smoking cabbage cigars and still worse dissipations." "To teach our children reverence in an irreverent age," he wrote, "this is the great task for Irishmen in America."[97] The task could succeed only if Catholics had control over the religious education of their children – which, in the United States, they manifestly had not.

Things looked very different, however, north of the border. What now struck McGee about Canada was not its colonial status or the need for revolution followed by annexation to the United States. Instead, he emphasized the "powerful position of the Catholic Church in Canada," and noted that Catholic institutes were spreading throughout Canadian towns and cities. Canada might be materially inferior to the United States, but it was "morally superior." "All civilization without religion is hectic and hollow," he wrote, echoing Balmez. Protestant America was by definition irreligious, but the One True Faith was thriving in British North America. Particularly important, and worthy of emulation, was the existence of Catholic separate schools in Canada; here was the surest safeguard against the corrupting influences of Protestant American culture. Americans, he argued, would do well to "study more closely the educational system of our northern neighbours."[98]

This, too, was a dramatic reversal of his position in 1849. While McGee's ultramontanism intensified his hostility to Britain and increased his sense of alienation in America, it also forced him to alter his previously negative impressions of Canada. The country might be part of the British Empire, but it was the bastion of Catholicism on the North American continent. There were new possibilities here, new roads that might yet be taken.

The Revolution of Antichrist
July 1852 – May 1853

In becoming an ultramontane journalist in Boston, McGee had effectively argued himself out of a job. His newspaper now shared the same sentiments as the well-established and clerically supported *Boston Pilot*, and it made little sense for two Catholic newspapers to compete for the city's Irish American readers. But if supply exceeded demand in Boston, the reverse was true in Buffalo, where the American-born Bishop John Timon presided over a rapidly expanding Irish Catholic population and needed the services of someone like McGee.

Buffalo was the classic American boomtown. As the largest grain port in the world, it was a magnet for Irish immigrants, many of whom had arrived through Canada during the famine migration of 1847. Over half the city's Irish Catholics lived in slum housing, with the men working in low-paying, unskilled seasonal jobs, and the women concentrated in domestic service. Irish Catholics were over-represented in the city's poorhouse and prisons, and quickly acquired a reputation for collective and individual violence, heavy drinking, and disorderly behaviour. As David Gerber has shown, the problems of poverty, internal divisions, political power and nativist hostility were approached through "two divergent Irish-American ideological constellations – one, clerical and conservative; the other, social democratic and republican."[1] In this struggle for the hearts, minds, and souls of the city's Irish Americans, Bishop Timon believed, McGee would make an excellent ally for the church.

Timon had good reasons to invite McGee to Buffalo, and McGee had good reasons to accept. He and Mary made the journey in July 1852, with their two children; Martha Dorcas now had a sixteen-month-old

Buffalo, 1853. The classic American boomtown, a magnet for Irish immigrants, and McGee's home during the peak of his ultramontane period (J.W. Hill, Library and Archives Canada, C-046096)

sister, Mary Euphrasia, or Frasa, as she was called.[2] "We have a very comfortable house and large garden with my favourite vegetable, *Cabbage*," Mary told Bella Morgan shortly after her arrival. "The neighbourhood is very pleasant, and our neighbours are all holy people ... The Bishop has called several times. I call him the 'Model Bishop' for I never saw one who completely gave the idea of what a Bishop should be, but him. Nothing can exceed his affability, humility and charity." This was a different world from the Irish ghettoes of Buffalo's First and Eighth Wards; it was middle class and respectable, though it was also, for Mary, rather isolating. "I sometimes feel very lonely here," she wrote, "and miss my old friends."[3]

As well as visiting the family, Bishop Timon provided McGee with crucial financial help, lending him $350 to cover his costs and encouraging his priests to subscribe collectively and publicly to his newspaper – which they duly did. Such a show of support, wrote McGee's close friend Vicar General Peter Bede, would set a good example to the laity and steer them in the right direction.[4] The newspaper was

John Timon, bishop of Buffalo (1797–1867). Born in Pennsylvania of Irish parents, Timon attempted to protect Irish Catholic immigrants from the snares of Protestantism and revolutionary Irish nationalism, and to promote Catholicism in his diocese of Western New York. To this end, he invited McGee to come to Buffalo in 1852, lent him money to run the *American Celt*, and controlled the paper's religious content. After McGee left Buffalo, the loan became a matter of dispute, and relations soured between the two men. "My advice, or rather my experience, is, that it is very unhappy for the man who is under pressing obligations to Bishops," McGee later told one of his friends. (Charles G. Deuther, *The Life and Times of the Rt Rev John Timon* [1870])

in effect a joint venture between McGee and Timon. While McGee remained "solely responsible for the general conduct of the paper," he placed it "under the control of the Bishop of the Diocese" in all matters concerning religion.[5] Religious matters received extensive coverage; the columns were full of news about Catholicism in Britain, Ireland,

and America, along with reports of local Catholic affairs. The new emphasis was reflected in the new title for his paper; in Buffalo, it became the *American Celt and Catholic Citizen* – synonymous categories, in McGee's view.

———•••••———

Over the next ten months in Buffalo, McGee became one of the most militant, outspoken, and uncompromising ultramontanists in the United States. He inhabited a world of absolute moral certainty, in which the Catholic Church stood alone against democratic demagogues, apostate Catholics, persecuting Protestants, radical liberals, and red republicans, all of whom were part of the "Revolution of AntiChrist."[6] The battle was simultaneously political and personal. It was impossible to attack the "isms," McGee believed, without attacking the people who held them. He began to use words like "lepers" and "vermin" to describe his political enemies; his polemical style was starting to mirror that of the revolutionary republicans whom he had fought in New York two years earlier.[7]

Much of his anger was directed against the "numerous army of demagogues" who afflicted American society. "A demagogue," he wrote, "is a 'mob-leader' or an 'orator of a faction.' He is one who is capable of any trick to insure his object ... He lives only in agitation, turmoil and sedition. All his lines are out in the troubled waters. He is a moral wrecker, who would evoke the whole fury of a popular tempest for the sake of the drift-wood it might cast up at his own door."[8] Typical of the species, McGee argued, were the American politicians who courted Irish Catholics during election campaigns, only to abandon them afterwards. Equally reprehensible were democratic ideologues such as Devin Reilly who sought to raise themselves on the ruins of legitimate authority. Reilly, like the McGee of 1848–49, was putting it about that the Catholic Church supported the enemies of liberty and was collaborating in Britain's oppression of Ireland. Nothing could be farther from the truth, countered the McGee of 1852; Irish bishops had consistently resisted British attempts to limit their power and were currently "in open antagonism to the Imperial Government" over the Ecclesiastical Titles Bill.[9]

In McGee's view, Reilly was part of a long-standing minority anticlerical tradition in Ireland – an "inky stream of unbelief, flowing sometimes in secret, and sometimes in the sun."[10] The stream had been dammed up in Ireland but continued to flow in the United States, where it converged with the powerful force of manifest destiny. The result? Radical republicans were attempting to annex Catholic countries in the New World and to absorb them into the Protestant democracy of the United States. His old enemy Joseph Brenan, now based in New Orleans, was a case in point; Brenan was currently supporting an American filibustering expedition against Catholic Cuba, even though the United States and Spain were at peace. The notion that American freebooters could "liberate" Cuba from its Catholic and colonial yoke, argued McGee, was nothing more than piracy in the guise of democracy, arrogance in the name of enlightenment, and aggression in the name of liberty.[11]

He applied the same logic to secret societies that "were proposed to be formed in America, for the liberation of Ireland." As American citizens, the Irish must uphold the constitution and respect the oath of allegiance, asserted McGee. Only if the United States and Britain were at war could Irish Americans do something about Ireland – and even then, it would be in their capacity as American soldiers rather than as freelance revolutionaries. This position was, of course, entirely consistent with his subsequent attack on Irish American Fenianism.[12]

———————

If demagoguery, anticlericalism, and revolutionary imperialism were dark and dangerous features of American life, an even greater threat to Irish Catholics lay in the Protestant character of the country. As well as reiterating his general arguments that Protestantism was a heretical sect and that Protestant Anglo-Saxons were conspiring against Catholic Celts, McGee emphasized the immediate consequences of anti-Catholic discrimination. "We charge that every Protestant *organization, or society, and almost every practical Protestant in the Union, is engaged in a social persecution of the Catholics at this hour*," he declared, "and that this persecution ranges from the Catholic Lawyer, Doctor, or Politician, down to the poor, pious, Kitchen-girl, who must either eat meat on fast days or go without a dinner."[13]

There was, in short, a glaring gap between theory and practice in the United States. Although Catholics were formally equal under the law, they were informally excluded from political office, "every honorable distinction," and employment opportunities. Precisely because of its informal, insidious nature, such discrimination was hard to fight; specific targets remained elusive, and McGee would have preferred "open to secret persecution" so that the enemies could be directly engaged.[14]

Among these enemies were the forces of the Crown. England, he wrote, "*employs numerous agents in the United States, to stir up sectarian hatred against the Catholic citizens.*"[15] And the agents were highly effective: "Our public (all but the Catholics) are helplessly moved to and fro, according as the wires are pulled, at London."[16] He had made similar accusations nine years earlier, during the Philadelphia riots. In both cases, the fact that he had no evidence was immaterial; McGee's premises locked him into a hermetically sealed and self-validating conspiracy theory, in which the very absence of evidence testified to the effectiveness of the conspirators and the secrecy of their agents.

As he considered the best way to respond to Protestant "social persecution," McGee experienced the same kind of tension between confrontation and caution that had characterized his earlier career. Part of him wanted to meet "argument by argument, organization by organization, force by force," and demanded a Catholic Convention to resist "injustice and oppression."[17] This was the McGee who had taken a hard line during the Philadelphia riots of 1844, who had described native Americans as cowards, and who reacted to Protestantism and Anglo-Saxonism with a militant Catholicism and a narrow Celticism. But another part of him stressed the importance of political prudence and recognized that confrontation could become counterproductive:

No-Popery excitement ... cannot be kept up except by a counter
Catholic irritation. It must die out for shere [sic] want of food,
or explode in a series of Charlestown rows. It is our part, as
good Catholics and good citizens, to keep cool, to meet ignorant

clamor with manly forbearance, to state our principles as explicitly as if writing a will, and to look to the morrow and the day
after, rather than the present noisy moment. By this course we
will defeat the conspirators, win converts, strengthen our ranks,
and finally secure the social establishment of Christianity on this
continent. By an opposite course we would merely be strengthening the hands of the Enemy.[18]

This was the McGee who had tried to defuse ethnoreligious tensions
by arguing that the Boston Irish should cancel their St Patrick's Day
parade in 1845, and who wrote that Irish Catholics should not allow
themselves to be provoked by the kind of Orange aggression that
occurred at Dolly's Brae in 1849. Significantly, McGee made his "keep
cool" remarks some six weeks after he had urged Catholics to meet
"force by force"; in the interim, it is highly likely that Bishops Fitzpatrick and Timon urged him to tone down his language.

⋅•••⋅

American Protestantism found its political analogue in American liberalism, which in turn opened the doors to "red republicanism," or
socialism, McGee argued. Liberals, after all, began with private judgment, while Catholics began with the Word of God. From here, liberals fell into a series of errors; they wanted to separate religion from politics, believed that all religious sects were equal, and maintained that
the state should control education. Equally erroneously, they thought
that man was perfectible, that democracy was the only legitimate form
of government, and that the people had an absolute right of insurrection against all illegitimate forms of government.

   Catholics knew better. Far from treating politics and religion as distinct entities, Catholics believed that politics should be subordinated
to Christian morality, as defined by their church. This meant rejecting
liberal notions about the equality of sects; all the others were wrong,
and misguided notions of religious equality pointed in the dangerous direction of religious indifferentism. It also meant rejecting state
schools and mixed education; only Catholic-controlled schools could
inculcate the true faith and preserve the religious foundation of society.

Unlike liberals, Catholics realized that man was incapable of perfection, that power emanated from God rather than from the people, and that different forms of society required different forms of government. Democracy was not the sole criterion of legitimacy, and people did not have an unconditional right of rebellion, though insurrections were permissible in certain circumstances – when oppression was intolerable, there were no other options, the people were united, and there was a reasonable chance of success.[19]

In developing these ideas, McGee adopted a kind of Catholic domino theory, in which Protestantism generated liberalism, liberalism generated revolutionary democracy, and revolutionary democracy generated socialism. The result was an international "anti-Christian conspiracy," whose principal American mouthpiece was Horace Greeley's *New York Tribune*; there was a direct line, McGee asserted, from Luther through Voltaire, Robespierre, and Fourier to Greeley.[20] Among those who had been lured by the "Socialist syren," he included his old friend and colleague Thomas Meagher, who arrived in the United States in the spring of 1852 after escaping from Van Diemen's Land.[21]

Shortly after Meagher settled in New York, McGee visited him at his Long Island home; it was their first meeting since the emergency session of the Irish Confederation's revolutionary council in July 1848, when Meagher advised McGee to rally the Confederates in Scotland. They got on well with each other, and McGee remarked that Meagher was "a sounder and stronger man" after his experiences in Australia.[22] The friendship, however, soon cracked under the pressure of ideological differences: while McGee had pulled hard to the right, Meagher remained very much the radical. In a series of speeches to enthusiastic Irish American audiences, Meagher blamed the Catholic Church for the failure of 1848, maintained that priests had no place in politics, and praised European revolutionaries such as Giuseppe Mazzini and Lajos Kossuth. Recognizing in Meagher the same "errors" that he himself had once committed, McGee moved to the ultramontane counterattack, urging Meagher to repudiate the socialism and "heathenism" of revolutionary European republicanism. There was also a personal edge; McGee contrasted Meagher's privileged Jesuit education with his own background. "My university," he wrote, "has been the wide

world, with all its disputes and classes [sic], delusions, trials, and experiences."[23] Gavan Duffy, it will be recalled, had written that the self-
educated and "underbred" McGee felt out of place and intimidated by
the confident and "dandified" Young Irelanders back in 1845; it appears
that old resentments were resurfacing in a new form.[24]

Relations between the two men worsened later in 1852, when Meagher's speaking tour took him to Buffalo. This time they did not meet,
and McGee used Meagher's speech as further evidence that he had
drifted into "the bloody and crooked channel of French Revolutionary
principles."[25] Writing to Duffy three weeks later, Meagher expressed
his anger at the "bigotry and intolerance" displayed by the Irish Catholic press in the United States, and the *American Celt* in particular.
McGee, he wrote, was doing "incalculable mischief," had betrayed the
principles of Young Ireland, and was utterly untrustworthy.[26]

By this time, McGee had alienated all the leading figures on both
the militant and the moderate wings of Young Ireland – all, that is,
except Duffy. In a public letter written in 1854, Duffy criticized Meagher's revolutionary liberalism and blamed him for the split. He said
that McGee had displayed "unflinching courage" in 1848, had demonstrated a "fixed devotion to Irish interests," and had been "systematically slandered by the Jacobins to an extent that would have blackened
a Saint of God." "Ah, my dear Meagher," Duffy concluded, "there are
few sacrifices I would not make to see him and you side by side again.
Till you are side by side, that new Irish nation will not be wholly at
one, or a terror to its enemies. Your unity is an indispensable prelimi-
nary." Indispensable as it may have been, it was clearly unattainable. As
Duffy lamented in his memoir, it was the fate of revolutionary exiles to
"fly at each others' throats."[27]

Taken together, McGee's ultramontane arguments could easily be con-
strued as a devastating critique of the United States. The country, after
all, was run by Protestants, and Protestants were heretics. Protestantism
produced myriad evils, ranging from religious indifferentism to nativism, and including demagoguery, filibustering, socialism, and rampant
materialism. An obvious question arises: How could McGee's ultra-

montanism be reconciled with democratic republicanism in America? His answer drew partly on a Burkean distinction between American and European forms of republican democracy, and partly on the belief – inspired by Balmez and Brownson – that Catholicism could save the United States from its own worst tendencies.

Like Burke, McGee drew a clear line between the American Revolution, which he interpreted as an act of secession from an intrusive and innovative colonial government, and the French Revolution, which he viewed as an ideologically driven attempt to restructure society on the basis of *a priori* political principles. "American Democracy," he said, "began with the beginning of the country, it is a native here, its constitution is formed to the climate, its growth was regular and orderly – it is never to be confounded with the ferocious and chimerical Democracy of old monarchical States."[28] History, circumstances, customs and traditions were crucial in forming the character of a state; because constitutions could not be "improvised like a sonnet, or established by a proclamation," it was totally wrong to imagine that American democracy was some kind of "model" for Europe.[29] Within the United States, he believed, the conservative republicanism of Washington, rather than the revolutionary democracy of Jefferson, was more closely attuned to the American condition.[30]

Far from being hostile to republican democracy in its proper conservative American form, the Catholic Church was well positioned to carry forward Washington's legacy into the mid-nineteenth century, McGee maintained. Catholicism provided a necessary counterweight to facile notions of liberalism and progress. Without the Catholic emphasis on authority, religious faith, and reverence for the Founding Fathers, republican institutions would remain vulnerable to the whims of private judgment, public opinion, and self-interest. Catholics did not make the mistake of confusing progress with materialism; they realized that true progress consisted in recognizing that "all Truth has been already discovered" and that "'the fear of the Lord is the beginning of wisdom.'"[31] Catholics formed a bulwark against demagogues, abolitionists, and filibusterers, all of whom threatened to destroy the Union. And Catholics stood for social stability and family values against liberal individualism and the emancipation of the passions. McGee had brought Balmez to Buffalo, and had made Catholicism essential for the health of the United States.[32]

Not just Catholicism, but *Irish* Catholicism. Through the Americo-Celtic Society that McGee formed in Buffalo, through his proposed auxiliary Irish Archaeological Society, by participating in the rapidly expanding Catholic institutes in America, and above all by sending their children to parochial schools, Irish Catholics could fulfill their divinely appointed mission to save the United States from the snares of Protestant liberalism.[33] The success of that mission hinged on providing a Catholic education for Catholic children. If the state tried to compel Catholics to educate their children in common schools, McGee wrote, then Catholics would simply "disobey the State": "It is to us, a question of life or death. As well may you touch the apple of my eye, or the core of my heart as my child. If I cannot obtain for it freedom of education, in America, it is full time for me to arise and go hence."[34]

This position was at once political and personal. He was writing as the father of two daughters, whose moral protection was of paramount importance to him – so much so that he was prepared to leave the United States rather than see them educated in common schools. But if he ever decided to leave, where would he go? Mexico was one possibility, Canada was another; either country, he wrote, would be "far preferable" to the tyranny of a Protestant majority in an unchecked democracy.[35] On balance, he thought that the Canadians had got it right. "Here," he wrote of Canada, "the State is made a partner in the work of Education; but the Parents, also, are partners. The State has the right of Inspection and approval; the parents have the establishment of the school, and the choice of the Teacher. Such a compromise, fairly carried out, we are prepared to accept, as a satisfactory substitute for the present system."[36]

Unless Americans adopted this kind of model, just about anywhere would be better than the United States – even England: "Better to languish and die under the red flag of England than live to beget children of perdition under the flag of a proselytizing republic."[37] The remark shocked many of his contemporaries, and has been read as the first sign that McGee was rejecting the United States and embracing his old enemy.[38] To write of languishing and dying in England, however, is hardly a form of embrace. McGee's point – meant to shame Americans into supporting parochial schools – was that unless the United States changed course, it was in danger of becoming even more oppressive than the most anti-Catholic nation in the world.

But it had not yet come to this; it was still possible to get the United States on the right track. Not that the immediate political scene looked promising. On one side, wrote McGee, were anti-Catholic Whigs, and on the other were cynical Democrats who believed that they could "use us, as tools and crutches, and then cast us away."[39] He showed relatively little interest in the 1852 presidential election, though he described himself as a Conservative Democrat, "in the American not in the Parisian sense." Had he been eligible to vote, he would probably have opted for the Democratic candidate Franklin Pierce, who had fought against anti-Catholic discrimination in New Hampshire.[40]

Rather than focusing on contemporary American politics, McGee looked to the long-term character of the United States. The Catholic Irish, he argued, had a fifty-year period in which to make their mark; the country was still developing its identity, and Irish immigration would dry up by the end of the century. Within the evolving national synthesis, they could "perpetuate by their example and inculcation, the essentially good parts of the Irish character." In short, they could bring out the best in the United States by bringing out the best in themselves.

————

And the best was something in which Irish Catholics deserved to take great pride. For what was their history but one of deep devotion to their faith in the face of terrible oppression and deprivation? This was the point that McGee drove home in his *History of the Attempts to Establish the Protestant Reformation*. Drawing not only on the notes he had taken at the British Museum but also on Cobbett's *History of the Protestant Reformation* and Mathew Carey's *Vindiciae Hibernia*, McGee's work was dedicated to Bishop Fitzpatrick and was intended to inspire Irish Americans to follow in the footsteps of their heroic Catholic forefathers.[41]

Irish history became the story of a downtrodden and impoverished Catholic people who resisted the attempts of their much more powerful Protestant persecutors to crush their religion. The attacks began in 1541, when Henry VIII became king of Ireland. McGee still clung to his earlier belief that the "compact of 1541" constituted "a proof and a full recognition by England of the absolute sovereignty and independence of the Irish nation"; but he now argued that Henry VIII had abused and exploited his power to begin the conquest of Catholic Ireland.[42] Henry VIII, wrote McGee, was "among the greatest criminals known to mankind," whose evil was rivalled only by that of Oliver Cromwell, "one of the most wicked and detestable of the fallen children of Adam."[43] Through treachery, violence, confiscations, and plantations, English Protestants had repeatedly tried to impose their heretical beliefs on Irish Catholics; they had tortured and murdered their way through the country and then tried to cover their tracks with lies and propaganda.

Having failed to destroy Catholicism in the seventeenth century, the Protestants tried again in the eighteenth century with the Penal Laws, letting loose their priest hunters to capture the clergymen who came into Ireland from the Continent. Towards the end of the eighteenth century, the persecution abated, but Catholics soon came under threat from a different quarter – from Wolfe Tone and the Protestant United Irishmen, who tried to dupe the people into supporting a secular revolutionary republic "on the French plan."[44] The failure of the rising of 1798 led to the Act of Union, and forced Ireland into the British imperial world: "Here ... was an ancient Christian nation merged into a vast irreligious, money-making empire, which embraced nearly one hundred million Mohammedans in Asia, a large barbaric population in Africa, and above twenty millions of heretics in Great Britain and her colonies."[45] Far from identifying the Catholic Irish with other subject peoples in the British Empire, McGee was clearly disgusted that Irish Catholics were lumped in with infidels and savages.

In the teeth of this catalogue of oppression, and against all the odds, the Catholic Celts of Ireland had strengthened and deepened their faith, fighting and dying to preserve their religion. Among their heroes were the leaders of the 1641 Rebellion: Roger O'Moore ("could heroism rise higher above the earth?") and Owen Roe O'Neill ("very few names in any history are more worthy of our honorable and pious remembrance").[46] Among their martyrs were Archbishop Dermot O'Hurley of Cashel, who endured severe torture before being hanged in Dublin in 1584, and Oliver Plunkett, "a man of rare sagacity, goodness, and energy," who was hanged, drawn, and quartered on trumped-up charges of treason almost a century later.[47] They were joined in the penal era by Father Nicholas Sheehy of Tipperary. He died, wrote McGee, "with religious firmness and composure," while his persecutors "met deaths violent, loathsome and terrible," in the best homiletic tradition.[48]

Defeated in Ireland, Catholics had served with distinction in the *ancien regime* French army. Their greatest achievement came during the battle of Fontenoy in 1745, when with the battle cry "Remember Limerick!" they flung themselves on the English enemy and "smote them like a torrent."[49] Irish Catholics endured and suffered for their faith, fought their oppressors when they could, and ultimately prevailed. Even the Act of Union turned out to be part of the Divine Plan; by bringing Irish Catholics into the British Empire, it enabled them to spread their religious influence throughout the world. "Catholicity," he wrote, "became aggressive in the British dominions from the time of the act of union."[50] His story ended in 1829 with Catholic Emancipation: "The Protestant establishment, after three centuries of such warfare as we have witnessed, stood humbled, and conscious of defeat, before the unconquered faith of the Irish nation. Wonderful result of God's grace, aiding and sustaining a weak people! Lesson of lessons to the pride and ambition of heresy backed by temporal power!"[51]

Once again, McGee was in full melodramatic mode, with powerful villains on one side, virtuous heroes and martyrs on the other, and the ultimate triumph of Catholic Irish good over Protestant English evil. Ironically, though, the very vehemence of his conservative Catholic anglophobia could easily feed into the revolutionary republican tradition that McGee repudiated. Anyone with Irish republican sympathies who read his book would be more likely to burn with anger about English Protestant bigotry and brutality than to embrace McGee's ultramontanism. And his *History* also left him vulnerable to attacks on its own ground; when McGee later formed an alliance with Canadian Protestants, ultramontane Catholics flung the book in his face. For neither the first nor the last time, McGee had laid himself open to subsequent charges of apostasy.[52]

While he was writing his *History of the Attempts to Establish the Protestant Reformation*, McGee kept a close eye on events in Ireland. In response to the Ecclesiastical Titles Bill, a group of disaffected Irish Liberal MPs and constitutional nationalists in the moderate Young Ireland tradition joined with supporters of the Tenant League to form a new political party, the Irish Brigade. Its central objectives were the repeal of the Ecclesiastical Titles Bill, the disestablishment of the Church of Ireland, and land reform; the party would oppose any government that failed to meet these demands. In the general election of July 1852, the Irish Brigade became the largest party in Ireland, with forty-eight MPs, including Duffy. It seemed that Duffy's constitutional nationalist strategy was finally paying dividends, even though the Catholic basis of the new party was significantly removed from Young Ireland's ecumenicalism.

McGee had no problem with this, of course; a Catholic party for a Catholic people was exactly what he wanted. Locating the Irish Brigade within the long tradition of resistance that he had described in his book, he declared that it stood for two "great and sacred principles" – "the Church and the Soil; the right to live and the right to worship." These were the two causes, he wrote, that ran all through modern Irish history, from the sixteenth century to the present; even the rising of 1848 was slotted into this narrative, despite the church's opposition.[53]

In two open letters to Duffy (whom he described simply as "an Irish M.P."), McGee spelled out his prescription for Irish politics. All parties *"must be founded on a basis theologically right,"* putting the "Church before the State, and the Eternal before the Temporal." In the Burkean tradition, he held that Irish politics must rest on the "hereditary characteristics of the People," who were "naturally aristocratic and full of veneration"; this meant that the true Irish statesman must be "conservative in his principles" and "versatile in his expedients." It also meant that an

"Irish political chief" must be Catholic; Protestant settlers had always been at war with Catholic natives, and Protestants such as Henry Grattan and Thomas Davis were only patriots to the extent that they had transcended their religious prejudices. What was needed, in fact, was a latter-day O'Connell – a great Catholic and Celtic hero who personified the natural virtues and aspirations of his countrymen.[54] Through the medium of ultramontanism, McGee had moved back into the world of *O'Connell and His Friends.* All the reservations about O'Connell's quasi-dictatorial powers were dropped; for the rest of his life, McGee would regard O'Connell as the greatest Irishman of the modern age.

If the Irish character was essentially Catholic and conservative, and if Ireland was "an old traditional, clannish country," it followed that republicanism was fundamentally anti-Irish. McGee's initial criticism of Irish republicanism had been based on pragmatism – that it was impossible, given the power imbalance between Ireland and Britain – but now he extended the argument and brought it onto new ground. "Ireland is not naturally suited for Republican, nor even for representative government, in the sense of our times," he wrote. "A strong infusion of moral and religious authority would be essential to hold a native constitution together for a single year." British rule must eventually be replaced with Catholic authoritarianism, in a constitution that balanced elected representation with a strong judiciary and the institutionalized power of Catholic bishops. Home rule really would be Rome rule; Ireland would become a theocracy, in which Protestants would be tolerated as a minority and republicanism would be rooted out of every crack and crevice in Irish life.[55]

As one of the most forceful and articulate ultramontanists in the United States, McGee was in high demand as a Catholic speaker. In November 1852 he made his first trip to Montreal, where he delivered lectures to the Young Men's St Patrick's Association on "The Celtic Race" and "Christendom."[56] During this visit, he almost certainly met Bernard Devlin, the Roscommon-born lawyer who had called for an Irish American invasion of Canada in 1848.[57] The two men subsequently cooperated on Irish Catholic colonization schemes in the American

West, only to become bitter enemies over the question of revolutionary Irish nationalism. Also in Montreal, McGee began his long friendship with Mary Ann Sadlier, one of the most popular Irish writers in
nineteenth-century North America; he published her stories in the
American Celt, praised her literary abilities, and corresponded with her
regularly. "There are *very* few things in this world so pleasant to me as
one of your letters," he told her. "I do not know, and never expect to
know any one who makes the paper talk as you do."[58]

After visiting Montreal, he travelled to New York, where the Catholic Institute had invited him to speak on the Reformation. His talk
was "very successful," reported James Sadlier, Mary Ann's husband
– so much so that McGee was invited back for a repeat performance in
January. "Many of the priests insist on bringing his paper back to New
York," Sadlier informed Orestes Brownson; Sadlier also reported that
Archbishop Hughes was "much pleased" with McGee's lecture. The
rift had been healed; McGee's ultramontanism had atoned for his anticlerical sins of 1848–49.[59]

If New York was becoming more attractive for McGee, Buffalo
appeared increasingly constricting; he was too far from the action, and
by the time European news reached Buffalo it was out of date on the
coast. As a result, the *American Celt* was losing its eastern subscribers and
getting deeper into debt – and debt, as we know, was one of McGee's
greatest fears. This was doubtless an important reason for his lecture
tours, which provided an alternative source of income. "During the
month of April," he told James Sadlier, "I was but one day at home."
His constant absences would have accentuated his wife's feelings of isolation and loneliness, while the pressures of running a newspaper on
the road probably took a toll on his health. By May 1853 he needed
a change. "On strong representations and inducements offered to me,
when last in [New] York," he wrote, "I am resolved to move the *Celt*
publication office there, on and after the 1st of June." "This will be my
last newspaper experiment," he added. "If I succeed, well – if not, I
will drop it, and try something else."[60]

CHAPTER THIRTEEN

A More Troubled Prospect
June 1853 – December 1854

McGee had left New York in July 1850 as a liberal nationalist with a reputation for anticlericalism; now he returned as Irish America's best known ultramontane journalist. Although his conservatism remained constant, it changed in emphasis during his New York years. In Buffalo, the *American Celt and Catholic Citizen* had been an "authorized ecclesiastical newspaper"; in New York, it became a secular conservative journal that was "Catholic in intention and tendency."[1] Forming a business partnership with James Mitchell ("he is a Catholic, of course"), and working closely with Bernard Killian, the former editor of the *Buffalo Sentinel*, McGee was no longer under direct clerical control and had more freedom of action.[2] The paper's title reverted to the *American Celt*, dropping the *Catholic Citizen*, and its ultramontane content became less pronounced.

Applying his conservative principles to changing circumstances, McGee's priorities were increasingly shaped by the growing sectional crisis in the United States, by the Crimean War's implications for Irish nationalism, by the revitalization of Irish American revolutionary republicanism, and above all by the accelerating nativist movement. The new challenges facing Irish Americans in 1853 and 1854 pushed him into a search for new answers and eventually edged him in new directions.

Although McGee's public career can be traced in detail during these years, his personal life remains something of a mystery. We know that it was marked by tragedy. At some stage in the early 1850s, either in Buffalo or in New York, his first-born daughter, Martha Dorcas, died.

Around the same time, the McGees had a son, Thomas Patrick Bede. He was named after Buffalo's vicar general, Patrick Bede, and was known in the family as Patty. Helping Mary to look after the children was her mother, Martha Caffrey, who came to New York in 1854 and lived with the family. In the absence of any personal correspondence, however, it is not possible to go any further.

Of one thing, though, we can be certain. For McGee, the family was a "Sacred Institution" that represented a refuge from and bastion against the social and political fragmentation that he increasingly associated with American life.[3] The family was inseparable from private property, which was "the vital principle of all society"; family relations mirrored property relations, "enabling a man to say '*my* house,' '*my* wife,' or '*my* children.'"[4] Patriarchy, property, and religion all found their focus in the family, and anything that threatened this nexus had to be resisted – whether it came from the familiar direction of state schooling or from new-fangled theories about women's rights.

When Lucretia Mott helped to organize the Whole World Temperance Convention in September 1853, asserting the right of women to participate in politics, McGee immediately dismissed the proceedings as a "shameless exhibition." The proper sphere for women was in the home, where they exerted enormous power and influence. "Are we not all," he exclaimed, "from infancy to old age governed by the ladies, God bless them!" Women should exert this power and influence through the "magic of modesty," rather than the "vanity, immodesty and impiety" of public displays. As long as they were worthy wives and mothers, they would receive honour and respect. All this talk about "women's rights" was a "farce" and a "humbug" – yet another bizarre manifestation of Protestantism and private judgment in the United States.[5]

It was no accident, in McGee's view, that the issue of women's rights was closely connected to the antislavery movement and was supported by abolitionists such as William Lloyd Garrison; radical democrats were threatening both traditional morality and the republic itself.[6] Particularly alarming in this respect was the phenomenal success of Harriet Beecher Stowe's *Uncle Tom's Cabin*, which was on its way to becoming the bestselling novel in nineteenth-century America. McGee was appalled by the book. He described Stowe as a "gifted and generous, but ill-educated and unprincipled novelist," who was driven entirely by "the passions and the affections," and who failed to think through the implications of her argument. Her work was a "libel on her country" and was "destined to do infinite harm."[7]

To make matters worse, *Uncle Tom's Cabin* was immensely popular in Britain, where a "cruel and blood-stained oligarchy" was using it to denigrate the United States. In full paranoid mode, McGee maintained that a bad review of the book in the *Times* was actually part of the British conspiracy to destroy the United States and take over the world. "A slashing review, all book-sellers know, is better to the sale than a panegyric," he commented. "In cutting it up with assumed savage good will, 'the leading journal' was most effectively serving the abolitionists, while apparently taking a conservative American tone. The trick took, admirably."[8] If the British were extraordinarily devious, the Irish American enemies of the book made their position abundantly clear. "Well clad and cared for," ran one letter in the *American Celt*, "Sambo becomes an object for the sympathy of England's Petticoat Diplomats, — to the exclusion of her own underground coal slaves who do not, like ours, enjoy 'a life of blissful ignorance,' but one of bestial intercourse and obscene barbarianism."[9] In one sentence, the correspondent had managed to insult Afro-Americans, women, and coal miners.

McGee's contention that Stowe's exposure of the "social sores of America" played into anti-American hands replicated the complaints of his countrymen that his own exposure of Irish American social problems played into anti-Irish hands.[10] He would neither have recognized nor accepted the irony. As far as he was concerned, there was far too much talk about black slaves; it was all so fashionable and sentimental, and there were other people who were much worse off – the Native Americans, for example, who faced the threat of "exterminating war under forms of law." As the original inhabitants of America, they had prior rights that could never be accorded to slaves; at the very least, they should be given their own land in the western plains, protected from the grasping ambition of white settlers.[11]

"It may seem strange that a person like me should thus earnestly advocate justice to the aboriginal tribes of North America," he wrote.

"Yet it is not strange. In the language of one of the great writers of my race – 'I am an Irishman, hating injustice.'"[12] His Catholicism was also a factor; the Catholic Church, McGee argued, had historically been sympathetic to Native Americans, and its members were among their "most zealous friends."[13] Yet McGee saw no contradiction between a putatively Irish Catholic hatred of injustice and his own acquiescence in slavery; indeed, he buttressed his view that slavery was not a "moral wrong" with the teachings of Irish American Catholic bishops.[14] A Native American who encountered such justice might well have taken heart; an Afro-American would have been well advised to take flight.

The key, as always with McGee, lay in his assessment of potential consequences. Allocating western land to Native Americans would save them from the threat of "extermination" without endangering the republic; abolishing slavery pointed towards civil war. Sectional tensions increased in the wake of the Kansas-Nebraska Act of 1854, which appeared to pave the way for the extension of slavery into Kansas, and which undermined McGee's hopes for a Native American territory in the west.[15] Although McGee remained sympathetic towards Native Americans, his principal concern was the impact of the Kansas-Nebraska Act on the American political system. The Democratic party had been "badly shaken" by the Act, and the Whig party had "broken into atoms." "A more extraordinary condition of parties, a more troubled prospect in the future," he wrote, "never before was observable, since America became free."[16]

In this atmosphere of uncertainty, two developments were especially troubling – the fact that many northern Whigs were gravitating towards nativism, and that many Democrats were moving leftwards, joining the radical Young America movement (whose members included Devin Reilly), and supporting revolution in Europe and filibustering in Latin America. McGee had long viewed nativism and revolutionary democracy as the greatest dangers facing Irish Catholics; now, with the break-up of the old party system, it seemed that these forces could no longer be contained. They were, he believed, American variants of a transatlantic threat; American nativism was inseparable from British anti-Catholicism, and American radicalism was part of a "far spread conspiracy, to substitute the Mob for God, Democracy for Religion, and the dagger of Anarchy, for the wand of Authority."[17] The Irish American component of this international revolutionary movement was given new hope and purpose with the arrival of John Mitchel in New York in 1853 and the outbreak of the Crimean War in the spring of 1854.

After escaping from Australia, Mitchel had joined the Irish exiles in New York, and along with Meagher he launched the New York *Citizen* at the beginning of 1854. When news of the Crimean War reached the United States, their thoughts turned immediately to a replay of 1848, only this time with the revolutionaries winning.[18] Mitchel helped to found the Irishmen's Civil and Military Republican Society, approached the Russian consul in New York in the hope of procuring Russian arms for an Irish revolution, and advocated an Irish American filibustering expedition to liberate Ireland.[19] "Every succeeding post (thank God!) is charged with War," he wrote in August. "To us it seems that the procedure should run thus. Proclamation of a Republic: – A Provisional Government, to be named by the Filibusteros: – Proclamation of absolute forfeiture into the hands of the government of all the lands and goods of every man who shall dare to bear arms against his country ... Proclamation that every occupant of every farm, who actually cultivates the same shall forthwith be entitled to purchase that farm for his own fee-simple for ever."[20]

McGee reacted to these developments with predictable horror. A Michelite republic, he wrote, "must needs be a reign of terror, a time of plots, a monster and the mother of monsters."[21] The belief that an Irish American revolutionary army could free Ireland, he argued, was proof of political insanity. Leaving aside the problem of raising money and the impossibility of getting past the British and American navies, the fact remained that a conservative and Catholic people completely rejected anti-Catholic Irish American republican revolutionaries, who were continually fighting among themselves. "The few persons who, like Mr. Mitchel, talk of invading Ireland from America, and imposing a foreign rule on the national life, would talk treason, only they talk nonsense," he wrote. "To impose a republic by invasive force, is just as

criminal as to impose a monarchy; to bring in the Reds, would be even
worse than McMurrough's crime of bringing in the Normans."[22]

Against all this, McGee advocated a course of "wise *moderation*"
between the extremes of republican separatism and loyalty to the
United Kingdom.[23] But the quest for the middle ground, now defined
in conservative Catholic terms, left him vulnerable to misinterpreta-
tion. Then, as now, anyone who vigorously repudiated revolutionary Irish nationalism was liable to be caricatured as an apologist for
British rule. When this happened to McGee, he strenuously defended
himself from charges of political apostasy, and clarified his attitude to
Young Ireland. The "respectable Cawtholic" who supported the British Whigs, he wrote, was as repulsive to him as "the sentimental assas-
sin of the Mazzini school."[24] Young Ireland had been quite correct to
assert Ireland's right of armed resistance to British rule, he maintained;
he also endorsed the Irish Confederation's attempt to build an independent Irish party. But everything else about the movement – its liberalism, its literature, its links with European revolutionaries, its ethics, its
educational policies, its "un-Catholic" and "anti-Catholic" position –
had been "radically wrong."[25] "All of that school have much to answer
for, the present writer among the rest," he declared. "We trust that we
will live long enough to make adequate atonement for early errors,
unconsciously adopted, and as unwittingly propagated."[26]

While the Mitchelites perceived revolutionary opportunities during
the Crimean War, McGee saw an opening for his middle way of limited self-government. "If '*freedom* for Ireland' can be had out of the
present European war," he wrote, "it will be a glorious compensation
for the calamities which may fall on the armies of Great Britain."[27]
"Freedom for Ireland," in McGee's view, meant a federal relationship
between Ireland and Britain, in which Ireland had a local legislature,
an internal militia, and a responsible privy council – in broad terms,
the O'Connellite position that he had embraced in 1844 and rejected
in 1847.[28]

His thinking was strongly influenced by the Burkean assumptions
that, as McGee put it, "human nature is no abstraction; that we must
take men and races as we find them, if we would do any practical good;
that politics is a practical science or art; that the *possible* best is the high-

est good in all questions of government." Britain and Ireland were too closely connected by language, communications, and trade to become separate entities; besides, Britain would remain powerful enough to defeat a republican separatist revolution in Ireland.[29] As he had argued a decade earlier, federalism would balance Ireland's desire for freedom with Britain's need for security, and would provide the foundation for further advances.

<hr />

Along with challenging Mitchel's plans for Ireland, McGee attempted to undermine his influence within the Irish American community. The Mitchelites, he argued, were very much a minority; he reckoned that they formed about one-fifth of the Irish American urban population and little more than one-twentieth in rural areas. Most Irish Americans, he maintained, were reformers rather than revolutionaries, and were "less exiles than emigrants; they have not been banished by the laws of their country, nor the triumph of an adverse party, but voluntarily chose to quit it for a more favored region."[30] The trouble was, though, that the revolutionary exiles were numerous enough to become a disruptive force among the emigrants and were trying to remodel Irish America after their own image.[31] And this must not be allowed to happen.

"We find, in Mr. Mitchel's New York writings, two qualities highly censurable," declared McGee, "and these are – *irreverence* and *imprudence*."[32] The "irreverence" came from Mitchel's criticisms of the Catholic Church.[33] In 1853 the visit of the counterrevolutionary papal nuncio, Gaetano Bedini, to the United States had occasioned a series of anti-Catholic demonstrations; Mitchel sympathized with the protesters, and condemned the Pope and the Catholic Church for siding with European despotism in Europe.[34] Eventually, Archbishop John Hughes launched a pseudonymous counterattack, as he had done against McGee five years earlier. But Mitchel came from a radical Presbyterian background and, in contrast to McGee, was personally untroubled by Hughes's disapproval. The Irish could never be free, Mitchel replied, unless and until they liberated themselves from clerical authority.[35] He was cheered on by Patrick Lynch of the *Irish American*, who added for

good measure that Father John Roddan, in his capacity as editor of the
Boston Pilot, ought to be "spat upon" for his attacks on the Irish republican press.[36]

All this only strengthened McGee's conviction that Irish republicanism was fundamentally anti-Catholic. Mitchel, he wrote, had
finally revealed himself as "an impotent enemy of the Catholic church,
throughout the world." As part of McGee's effort to atone for his earlier
errors, he fully supported the archbishop. Just as Hughes had argued in
1849 that all good Catholics should shut their doors to McGee's New
York Nation, McGee now argued that all good Catholics should shut
their doors to Lynch's Irish American.[37]

So much for Mitchel's "irreverence." The charge of "imprudence"
stemmed from Mitchel's views on slavery. While McGee put national
unity above slavery and was strongly opposed to abolitionism, he none-
theless hoped that "moral and legal" means would eventually bring
freedom to Afro-Americans.[38] Mitchel, in contrast, had consistently
and unequivocally supported slavery and saw no reason to mince his
words on the subject. "We deny that it is a crime, or a wrong, or even
a peccadillo, to hold slaves, to buy slaves, to sell slaves, to keep slaves
to their work, by flogging or other needful coercion ..." he wrote in
the second issue of the Citizen. "We, for our part, wish we had a good
plantation well-stocked with healthy negroes in Alabama."[39]

His wife Jane concurred. "You will find it difficult to believe (as I
did myself at first) but it is no less true that the negroes are happier in
their state of slavery than when they get their freedom," she informed
a friend.[40] Many of Mitchel's readers, however, did not concur; he was
inundated with angry letters, and McGee was more than willing to
join the attack. In April 1847, when Mitchel first publicly declared his
support for slavery, McGee had attempted to avoid the issue, on the
grounds that it would divide the Irish Confederates. Now he drew
attention to the subject, precisely because it was sowing dissension in
republican ranks.[41]

A further line of attack was afforded by rumours in the late spring of
1854 that Mitchel was organizing a new secret society among the Irish
in America – presumably, the Irishmen's Civil and Military Republican Society. Such societies had long been the bane of Irish life, stated
McGee, and had only succeeded in providing tyrannical governments

with pretexts for oppressive legislation. In the United States, the organizers of secret societies were guilty of a "three-fold crime against their
Race": they tried to seduce the Irish people from the "moral control of
the Church," which had consistently condemned such organizations;
they were a divisive force that distracted Irish Americans from "unity
of moral purpose"; and they played into the hands of nativists, who
used the existence of Irish American secret societies as an argument for
their own anti-Irish secret societies.[42]

There was also a deeper sense in which McGee believed that Irish
American republicanism and American nativism were reinforcing one
another. Every time that Mitchel and Meagher opened their mouths
about Irish Catholics being controlled by priests and bishops who were
hostile to liberty, McGee wrote, they were providing American nativists with ammunition that Catholicism and American republicanism
were fundamentally incompatible.[43] This was, of course, a complete
reversal of his earlier position that Irish American anticlericalism actually undercut nativism by demonstrating that Irish immigrants were
not puppets of the Catholic Church. In effect, he concluded, Irish
American republicans were functioning as recruiting agents for the
nativist movement that was sweeping through America in 1854. And
nativism, he believed, was by far the greatest danger that faced Irish
Catholics in the United States.

McGee's fears were focused on the so-called Know-Nothing movement, which emerged in 1854 from a cluster of local nativist parties
and secret societies whose members claimed to "know nothing" about
such organizations – hence the name. Gathering momentum with the
formation of the American Party in July, the Know-Nothing movement was an unstable compound of antislavery Northern Whigs, disaffected Democrats, and proslavery Southern Whigs. An expression of
indigenous American nationalism, it insisted that immigrants must not
be allowed to vote until they had lived in the United States for at least
twenty-one years, and it stood for a common public school system.[44]

Most of its supporters were strongly anti-Catholic, but much more
than straightforward bigotry was going on. Millard Fillmore, the
former Whig president who was a leading figure in the movement

The American River Ganges. Although this cartoon by Thomas Nast was first published in 1871, it captures the fears of the Know-Nothing movement during the 1850s – that Catholic power in America would destroy the public school system, devour civil and religious liberty, and persecute Protestants. (*Harper's Weekly*, 1875)

and a member of Know-Nothing Lodge 107, gave money to the new Catholic cathedral in Buffalo and praised the charitable work of Catholic priests.[45] Such nuances meant little or nothing to McGee. From his perspective, the salient features of the movement were its hostility to the Catholic Church, its attempt to restrict the political rights of immigrants, its rejection of separate schools for Catholics, and its unprecedented political growth.

As before, McGee located American nativism within a British-based Anglo-Saxon conspiracy against Catholicism, with Orange immigrants serving as shock troops.[46] The Philadelphia-based American Protestant Association, he argued, was an Orange organization in all but name; its members bedizened themselves with Orange shawls and ribbons, and toasted the "Glorious, Pious and Immortal Memory" of William III.[47] The same pattern occurred in New York, he maintained: "North of

Ireland Orangeism lives now in the vicinity of Nassau St., New York, and shows marks of his father – Satan – who is the Alpha and Omega of all such things!"[48] Apocalyptic imagery gripped his mind: "If this be not the battle before Anti-Christ, it looks very like it."[49]

But the forces of Antichrist also spoke with American accents; there was an "unholy alliance" between "the trans-planted, house-wreck-ing, bloodthirsty Orangeman of the North of Ireland" and the native-born American "young rowdy, of scarcely twenty summers, with hell stamped upon every feature, and slung shots dangling in his sleeve." "With no creed but hatred," he wrote, "and no password softer than Extermination, they band together in a common brotherhood."[50]

McGee dated the renewed threat to the fall of 1853, when nativist secret societies, backed up by a significant section of the American press, formed an "illegal, unconstitutional and anti-American" conspiracy against Irish Catholic immigrants, and when nativist mobs started killing Irishmen on the streets.[51] By the spring of 1854, nativism had spread from its centre in New York to Massachusetts, "where the shreds and tatters of Puritan bigotry stand invitingly before it."[52] When the Scottish evangelist John Sayers Orr, popularly known as the Angel Gabriel, trumpet-blasted his way through New England, he left a trail of anti-Catholic riots in his wake – as he had done in Scotland earlier in the decade.[53] Attacks on Irish Catholic neighbourhoods, church burnings, assaults on priests (including the tarring and feathering of a priest in Maine), police brutality, marches, demonstrations, riots, and assassinations – all appeared to be part of the new reality in the United States.

Meanwhile, at the political level, nativists were making unprecedented gains. Know-Nothing mayors had been elected in Washington and Philadelphia, the American Party was making inroads into the South, the nativist movement was drawing in more and more Whigs, and even Franklin Pierce's Democratic administration was moving to the right.[54] American newspapers were arguing that the Irish were "deplorably clannish, misguided, and prone to violence," and that they had brought the nativist reaction upon themselves.[55] "From Maine to Florida, and from our own threshold to St. Paul's, Minnesota, with but five exceptions," McGee wrote, "the American press has wilfully and knowingly stifled truth, and shielded error wherever and whenever our race or our religion was attacked or defended."[56] What had begun as lower-class bigotry was moving up the social scale, acquiring the semblance of respectability, and attempting to "organize an absolutism of power" over immigrants in general, and Irish Catholics in particular.[57]

And then, in the middle of all this, came a bombshell: Orestes Brownson – the American-born Catholic convert who was one of McGee's "three masters" – declared that he supported "Native Americanism," and called for the permanent exclusion of immigrants from the franchise.[58] This did not mean, of course, that Brownson approved of the anti-Catholic element within nativism or supported the Know-Nothing movement. On the contrary, he intended to undermine anti-Catholicism by showing that native-born Catholics were good American citizens who did not want foreigners meddling in their affairs. The fact that most of these foreigners were Catholic was merely coincidental, in Brownson's view; Americans must distinguish between anti-Catholic sentiment, which was reprehensible, and anti-foreigner sentiment, which was understandable and, in certain circumstances, perfectly acceptable.[59]

It was not the Catholicism of most Irish immigrants that generated so much hostility, Brownson contended. The problem was that they formed their own militias, boasted that they could make or break American political parties, asserted their separate identity, arrogated to themselves a central role in the American Revolution, and criticized the American way of life.[60] "A man may scold his own wife, for she is his, and it is all in the family," he explained; "but let a stranger attempt the same thing, and the husband, if half a man, will knock him down, or at least turn him out of doors, with a significant kick behind, not likely to be soon forgotten."[61]

In fact, Brownson argued, native Americanism, shorn of its anti-Catholic features, was a positive expression of nationality and was thus worthy of respect. The inescapable reality was that the "population of English origin and descent are the predominating class," and all immigrants, including the Irish, "must ultimately lose their own nationality and become assimilated in general character to the Anglo-American race." The Irish were guests in the American house and must abide by its rules.[62]

As he read these arguments, McGee felt a rising sense of anger. In his view, Brownson's distinction between anti-Catholic and anti-foreign sentiments was not only untrue – it was the very reverse of the truth. All McGee's experiences had taught him that anti-Catholicism was the lifeblood of nativism, and that the Irish were being targeted precisely because of their Catholicism. "The Irish Catholics," he wrote, "are the *only wide-spread body of Christians on this continent, who have a dogmatic faith, and who refuse to compromise with the world* ... Their glorious privilege is – and they know it – to feel an infallible certainty that they are right, and that all others are wrong, in religion."[63] And if even Brownson was endorsing nativism, what hope was there for the Irish in America? McGee fell back on familiar ground: there was no fixed American identity; the American character was being shaped by a continuing process of mutual cultural accommodation; the Anglo-Saxons constituted a minority of white Americans, and this minority must be prevented from imposing its will on the majority.[64] But all these arguments could not conceal a wrenching sense of betrayal and a growing feeling of isolation.

"My most painful duty of the year was to find myself opposed to one whom I had long honored as a master, and respected as a friend," McGee wrote in December 1854. "But I had no option: for the cause of my persecuted people, I would equally dissent from my own father, had he been the author of some of the political sentiments put forward by Dr. Brownson."[65] Along with the Protestant enemy to the front, McGee now had an American Catholic enemy at the rear. The United States was becoming less and less congenial with every passing month.

As part of his counterattack, McGee delivered a series of lectures, which he published as *The Catholic History of North America*. Dedicated to "Mary, Immaculate, the ever-blessed Mother of God, under whose auspices America was Discovered and Explored," the book argued that Catholicism was the driving force behind European expansion to the

New World.[66] Catholic missionaries had made "the only systematic attempts to civilize and Christianize the aborigines," and "Catholic blood, talent, and treasure" had been largely responsible for American independence.[67]

Earlier in his career, McGee had emphasized the Irish rather than the specifically Catholic contribution to the American Revolution. The problem with this, as Brownson had recognized, was that the leading Irish American patriots were Protestants; McGee had fashioned a weak weapon against anti-Catholic nativism.[68] By placing Catholics in the forefront of the revolution while continuing to acknowledge the "Scotch-Irish" presence, McGee now put himself in a much stronger position. The bulk of the Continental Army had consisted of Irish Catholics, he asserted, and Catholic landowners and merchants had played a prominent part in the War of Independence. Nor should it be forgotten, he added, that French Catholics played a crucial role in defeating the British army at Yorktown.[69] Who, then, could argue that Catholicism was somehow antithetical to American liberty?

This was all well and good as far as it went. But it did not go beyond the converted; all the arguments in the world were useless in the face of Know-Nothing prejudice. "Reason!" McGee exclaimed. "You might as well reason with the floods of Niagara against falling over the rocks."[70] But if rational argument was inadequate, there were other strategies that Irish Catholics could employ to undermine nativism. Within their own communities, they could work to isolate Irish demagogues, whose mob politics contributed to the nativist backlash. They could also follow Father John Roddan's advice and simply abstain from the gubernatorial and state elections that were being held in November 1854. By refusing to become political targets, Irish Catholics would deprive nativism of its ostensible raison d'être.

The risk, of course, was that political abstinence would open the doors to nativism. But if that happened, at least Irish Catholics would know exactly where they stood in Protestant America.[71] Besides, the very act of bringing the Know-Nothings out into the open would expose them as the self-seeking bigots that they were. "Responsibility," McGee predicted, "will be their ruin."[72] And if the worst came to the worst, Irish Catholics could take some comfort from the fact that the Supreme Court would block unconstitutional Know-Nothing legislation.[73]

As the elections drew nearer, McGee found the "political abstinence" line increasingly difficult to sustain, and he began to recommend that Irish Catholics vote for any candidates who were pledged to equal rights for adopted citizens – if they could find any.[74] When the results came through, Irish Catholics indeed knew where they stood. In New Jersey, the Know-Nothings had "won everything they played for"; in Massachusetts, they "made a clean sweep"; they triumphed in Pennsylvania and Indiana, "carried the cities of Philadelphia, Baltimore, Norfolk, Louisville, St. Louis and New Orleans," and came close to victory in New York.[75] Know-Nothingism, McGee subsequently observed, had "swept the country with a hurricane force."[76]

"It is no chimera with which we have to deal," he wrote; "no local nor short-lived conspiracy, as we shall all probably discover in 1856."[77] The Know-Nothings would probably elect the next president in 1856; the United States Constitution would be "strangled in secret," and Irish Catholics would become victims of *"penal laws, or a massacre."* "All of us who have health and strength *can*, if we are driven to it, choose a new country, beyond the range of the present persecution, should it grow hotter and more intolerable," he wrote.[78] It was time to start looking for escape routes; it was time to start looking north.

Of course, McGee already believed that Canada had one important advantage over the United States – its educational system. In the United States, he wrote, the common schools were designed to assimilate children to the dominant Protestant culture, and constituted a major long-term threat to Catholicism; but in Canada, publicly funded separate schools and parental input into the choice of teachers encouraged diversity and allowed the Catholic faith to flourish. In this respect, he considered that Canada provided a healthier environment for Irish Catholic immigrants.[79]

This did not mean that McGee embraced other aspects of Canadian life. After all, Canada was part of the British Empire, and one of its most powerful institutions was the Orange Order – not exactly attractive features, from his perspective. Nor was British North America immune to sectarian riots. As recently as June 1853, the visit to Montreal of the ex-priest and anti-Catholic lecturer Alessandro Gavazzi had culminated in confrontation and bloodshed. After a crowd of Irish Catholics attempted to break up his meeting, violence had spilled out onto the streets. A detachment of troops opened fire, killing several people and wounding many more. McGee fixed the blame on the Orange Order, which he accused of inviting Gavazzi to Montreal in a calculated attempt to provoke the city's Catholic population. "It is notorious," he declared, "that there exists in Canada a wide-spread secret society, called 'Orangemen,' whose charter-oath binds them '*to wade knee deep in Papist blood*.'"[80]

He was equally convinced that Canadian Protestants had begun "a formal conspiracy, to strip the Catholics of property and power." The conspirators consisted of Orangemen, their supporters among the civil and military authorities, and the anti-Catholic radicals grouped around George Brown, editor of the Toronto *Globe*. McGee claimed that their activities met with the approval of the British government, which was pretending to acquiesce reluctantly in anti-Catholic policies that it secretly supported.[81] In a familiar pattern, McGee's passions had driven him into paranoia; the Orange charter oath about wading knee deep in Papist blood was a complete myth, and the "formal conspiracy" against Catholics existed only in his imagination – as a number of his Canadian readers were quick to point out.[82]

For most of 1854, McGee remained singularly unimpressed with the view that Irish Catholic Canadians enjoyed "more real liberty than you have in the United States."[83] In June, he declared that Britain's "wily statesmen" were drawing up plans for a "Northern Monarchy" that would embrace all the British American provinces and would be headed by one of Queen Victoria's sons. (In yet another ironic twist to McGee's career, he adopted this plan himself less than four years later.)[84] In early August, when the Know-Nothing movement was assuming frightening proportions, McGee was still advising Irish immigrants to choose the United States over Canada. "Bad as our bigots are," he wrote, they were by no means a majority and would be defeated after a "hard battle for seven or ten years."[85]

By November, however, the election results deepened his pessimism about the United States; nativism was much more pervasive than he had thought, and the outcome of the battle was by no means certain. In these circumstances, he decided to conduct a thorough investigation of the condition of Irish Catholics in Canada, to sound out the situation for himself. He left the management of the *American Celt* in the hands of Bernard Killian, and travelled north to Montreal.[86]

During his previous visit to the city, in 1852, McGee had been primarily concerned with disseminating his ultramontane message; this time, his purpose was to compare the United States and Canada East as a home for Irish settlers. Approaching Montreal, he was struck by "the glitter of a hundred crosses crowning the tin-covered domes and spires, which glisten like silver in the sun." "Within the city everything is in harmony with this first impression," he wrote. "The high-walled and deep-gated nunneries, the clergy, secular and regular, walking abroad in their proper habits, the courtesy of the laity, even of Protestants, who lift their hats whenever a priest passes – all things and signs speak the Christian city."[87]

Here was a place where Irish Catholics belonged; they could educate their children in their own schools, send them to their own colleges, and keep them within the faith. Here, children obeyed and respected their parents, in contrast to the United States, where it was the parents who obeyed their children. In this Catholic atmosphere, Canadians had achieved a higher quality of life than Americans. There was a "heavy balance of healthiness in favor of Canada"; Canadian mortality rates were lower, and even Canadian eating habits were better. "Indigestion is an uncommon complaint," he commented, "as the doctors confess with a melancholy unanimity." "With us," he wrote, "life is a fevered and eager race, with them a slow and merry procession."[88]

Although Canada East was best suited to commerce and manufacturing, there were also great opportunities for agricultural settlement. The Eastern Townships beckoned – a region, he was told, that contained a population of only 80,000 and had the same amount of arable land that existed in a third of Ireland. This land was available in two-hundred-acre lots, on terms that were "nearly as reasonable" as in the United States. "If the Irish in New England should ever be compelled to move *en masse*," McGee wrote, "it is pleasant to know that there is a vast, fertile, and thinly inhabited territory in their immediate neighborhood, where, if they be wise for their own interests, they may *realize* many of the fond hopes bigotry has forever blasted for them in our Eastern states."[89]

Paranoia had given way to paradox: In this corner of the British Empire — an empire that McGee still regarded as a force of great evil — lay a Catholic haven, a potential place of refuge for Irish Americans. How could this be explained? A key factor, McGee believed, was the proximity of Canada to the United States. Realizing that oppressive colonial rule would drive Canada into the arms of the republic, British authorities had granted Canada responsible government and had generally chosen not to exercise their imperial veto over local legislation.[90] And in Montreal at least, Orangeism was barely visible; the Gavazzi riot now appeared as the exception rather than the rule. Canadian political institutions were "substantially the same" as those in America, only without "the despotism of the mob and the proscriptive patterns of an illiberal *nativism*."[91]

McGee was not exclusively wedded to Canada as a haven for Irish American Catholics; the American West, he believed, could also fulfill this function. After visiting Montreal, he travelled to St Louis to investigate the "farming states" beyond the Mississippi. Although he lacked the time to conduct a detailed analysis, the general situation was clear. Millions of acres of land were opening up for settlement, and the land was being sold at a rapid rate; the Irish had to move quickly, he wrote, if they were to seize the opportunity.[92]

More important at this stage than the pull of a potential destination was the push of prejudice — what he saw as the increasingly intolerable religious, political, social, and economic conditions of Irish Catholic immigrants in the United States. Anti-Catholic pressure, he believed, was building; there were conspiracies on every side, from radical Irish American republicans to bigoted American nativists, aided and abetted by abolitionists, with the British government in the background, pulling the strings. And all this was occurring within the context of the break-up of the old American party system. The future was uncertain and sometimes terrifying. Some kind of safety valve was needed, in the west or north. If Irish Americans were to realize the opportunities in the north, they must shake off their repugnance of living under the Union Jack – a repugnance that McGee had shaken off himself. "The British flag does indeed fly here," he wrote of Canada, "but it casts no shadow."[93] He now had to convince his countrymen that he was right.

CHAPTER FOURTEEN

A Rather Isolated Position
January 1855 – April 1857

"Thomas as usual is away from home," Mary McGee told Bella Morgan in July 1856.[1] When she wrote these words, her husband was on an extended tour of Nova Scotia and New Brunswick; it was one of four major trips he made to British North America that year. In 1855 he spent almost half the year away from New York, including a three-month visit to Ireland and England, and journeys to Canada West and Canada East.[2] His restlessness was symptomatic. As McGee became increasingly disillusioned with the United States, he spent less and less time in the country. The man was voting with his feet.

Among these journeys, his visit to Ireland in February 1855 was of special significance. The Young Ireland prisoners, including Smith O'Brien, had been pardoned the previous year, and it was now safe for McGee to return.[3] In this new climate, his old friend Richard Baptist O'Brien, the founder of the Catholic Young Men's Societies in Ireland, invited him on a speaking tour.[4] McGee immediately accepted; it would give him the opportunity to visit old haunts, see his father and family, and reconnect with Gavan Duffy, who had told McGee of his plans to leave Ireland for Australia.[5]

The visit also enabled him to take the pulse of post-famine Ireland and to inform Irish audiences about his experiences in the United States. Just over six years earlier, McGee had slipped out of Tremone Bay at a time of famine and revolution. A changed man in a changed country, he now penned a series of articles entitled "Ireland Revisited," which provided a vivid account of what he called the "silent revolution" that was modernizing Irish society.[6]

On the economic and social front, McGee registered the central characteristics of post-famine Ireland – the consolidation of holdings, the switch from tillage to pasture, and the disappearance of "the cottier and conacre class." He found much to applaud about the new situation; the harvests had been good, wages were increasing, and railways were transforming the country.[7] "The railroad," he remarked later in the year, "has banished the fairies from Ireland, it has waked up the intellectual facilities of the agricultural classes, [and] introduced among them habits of punctuality and industry."[8]

But there were also some disturbing developments. "The whole style of Irish thinking and talking has changed, or is fast changing," he observed; "all classes seem more serious than formerly, more business-like, more selfish."[9] This was particularly true of the farmers, who had been frightened into "the extreme of parsimony" by the famine and were increasingly exploiting their labourers.[10] "I regret to state that the farmers are often more tyrannical with them in turn, than the landlords are with the farmers," a priest informed McGee. "I could tell you instances of this kind which would astonish and shock you, at the inhumanity of men, themselves of the people, themselves protesting against oppression, and themselves ever ready to oppress their hired servants."[11]

Along with increased class tensions, McGee discovered a general disillusionment with nationalist politics. "There is a 'what's the use?['] sort of air about almost every person I meet," he wrote.[12] And no wonder. As an Irish MP (probably Duffy) told him, "O'Connell's failure, the '48 failure; the potato failure; the Parliamentary failure, all within ten years, will certainly justify, to some extent, the general distrust and disgust the people feel towards politics and politicians." The "Parliamentary failure" had been hastened by the defection of two leading MPs, John Sadleir and William Keogh, from the Irish Brigade, and was viewed by McGee as symptomatic of a declining "public spirit."[13] On the other hand, McGee was heartened by the "general 'revival' of Catholicity" in Ireland. New churches were being built, the religious orders were growing in strength, and the Catholic University was increasing in influence.[14] If Irish nationalism was receding, Irish Catholicism was moving into the ascendant – a trajectory that perfectly matched the changes within McGee himself.

——•··•··•——

The "Ireland Revisited" series included some revealing reports of McGee's conversations with people he met on his travels. On the road from Bagnalstown to Bunclody, he got talking with his coachdriver, Mike, who told him that wages and prices had risen and that there was more work than before. They began to discuss the war. "Didn't the English get a terrible handlin' in the Crimea, sir?" said Mike. "They did so, thank God," replied McGee. "Forty thousand men lost in one year. Unfortunately, most of them were our poor countrymen, Mike." Mike was unmoved. "Them fellows that take the shillin', sir, are small loss. They are mostly poor pilgarlicks, picked up at fairs and markets, too lazy to work, and just good enough to be shot at."

McGee then asked Mike about the prophecies of Columcille, which had been circulating in the countryside. "A great many believes in it, sir," came the reply. "And about them prophecies, there's a thing I know myself; that the ould parish priest of Ferris, who died twenty years ago, always believed them prophecies. Till his dying day he was ever and always sayin that another Bonypart would have France, and that France would humble England before the children he had christened were dead. Dozens of men remember these sayin's, and since the war, they're flying all round the country. More than that, even the gentlemen have got a notion that England's reign is nearly over."[15] Significantly, and somewhat surprisingly for an ultramontanist, McGee found this heartening. Despite the decline of nationalism, the fact that people were equating British defeats in the Crimea with the "*pseudo* 'prophecies' of Saint Columbcille" demonstrated to McGee that there was still some spirit left in the country.[16]

Higher up the social scale, however, McGee encountered people such as the "ex-Mayor and leading politician of a provincial town" whose patriotism had waned as his prosperity had waxed. When the politician congratulated him for changing his views, McGee bristled. It was true, McGee said, that he now had very different views about mixed education and the relation between religion and politics. "But if you mean that I have now, or ever had, any doubt of the right of Ireland to deliver herself from foreign oppression by the shedding of any quantity of British blood, you are totally wrong."[17]

As the conversation continued, the politician argued that Ireland was not oppressed; Ireland had "freedom of worship, of speech, of the press, and of trade," and lived under the best form of government in the world. "Standing on his Kidderminster carpet, and looking from his drawing-room windows," McGee wrote, "he, indeed, could not see 'what the Irish wanted.'" What about disestablishing the Church of Ireland and reforming the land system? That was all very well in principle, the politician replied, but would never happen in practice; such bills would never get past the Protestant House of Lords. Surely, said McGee, concerted political action could push through reforms. "My dear fellow," replied the ex-mayor, "Irish politics are all a farce. If you have a brazen face and a noisy tongue you can lead the mob anywhere for a while, but if you talk common sense no one will listen to you."[18]

McGee also got into a discussion with a Dublin mechanic and former Young Irelander, who told him that most people had abandoned the Confederates and that the few who remained were "split into fifty factions." Before long, the conversation turned to religion. When the mechanic criticized the recently proclaimed dogma of the Immaculate Conception, on the grounds that it provided "an opening to scoffers against our religion," McGee gave him a stern admonition. The church was right to declare that Mary had never been stained with original sin; the mechanic was taking "the Devil's side of this question" and had no right to his own opinion. "Rome has spoken," McGee told him, "and that is enough for you, for me, and for all Catholics." It was, he remarked, "lamentable to find such errors afloat, among a generally religious people."[19]

These conversations not only shed light on changing attitudes in post-famine Ireland; they also provide a fascinating snapshot of McGee's mind in the spring of 1855. He still adhered to the extreme theoretical position that limitless quantities of British blood could be shed for the cause of Irish freedom, while arguing that the best practical course of action was to work for disestablishment and land reform through constitutional means. His hostility to the British Empire remained unabated, and he thanked God for the Russian victories over the British army – Irish soldiers and all – in the Crimea. And he took a hard line against anyone who criticized or questioned the teachings of the Catholic Church: to elevate private judgment above Catholic dogma was to align oneself with Satan.

•━•••━•

McGee's conservative Catholicism also informed his Irish lectures about conditions in the United States. He spoke about the moral dangers of American life – the break-up of family life ("the family," he asserted, "is not an American institution"), the lack of order, and the frenetic focus on acquiring wealth. "If I were asked to give, in one word, the definition of American public opinion, so far, I would use only the word – *excitement*," he said. "We cannot exist without an annual *excitement*, native or foreign, real or imaginary. Sometimes it is a great principle that works us into a fury, sometimes a horrible fiction, sometimes a fashion of the day. A picturesque demagogue, a literary lion, a northern nightingale, a dancing girl will do. If not supplied from these sources, then we must fall back on ... good old Popery." Irish Catholics would be better off staying at home, he wrote, even as he chose not to follow his own advice. The United States was no longer a refuge for the Irish – it had become "a vast fortress armed against them." If Irish Catholics had to leave home, he declared, they would be better off going to Canada.[20]

Such words did not go down well in the Great Republic. Orestes Brownson, as a good American nationalist, was appalled that McGee would criticize the United States in front of a foreign audience; the two men were driven further apart than ever.[21] Irish American republicans were even more incensed; they spread rumours that McGee had conferred with the British consul in New York before his trip, and that his visit had been undertaken "in the interests of the British government" – something that is rather hard to square with McGee's continuing anglophobia.[22] John McClenehan, who had taken over the New York *Citizen* from John Mitchel, went on the offensive, declaring that the newspaper's articles had exposed "Darkey" McGee as "a mischievous, drunken, ribald sweep," a traitor and a spy, and had given him "a kick in the fundament with the toe of our boot that made him writhe and yell."[23] Rather than writhing and yelling, McGee decided to do something more substantive – to sue McClenehan for libel. Eventually, though, he dropped the charge, on the grounds that the Irish republican movement had become so faction-ridden that it was effectively destroying itself.[24]

In explaining the United States to his Irish audiences, and in explaining Ireland to his American readers, McGee's dominant tone was one of pessimism. A few months later, Duffy declared that there was "no more hope for the Irish Cause than for the corpse on the dissecting table," and McGee had clearly caught some of his mood.[25] After he returned to the United States, there was a major shift in the focus of his writings; rather than looking back across the Atlantic, he increasingly turned his attention to the continental north and west, where it might be possible to find a new home and new hope for his countrymen.

McGee cut his trip short in early April and rushed back to New York because of "imperative personal duties," about which we can only speculate.[26] There was no sign of any trouble in a letter that Mary wrote to Bella Morgan some three weeks earlier. Mary was pregnant at this time and would give birth in the summer to a daughter, Rose, named after one of McGee's sisters; it is possible her health was suffering and that she needed her husband's support.[27] Whatever the reason, McGee was back at work later in the month, resuming his struggle against American nativism.[28]

"It is no longer with a local mob we have to deal," he had written just before his departure, "but with the entire confederacy, revolutionized into one vast Secret Society."[29] By the summer of 1855, however, it was clear that his dark predictions about the Know-Nothings becoming the majority party and capturing the presidency were not materializing; the Know-Nothing movement was splitting over slavery, and the American Party was losing momentum.[30] Yet McGee took little comfort from this development. Even though Know-Nothingism as an organized political force was dissipating, he was convinced that the anti-Catholic spirit that sustained it remained as strong as ever.[31] His earlier fears about the possibility of a "massacre" found a measure of confirmation in the "Bloody Monday" riots of August 1855 in Louisville, when a Know-Nothing crowd attacked Irish and German Catholics, leaving around a hundred dead.[32]

A "strong tide of prejudice," McGee believed, ran through all American political parties, including the Democrats.[33] His loose identification with the conservative wing of the party came to an abrupt end in May 1856, over the Philemon Herbert and Thomas Keating affair. Philemon Herbert was a Democratic congressman from California; Thomas Keating was an Irish waiter in a Washington hotel. At breakfast one morning, Herbert complained about the service and called Keating "a damned Irish son of a b—h." As the argument escalated, Herbert grabbed Keating by the collar, pulled out a pistol, and shot him through the heart.

Despite his action, Herbert was let out on bail, allowed to return to the House of Representatives, and protected by seventy-nine Democrats who voted against a public inquiry. "What then does it mean?" McGee asked. "Or can it mean anything but one thing – that an Irishman born, however peaceable or loyal, is only fit to be used by the Democratic party, and when used, set up for a target, and shot with impunity." "A few days ago the blood of Thomas Keating was on the hands of but one Democrat," he wrote; "it has spread since then, and it is now upon the souls of the 79, who refused all inquiry. It is on the Democratic party, as a party, and accursed be he who helps such a party into power, until that blood is lawfully purged away."[34]

The event left a deep mark on McGee; he was still fuming about it after he moved to Canada.[35] It almost pushed him, by way of reaction, towards the Republicans; at least they supported an inquiry into Keating's murder, and they were trying to outbid the Democrats for Catholic support.[36] But any possibility of a rapprochement with the Republicans ended during the presidential campaign of 1856, when McGee became convinced that they were tapping into anti-Catholic prejudices.[37] The result was a "plague on both your houses" attitude. The Catholic Irish, he wrote, should have nothing to do with either party; they should keep their heads down and do nothing that would "arouse the Protestant sentiment of the country" against them.[38]

This left him, as he put it, in "a rather isolated position."[39] Almost all the other Irish Catholic newspapers supported the Democrats, and their urban readers turned out heavily for James Buchanan, the Democratic presidential candidate. By supporting the party that shielded the murderer of Keating, McGee argued, Irish Catholics had abandoned their self-respect; by expressing that support through demagoguery, machine politics, and a mob mentality, they had brought disgrace upon themselves. All this sowed "the bitter seeds of future trouble." "We assert now, and we ask readers to bear in mind our assertion," he wrote, "that the indecent exhibition of their Irish stock by the Democratic managers in 1856, will lead within a few years, to a fundamental alteration of the naturalization laws."[40]

Along with his growing hostility to American political life and his exasperation with Irish Catholics who embraced its worst features, McGee became increasingly angry about the social conditions facing his countrymen in urban America. The problems began even before they landed, he wrote; on the transatlantic voyage, Irish immigrants were cut off from the control of the church and exposed to all kinds of temptations. When they disembarked, they were greeted by "labor-brokers," who sent them off to the public works, where they were exploited. They took shelter in substandard shanties, "without Priest or Police, but never without bad brandy."[41] In the slums of New York and Boston, McGee asserted, the Irish tenant was "as much a slave, as the Irish tenant of a quarter acre ever was, in Cork or Connaught."[42]

Indeed, he believed that Irish immigrants in urban ghettoes were, if anything, even worse off than they had been at home. Citing the New York Legislative Committee's report on tenement houses in Brooklyn, McGee described the overcrowding, squalor, unsanitary conditions, fire traps, and extortionate rents that created a "hell on earth" for their largely Irish inhabitants.[43] In these conditions, traditional moral boundaries broke down; the report described "drunken and diseased adults of both sexes lying in the midst of their filth; idiotic and crippled children suffering from neglect and ill-treatment; *girls, just springing into womanhood living indiscriminately in the same apartment with men of all ages and of*

Constitution Wharf. Irish immigrants arriving in Boston, where some were greeted by friends and relatives, as above, and others were exploited by a variety of "labor-brokers" and conmen. McGee believed that the Catholic Church could play a large role in protecting vulnerable immigrants, and supported the establishment of immigration stations such as Castle Garden in New York.

all colors; babes left so destitute of care and nourishment as to be fitted only for a jail or hospital in after years, if they escape the blessing of an early grave."[44] Men and women who might have remained under the care and guidance of the Catholic Church in rural Ireland had become "mixed up with a motley population of sailors, negroes, and the most degraded natives" in the slums of America. They were becoming contaminated with corruption, and their children were turning away from the faith.[45]

A graphic example of this degradation, in McGee's view, was the notorious prize fight between Charley Lynch and Andy Kelly at the Palisades, New Jersey, in September 1856. Described by contemporaries as "one of the most brutal, atrocious and revolting ever known," the fight lasted two hours and fifteen minutes, until Kelly collapsed at the beginning of the eighty-sixth round, dying shortly afterwards.

With feelings of "deep disgust and humiliation," McGee pointed out that "the names of nearly all the actors in that brutal conflict suggest only too plainly their paternity." Ireland, he lamented, had "the discredit of swarming the great cities with a horde of hardy, vulgar ruffians, unmatched in any former state of society."[46]

But the "lost second generation"[47] was not only a product of urban squalor; it was also the result of broader homogenizing pressures in the United States. "Americanize, Americanize! is the cry of the mob and the press," McGee wrote. In practice, he argued, Americanization meant Protestantism (the latest symptom of which was New York's Free Love Society), a "very lively hatred of Rome and its religion," and a belief in "the divine appointment of the Anglo-Saxon to civilize the earth."[48]

This was bad enough; still worse was the evidence that the Irish were joining the "clamor for uniformity" and becoming agents in the destruction of their own identity. He noted reports that Irish immigrants were changing their names to appear more American, adding that such stories matched his own observations: "Among women the sweet old names, Grace, Rose, Winnifred, Kathleen, Bride, Aileen, Eva, Anne, Sarah, Margaret, are fast dying out. We can hardly restrain our indignation while we speak of it."[49]

Religious prejudice, political manipulation, economic exploitation, social degradation, and cultural conformity – all these forces were destroying the Irish identity and Catholic morality in the United States, according to McGee. Against this background, his view that Irish Catholics should get out of the cities and form their own communities on the land acquired a new urgency. McGee had made sporadic but enthusiastic references to western colonization both before and after his Young Ireland years. He had written poems such as "The Army of the West" and "The Shanty" to encourage earlier settlement schemes, and in 1852 he had supported associations "for the formation of Catholic Colonies out west."[50] Now, in the mid-1850s, he approached the subject with a new intensity and fixity of purpose. Colonization, he was convinced, offered the only salvation for Irish Catholics in urban America;

consequently, he devoted most of his formidable energy to the cause – so much so, in fact, that he soon became known as "Moses McGee."[51]

As McGee acknowledged, there was nothing original about this idea. In 1817, United Irish *émigrés* such as William MacNeven and Thomas Emmet had attempted to create an Irish colony in Illinois, only to be rebuffed by a slim majority in Congress.[52] Bishop Benedict Joseph Fenwick of Boston had established a Catholic Irish colony, Benedicta, in Maine in 1834, and other clerical initiatives had been taken in Wisconsin and Indiana.[53] But McGee was planning something on a much grander scale. His plan was to take anywhere between 50,000 and 200,000 Irish Catholic immigrants out of the cities, and to transplant them to new land, where they would be controlled by their priests and inoculated against the contamination of Protestantism and revolutionary republicanism.[54]

In these self-governing communities, Irish immigrants would become respectable, independent farmers, rather than exploited wage labourers.[55] Catholics would marry Catholics, bring their children up in the faith, and be "morally certain of moulding the minds" of their children.[56] McGee's ideal image of Ireland would be redrawn on the blank slate of new territory in North America. Not only those who left would benefit but also those who stayed behind. Removing large numbers of Irish from the cities would produce a labour shortage and thus higher wages for those who remained; it would also make native-born Americans realize that they could no longer push the Irish around or take them for granted.[57] The colonization project, McGee announced, should be launched under the banner of "Shin Fane," which he translated as "Ourselves for Ourselves." He had beaten Arthur Griffith to the name by half a century.[58]

Having made the case for a Catholic Irish colony, McGee was faced with the question of its location. His central criterion appeared to be the availability of good land, whether in the American West or in Canada. Indiana and Iowa were possible destinations, along with the Ottawa Valley and Bruce Peninsula regions of Canada West.[59] On balance, though, he preferred Canada; the American West was already becoming infected with Protestant prejudice, while Canada was closer and more accessible to the Irish population in New York.[60] Recognizing that his readers would have the same reluctance about living in the British Empire that he himself had once felt, McGee re-emphasized his earlier distinction between Britain and Canada. The British government, he wrote, was "an hereditary oligarchy of the meanest and most oppressive sort," and Irishmen owed it their "stern hereditary hatred."[61] But Canada enjoyed *de facto* independence, and was not tainted by landlordism, a state church, or a corrupt court.[62]

There was, however, another problem with respect to Canada – the growing power of the Orange Order, especially in Canada West. How could McGee lead Irish Catholics into one of the most Orange places on the planet? What kind of deliverance was that? The answer came during an extended trip to Canada West in the summer of 1855, when he concluded that most Canadian Protestants were not Orangemen, and that the Orange Order in Canada was significantly different from its Irish parent. "The Canadian Order is largely modified," he wrote; "is far more political than religious, and (except on the 12th, when they go mad, of course), I am assured by the most respectable Catholics in Canada West, that they have no better neighbors all the rest of the year, than these same Orangemen."[63]

Even on the Twelfth of July in Toronto, he reported, Orangemen left the Catholic clergy alone. Conditions of social equality between Catholics and Protestants were more important in Canada than atavistic memories of Aughrim and the Boyne. An Irish Catholic in Canada, McGee remarked, "does not lower his note on entering a hotel or a steamboat, he is not obliged to bite his lip and be silent in mixed society; his feelings and opinions are habitually respected, and he holds his head high, without once straining a muscle."[64]

McGee's Irish Catholic Canadian readers were quick to endorse his arguments.[65] From St Thomas, Peter Murtagh wrote that the relatively strong position of Irish Catholics in Canada was the product of two forces – the French fact, which meant that almost half the province's MPs were Catholic, and the abundance of resources, which meant that there was less competition between Protestants and Catholics.[66] Advice began coming in about possible sites for an Irish Catholic colony in Canada – the Bruce Peninsula, the Eastern Townships, or the counties of Lambton, Essex, and Kent.[67] It was one thing, though, to make these suggestions, and another thing altogether to put them into practice. And this is where Dean Thadeus T. Kirwan, from London in Canada West, entered the picture.

———•·•·•———

An immigrant from County Clare, Kirwan had been saying since the beginning of the famine that Irish immigrants to North America should settle in the countryside rather than the towns.[68] McGee and Kirwan had first met during McGee's tour of Canada in July 1855 and doubtless discussed the subject of colonization.[69] In November, Kirwan wrote to the *American Celt*, pointing out that the Canadian government had just opened up free land in the Owen Sound district, and calling for a convention in Buffalo that would promote and plan Irish Catholic colonies in the American West or in Canada.[70] McGee enthusiastically endorsed the idea and provided maximum publicity in his newspaper. Kirwan announced that the convention would assemble on 12 February 1856 and suggested that it meet every year; McGee expected it to become "the Congress of the emigrant."[71]

In the course of selecting delegates to the Buffalo Convention, a pro-McGee Irish Catholic network was forming in Canada. It included Peter Murtagh from St Thomas, Father John H. McDonagh of Perth (later the subject of McGee's well-known poem "The Priest of Perth"), John O'Donohoe of Toronto and George Clerk, the ultramontane editor of Montreal's *True Witness*.[72] Also from Montreal was Bernard Devlin, president of the Young Men's St Patrick's Association, who claimed that the idea of a convention had actually originated with his organization the previous year.[73]

Over the three days of the Buffalo Convention, almost a hundred delegates converged on the city. Forty-three of them came from Canada, including ten priests; almost half of the fifty-five American delegates were clergymen. Among the laity were "judges, lawyers, aldermen, editors, captains of military companies, merchants, farmers, and mechanics," some of whom had travelled a thousand miles to attend.[74]

As they assembled, tensions quickly emerged. George Clerk, who had travelled down with Bernard Devlin, got into a fierce row with some of the local Catholic clergy who opposed the project; Buffalo's Irish American republicans also denounced the scheme. Within the convention itself, some of the American delegates had been mandated to support colonization only within the United States; there was, Clerk recorded, "a little jealousy of Canada."[75] To counter such criticisms, the convention pointed out that it was not a "Canadian Colonization Society"; it was an "Irish and Catholic Convention for the Promotion of Actual Settlements" wherever conditions were suitable. Canadians and Americans had roughly equal representation on committees, and the Canadian president, Thadeus Kirwan, sat on the "Supreme Directory" with two American vice presidents.[76]

McGee was not a member of the Supreme Directory, but he worked with his fellow ultramontane journalist Clerk in drawing up the convention's Address to Irish Catholics, and chaired its finance committee.[77] In its report, the committee estimated that Irish immigrants had around $48 million in savings banks. Asserting that "the best of all banks ... is the unshaken soil of the earth," the committee argued that this money could be invested in joint stock companies, which would lend money to settlers at competitive interest rates. In the case of "the poor settler, who is a sober man and otherwise desirable," the companies would defer interest charges until his land became profitable; further financial assistance would be provided through periodic church collections. The committee also resolved that every township should reserve forty acres of land "for a church, school, and priest's farm, the deed to be made out to the proper ecclesiastical authority."[78]

The proceedings gave "weight and importance" to the colonization question, bringing it to the attention of leading politicians in Canada and the United States, McGee noted. He contrasted the constructive work at Buffalo with the "disgraceful bar-room battles" at the recent Irish American republican convention in New York.[79] But he was aware that much work remained to be done; it was essential to develop a "regular *system* of action" that would begin the process of settlement.[80]

By the spring of 1856, it seemed that progress was indeed being made. The Buffalo Convention had received some positive publicity, Mary Ann Sadlier's *Con O'Regan* (serialized in the *American Celt*) provided literary support, and plans to finance the first township – to be called

St Patrick and located in Nebraska – were underway.[81] But the initial enthusiasm proved hard to sustain, and complaints about the "inaction" of some delegates soon began to surface.[82] Land was becoming available in the Ottawa Valley and the Bruce Peninsula, but local colonization societies had failed to reach their minimum contributions, and the Supreme Directory did not have sufficient purchasing power. Opportunities were slipping through fingers, and time was running out.[83]

During the summer, McGee co-authored a report on the situation. It cost $25,000 to buy one township. For the proposed township of St Patrick, $17,250 had been pledged, but only $1,950 had actually been raised.[84] To reinvigorate the movement, some members called for a second convention, to be held in Chicago.[85] McGee supported the idea, but there were no takers. "The apathy, the selfishness, of which we complain, must not be suffered to pass unpunished," he wrote. "We call especially on those who were at Buffalo to say, whether they were in jest or in earnest on that solemn occasion ... We put these plain questions: shall the colonization cause be abandoned? or, will increased and better efforts be made in 1857, to bring it to a successful issue?"[86]

The very act of posing the questions provided the answer; the colonization cause turned out to be a total failure. A number of reasons have been adduced, ranging from the demise of the Know-Nothing movement to the high demand for Irish labour in the cities and the closing of the principal land offices in the United States during the summer of 1856.[87] More significant is the fact that many Irish immigrants were already moving west of their own volition; 85 percent of the Irish who landed in New York during the famine did not stay there, and the census of 1870 shows that over half the Irish-born Americans lived outside the cities.[88] The movement from the cities that McGee was trying to achieve collectively was occurring individually, in a stepwise pattern of migration. As Archbishop Hughes argued, "There is a natural process by which this result is perpetually going on." Irish immigrants, Hughes pointed out, were travelling west in search of work, gathering experience and knowledge of their new neighbourhoods, building up their capital, and acquiring land or other property. And that, he insisted, was exactly the way it should happen.[89]

There was, however, another important reason for the collapse of colonization – the opposition of a large section of the Catholic Church. Although the project generated significant Catholic support in Canada and the American West, many bishops, priests, and prominent laymen in the East came out strongly against colonization. Among them was Father John Roddan, one of the key figures in McGee's conversion to ultramontanism. In January 1855, more than a year before the Buffalo Convention, the *Boston Pilot* published a letter condemning Canadian colonization schemes as *"uncatholic and unpatriotic."*[90] Commenting on the letter, Roddan argued that a *"wholesale* emigration, *stampede*, or second Exodus" was an act of cowardice. Instead of running away from Know-Nothingism, Irish immigrants should confront and defeat it at home.[91]

This marked the beginning of a sustained attack on McGee's plans and on his positive image of Canada. How, asked Roddan, could McGee possibly raise the vast amount of money that was needed to settle large numbers of impoverished city dwellers in rural areas? And who in their sane senses would encourage Irish Catholics to leave a country where nativism was declining for one where Orangeism was in the ascendant?[92] In Canada, Roddan declared, Irish Catholics were excluded from political power, forced out of Orange townships, insulted every Twelfth of July, and subjected to systematic discrimination. And what made McGee think that the British government and Canadian Protestants would welcome a massive influx of Irish Catholics into Canada?[93]

Apparently confirming Roddan's position, three thousand Irish Protestants packed themselves into Toronto's St Lawrence Hall just before the Buffalo Convention and denounced what they saw as a plan "to swamp the Protestants of Canada, by bringing in to the Province Eight hundred thousand unenlightened and bigotted Romanists"; the numbers escalated with the fear. The main speaker was John Holland, the Orange Order's grand secretary of British America. "Wherever these people predominate," he told a cheering crowd, "there the peace and happiness and comfort of the community is destroyed." "These people" had no mind of their own, he explained; they were mentally enslaved by their priests, and the results were plain to see – they were "bad farmers," with a well-deserved reputation for drinking, fighting, and rioting. Would the "great Protestant city of Toronto" ever allow itself to be dominated by Roman Catholics? Holland asked. "Never!" came the resounding reply. The Protestants were once again under siege, and it was Toronto's Orangemen who would save them.[94]

All this was grist to the mill of McGee's Catholic critics. Permeating Roddan's comments was a sense of bewilderment that McGee, of all people, could endorse colonization in a place like Canada. After all, Roddan wrote, McGee had been "the most cordial hater of the English flag we ever saw" and "an almost insane hater of the British government." Throughout his American career, McGee had insisted that Irish immigrants must become American citizens and stand their ground against nativism. Yet here he was, encouraging his countrymen to live under the Union Jack, and urging them to abandon the United States. Nothing could be better calculated to confirm the Know-Nothing argument that Irish Catholics were not truly committed to the American way of life.[95] McGee's views, declared Roddan, were "beyond our comprehension."[96]

Not only was McGee running away, just as he had done in 1848, alleged Roddan, but he was running away from the phantoms of his own imagination.[97] It was true that Irish Catholics faced serious difficulties in the United States, but McGee had magnified them out of all proportion; by fixating on everything that was bad about America – the riots, massacres, robberies, and rapes – McGee and the Canadian Catholic press were making it look as if "hell is let loose in the United States," while "Paradise, or something very like it, is established in Canada."[98] "This," commented Roddan, "is neither fair nor kind treatment."[99]

***

Well before the Buffalo Convention, then, colonization had been subjected to a barrage of criticism. Immediately afterwards, McGee was hit from a new direction when the New York *Freeman's Journal* – the "official organ" of the New York diocese – charged that the convention had been manipulated by "secret wire-pullers" in the form of British agents and Canadian land speculators.[100] The attacks in the *Freeman's Journal* were themselves the work of a secret wire-puller – Archbishop Hughes. Once again, the two men were on a collision course.

But Hughes could not, at this stage, openly denounce the project. During McGee's lecture tour of New York in the winter of 1855–56, someone had handed McGee a potentially explosive document about anti-Irish machinations within the Catholic Church in Newburgh. Although the details remain unknown, Hughes feared that McGee would go public with the document if the two men got into a debate; as a result, Hughes told Brownson, "the power of correction on my part has been very much diminished."[101] Only when it became clear later in the year that McGee would not divulge the information did Hughes go directly on the offensive.

And go on the offensive he did. McGee, he wrote, was exaggerating the miseries of the Irish in New York and tarring the entire second generation of Irish Americans with the brush of its "lowest and most degraded" characters.[102] Canada was the worst place imaginable for Irish Catholics, and McGee was the worst person to lead them anywhere. The man was constantly whining about conditions that his own earlier liberalism had helped to create, and he could not even manage his own affairs, let alone anyone else's – presumably, a reference to McGee's drinking.[103] Hughes said that he himself, in his youth, had dreamt of establishing an Irish Catholic colony in Wisconsin; now, however, he realized that such schemes were "all nonsense." As in 1849, Hughes was attacking in McGee something that he had rejected within himself.[104]

In December 1856, Hughes urged Irish Catholics to consider "withdrawing their support" from a number of Irish American newspapers, including the *American Celt*;[105] and three months later he made a dramatic intervention against colonization at a public meeting on Broadway. McGee had invited Father Jeremiah Trecy, one of the Iowa delegates at the Buffalo Convention, to speak in support of the St Patrick's colony that was being planned in Nebraska.[106] As Trecy talked about the project, Hughes sat in the gallery, concealing himself beneath an overcoat and muffler. When the speech was over, Hughes stood up and attacked Trecy with "considerable asperity." It was a classic political ambush.[107]

No holds were left unbarred. Hughes chastised Trecy for daring to speak in his diocese without permission. He dismissed pro-colonization Catholics as dupes of unscrupulous land speculators – not deeming it worthwhile to provide any evidence for his assertion. He accused his enemies of spreading lies that he opposed colonization on the grounds that it would depopulate eastern dioceses – forgetting that he had made that very argument himself only three months earlier.[108] He derided the delegates at the Buffalo Convention as hypocrites who had never actually lived in the West themselves – ignoring the fact that many of them were missionaries who had worked there for years.

It was down and dirty, in a most unchristian kind of way. But in one crucial respect, Hughes was right. Projects like St Patrick's, he asserted, were bound to fail, and their embittered victims would turn against their clerical leaders and possibly even the church itself. Although there is no evidence that the two hundred Irish Catholics who settled at St Patrick's abandoned the faith, they certainly abandoned the township. After struggling to survive on poor land in a poor location, they cut their losses and moved on. Within a decade, St Patrick's was deserted and the project had collapsed.[109]

While Roddan, Brownson, and Hughes were shouting in one ear, McGee's Irish American republican enemies were shouting in the other. From the republican view, the point was not to resettle Irish immigrants in the American West or, even worse, in Canada; it was to fight for freedom in Ireland. Where Roddan had been perplexed by McGee's position, Irish American republicans had a ready explanation at hand – the traitor McGee was driven by personal ambition. By seducing Irish Catholics into newly planted colonies, wrote Felix O'Driscol from New York, McGee hoped to "have a seat in the colonial parliament; or if in Iowa, or Minnesota ... have a chance of being elected to Congress!"[110] "We have now done with McGee," declared John McClenehan at the end of a hate-filled harangue about his treachery, hypocrisy, cowardice, and dishonesty. "Let him take his carcase to Canada."[111]

McGee's reaction to these attacks consisted largely of reiterating his earlier arguments.[112] Against the view that individual western migration was already occurring, he wrote that Irish Catholics could protect and preserve their religion only in communal settlements.[113] Against the view that he was exaggerating the plight of urban Irish Catholics, he insisted that his countrymen had experienced "a bitter social persecution" and were politically powerless to improve their condition.[114] And against the view that Irish Canadian Catholics faced at least as much discrimination as their American counterparts, he declared that Canada had "more social freedom, and a purer moral atmosphere" than New England and New York.[115]

How persuasive was his defence? On the subject of colonization, McGee's critics had the stronger case, leaving aside Hughes's unfounded and unfair accusations. McGee made a powerful theoretical argument for the benefits of moving impoverished and ghettoized Irish Catholics onto the land, but Hughes and Roddan were right to emphasize the immense logistical difficulties of actually getting them there. Just try it and see, Roddan told McGee. If the plan failed, which was virtually certain, "you can console yourself for the failure by assigning all sorts of reasons excepting the true one – viz., that the scheme is the wildest one that was ever heard of."[116] The history of Irish Catholic colonization schemes had been one of unremitting failure; the dismal fate of the St Patrick's colony was part of a much larger picture.

Yet there was also a sense in which the arguments of Hughes and Roddan were self-fulfilling; by opposing colonization in the 1850s, they helped to ensure its defeat. When the hierarchy was united, as it was in the 1880s, Irish Catholic colonies on a limited scale – nothing like the 50,000 to 200,000 originally projected by McGee – were established in Minnesota and Nebraska. For the organizers of those colonies, McGee was an inspirational and heroic figure; Bishop John Ireland, for example, praised the "enlightened views of D'Arcy McGee and those who took part with him in the famous Buffalo colonization convention of 1856."[117] McGee, in this respect, had achieved a degree of posthumous success – another emerging pattern in his career.

On the condition of Irish Catholics in the United States, there is much evidence to back up McGee's comments about the exploitation, unemployment, petty crime, and squalid housing conditions that characterized the urban ghettoes. The political and social power of the nativist movement had been growing, and it reached its peak during the mid-1850s; in these circumstances, his sense of alienation was perfectly comprehensible. Nor were his observations about ward bosses and corrupt Irish American political machines off the mark; such activities had already become notorious and would become even more so later in the century.[118]

Nevertheless, McGee's critics had a point when they accused him of generalizing from the worst features of Irish American life. As we have seen, most Irish Catholics did not live in the cities (although this did not mean that they were rural dwellers, either), and modern historians have emphasized the variegated and diverse nature of the mid-nineteenth-century Irish American experience. The Catholic Irish in places such as Albany, for example, faced much less discrimination than their counterparts in the larger cities; the "No Irish Need Apply" syndrome has been exaggerated; and Irish Americans were conspicuous for their upward social mobility. They weathered the nativist storm, became an important presence within the Democratic party, and effectively took over an expanding American Catholic Church. During the mid-1850s, though, it was the malign features of Irish American life that gripped McGee's mind.[119]

When it came to Canada, both McGee and his opponents were highly selective in their assessment of the condition of Irish Catholics; there were so many local and regional variations that enough evidence could be found to support any predetermined position, positive or negative.[120] McGee's critics were right to argue that the Orange Order was one of the most powerful organizations in English-speaking Canada, and could point to particular places where local Orange majorities were fiercely anti-Catholic; the reaction of Toronto's Orangemen to the Buffalo Convention was a case in point. At the same time, leaders of the Canadian Orange Order had reached political accommodations with other groups, including conservative French Canadian Catholics; in this sense, McGee was quite right to argue that Orangeism in Canada was different from the Orange Order at home.[121]

Similarly, McGee's critics were correct to point out that Irish Canadian Catholics were underrepresented at all levels of government. On the other hand, the presence of a powerful French Catholic bloc in the legislative assembly meant that Irish Catholics could secure legislation that was impossible in the United States. Separate schools were the best example of this, and it is not surprising that McGee seized on this point; it was, after all, of paramount importance for him, in personal and public terms.

As for the economic condition of Irish Canadian Catholics, there is no doubt that they were overrepresented in the urban working class; in mid-nineteenth-century Toronto, for example, more than half the Irish Catholics were skilled or semi-skilled workers.[122] But the cities were not typical. Most Irish Catholics lived in the countryside, and their single largest occupation was farming – a fact that was not lost on McGee.[123] By 1871, the occupational profile of Irish Catholics was fairly close to that of the Canadian population as a whole, though regional variations remained important, and Catholics were at a moderate disadvantage compared with Irish Protestants.[124] The significance of the difference between Irish Protestants and Irish Catholics remains a matter of lively controversy within Canadian historiography; modern scholars, like their nineteenth-century predecessors, are debating whether the glass is half empty or half full.[125] On balance, though, the evidence indicates that McGee had a good case, even if things were not nearly as rosy as he claimed during the mid-1850s.

———

Of more immediate significance than the validity of his arguments, however, was the fact that they left him on the margins of Irish America. Irish American republicans had turned against him in 1849 and had been dogging his steps ever since. His conversion to ultramontanism brought him powerful new allies in the Catholic Church. But his growing criticism of American life, his support for colonization, and his positive image of Canada produced a serious rift with Brownson and Roddan, his former mentors, and opened up a new conflict with Archbishop Hughes. Meanwhile, McGee's disillusionment with the Democratic party put him out of step with most Irish Catholic American voters. It is both revealing and ironic, given his earlier emphasis on naturalization, that McGee never actually took out citizenship papers, even though he had been eligible to do so since November 1853; during the mid-1850s, he found it impossible to commit himself to a country from which he had become increasingly alienated.[126]

Not surprisingly, sales of the *American Celt* began to plummet. At the end of 1856 he was threatening to publish a "black list" of "DIS- HONOURABLE DEFAULTERS" on their subscriptions – a sure sign of trouble.[127] By that time, however, he had already decided to leave for Canada. The previous July, he had made his intentions clear to Armand de Charbonnel, the bishop of Toronto:

> Disappointed in this country of that religious freedom and equal justice, which was the hope of so many emigrants, I have all but resolved, to make my future home & that of my children, in the valley of the Ottawa, probably at Ottawa city ... My hope is to bring up my children unstainted [sic] and unmarked by false systems of education, or *mis*education, and as I cannot isolate them in this state of society, I am most anxious to take them, with that view, to Canada ... I will not conceal from your Lordship, that being in my 32nd year and having a passion for political studies, I would fain hope to enter your Parliament, and render some service in the battle, which your Lordship is so heroically fighting for the souls of the children of your province.[128]

In Canada, McGee could realize his long-standing ambition to become an elected politician, use his position to advance the cause of Catholicism, and ensure that his children were brought up in the true faith.

Shortly after writing his letter to Bishop Charbonnel, McGee broadened his knowledge of British North America with a tour through the Maritimes. As with his visits to the Province of Canada, he liked what he saw. The Catholic Irish in New Brunswick, he wrote, enjoyed "something like equal social consideration," had contributed to the victory of John Hamilton Gray's Tory party, and were actively involved in the government.[129] In Nova Scotia, he was equally struck by the "easy tone of confidence and equality" among all classes, and attended a dinner at which Protestants toasted the health of the Catholic archbishop.[130]

By September 1856 he was back in Montreal, speaking to the city's Colonization Society, and arguing that Canadians should do more to attract European immigrants by publicizing the positive features of their country.[131] During his visit, some of Montreal's leading Irish Catholics, including Bernard Devlin and James Sadlier, sounded him out about starting a newspaper in the city. The existing English-language Catholic newspaper, George Clerk's *True Witness*, did not pay sufficient attention to Irish affairs, they told him; there was an opening for "an independent liberal paper in politics, which would at the same time more particularly devote itself to the expression and advancement of Irish feeling and interest in this Community."[132]

It seemed unlikely that Montreal's Catholic Irish community could support two newspapers; the general consensus was that competition from McGee would sink the *True Witness* – something that obviously did not sit well with Clerk. Describing McGee as a divisive force whose presence would be "injurious to *Catholic* interests," Clerk enlisted the senior French Canadian clergy against the project; Montreal's Irish clergy, in contrast, came out in favour of McGee.[133] When he learned of the split, McGee backed off. "I must either give up Canada, or at least give up Montreal, for the present," he told Sadlier in October.[134]

But the momentum proved to be unstoppable. The Canadian network that he had built up during his colonization campaign and in his previous visits swung into action, with significant support emerging from liberal Irish Catholics in Toronto. By the spring of 1857 the plans were in place. McGee informed James Moylan, one of his Canada West backers, that his newspaper would be "tri-weekly; strictly secular, with a considerable tinge of literature."[135] It would be called, appropriately enough, the *New Era*. Yet McGee and his Canadian allies had more than a newspaper in mind; part of the arrangement was that he would run in the next election as the candidate representing Montreal's Irish community.[136] The *New Era* was conceived as the means to a larger objective — a new political career, and a new beginning in a new country.

———

It is tempting at this point to fall into a familiar rhetorical refrain — that McGee's career before 1857 had been marked by unremitting failure, and that Canada opened the door to unprecedented success. Gavan Duffy certainly felt that way; he believed that McGee had wasted his energy in a series of unproductive polemical wars in the United States but finally came into his own as a statesman in Canada.[137] Robin Burns, in his biography of McGee, made much the same point; every pre-Canadian movement with which McGee had been involved, he wrote, from the Irish Confederation to the Buffalo Convention, had fallen apart: "After two decades of frustration and bitter failure in Ireland and the United States, McGee found a place in British North America."[138]

Yet, McGee did not see his past as a story of frustration and failure. Rather, he viewed himself as someone who had laboured long and hard under conditions of great adversity to elevate his countrymen on both sides of the Atlantic. This had been his self-image in 1847 while defending the record of the Irish Confederation against its critics; it was also the stance he assumed against his growing number of American enemies during the mid-1850s. "A thousand lectures; six volumes of historical compilations; ten volumes of newspapers; many unacknowledged magazine labors; — all these, within twelve years, we undertook and performed, for the honor and credit of Irish character, especially as placed in the United States," he declared in 1854.[139]

Equating advocacy with accomplishment, McGee reminded his readers that he had pushed for emigrant education, that he had asserted the claims of the Celts against Anglo-Saxon supremacy, and had helped to sustain and create an Irish American literary tradition. He was particularly proud of his "Irish Authors and Authoresses" sketches of 1842–44, and of being the "first Historiographer of the Exodus" in his *History of the Irish Settlers in North America*. Among his other causes, he listed "the preference of Country to Town life by all those who can live in the country, the perpetuation of the Faith of our Fathers among

our posterity, the absence of all offensive street displays of Irishism on
St. Patrick's Day or any other day, direct steam communication with
Ireland, Naturalization according to law, no office-seeking, and the
cultivation of friendly relations with our brethren in Canada."[140] The
fact that McGee felt compelled to justify himself in this way tells its
own story. Yet the character of his self-justification is revealing: it was
the effort that mattered, much good had been done in a difficult situation, and the problem lay not in his vision of the future but in the realities of American life.

McGee's American career from 1848 to 1857 contained familiar patterns and remarkable transformations as he journeyed from revolutionary republicanism to moral-force nationalism, from moral-force
nationalism to ultraconservative Catholicism, and from ultraconservative Catholicism to the Buffalo Convention, colonization, and Canada.
Anger, passion, and idealism pushed him to extremes, while reflection,
reason, and pragmatism pulled him towards the centre; the centrifugal
was constantly at war with the centripetal. His anger about Britain's
perceived responsibility for the famine, and Britain's suppression of
the Irish Confederates, impelled him towards anglophobia and republicanism, to the point of believing that a revolution in Canada could
provide a measure of revenge for oppression in Ireland. Similarly, his
anger at what he saw as the Catholic Church's complicity with British
oppression drove him towards an intense anticlericalism, to the point
that he clashed head-on with Bishop Hughes.

It was Duffy who pointed out that he was becoming consumed
with anger, who persuaded him that revolution was an impossibility in
post-famine Ireland, and who pulled him back to the centre. Following Duffy's lead, McGee adopted a Burkean emphasis on gradualism,
viewed Irish independence as the culmination of piecemeal reforms,
and settled in for the long haul. But the centre could not hold. From
one side it was being challenged by revolutionary republicans, and
from the other it faced the growing and greater threat of nativism. As
he became convinced that there was a transatlantic Anglo-Saxon Protestant conspiracy against Catholic Celts, his old reactive tendencies re-

appeared in a new form. Now, he swung hard to the right, embracing an ultramontane position that he had once equated with dictatorship and censorship. Once again, he entered a world of moral absolutes, and located himself within an apocalyptic struggle between good and evil, with ultramontanism performing the same kind of idealistic function that he had previously found in revolutionary republicanism. Ultramontanism and revolutionary republicanism may have been diametrically opposed to one another, but they shared one critically important characteristic – an imaginative and aspirational idealism against which reality was judged, and through which their adherents occupied the pure and unsullied moral high ground. McGee is a classic example of the way in which opposites can unite.

Just as McGee's revolutionary republicanism of 1848–49 gave way to "wise moderation," his ultramontanism receded from its high-water mark of 1851–53. This time, as far as we know, there was no input from someone like Duffy. After McGee left Buffalo for New York in 1853, and wrote a secular newspaper in changing circumstances, his ultramontanism gradually became less visible and less intense. Nevertheless, the defence of Catholicism, particularly in its Irish form, remained his central priority; we see this in his continuing counterattacks on republicanism and nativism, and we see it in such books as the *Catholic History of North America* and his biography of Bishop Maginn. But the specific way in which McGee chose to defend Catholicism – by encouraging Irish Catholics to live in Canada, and advocating colonization schemes – alienated the very ultramontanists who had played such a prominent role in his conversion. Having broken with Brownson and Roddan, McGee began to move back to the pragmatic centre, without abandoning his core belief that Catholicism was the One True Faith and that all other religions were wrong.

In his growing pragmatism, his conviction that politics should be guided by moderation, his Burkean view that the possible best was the actual best, McGee was slowly turning into a socially conservative Catholic liberal – certainly, that was how his Canadian supporters saw him in 1857. This was a form of liberalism that rejected common schools, the view that one religion was as good as another, and the intrinsic superiority of democracy. But it was also a form of liberalism that accepted diversity, and attempted to balance authority and liberty through reasonable compromises that were grounded in history, conditioned by circumstances, and guided by potential consequences. And Canada, McGee was convinced, was precisely the place where such liberalism could flourish, where his religion could prosper, where his nationalism could find new expression, and where his political ambitions could be realized.

In Ireland, McGee had been an extreme republican; in the United States he had been an extreme Catholic; in Canada, he would become an extreme moderate.

Notes

ABBREVIATIONS

AO   Archives of Ontario
CUA   Concordia University Archives (Thomas D'Arcy McGee
       Collection)
LAC   Library and Archives Canada
NAI   National Archives of Ireland
NLI   National Library of Ireland
RIA   Royal Irish Academy
TCD Trinity College Dublin

CHAPTER ONE

1 On the movements and demeanour of the "solitary figure," see "Judge William Buell Richards' Trial Notes, Testimony of Edward Stow [Storr]," CUA, PO30 HA259, folder 7; *Canadian Freeman*, 23 April 1868; *Guelph Evening Mercury*, 11 and 17 April 1868; *Trial of Patrick J. Whelan*, 81. On the weather conditions that night, see *Trial of Patrick J. Whelan*, 7–8.

2 For the state of McGee's health, see McGee to C.P. Meehan, 8 February 1868, CUA, PO30 HA261, folder 21; McGee to John A. Macdonald, 18 October 1867, Charles Murphy Papers, LAC, MG27 III B8 [Murphy Papers], f. 14232; and McGee to Macdonald, 11 January 1868, John A. Macdonald Papers, LAC, MG26A [Macdonald Papers], vol. 59, C1508, f. 23938. On his abstinence from alcohol, see McGee to Meehan, 6 April 1868, CUA, PO30 HA261, folder 7; for MacFarlane's comments, see *Irish Canadian*, 16 September 1868.

3 House of Commons, *Debates, First Session – First Parliament*, 6 April 1868, 468–71. For Burke's views on representation, see "Mr. Edmund Burke's Speech, November 3, 1774," in *Writings and Speeches*, 3:64–70.

4 McGee to the Earl of Mayo, 4 April 1868, Murphy Papers, f. 21586. Although the letter was begun on Saturday, 4 April, it was not completed until 6 April; see McGee to Meehan, 6 April 1868, CUA, PO30 HA261, folder 7. Mayo kept McGee's letter "as a memento," he said, "of one whose talents courage and character, I in concurrence with my country men entertain the deepest admiration and respect – whose life was sacrificed to his Patriotism and whose untimely and cruel Death I look upon as a national Calamity." See Mayo to Brown Chamberlin, 8 June 1868, Brown Chamberlin Papers, LAC, MG24 B19, vol. 3, f. 22.

5 McGee to Charles Tupper, 6 April 1868, Murphy Papers, ff. 14314–15; McGee to Meehan, 6 April 1868, CUA, PO30 HA261, folder 7; Timothy Daniel Sullivan to McGee, 18 February 1862, CUA, PO30 HA253, folder 5.

6 Rees and Rees, *Celtic Heritage: Ancient Tradition in Ireland and Wales*, 88.

7 McGee to Charles Tupper, 6 April 1868, Murphy Papers, f. 13414.

8 McGee to Mrs Sadlier, 18 February 1867, James Sadlier Papers, LAC, MG24 C16; McGee to Macdonald, 3, 11, and 15 February 1868, Murphy Papers, ff. 14234–42; Macdonald to Archbishop Connolly, 1 June 1868, Macdonald Papers, vol. 514, C26, ff. 814–17.

9 *Irish Canadian*, 24 January 1866; R. Wright to Macdonald, 10 April 1868, Macdonald Papers, vol. 341, C1707, ff. 155929–30; *Trial of Patrick J. Whelan*, 26–7, 31–2, 33–6; McGee to Macdonald, 25 February 1868, Murphy Papers, ff. 21583–4.

10 *Montreal Gazette*, 19 April 1864; Slattery, *The Assassination of D'Arcy McGee*, 441, 451–2; *Canadian Freeman*, 23 April 1868.

11 [Toronto] *Globe*, 28 August 1863; McGee, "The Future of Canada," in *Ottawa Citizen*, 1 December 1863; McGee to the Earl of Mayo, 6 April 1868, Murphy Papers, f. 21586.

12 *Trial of Patrick J. Whelan*, 9–11; *Canadian Freeman*, 10 September 1868; "Coroner's Inquest as to the Death of D'Arcy McGee," CUA, PO30 HA259, folder 1. McGee, it should be added, would not have approved of this opening: "To commence a mans [sic] life by describing his tombstone," he once wrote, "would be rather unartistic." See McGee to Charles Gavan Duffy, 5 March 1846, Charles Gavan Duffy Papers, NLI, MS 5756, f. 303.

13 For a brief discussion of McGee's funeral in the general context of nineteenth-century parades, see Goheen, "Symbols in the Streets: Parades in Victorian Urban Canada," 237–43.

14 *Canadian Freeman*, 16 April 1868; William Forster to Macdonald, 14 April 1868, Macdonald Papers, vol. 341, C1709, ff. 155944–7; Ewyn Bruce Mackinnon to Charles Murphy, n.d. [February – March 1925], Murphy Papers, ff. 18243–5.

15 Berger, *The Sense of Power: Studies in the Ideas of Canadian Imperialism, 1867–1914*, 49–52; William Foster (not to be confused with William Forster, above), *Canada First; or, Our New Nationality; An Address*, 32–3; Jonathan E. Donnelly to Charles Murphy, 6 February 1925, Murphy Papers, f. 17771.

16 *Irish World*, 2 February 1878.

17 H.C. Moore to George-Étienne Cartier, 20 April 1868, Macdonald Papers, vol. 59, C1508, f. 24039; W. Lambert to Gilbert McMicken, 7 May 1868, Macdonald Papers, vol. 240, C1666, ff. 106830–1; Rev. E.P. Roche to Bishop Horan, 15 April 1868, Bishop Edward John Horan Papers, Archives of the Archdiocese of Kingston, Ontario, DC18 C18/19; MacNeil Clarke to Macdonald, 8 April 1868, Macdonald Papers, vol. 184, C1586, f. 76978; Statement of John Clare, 16 April 1868, Macdonald Papers, vol. 184, C1586, f. 76970.

18 Joseph Workman to Charles Clarke, 14 April 1868, Charles Clarke Papers, AO.

19 McGee, *Memoir of Charles Gavan Duffy, Esq., as a Student, Journalist, and Organizer*, 9.

20 John Mitchel to his sister, 5 March 1849, Hickey Collection, NLI, MS 3226; Michael Doheny to William Smith O'Brien, 20 August 1858, William Smith O'Brien Papers, NLI, MS 446, f. 3058; Richard O'Gorman to Smith O'Brien, 1 January 1859, O'Brien Papers, NLI, MS 446, f. 3082; Thomas Meagher to Charles Gavan Duffy, 17 January 1853, Duffy Papers, NLI, MS 5757, f. 387.

21 Duffy, "Principles and Policy of the Irish Race," *Nation*, 29 April 1854; McGee to Mary McGee, 31 March 1859, Thomas D'Arcy McGee Papers, LAC, MG27 I E9; McGee to [James] Sadlier, 9 May 1853, Buffalo and Erie County Historical Archives, MSS A00-385; McGee to Macdonald, 18 October 1867, Murphy Papers, ff. 14232–3.

22 McGee to William Smith O'Brien, 12 July 1847, O'Brien Papers, NLI, MS 438, f. 1925. See also McGee to O'Brien, 29 June 1847, O'Brien Papers, MS 438, f. 1917, and Meagher to O'Brien, n.d. [12 July 1847], O'Brien Papers, MS 440, f. 2203.

23 Quoted in Duffy, *Young Ireland: A Fragment of Irish History, 1840–45*, 2:198; Duffy, *My Life in Two Hemispheres*, 1:128; McGee, *Eva MacDonald: A Tale of the United Irishmen, and Their Times*, passim; McGee, *Historical Sketches of O'Connell and His Friends*, 182–3, 205.

24 *Boston Pilot*, 23 March 1844; Mercy Ann Coles, "Reminiscences of Canada in 1864," Mercy Ann Coles Papers, LAC, MG24 B66.

25 Alexander Campbell to Macdonald, 25 January 1867, Macdonald Papers, vol. 194, C1589, 80800–1.

26 [James Ryan], *Two Trimmers Trimmed: The Dismissal of James Ryan from the Executive Council, after a Service of Twenty-Five Years,* by Mssrs. Lee and Himsworth, Clerks [1869], 2–3, 7–8, in Macdonald Papers, vol. 341, C1709, ff. 156147–54; Mary McGee to Thomas Devine, 20 August 1863, CUA, PO30 HA254, folder 7.

27 Skelton, *The Life of Thomas D'Arcy McGee,* 415; *Irish Canadian,* 8 January 1868.

28 *American Celt*, 15 November 1851; [New York] *Nation*, 3 February 1849; *Boston Pilot*, 22 June 1844; Bishop's Journal 3, 22 November 1844, Boston Archdiocesan Archives.

29 *American Celt*, 26 July 1851.

30 [New York] *Nation*, 2 December 1848, 31 March 1849; *American Celt*, 24 December 1852.

31 *American Celt*, 31 May, 26 July, 23 August, and 20 December 1851.

32 Hughes, "Reflections and Suggestions in Regard to What Is Called the Catholic Press," 653.

33 *American Celt*, 19 April, 3 May 1851; *Boston Pilot*, 24 May 1851; Burns, "Thomas D'Arcy McGee: A Biography," 242.

34 Alexander Campbell to Macdonald, 28 November 1866, Macdonald Papers, vol. 194, C1589, ff. 80718–19.

35 John Dillon to McGee (draft letter), 22 May 1849, John Blake Dillon Papers, TCD, MS 6455, f. 107b; Dillon to Ady Dillon, Dillon Papers, 29 May 1849, f. 110; Dillon to Ady Dillon, 7 July 1849, f. 123; Dillon to Ady Dillon, n.d. [October–December 1849], f. 131.

36 Thomas Meagher to Duffy, n.d. [1852], Charles Gavan Duffy Papers, Royal Irish Academy, MS 12 P19, f. 5; Meagher to Duffy, 17 January 1853, Charles Gavan Duffy Papers, NLI, MS 5757, f. 387.

37 George Clerk to Bishop Horan, 26 June 1865, Bishop Edward John Horan Papers, Archives of the Archdiocese of Kingston, Ontario, D12 C33/20.

38 Charles Gavan Duffy, "Principles and Policy of the Irish Race. To Thomas Francis Meagher," *Nation*, 29 April 1854; *Irish People*, 3 June 1865.

39 James Moylan to Henry Morgan, n.d., Murphy Papers, f. 14324.

40 Thomas Connolly to Paul Cullen, 1 May 1868, Paul Cullen Papers, Dublin Diocesan Archives, file III, 334/8/11/12. For Connolly's letter of introduction for McGee, see Connolly to Cullen, 25 May 1865, Cullen Papers, file

11, 327/1/11/14. "Whatever may be said of the merits or demerits of his early political career," commented Connolly, "one thing is quite certain that his public acts for the last fifteen years [sic] in British America have won for him a position which no Irishman nor indeed a man of any other country has ever yet attained."

41 Howell, *Eighteenth-Century British Logic and Rhetoric*; [New York] *Nation*, 28 October 1848.

42 Perhaps significantly, McGee found Cobbett difficult to pin down, and wrote of his "strange and curious mind." See *Boston Daily Times*, 5 September 1850.

43 *American Celt*, 31 August 1850; [New York] *Nation*, 5 May 1849; McGee, *Canadian Ballads and Occasional Verses*, 12–16.

44 Sadlier, ed., *Poems of Thomas D'Arcy McGee*, 73–4, 84–5, 155–6, 163–4; McGee, *Canadian Ballads*, 44–6.

45 Virgo, ed., *Selected Verse of Thomas D'Arcy McGee*, xviii, xx–xxi. The book presents McGee as a kind of Red Tory who left the United States because of slavery, who attacked privilege, and who defended the poor; in fact, McGee opposed abolitionism in the United States and consistently put national unity above issues of privilege or poverty.

46 Vance, *Irish Literature: A Social History*, 121, 154.

47 Lady Ferguson, *Sir Samuel Ferguson in the Ireland of His Day*, 1:139; Duffy, *My Life*, 1:128n; Sadlier, *Poems of Thomas D'Arcy McGee*, 43–4, 47–8.

48 Duffy, *My Life*, 1:315; Richard O'Gorman to William Smith O'Brien, 12 December 1852, O'Brien Papers, NLI, MS 445, f. 2842; R. Garrett to Charles Murphy, 30 January 1925, Murphy Papers, f. 17678; George B. Meadows to Mr Justice Anglin, 7 March 1925, Murphy Papers, ff. 19586–8.

49 Cameron, *Memoirs of Ralph Vansittart*, 149; [New York] *Nation*, 27 January 1849; *Nation*, 7 February, 19 September 1846.

50 *American Celt*, 20 December 1856; see also [New York] *Nation*, 24 November, 29 December 1849; *New Era*, 2, 21, 30 January 1858; *Canadian Freeman*, 27 January 1860.

51 [New York] *Nation*, 27 January 1849; *Nation*, 14 August 1852.

52 *American Celt*, 20 December 1856.

53 Sandford Fleming to Henry Morgan, 15 April 1895, Henry Morgan Papers, LAC, MG29 D61, ff. 5244–5.

54 Duffy, *Young Ireland*, 1:197; *Boston Pilot*, 23 September 1843; [New York] *Nation*, 5 January 1850; Ross, *Getting into Parliament and After*, 3–4.

55 Ross, *Getting into Parliament and After*, 3–4; *American Celt*, 11 August 1855.

56 *Irish Canadian*, 20 April 1864; [New York] *Nation*, 27 January 1849.

57 *True Witness*, 7 January 1859; *American Celt*, 26 February 1853.

58 *Canadian Freeman*, 13 August 1858; *American Celt*, 15 March 1851, 27 November 1852.

59 *True Witness*, 21 November 1856.

60 *Boston Pilot*, 23 September 1843, 23 August 1845; McGee, *Historical Sketches of O'Connell and His Friends*, 17, 183; *Irish Canadian*, 16 August 1865; *Montreal Herald*, 16 March 1861.

61 [New York] *Nation*, 28 October 1848, 29 December 1849.

62 *American Celt*, 18 November 1854, 15 March 1851; *Nation*, 12 July 1851; *American Celt*, 4 October 1851.

63 *True Witness*, 21 November 1856; *New Era*, 26 September, 3 and 6 October 1857.

64 *Boston Pilot*, 23 August 1845; *American Celt*, 20 December 1851; *True Witness*, 9 December 1853; McGee, *A History of the Attempts to Establish the Protestant Reformation in Ireland*, 190, 251–2; *True Witness*, 21 November 1856.

65 *American Celt*, 13 November 1852; *True Witness*, 21 November 1856. McGee's interpretation of Burke has much in common with that of O'Brien's in *The Great Melody: A Thematic Biography of Edmund Burke*.

66 Chapman, *The Celts: The Construction of a Myth*; James, *The Atlantic Celts: Ancient People or Modern Invention?*

67 *Boston Pilot*, 8 February 1845.

68 McGee, *Historical Sketches of O'Connell and His Friends*, 7.

69 *Nation*, 19 September, 28 November 1846, 9 January 1847.

70 [New York] *Nation*, 9 December 1848; *American Celt*, 4 January 1851.

71 *American Celt*, 17 May 1851, 8 January 1853.

72 *American Celt*, 13 November 1852.

73 *New Era*, 9 January 1858; *True Witness*, 12 February 1858.

74 Tolkien, "English and Welsh," 29–30.

75 *Nation*, 15 May 1847; [New York] *Nation*, 20 October 1849; McGee, *Historical Sketches of O'Connell and His Friends* and *The Irish Writers of the Seventeenth Century*, passim; *Boston Pilot*, 18 May, 17 August, 28 September, 26 October 1844.

76 *American Celt*, 14 April 1855.

77 [New York] *Nation*, 1 September 1849.

78 *Boston Pilot*, 2, 24 February 1849, 15 February 1851.

79 [New York] *Nation*, 25 August 1849.

80 *American Celt*, 7 January 1854.

81 *American Celt*, 14 April, 18 August 1855.

82　See, for example, *Canadian Freeman*, 14 April 1864, where McGee compared Fenianism to cholera.

83　Harvey, *Thomas D'Arcy McGee*; Brady, *Thomas D'Arcy McGee;* Skelton, *Life of Thomas D'Arcy McGee*; Phelan, *Ardent Exile*.

84　Brady, *Thomas D'Arcy McGee*, 175–6.

85　They both, for example, omitted the words "the moral" from Gavan Duffy's statement that "McGee resembled [Thomas] Davis in everything but in the moral qualities, where Davis was unapproachable" – an omission that puts a significantly different spin on Duffy's meaning. They also omitted Duffy's verdict that the "painful struggles" of McGee's youth helped to explain "whatever defects marked McGee's character in after-life." See Skelton, *Life of Thomas D'Arcy McGee*, 113; Phelan, *Ardent Exile*, x; Duffy, *Young Ireland*, 2:216, and *Four Years of Irish History*, 17–18.

86　Phelan, *Ardent Exile*, 301.

87　Ibid., 8, 98, 143–4, 153, 238. For a withering critique of such stereotyping, see Akenson, *Being Had: Historians, Evidence, and the Irish in North America* and *Small Differences: Irish Catholics and Irish Protestants, 1815–1922. An International Perspective*.

88　O'Driscoll and Reynolds, eds, *The Untold Story: The Irish in Canada*, xiv–xv, xvii, 103–53, 453.

89　Ibid., xii, xv, 453–554.

90　*Daily News*, 14 April 1868; [New York] *Nation*, 11 November 1848.

91　Phelan, *Ardent Exile*, 92, 100; Brady, *Thomas D'Arcy McGee*, 26, 35–7; Harvey, *Thomas D'Arcy McGee*, 5; Skelton, *Life of Thomas D'Arcy McGee*, 188.

92　Sadlier, ed., *The Poems of Thomas D'Arcy McGee*, 586; *Dublin Evening Mail*, 16 May 1865.

93　John Joseph McGee to John J. O'Gorman, 26 March and 7 April 1925, J.J. O'Gorman Papers, LAC, MG30 D20, folder 1. For reports of the Orange Lambs in Bradford, see *Canadian Freeman*, 27 January and 3 February 1860; for the Peterborough St Patrick's Day "outrages," see *Peterborough Examiner*, 19 March 1863, and *Peterborough Review*, 20 March 1863.

94　John J. O'Gorman, "McGee the Catholic Lay Apostle," O'Gorman Papers, LAC, MG30 D20, folder 5.

95　Toner, "The Rise of Irish Nationalism in Canada, 1858–1884," 39, 67–8, 151.

96　Wilson, "The Fenians in Montreal, 1862–68: Invasion, Intrigue, and Assassination," 109–33.

97 Toner, it should be noted, does not go as far as Malcolm Brown, who contended that McGee "had turned venomously anti-Irish." See Brown, *The Politics of Irish Literature from Thomas Davis to W.B. Yeats*, 134.

98 Slattery, *The Assassination of D'Arcy McGee*, 337; Skelton, *Life of Thomas D'Arcy McGee*, 415–16.

99 Slattery, "*They Got to Find Mee Guilty Yet*," 396.

100 Burns, "D'Arcy McGee and the New Nationality," 8, 55, 61–2, 74–5, 90–3.

101 Burns, "Thomas D'Arcy McGee: A Biography," x.

102 Ibid., vi, 365.

103 *New Era*, 21 July 1857; *Montreal Herald*, 16 March 1861.

104 Macdonald to Frank Smith, 17 July 1871, Macdonald Papers, vol. 519, C30, ff. 40–1.

105 McGee to Moylan, 27 October 1865, James G. Moylan Papers, LAC, MG29 D15 1.

106 [New York] *Nation*, 9 December 1848.

107 McGee to Moylan, 27 October 1865, Moylan Papers, LAC, MG29 D15 1.

108 O'Gorman to Smith O'Brien, 12 December 1852, O'Brien Papers, NLI, MS 445, f. 2842.

CHAPTER TWO

1 *Boston Pilot*, 9 July 1842.

2 *Nation*, 15 May 1847; Dorcas McGee to Bella Morgan, 28 March 1842, CUA, PO30 HA254, folder 21; D'Arcy McGee to Bella Morgan, 30 June 1842, folder 22.

3 *Boston Pilot*, 9 July 1842.

4 On the United Irishmen and Irish American nationalism, see Wilson, *United Irishmen, United States: Immigrant Radicals in the New Republic*, 153–71. On the Republican Wife and Mother, see Lewis, "The Republican Wife: Virtue and Seduction in the Early Republic," 689–721, and Kerber, "The Republican Mother and the Enlightenment: An American Perspective," 187–205. For a discussion of the "ancient splendour – present misery" motif in Irish historical writing, see MacCartney, "The Writing of History in Ireland, 1800–1830," 347–62.

5 D'Arcy McGee to Bella Morgan, 11 July 1842, CUA, PO30 HA254, folder 24; *Boston Pilot*, 9, 23 July, 6 August 1842; D'Arcy McGee to Bella Morgan, 16 September 1842, CUA, PO30 HA254, folder 26; D'Arcy McGee to Bella Morgan, 9 November 1842, folder 26; James McGee to D'Arcy McGee, 26

July 1843, folder 10. When the report of McGee's Independence Day speech reached Wexford, he was identified as "the young man who so eminently distinguished himself at the Temperance Soirees in this town"; see *Wexford Independent*, 24 August 1842. The first "One of the Macs" article appeared in the *Wexford Independent*, 25 February 1843.

6 Irish Coastguard Establishment Books, National Archives of the United Kingdom, Mfm. ADM 175, Records for Rush and Point of Garron. Confirmation that the family lived together in Cushendall comes from Conyngham, *The Irish Brigade and Its Campaigns*, 548, where it is stated that James McGee, D'Arcy's brother, was "born in 1830, near the village of Cushendall," and from the Australian birth certificate of D'Arcy McGee's grandnephew, James McHugh, which states that McGee's sister Anna Maria was born in County Antrim. Anna – or Anne – Maria was born in 1828; see Dorcas Morgan to Bella Morgan, 21 August 1841, CUA, PO30 HA254, folder 20. I thank Brendan and Jenny Meegan for supplying the information about the Coast Guard Records and the birth certificate of James McHugh. See also Meegan and Meegan, "Thomas D'Arcy McGee," 56–74.

7 McGee, *A History of the Attempts to Establish the Protestant Reformation in Ireland*, 104n. McGee was drawing on Carte, *The Life of James, Duke of Ormond*, 1:379; for a modern example of the myth, see Schama, *A History of Britain: The British Wars 1603–1776*, 205. On the debunking of the story, see McSkimin, *The History and Antiquities of the County of the Town of Carrickfergus*, 44–5, and Donaldson, *Historical, Traditional, and Descriptive Account of Islandmagee*, 37–40, 72–3.

8 "1641 Depositions, County Antrim," TCD, MS 838.

9 James McGee to D'Arcy McGee, 26 July 1843, CUA, PO30 HA254, folder 10; *Wexford Independent*, 22 April 1843.

10 Cameron, *Memoirs of Ralph Vansittart*, 149; Duffy, *Four Years of Irish History, 1845–49: A Sequel to Young Ireland*, 18; Dorcas McGee to Bella Morgan, 21 August 1841, CUA, PO30 HA254, folder 20.

11 Marriage records for the Catholic Parish of Wexford, 2 March 1840; Baptism records for the Catholic Parish of Wexford, 6 August 1840. I thank Brendan and Jenny Meegan for this information.

12 Dorcas McGee to Bella Morgan, 21 March 1841, CUA, PO30 HA254, folder 19; D'Arcy McGee to Bella and Charles Morgan, 3 August 1845, CUA, PO30 HA256, folder 7.

13 Griffith's Valuation, 1853, 187, NLI; Dorcas McGee to Bella Morgan, 21 March 1841, CUA, PO30 HA254, folder 19.

14 Hedge schools were clandestine Catholic schools that emerged during the Penal Laws, when Catholics were banned from educating their children in their own religion. Banim, *Here and There through Ireland*, part 1, 202–3. See also Akenson, *The Irish Education Experiment: The National System of Education in the Nineteenth Century*, 45–58, and McManus, *The Irish Hedge School and its Books*, 118–34.

15 *Boston Pilot*, 8 February 1845. See also *Boston Pilot*, 18 October 1845, and Malcolm, *"Ireland Sober, Ireland Free": Drink and Temperance in Nineteenth-Century Ireland*, 52–5, 101–50.

16 *Wexford Independent*, 11 April 1840. This is the first of three stanzas.

17 Banim, *Here and There through Ireland*, 203; *Wexford Independent*, 22 January, 2 July 1842; McGee, *Historical Sketches of O'Connell and His Friends*, 198.

18 Malcolm, *"Ireland Sober, Ireland Free,"* 127–31; Dorcas McGee to Bella Morgan, 21 August 1841, CUA, PO30 HA254, folder 20.

19 *Boston Pilot*, 9 September 1843. On the relationship between the reality of voluntary migration and the myth of exile, see Miller, *Emigrants and Exiles: Ireland and the Irish Exodus to North America*.

20 Dorcas McGee to Bella Morgan, 21 March 1841, CUA, PO30 HA254, folder 19; 21 August 1841, folder 20; and 28 March 1842, folder 21.

21 McGee to Bella Morgan, 28 March 1842, CUA, PO30 HA254, folder 21; *Wexford Independent*, 9 April 1842.

22 "Farewell to my Friends," in *Wexford Independent*, 16 April 1842; "To Wexford in the Distance," "Lines Dedicated to the Memory of a Beloved Mother and Two Dear Sisters," and "To My Wishing Cap," in Sadlier, ed., *Poems of Thomas D'Arcy McGee*, 578, 577, 111–12; McGee to Bella Morgan, 30 June 1842, CUA, PO30 HA254, folder 22, and 30 September 1843, folder 28; McGee to Bella Morgan, 3 October 1846, CUA, PO30 HA256, folder 8.

23 Wilson, *United Irishmen, United States*, 100.

24 Akenson, *The Irish Diaspora: A Primer*, 217–69; Byron, *Irish America*, 54–9, 268–99; Jensen, "'No Irish Need Apply': A Myth of Victimization," 405–29. See also Doyle, "The Irish as Urban Pioneers in the United States, 1850–1870," 36–61.

25 The classic work is Handlin, *Boston's Immigrants: A Study in Acculturation*. See also O'Connor, *The Boston Irish: A Political History*.

26 Billington, *The Protestant Crusade, 1800–1860: A Study of the Origins of American Nativism*, 53–84; O'Connor, *Boston Irish*, 42–52; Morse, *Foreign Conspiracy against the United States*; Monk, *Awful Disclosures, by Maria Monk, of the Hotel Dieu Nunnery of Montreal*; Handlin, *Boston's Immigrants*, 186–91; Knobel, *"America for the Americans": The Nativist Movement in the United States*, 54.

27 *Wexford Independent*, 25 February 1843. In 1846 the legislature voted $10,000 to compensate the Ursulines, but the offer was rejected; see Handlin, *Boston's Immigrants*, 189.

28 McGee to Bella Morgan, 9 November 1842, CUA, PO30 HA254, folder 26; *Boston Pilot*, 23 July, 6 and 27 August 1842; McGee to Bella Morgan, n.d. [September 1842], CUA, PO30 HA254, folder 27, and 30 September 1843, folder 28.

29 *Boston Pilot*, 24 September 1842, 20 May 1843, 15 October 1842.

30 *Boston Pilot*, 8 October 1842, 7 October 1843, 10 February 1844.

31 *Boston Pilot*, 7 January 1843, 9 March 1844. McGee's understanding of Persian fire worshippers was clearly influenced by Thomas Moore's famous narrative poem *Lalla Rookh*; see *Boston Pilot*, 22 October 1842.

32 *Boston Pilot*, 9, 23 March 1844. See also McGee's comments in *Boston Pilot*, 2 August 1845, where he argues that many Scots "find it easier to plagiarize than to originate."

33 Vance, "Celts, Carthaginians, and Constitutions: Anglo-Irish Literary Relations, 1780–1820," 227; William Jones, "On the Musical Modes of the Hindus," 197; Marsden, *The History of Sumatra*, 196.

34 *Boston Pilot*, 7 January 1843, 13 August 1842, 15 July 1843.

35 McGee to Bella Morgan, n.d. [1842], CUA, PO30 HA254, folder 27; 9 November 1842, folder 26; 30 September 1843, folder 28; 1 November 1843, folder 30; Dorcas McGee to Bella Morgan, 13 December 1843, CUA, PO30 HA254, folder 33; McGee to Bella and Charles Morgan, 3 August 1845, CUA, PO30 HA256, folder 7.

36 *Boston Pilot*, 17, 24 June 1843.

37 *Wexford Independent*, 22 April 1843; *Boston Pilot*, 1 July, 5 August 1843.

38 *Boston Pilot*, 30 September 1843.

39 *Boston Pilot*, 7 October 1843.

40 *Hartford Daily Times*, 22, 27 September, 14 October 1843.

41 McGee, *Speech Delivered before the Repealers of Watertown, Mass., and the Adjoining Towns, on the Repeal of the Union*, 3–5; *Wexford Independent*, 21 June 1843.

42 *Boston Pilot*, 21 October 1843.

43 Ibid.

44 O'Connell to Paul Cullen, 9 May 1842, in O'Connell, ed., *The Correspondence of Daniel O'Connell*, 7:158: "If the Union were repealed and the exclusive system abolished, the great mass of the Protestant community would with little delay melt into the overwhelming majority of the Irish nation. Protestantism would not survive the Repeal ten years. Nothing but perse-

cution would keep it alive and the Irish Catholics are too wise and too good to persecute."

45 Wilson, *United Irishmen, United States*, 13–14.

46 *Nation*, 17 June 1843; Duffy, *My Life*, 1:86; Davis, *The Young Ireland Movement*, 40.

47 *Nation*, 3 June, 22 July 1848.

48 McGee, *Speech Delivered before the Repealers of Watertown*, 3–4, 22–3; *Boston Pilot*, 6 January 1844.

49 *Boston Pilot*, 9 March 1844.

50 McGee to Bella Morgan, 9 February 1844, CUA, PO30 HA256, folder 5, and 2 March 1844, folder 6.

51 *Boston Pilot*, 9, 23 March 1844.

CHAPTER THREE

1   *Boston Pilot*, 13 April 1844; McGee to James Moylan, 3 September 1858, James G. Moylan Papers, LAC, MG29 D15 1.

2   *Boston Pilot*, 10, 31 August 1844.

3   *Boston Pilot*, 1 March 1845.

4   Kendle, *Ireland and the Federal Solution: The Debate over the United Kingdom Constitution, 1870–1921*, 9–10.

5   *Boston Pilot*, 30 November 1844.

6   *Boston Pilot*, 15 March 1845.

7   *Boston Pilot*, 22 February 1845, 28 September 1844.

8   *Boston Pilot*, 27 April 1844.

9   Knobel, *"America for the Americans": The Nativist Movement in the United States*, xvii–xviii, 46–8; Higham, *Strangers in the Land: Patterns of American Nativism 1860–1925*, 61; Berthoff, *British Immigrants in Industrial America, 1790–1950*, 189–90; Gordon, *The Orange Riots: Irish Political Violence in New York City, 1870 and 1871*, 22. On the growth of the Catholic Church, see Gaustad and Barlow, *New Historical Atlas of Religion in America*, 155–9.

10 For the fullest account of the riots, see Feldberg, *The Philadelphia Riots of 1844: A Study of Ethnic Conflict*, 99–119. See also Billington, *The Protestant Crusade, 1800–1860: A Study of the Origins of American Nativism*, 220–37; Knobel, *"America for the Americans,"* 59–61; *Boston Pilot*, 11, 18 May 1844.

11 [New York] *Freeman's Journal*, 9, 11 May 1844. See also Henry Joseph Browne, "Biography of John Hughes," typescript, box 16, chapter 8, 5–15,

Browne Papers, Rare Book and Manuscript Library, Columbia University. The "second Moscow" story first appeared in Hassard, *Life of John Hughes, First Archbishop of New York*, 276, where it was reported as a private conversation between Hughes and a priest who had "escaped from Philadelphia." From here, it was quoted as a public declaration in Shaw, *Dagger John: The Unquiet Life and Times of Archbishop John Hughes of New York*, 197, and has now entered the mainstream of Irish American history. See, for example, Kenny, *The American Irish: A History*, 82.

12 Grozier, "The Life and Times of John Bernard Fitzpatrick: Third Roman Catholic Bishop of Boston," 174–7; *Boston Pilot*, 18 May 1844.

13 *Boston Pilot*, 18 May 1844.

14 Feldberg, *The Philadelphia Riots of 1844*, 112, 118–19.

15 *Boston Pilot*, 22 June 1844. See also Wilson, *United Irishmen, United States*, 61–2, 176–8.

16 *Boston Pilot*, 22 June 1844.

17 Handlin, *Boston's Immigrants*, 199; [New York] *Citizen*, 17 November 1855; *Boston Pilot*, 13 July, 16 November 1844; McGee, *A History of the Irish Settlers in North America, from the Earliest Period to the Census of 1850*, 146.

18 *Boston Pilot*, 6 July, 5, 26 October 1844.

19 McGee, "The Priest Hunter: A Tale of the Irish Penal Laws," 264–9. McGee also published two religious poems for the magazine: "The Backwoodsman and the Jesuit," 4 (August 1843): 316–17, and "The Progress of Christianity. A Poem – In Three Parts," 6 (July, August, and September 1844): 287–9, 357–9, 430–2).

20 *Boston Pilot*, 18 May, 6 July, 28 September 1844.

21 Morse, *Foreign Conspiracy against the Liberties of the United States*; Bishop's Journal 3, 22 November 1844, Boston Archdiocesan Archives.

22 *Boston Pilot*, 8 February 1845.

23 *Boston Pilot*, 31 August, 7, 21, 28 September, 30 November 1844, 25 January, 8 February 1845.

24 *Boston Pilot*, 11 January, 22 February 1845.

25 *Boston Pilot*, 21 January 1843, 5 April 1845; McGee, *Eva MacDonald*, n.p.; *Wexford Independent*, 21 June 1843; Grattan, *Civilized America*, 2:47. As it turned out, Grattan's views on Anglo-Irish relations were those which McGee himself would eventually adopt in the late 1850s – "justice to Ireland" within the Union; see *Civilized America*, 50.

26 McGee, *Eva MacDonald*, 28, 31, 36; McGee to Charles Tupper, 6 April 1868, Charles Murphy Papers, LAC MG27 III B8, ff. 14314–15.

27 McGee, *Historical Sketches of O'Connell and His Friends*, 7, 42, 51, 55–7, 163, 190–1. On the career of Thomas Furlong, see Mythen, *Thomas Furlong: The Forgotten Wexford Poet*.

28 McGee, *Historical Sketches of O'Connell and His Friends*, 89, 129, 191–2; O'Connell, quoted in Madden, *United Irishmen: Their Lives and Times*, 3:178–9.

29 For example, McGee mistakenly thought that Mathew Carey was a survivor of the rising of 1798; he idealized Thomas Addis Emmet (among others); and he anticipated the "How the Irish saved civilization" myth that became popular during the late twentieth century. See McGee, *Historical Sketches of O'Connell and His Friends*, 59, 200, 205.

30 *Boston Pilot*, 1 March 1845.

31 Ignatiev, *How the Irish Became White*, 9–10, 23–4.

32 *Boston Pilot*, 26 October, 16 November 1844. This is not to argue, *pace* Ignatiev, that the Irish "became" white; see Wilson, "Whiteness and the Irish Experience in North America," 153–60.

33 *Boston Pilot*, 6 July 1844, 26 April, 10 May 1845.

34 *Nation*, 5 April 1845; *Boston Pilot*, 3, 10 May 1845.

35 *Boston Pilot*, 26 April, 3 May 1845.

36 *Boston Pilot*, 10 May 1845.

37 *Boston Pilot*, 28 December 1844, 29 March 1845. On the Montreal riots, see *Montreal Pilot*, 2, 4, 6, 13, 18, 20 December 1844, and *Montreal Transcript*, 3, 5, 7, 10 December 1844.

38 *Boston Pilot*, 5 October 1844, 29 March, 19 April 1845.

39 *Boston Pilot*, 19 April 1845. See also *American Celt*, 14 April 1855, and *Boston Pilot*, 15 February 1851.

40 *Boston Pilot*, 1 March 1845.

41 *Boston Pilot*, 15 March 1845.

42 *Boston Pilot*, 15 April 1845.

43 *Boston Pilot*, 15 March, 5 April 1845.

44 Father John McCaffrey to Orestes Brownson, 15 December 1848, Orestes A. Brownson Papers, University of Notre Dame.

45 Duffy, *Four Years of Irish History*, 18–19; James E. McGee, *The Men of '48*, 204; McGee to Bella and Charles Morgan, 3 August 1845, CUA, PO30 HA256, folder 7; *Boston Pilot*, 17 May 1845.

46 See, for example, *Boston Pilot*, 7 January and 3 June 1843, 15 February and 17 May 1845.

47 McGee to Bella Morgan, 9 February 1844, CUA, PO30 HA256, folder 5.

48 *Boston Pilot*, 19 October 1844.

CHAPTER FOUR

1 McGee to Bella and Charles Morgan, 3 August 1845, CUA, PO30 HA256, folder 7; Ó Gráda, *Ireland Before and After the Famine: Explorations in Economic History, 1800–1925*, 35–6; *Boston Pilot*, 12 July, 8 November 1845.

2 McGee to Archdeacon O'Brien, 15 June 1866, Archdeacon O'Brien Papers, LAC, MG24 C20; [New York] *Nation*, 27 January 1849; *Nation*, 14 August 1852; *Boston Pilot*, 26 July 1845.

3 McGee to Bella and Charles Morgan, 13 August 1845, CUA, PO30 HA256, folder 7; James McGee to McGee, 26 July 1843, CUA, PO30 HA254, folder 10.

4 *Boston Pilot*, 12 July 1845.

5 McGee to Bella and Charles Morgan, 3 August 1845, CUA, PO30 HA256, folder 7; Duffy, *My Life*, 1:93, 96, 99–106; Davis, *Young Ireland Movement*, 45–6, 61–6; MacDonagh, *The Emancipist: Daniel O'Connell 1830–1847*, 253–7.

6 Duffy, *My Life*, 1:115–17; Davis, *Young Ireland Movement*, 66.

7 Davis, *Young Ireland Movement*, 68–71; MacDonagh, *The Emancipist*, 267–70.

8 *Boston Pilot*, 28 September 1844, 25 January and 23 August 1845. In the event, McGee did not take a degree at Trinity; the demands of journalism and politics got in the way.

9 McGee, *Memoir of Charles Gavan Duffy*, 13, 32; McGee to Duffy, 8 May 1849, in Duffy, *My Life*, 2:5.

10 Duffy, *Young Ireland*, 197; Duffy, *My Life*, 1:121, 128; Duffy, *Four Years of Irish History*, 20. For an example of a hostile reference to the "Kanuck Darky McGee," see Matthias D. Phelan to the editor of the *Irish People*, 14 June 1865, in NAI, Fenian Briefs, carton 2, envelope 3, f. 121.

11 MacDermott, *Songs and Ballads of Young Ireland*, 369; Grozier, "Life and Times of John Bernard Fitzpatrick," 11; *Boston Pilot*, 25 October 1845.

12 Duffy, *Young Ireland*, 198; *Boston Pilot*, 11 October 1845; *Nation*, 20 November 1847; [New York] *Nation*, 3 February 1849.

13 He later found the words – in one of his most moving poems, "Eugene O'Curry"; Sadlier, *Poems of Thomas D'Arcy McGee*, 457–60. See also Duffy, *Young Ireland*, 197; *Boston Pilot*, 2 August 1845; McGee to T.D. O'Sullivan, 15 August 1862, NLI, Young Ireland Miscellaneous Letters, MS 10,517.

14 [New York] *Nation*, 3, 24 February 1849.

15 *Boston Pilot*, 2 August 1845; [New York] *Nation*, 3 February 1849.

16 *Boston Pilot*, 18 October 1845; Duffy, *My Life*, 1:121, 2:24; *Nation*, 22 January 1848; Sadlier, *Poems of Thomas D'Arcy McGee*, 142–3; Lambkin, "Moving

Titles of a Young Ireland Text: Davis, Duffy and McGee and the Origins of *Tiocfaidh Ar Lá* [Our day will come]," 103–11.

17 *Boston Pilot*, 9 August 1845.

18 *Boston Pilot*, 9 August 1845.

19 *Boston Pilot*, 25 October 1845. On Young Ireland attitudes to Orangeism, see Davis, *Young Ireland Movement*, 215–19.

20 *Boston Pilot*, 9 August 1845; Duffy, *Young Ireland*, 211; Duffy, *My Life*, 1:125–6.

21 Duffy, *Four Years of Irish History*, 7–12, 15–17; Duffy, *My Life*, 1:129n; Davis, *Young Ireland Movement*, 76–7, 82–4.

22 *Boston Pilot*, 11 October 1845; Duffy, *My Life*, 1:128; Duffy, *Four Years of Irish History*, 17; Duffy, *Young Ireland*, 216.

23 Ó Gráda, *The Great Irish Famine*, 24–5, 39–40; Kinealy, *This Great Calamity: The Irish Famine, 1845–52*, 34–5; Gray, *Famine, Land, and Politics: British Government and Irish Society*, 102; Donnelly, *The Great Irish Potato Famine*, 1–3, 41–7.

24 *Boston Pilot*, 8 November 1845.

25 *Boston Pilot*, 22 November 1845; Donnelly, *Great Irish Potato Famine*, 48.

26 Davis, *Young Ireland Movement*, 196; Duffy, *Fours Years of Irish History*, 43–7; *Boston Pilot*, 8, 22 November 1845.

27 *Boston Pilot*, 27 December 1845; [MacNeven], *An Argument for Independence, in Opposition to an Union*, 23; Donnelly, *Great Irish Potato Famine*, 214–15; Bourke, *"Visitation of God?" The Potato and the Great Irish Famine*, 52.

28 *Boston Pilot*, 8 November 1845; Donnelly, *Great Irish Potato Famine*, 49–56; Ó Gráda, *Great Irish Famine*, 40.

29 *Boston Pilot*, 22 November 1845; Davis, *The Young Ireland Movement*, 194; Woodham-Smith, *The Great Hunger: Ireland 1845–1849*, 89.

30 *Boston Pilot*, 31 January 1846.

31 *Boston Pilot*, 21 February, 7 March 1846; McGee to Bella Morgan, 3 October 1846, CUA, PO30 HA256, folder 8. Robert White was probably the Robert Whyte who wrote *The Ocean Plague*, a graphic account of conditions on board a "coffin ship."

32 *Nation*, 28 November 1846; *Boston Pilot*, 26 December 1846.

33 *Freeman's Journal*, 11, 13, 16, 18, 20, 22 December 1845. Although "our London Correspondent" was not explicitly identified as McGee, the evidence suggests that he was the author. His last "Journal from Ireland" article for the *Boston Pilot* was dated 1 December 1845; the first article from "Our London Correspondent" was written on 9 December; on some occa-

sions, the London Correspondent signed himself "T"; and McGee became the paper's "Parliamentary Correspondent" at the beginning of the 1846 session.

34 McGee to Duffy, 5 March 1846, Charles Gavan Duffy Papers, NLI, MS 5756, f. 303; *Boston Pilot*, 21, 28 February 1846; *Nation*, 7 February 1846.

35 *Freeman's Journal*, 12, 14, 27 February 1846.

36 *Nation*, 17 February 1846; *Freeman's Journal*, 12, 19 February, 26, 30 March 1846.

37 *Freeman's Journal*, 13, 14, 23, 27 February 1846.

38 *Freeman's Journal*, 5, 7, 10, 23 February, 2 March 1846; *Nation*, 19 September 1846.

39 *Nation*, 14 February 1846; *Freeman's Journal*, 12 February 1846.

40 *Nation*, 21 February 1846; *Freeman's Journal*, 20 February, 17, 26 March, 9 April 1846.

41 *Freeman's Journal*, 26 March 1846; *Nation*, 19 September 1846.

42 McGee to Bella Morgan, 3 October 1846, CUA, PO30 HA256, folder 8; James E. McGee, *The Men of '48*, 204–5.

43 McGee to Duffy, 13 April 1846, Duffy Papers, NLI, MS 5756, f. 325; McGee to Duffy, 5 March 1846, ibid., f. 303; Duffy, *Four Years of Irish History*, 19–20.

44 Thomas D'Arcy McGee, *The Irish Writers of the Seventeenth Century*, 244, 247–9.

45 Ibid., 248, 82.

46 Ibid., 83, 239; *Freeman's Journal*, 11 February 1846.

47 McGee to Duffy, 5 March 1846, Duffy Papers, NLI, MS 5756, f. 303; McGee to Duffy, 13 April 1846, ibid., f. 325; McGee, *History of the Attempts to Establish the Protestant Reformation in Ireland*, 12. In [New York] *Nation*, 17 February 1849, McGee wrote that he had stayed in London throughout the parliamentary session of 1846.

48 Sloan, *William Smith O'Brien and the Young Ireland Rebellion of 1848*, 149–57; Davis, *Young Ireland Movement*, 93–4; [New York] *Nation*, 17 February 1849.

49 [New York] *Nation*, 19 May 1847; Kennedy et al., *Mapping the Great Irish Famine: A Survey of the Famine Decades*, 36–9.

50 Burns, "Thomas D'Arcy McGee," 119; *Nation*, 28 November 1846.

51 Donnelly, *Great Irish Potato Famine*, 192; Davis, *Young Ireland Movement*, 96.

52 Nowlan, *The Politics of Repeal: A Study in the Relations between Great Britain and Ireland, 1841–50*, 108–10; Davis, *Young Ireland Movement*, 95–106.

53 Sloan, *William Smith O'Brien and the Young Ireland Rebellion of 1848*, 165–6; Davis, *Young Ireland Movement*, 105; Duffy, *Four Years of Irish History*, 249–58; *Nation*, 12 September 1846.

54 *Nation*, 19 September 1846.

55 *Nation*, 19 September 1846; McGee to Bella Morgan, 3 October 1846, CUA, PO30 HA256, folder 8.

56 McGee to Bella Morgan, 3 October 1846, CUA, PO30 HA256, folder 8.

57 *Wexford Independent*, 2 January 1847.

58 *Nation*, 7 November 1846; McGee to Duffy, 31 October 1846, Charles Gavan Duffy Papers, RIA, MS 12, P19; *Irish Tribune*, 24 June 1848.

59 Davis, *Young Ireland Movement*, 109–11; Nowlan, *Politics of Repeal*, 111–12; Duffy, *Four Years of Irish History*, 298–9, 305–7; Doheny, *Felon's Track*, 113.

60 *Nation*, 7 November 1846; James McGee, *Men of '48*, 202–3, 205.

61 *Nation*, 28 November 1846.

62 *Nation*, 5 December 1846; Nowlan, *Politics of Repeal*, 112–13; *Irish Tribune*, 24 June 1848.

63 Davis, *Young Ireland Movement*, 111–16.

CHAPTER FIVE

1 Ó Gráda, *Black '47*, 34–41; Donnelly, *Great Irish Potato Famine*, 214–15; Bourke, *"The Visitation of God?"* 159–69; Solar, "The Great Famine," 112–33.

2 Nowlan, *Politics of Repeal*, 165. On British policies during the famine, see Gray, *Famine, Land, and Politics*, and Kinealy, *This Great Calamity*. See also Haines, *Charles Trevelyan and the Great Irish Famine*.

3 Ó Gráda, *Black '47*, 66–72, 157–92.

4 *Nation*, 16 January 1847.

5 *Nation*, 23 January 1847.

6 *Nation*, 9 January 1847.

7 Ibid.; Stewart, *Narrow Ground*, 27.

8 *Nation*, 9 January 1847; McGee, *History of the Irish Settlers*, 135–6, 140; Donnelly, *Great Irish Potato Famine*, 209–21.

9 Davis, *Young Ireland Movement*, 117–20; Nowlan, *Politics of Repeal*, 125–9; Sloan, *William Smith O'Brien and the Young Ireland Rebellion*, 179–81.

10 *Irish Tribune*, 24 June 1848; James Fintan Lalor to John Mitchel, 25 June 1847, Charles Gavan Duffy Papers, RIA, MS 12 P15; Davis, *Young Ireland Movement*, 120.

11 Proceedings of the Council of the Irish Confederation, 19 January 1847, RIA, MS 23 H44; *Nation*, 23 January, 6 March 1847.

12 *Nation*, 6 March 1847.

13 Mitchel to O'Brien, 19 March 1847, 24 April 1847, William Smith O'Brien Papers, NLI, MS 438, f. 1882.

14 Mitchel to O'Brien, 24 April 1847, O'Brien Papers, NLI, MS 438, f. 1882.

15 Mitchel to O'Brien, 19 March 1847, O'Brien Papers, NLI, MS 438, f. 1845; Duffy, *My Life*, 1:234–8.

16 Duffy, *My Life*, 1:236; McGee to Lalor, 8 March 1847, James Fintan Lalor Papers, NLI, MS 340, f. 108.

17 Lalor to McGee, 13 March 1847, Lalor Papers, NLI, MS 340, f. 61; McGee to Lalor, 20 March 1847, f. 103; McGee to Lalor, n.d. [26 March 1847], f. 104.

18 Duffy, *My Life*, 1:242–3.

19 McGee to Lalor, 20 March 1847, Lalor Papers, NLI, MS 340, f. 105; Lalor to Mitchel, 25 June 1847, Duffy Papers, RIA, MS 12 P15, vol. 1, f. 3.

20 *Nation*, 10 April 1847.

21 *Nation*, 10 April 1847; Proceedings of the Council of the Irish Confederation, 17 April 1847, Correspondence Book of the Irish Confederation, RIA, MS 23 H41; Quinlan, *Irish Boston*, 53–6.

22 McGee, *Memoir of the Life and Conquests of Art Mac Murrough*, xi–xiv, 107.

23 *Nation*, 10 April, 22 May 1847.

24 Ó Gráda, *Black '47*, 72–3; Gray, *Famine, Land, and Politics*, 300–1.

25 *Nation*, 3, 17 April 1847.

26 *Nation*, 17, 24 April, 5 June 1847.

27 Elgin to Gray, 7 May 1847, Doughty, ed., *Elgin–Grey Papers*, 1:35.

28 *Nation*, 24 April, 21 July 1847; Mitchel, *Last Conquest of Ireland*, 219.

29 *Nation*, 24 April, 15 May, 26 June, 16 October 1847.

30 *Nation*, 24 April, 15 May 1847.

31 *Nation*, 22, 29 May, 5, 12 June 1847. One of the "Two Irish Girls" was Adelaide Hart, who later that year married John Dillon; see Duffy, *Four Years of Irish History*, 95–6n, and Ó Cathaoir, *John Blake Dillon*, 1.

32 *Nation*, 26 June, 10 July 1847; McGee to O'Brien, 7 July, 1847, O'Brien Papers, NLI, MS 438, f. 1920.

33 *Nation*, 10 July 1847; McGee to O'Brien, 7 July 1847, O'Brien Papers, NLI, MS 438, f. 1920.

34 *Nation*, 13 November 1847; Duffy, *My Life*, 1:202; *Nation*, 15 January 1848.

35 Proceedings of the Council of the Irish Confederation, 1 May 1847, RIA, MS 23 H44; Davis, *Young Ireland Movement*, 127, 131; Duffy, *My Life*, 1:209.

36 *Nation*, 15 May, 10 July 1847; Duffy, *My Life*, 2:24.

37 *Nation*, 12 June 1847.

38 Duffy, *Four Years of Irish History*, 406–10.

39 O'Gorman to O'Brien, 17 July 1847, O'Brien Papers, NLI, MS 438, f. 1929.

CHAPTER SIX

1 *Irish Tribune*, 24 June 1848; Proceedings of the Council of the Irish Confed-
eration, 26, 28, 29 June 1847, RIA, MS 23 H44; Meagher to O'Brien, n.d. [12
July 1847], William Smith O'Brien Papers, NLI, MS 440, f. 2203; Duffy, *My
Life*, 1:231.

2 Sadlier, ed., *Poems of Thomas D'Arcy McGee*, 425–30; Meagher to O'Brien,
n.d. [12 July 1847], O'Brien Papers, NLI, MS 440, f. 2203; McGee to Bella
Morgan, 28 June 1849, CUA, PO30 HA256, folder 10; Nora Barnacle, quoted
in Ellmann, *James Joyce*, 159. For Mary's attitudes to and experiences with
Thomas, see Mary McGee to Bella Morgan, 2 August 1852, CUA, PO30
HA256, folder 13, and 21 July 1856, folder 15; Mary McGee to Thomas
Devine, 20 August 1863, CUA, PO30 HA254, folder 7; Mary McGee to Bella
Morgan, 1 June 1868, CUA, PO30 HA256, folder 17, and 19 January 1870,
folder 19. Thomas's tenderness towards his children comes out clearly in
his letters to his daughter Peggy. See McGee to Peggy, n.d., CUA, PO30
HA256, folder 15; McGee to Peggy, n.d. [1863], CUA, PO30 HA254, folder
17; McGee to Peggy, 5 August 1866, CUA, PO30 HA256, folder 16, and 19
April 1867, folder 2.

3 *Nation*, 10 July 1847; Davis, *Young Ireland Movement*, 118–19; McGee to
O'Brien, 20 September 1847, O'Brien Papers, NLI, MS 439, f. 1998.

4 Koseki, *Dublin Confederate Clubs*, 2–5.

5 Ibid., 8; *Nation*, 10 July, 14 August 1847.

6 *Nation*, 14, 28 August, 11 September 1847; Hughes, "Lecture on the Antecedent Causes of the Irish Famine," in *Complete Works*, 1: 545, 556.

7 McGee to O'Brien, 14 August, 1 and 9 September, 4 and 6 October, 2
December 1847, O'Brien Papers, NLI, MS 439, ff. 1960, 1974, 1985, 2006,
2008, 2028; *Nation*, 13 November 1847.

8 *Nation*, 14 August 1847.

9 On Urquhart, see Robinson, *David Urquhart*; Anderson, *A Liberal State at
War*, 140–3; Taylor, "The Old Radicalism and the New," 23–43.

10 Duffy, *My Life*, 1:211–14; *Boston Daily Times*, 27 September 1850; McGee to
Urquhart, 30 August, 8 September 1847, Urquhart Papers, 1/J6, Balliol College, Oxford University.

11 McGee to Urquhart, 30 August 1847, Urquhart Papers, 1/J6.

12 McGee to Urquhart, 2, 8 September 1847, Urquhart Papers, 1/J6.

13 McGee to Urquhart, 8 September 1847, Urquhart Papers, 1/J6.

14 McGee to Urquhart, 8 September 1847, Urquhart Papers, 1/J6; McGee to O'Brien, 9 September 1847, O'Brien Papers, NLI, MS 439, f. 1985.

15 Kennedy and Johnson, "The Union of Ireland and Britain," 34–44; *Nation*, 18 September 1847; Urquhart to McGee, 4 September 1847, Urquhart Papers, 1/J6.

16 *Nation*, 18 September 1847.

17 *Nation*, 2 October 1847; Urquhart to McGee, 8 October 1847, and McGee to Urquhart, 12 October 1847, Urquhart Papers, 1/J6.

18 *Nation*, 16 October, 11 December 1847.

19 *Nation*, 16 October 1847; Burns, "Thomas D'Arcy McGee," 146.

20 Proceedings of the Council of the Irish Confederation, 27 October, 20 December 1847, RIA, MS 23 H44; *Irishman*, 7 July, 25 August 1849.

21 *Irish Canadian*, 14 June 1865.

22 McGee to Bella and Charles Morgan, 3 August 1845, CUA, PO30 HA256, folder 7; Urquhart to McGee, 8 October 1847, and McGee to Urquhart, 12 October 1847, Urquhart Papers, 1/J6.

23 McGee to Urquhart, 12 October 1847, Urquhart Papers, 1/J6.

24 Davis, *Young Ireland Movement*, 107, 134; Sloan, *William Smith O'Brien and the Young Ireland Rebellion*, 193–4.

25 *Nation*, 20 November 1847.

26 *Nation*, 20, 27 November 1847; McGee to O'Brien, 25 November 1847, O'Brien Papers, NLI, MS 439, f. 2021.

27 Sloan, *William Smith O'Brien and the Young Ireland Rebellion*, 225.

28 *Nation*, 13 November 1847; Nowlan, *Politics of Repeal*, 153–5.

29 Duffy, *Four Years of Irish History*, 458–9.

30 Nowlan, *Politics of Repeal*, 166–7.

31 *Nation*, 4 December 1847; McGee to O'Brien, 2 December 1847, O'Brien Papers, NLI, MS 439, f. 2028; Sloan, *William Smith O'Brien and the Young Ireland Rebellion*, 199–201.

32 O'Gorman to O'Brien, 3 December 1847, O'Brien Papers, NLI, MS 439, f. 2030; *Nation*, 18 December 1847.

33 Duffy to O'Brien, 11 December 1847, O'Brien Papers, NLI, MS 441, f. 2235; O'Gorman to O'Brien, 14 December 1847, O'Brien Papers, NLI, MS 439, f. 2033; McGee to O'Brien, 30 December 1847, O'Brien Papers, NLI, MS 439, f. 2040.

34 McGee to O'Brien, 30 December 1847, O'Brien Papers, NLI, MS 439, f. 2040.

35 Proceedings of the Council of the Irish Confederation, 31 December 1847, RIA, MS 23 H44; Duffy to O'Brien, 11 December 1847, O'Brien Papers, NLI, MS 441, f. 2235; McGee to O'Brien, 30 December 1847, O'Brien Papers, NLI, MS 439, f. 2040.

CHAPTER SEVEN

1 *Nation*, 5 February 1848; Davis, *Young Ireland Movement*, 146.

2 M.J. Barry to O'Brien, 5 January 1848, William Smith O'Brien Papers, NLI, MS 441, f. 2349; O'Gorman to O'Brien, 18 January 1848, ibid., f. 2355; Meagher to O'Brien, n.d. [January 1848], ibid., f. 2298; *Nation*, 5 February 1848.

3 Proceedings of the Council of the Irish Confederation, 17, 21, 22, 24, 25 January 1848, RIA, MS 23 H44; *Nation*, 26 February 1848.

4 *Nation*, 8 January 1847.

5 *Nation*, 15 January 1848; Proceedings of the Council of the Irish Confederation, 12 January 1848, RIA, MS 23 H44.

6 McGee to O'Brien, 20 January 1848, O'Brien Papers, NLI, MS 441, f. 2358; Proceedings of the Council of the Irish Confederation, 24 January 1848, RIA, MS 23 H44.

7 Proceedings of the Council of the Irish Confederation, 31 January 1848, RIA, MS 23 H44; *Nation*, 5 February 1848; Duffy, *Four Years of Irish History*, 518–20.

8 *Nation*, 12 February 1848; McGee to Urquhart, 8 September 1847, Urquhart Papers, 1/J6, Balliol College, Oxford University.

9 *Nation*, 12 February 1848.

10 Ibid.; Proceedings of the Council of the Irish Confederation, 5, 7 February 1848, RIA, MS 23 H44.

11 Koseki, *Dublin Confederate Clubs*, 12; Owens, "Popular Mobilisation," 54; Davis, *Young Ireland Movement*, 145.

12 Sloan, *William Smith O'Brien and the Young Ireland Rebellion*, 209; *Nation*, 4 March 1848.

13 *Montreal Gazette*, 17 August 1867. On the Revolutions of 1848, see Stearns, *Revolutions of 1848*; Jones, *The 1848 Revolutions*; Evans and Von Strandmann, *Revolutions in Europe*.

14 *Nation*, 8 January, 4 March 1848.

15 *Nation*, 4 March 1848; Paine, *Rights of Man, Part Second*, in *Complete Writings*, 1:355; Sloan, *William Smith O'Brien and the Young Ireland Rebellion*, 209.

16 Meagher to Duffy, Thursday, n.d. [2 March 1848], Charles Gavan Duffy Papers, NLI, MS 5757, f. 95; *Nation*, 11 March 1848.

17 *Nation*, 4 March 1848; *Montreal Gazette*, 17 August 1867.

18 *Nation*, 11 March 1848; Sloan, *William Smith O'Brien and the Young Ireland Rebellion*, 215–16. On links between Repealers and Chartists, see Saville, *1848*, 72–4.

19 Proceedings of the Council of the Irish Confederation, 11, 14 March 1848, RIA, MS 23 H44; *Nation*, 18 March 1848.

20 *Nation*, 18 March 1848.

21 O'Gorman, "Narrative of 1848," 23 May 1881, Duffy Papers, NLI, MS 5886, ff. 6–7; *Nation*, 18 March 1848.

22 *Nation*, 18 March 1848.

23 *Nation*, 18, 25 March; Nowlan, *Politics of Repeal*, 184–5.

24 *Nation*, 11, 18 March 1848; Duffy, *My Life*, 1:261.

25 *Nation*, 25 March 1848; O'Gorman, "Narrative of 1848," 23 May 1881, Duffy Papers, NLI, MS 5886, ff. 9–11; Koseki, *Dublin Confederate Clubs*, 18.

26 Duffy to O'Brien, n.d. [late February 1848], O'Brien Papers, NLI, MS 441, f. 2344; Duffy, *Four Years of Irish History*, 537.

27 *Nation*, 11 March, 8 April 1848.

28 *Nation*, 8, 29 April 1848.

29 Proceedings of the Council of the Irish Confederation, 27, 29 March 1848, RIA, MS 23 H44; O'Gorman, "Narrative of 1848," 23 May 1881, Duffy Papers, NLI, MS 5886, f. 9; Sloan, *William Smith O'Brien and the Young Ireland Rebellion*, 217–21; Nowlan, *Politics of Repeal*, 187–92.

30 McGee to O'Brien, April 1848, O'Brien Papers, NLI, MS 442, f. 2410; *Nation*, 8 April 1848.

31 *Nation*, 25 March 1848; Sloan, *William Smith O'Brien and the Young Ireland Rebellion*, 222–3.

32 *Nation*, 6 May 1848; Sloan, *William Smith O'Brien and the Young Ireland Rebellion*, 225–8.

33 Proceedings of the Council of the Irish Confederation, 1, 2, 5 May 1848, RIA, MS 23 H44; M.J. Barry to O'Brien, 22 April 1857, O'Brien Papers, NLI, MS 445, f. 2950.

34 McGee to O'Brien, April 1848, O'Brien Papers, NLI, MS 442, f. 2410; Koseki, *Dublin Confederate Clubs*, 20; Proceedings of the Council of the Irish Confederation, 6 May 1848, RIA, MS 23 H44.

35 Owens, "Popular Mobilisation," 55; *Nation*, 1, 8, 15, 22, 29 April 1848.

36 *Nation*, 8 April 1848.

37 *Nation*, 8 April 1848; reports of informant "CD," 14, 15 April 1848, TCD, MS 2040, ff. 17, 22; report of informant "AB," 21 June 1848, TCD, MS 2037, f. 12.

38 *Nation*, 6 May 1848; reports of informant "AB," 4, 6 May 1848, TCD, MS 2037, ff. 3, 7.

39 McGee to O'Brien, April 1848, O'Brien Papers, NLI, MS 442, f. 2410; Nowlan, *Politics of Repeal*, 203.

40 Nowlan, *Politics of Repeal*, 203–5.

41 Koseki, *Dublin Confederate Clubs*, 23; reports of informant "EF," 26, 31 May 1848, 1 June 1848, TCD, MS 2038, ff. 32, 34.

42 O'Gorman, "Narrative of 1848," 23 May 1881, Duffy Papers, NLI, MS 5886, ff. 11–12; *Nation*, 3 June 1848.

43 Jane Verner Mitchel to John Martin, 17 July 1848, and Jane Verner Mitchel to — [John Martin?], n.d. [1848], Meloney-Mitchel Papers, Columbia University, New York.

44 *Nation*, 3 June 1848.

CHAPTER EIGHT

1 O'Gorman, "Narrative of 1848," 23 May 1881, Charles Gavan Duffy Papers, NLI, MS 5886, ff. 7–8.

2 *Montreal Gazette*, 17 August 1867; McGee, *Historical Sketches of O'Connell and His Friends*, 68; *Nation*, 3 June 1848.

3 Owens, "Popular Mobilisation," 55–6; Koseki, *Dublin Confederate Clubs*, 24–6; *Nation*, 3 June 1848.

4 Duffy, *Four Years of Irish History*, 606–11. Duffy did not identify the sixth person on the committee, describing him only as "another gentleman still living."

5 *Irish Felon*, 1 July 1848.

6 Anglin to Brenan, 3 July 1848, James Fintan Lalor Papers, NLI, MS 340, f. 1. Anglin managed to conceal this part of his past not only from his contemporaries but also from his biographer; see Baker, *Timothy Warren Anglin*, 9–11.

7 *Nation*, 3 June 1848.

8 "The Value of an Irish Harvest," *Nation*, 1 July 1848. The article was so incendiary that the government used it against Duffy during his trial for high treason in 1849. McGee's authorship of the article was affirmed by Mary McGee during Duffy's trial; see [New York] *Nation*, 17 March 1849.

9 *Nation*, 15 July 1848.

10 *Irish Tribune*, 24 June 1848; reports of informant "CD," 22 June, 1 July, 1848, TCD, MS 2039, ff. 9, 20.

11 *Nation*, 17 June, 15 July 1848; Duffy, *Four Years of Irish History*, 622–3; Deposition of William A. Wilson, *Treanor vs Donahoe*, Minutes of Evidence, 7 February 1851, Supreme Judicial Court for Suffolk County, Mass., docket 247, f. 13, Supreme Judicial Court Archives, Boston.

12 *Nation*, 10 June 1848.

13 *Boston Pilot*, 21 October 1848; Nowlan, *Politics of Repeal*, 206–8; Sloan, *William Smith O'Brien and the Young Ireland Rebellion*, 235–7; Kerr, *"A Nation of Beggars?"* 132–45.

14 Kerr, *"A Nation of Beggars?"* 149–51, 155–6; Duffy, *Four Years of Irish History*, 628–30; [New York] *Nation*, 17 February 1848.

15 Koseki, *Dublin Confederate Clubs*, 30; *Boston Pilot*, 21 October 1848; O'Gorman, "Narrative of 1848," 23 May 1881, Duffy Papers, NLI, MS 5886, ff. 12–13.

16 *Irish Felon*, 15 July 1848; *Nation*, 15 July 1848; Duffy, *Four Years of Irish History*, 624–6. Duffy erroneously dated his own arrest as 9 July 1848.

17 Duffy, *Four Years of Irish History*, 680; Sloan, *William Smith O'Brien and the Young Ireland Rebellion*, 243–4; *Irish Felon*, 22 July 1848; *Nation*, 22 July 1848.

18 *Nation*, 22 July 1848; Sloan, *William Smith O'Brien and the Young Ireland Rebellion*, 245–6.

19 Duffy, *Four Years of Irish History*, 638–9; reports of informant "EF," 22, 23 July 1848, TCD, MS 2038, ff. 61–2; report of informant "CD," 21 July 1848, TCD, MS 2039, f. 39.

20 Duffy, *Four Years of Irish History*, 641–2; Sloan, *William Smith O'Brien and the Young Ireland Rebellion*, 246–50.

21 Duffy, *Four Years of Irish History*, 644; reports of informant "EF," 26 July, 1 August 1848, TCD, MS 2038, ff. 64, 68; report of informant "CD," 24 July 1848, TCD, MS 2039, ff. 42–3.

22 *United Irishman*, 1 April 1848; [New York] *Nation*, 28 July 1849; Cavanagh, *Memoirs of Meagher*, 245.

23 [New York] *Nation*, 28 July 1849. See also the *Times*, 25 July 1848: "It was rumoured that warrants were out against Mr. Meagher and Mr. Darcy M'Gee; but on inquiry I find that such is not the fact, and that as yet these gentlemen are free to spout treason without let or hindrance. They are, beyond comparison, the two most dangerous men in connexion with the movement."

24 [New York] *Nation*, 28 July 1849; Duffy, *Four Years of Irish History*, 679.

25 [New York] *Nation*, 28 July 1849; Warrant for the Arrest of Thomas Darcy McGhee [sic], 28 July 1848, NLI, MS 7910.

26 [New York] *Nation*, 28 July 1849.

27 Duffy, *Four Years of Irish History*, 653; Koseki, *Dublin Confederate Clubs*, 35–6.

28 Sloan, *William Smith O'Brien and the Young Ireland Rebellion*, 250–9; Duffy, *Four Years of Irish History*, 658.

29 Sloan, *William Smith O'Brien and the Young Ireland Rebellion*, 259–75; Cavanagh, *Memoirs of Meagher*, 273.

30 Sloan, *William Smith O'Brien and the Young Ireland Rebellion*, 275–81, 285.

31 *Nation*, 10 June 1848; O'Gorman, "Narrative of 1848," 23 May 1881, Duffy Papers, NLI, MS 5886, ff. 19–20; Duffy, *Four Years of Irish History*, 690n.

32 [New York] *Nation*, 28 July 1849; *Boston Pilot*, 1 March 1845; *Nation*, 8 April 1848; Owens, "Popular Mobilisation," 58.

33 [New York] *Nation*, 28 July 1849; Blake to Redington, 18 September 1848, and Mulreany to Blake, 20 October 1848, Outrage Reports 1848, NAI, box 1514, ff. 239, 267.

34 *Nation*, 15 March 1851.

35 Ibid.

36 Ibid.; Blake to Redington, 18, 28 September 1848, Outrage Reports 1848, NAI, box 1514, ff. 239, 250; O'Gorman, "Narrative of 1848," 23 May 1881, Duffy Papers, NLI, MS 5886, ff. 1–22. There actually was a student named John Kelly at Maynooth; he was from County Tyrone and was away from the college on his summer vacation; see Renham to Redington, 24 September 1848, Outrage Reports 1848, NAI, box 1514, f. 246.

37 Blake to Redington, 18, 28 September 1848, Outrage Reports 1848, NAI, box 1514, ff. 239, 250. An example was indeed made; James O'Donnell was imprisoned under the suspension of habeas corpus; see Duffy, *Four Years of Irish History*, 756.

38 Blake to Redington, 15 October 1848, Outrage Reports 1848, NAI, box 1514, f. 265; *Nation*, 15 March 1851.

39 McGee, *Life of Maginn*, 170; [New York] *Nation*, 17 February 1849; Beattie, ed., *Thomas D'Arcy McGee*, 1; Duffy, *Four Years of Irish History*, 774; *Canadian Freeman*, 23 April 1868; [Castlemain] *Mount Alexander Mail*, 22 July 1868. I thank Jenny Meegan for this reference.

CHAPTER NINE

1 *Nation*, 22 April, 24 June 1848; Duffy, *Four Years of Irish History*, 609–10; Ó Cathaoir, ed., *Young Irelander Abroad*, 2. For Binns's background, see Wilson, *United Irishmen, United States*.

2 *New York Daily Tribune*, 15 August 1848.

3 *New York Daily Tribune*, 21 August 1848.

4 *New York Daily Tribune*, 22 August 1848; for Devlin's speech, see *New York Daily Tribune*, 25 August 1848.

5 *New York Daily Tribune*, 28 August 1848.

6 [New York] *Nation*, 4 November 1848.

7 [New York] *Nation*, 23 December 1848.

8 Also published in the *Boston Pilot*, 21 October 1848.

9 *Boston Pilot*, 21 October 1848.

10 *Boston Pilot*, 28 October 1848.

11 *Limerick Reporter*, 7 November 1848; *Dublin Evening Post*, 18 November, 2 December 1848.

12 *Dublin Evening Post*, 7 November 1848.

13 *Times*, 7 February 1849.

14 [New York] *Nation*, 23 December 1848.

15 *Irishman*, 7, 14 July 1849.

16 See, for example, the *Citizen* [New York], 17 November 1855, which erroneously maintained that McGee published his letter "while O'Brien and Meagher were yet to be tried."

17 *La Minerve*, 21 February 1861; *Canadian Freeman*, 19 September 1861.

18 *Canadian Freeman*, 8 October 1858.

19 [New York] *Nation*, 28 October and 2, 16 December 1848.

20 [New York] *Nation*, 11 November 1848.

21 [New York] *Nation*, 2 December 1848.

22 Reports of informant "CD," 13, 14 November 1848, and 20, 25 January 1849, TCD, MS 2039, ff. 112–13, 195, 199–200.

23 Report of informant "CD," 17 April 1849, TCD, MS 2040, f. 65. See also Duffy, *Four Years of Irish History*, 760–6.

24 Reports of informant "CD," 16 December 1848, and 12 February, 3, 9 March 1849, TCD, MS 2039, ff. 161, 209, 216–17, 221.

25 Compare [New York] *Nation*, 2 December 1848, with report of informant "CD," 30 December 1848, TCD, MS 2039, f. 173; and compare [New York] *Nation*, 21 April 1849, with report of informant "CD," 21 May 1849, TCD, MS 2040, f. 103.

26 [New York] *Nation*, 16 December 1848.

27 [New York] *Nation*, 30 December 1848, 6 January 1849.

28 [New York] *Nation*, 23 December 1849.

29 [New York] *Nation*, 6 January 1849.

30 There were five letters in all; see [New York] *Freeman's Journal*, 13, 20, 27 January, 3, 10 February 1849.

31 Quoted in Shaw, *Dagger John*, 304–5.

32 Hughes, "Address to the National Brotherhood of St. Patrick," 22 July 1862, in *Complete Works*, 2:527.

33 Ibid., 2:528.

34 Hughes, "The Question of Ireland," in *Complete Works*, 2: 793–4.

35 [New York] *Freeman's Journal*, 13 January 1849.

36 Ibid. For the charges of cowardice, see also 20 January, 10 February 1849.

37 [New York] *Freeman's Journal*, 3 February 1849.

38 [New York] *Freeman's Journal*, 13 January 1849. For the views of McGee and Hughes in 1844, see above, 79–80.

39 [New York] *Freeman's Journal*, 27 January 1849.

40 [New York] *Freeman's Journal*, 13 January 1849.

41 Ibid.

42 [New York] *Freeman's Journal*, 20, 27 January 1849.

43 Father John McCaffrey to Orestes Brownson, 17 January 1849, Orestes A. Brownson Papers, University of Notre Dame.

44 [New York] *Nation*, 20 January 1849.

45 [New York] *Freeman's Journal*, 27 January 1849.

46 [New York] *Nation*, 20 January 1849.

47 [New York] *Nation*, 10 February 1849.

48 "Resolutions and Promises of T. Darcy McGee," 15 February 1849, McMaster and McGee Correspondence, box 3, Henry J. Browne Papers, Columbia University, New York. The document is not in McGee's handwriting and is probably a copy of the first draft of an agreement drawn up by McMaster and McGee.

49 Burns, "Thomas D'Arcy McGee," 203; McGee to Duffy, 18 May 1849, in Duffy, *My Life*, 2:5.

50 [New York] *Nation*, 31 March 1849.

51 [New York] *Nation*, 14 July, 25 August 1849; see also 1 September 1849.

52 Diary of Charles Hart, 24 February 1849, in Ó Cathaoir, ed., *Young Irelander Abroad*, 43.

53 Doheny, *Felon's Track*, 155, 163–70.

54 [New York] *Nation*, 10 February 1849.

55 [New York] *Nation*, 27 January 1849.

56 [New York] *Nation*, 21 April 1849.

57 [New York] *Nation*, 10, 17 March 1849.

58 [New York] *Nation*, 3, 10, 31 March, 21 April 1849.

59 [New York] *Nation*, 17 February 1849.

60 [New York] *Nation*, 5 May 1849.

61 [New York] *Nation*, 3 March 1849.

62 Loughlin, "Allegiance and Illusion," 491–513.

63 [New York] *Nation*, 21 April 1849.

64 [New York] *Nation*, 31 March, 5 May 1849.

65 Contrast *Nation*, 2, 19, 26 February 1848 with *Nation*, 4 March and 6 May 1848.

66 Report of informant "EF," 3 June 1848, TCD, MS 2038, f. 36; report of informant "CD," 15 April 1848, TCD, MS 2040, f. 22.

67 Senior, *Fenians and Canada*, 27–31.

68 Diary of Charles Hart, 16 October 1848, in Ó Cathaoir, *Young Irelander Abroad*, 36.

69 [New York] *Nation*, 31 March 1849.

70 [New York] *Nation*, 20 January 1849.

71 [New York] *Nation*, 21 April 1849.

72 [New York] *Nation*, 28 April 1849.

73 Ibid.

74 [New York] *Nation*, 5 May 1849.

75 Ibid.

76 *Montreal Herald*, 25 July 1867.

CHAPTER TEN

1 [New York] *Nation*, 26 May, 9 June, 14, 21 July 1849.

2 Duffy to McGee, 23 February 1849, *Irish Monthly*, 1883, 377–8.

3 McGee, *Memoir of Charles Gavan Duffy*, 26–7.

4 McGee to Duffy, 8 May 1849, in Duffy, *My Life*, 2:5–6.

5 [New York] *Nation*, 12 May 1849.

6 [New York] *Nation*, 15 September 1849.

7 [New York] *Nation*, 28 July 1849.

8 [New York] *Nation*, 29 September 1849. See also *Nation*, 1 September 1849, and [New York] *Nation*, 28 July 1849.

9 [New York] *Nation*, 9, 16 December 1848.

10 [New York] *Nation*, 12, 19 May 1849.

11 Dillon to McGee (draft letter), 22 May 1849, John Blake Dillon Papers, TCD, MS 6455, f. 107b.

12 Dillon to Ady Dillon, 7 July 1849, Dillon Papers, MS 6455, f. 123.

13 Dillon to Duffy, 19 May 1849, Dillon Papers, MS 6455, f. 106a; Dillon to Ady Dillon, 29 May 1849, ibid., f. 110.

14 Dillon to Ady Dillon, n.d., ibid, f. 131.

15 Duffy, *My Life*, 2:266.

16 *Irishman*, 7 April, 5 May 1849. The other editor of the *Irishman* was Bernard Fullam.

17 One of the letters, under the pseudonym Frater, was from Bernard Brady, who distributed the New York *Nation* in Dublin; see report of informant "CD," 12 May 1849, TCD, MS 2040, f. 92, and *Irishman*, 12 May 1849. For the paper's response to James McGee's letter, see *Irishman*, 19 May 1849.

18 [New York] *People*, 26 May 1849, quoted in [New York] *Citizen*, 10 November 1855.

19 Duffy, *Four Years of Irish History*, 775n.

20 *Irishman*, 7 July, 25 August 1849.

21 *Nation*, 8 December 1849.

22 [New York] *Nation*, 12 May 1849.

23 [New York] *Nation*, 9 June 1849.

24 [New York] *Nation*, 15 March 1850.

25 [New York] *Nation*, 27 October 1849. For the view that such "No Irish need apply" signs were largely an urban myth, see Jensen, "No Irish Need Apply," 405–29. The views of McGee's Canadian correspondents on annexation can be found in the [New York] *Nation*, 12 May, 9, 30 June, 21 July, 3 November 1849, and 9 February, 16 March 1850.

26 [New York] *Nation*, 2 June 1849.

27 [New York] *Nation*, 14 July 1849.

28 [New York] *Nation*, 16 March 1850, 29 December 1849.

29 *Nation*, 12 February 1848.

30 [New York] *Nation*, 13 April 1850.

31 See, for example, *American Celt*, 15 March 1851.

32 [New York] *Nation*, 18 August 1849.

33 [New York] *Nation*, 14 July, 11, 18 August, and 20 October 1849.

34 [New York] *Nation*, 8 September 1849.

35 Ibid.

36 [New York] *Nation*, 11 August 1849.

37 *Nation*, 1 September 1849.

38 [New York] *Nation*, 8 September 1849.

39 McGee, *Memoir of Charles Gavan Duffy*, 4.

40 [New York] *Nation*, 9 March 1850.

41 [New York] *Nation*, 8 September 1849.

42 Ibid.

43 [New York] *Nation*, 29 December 1849.

44 [New York] *Nation*, 19 May 1849.

45 *Nation*, 1 September 1849.

46 [New York] *Nation*, 27 October 1849.

47 *Irish American*, 23 September 1849.

48 [New York] *Nation*, 24 November 1849.

49 [New York] *Nation*, 1 December 1849.

50 *Boston Pilot*, 16 February 1850.

51 See, for example, *Irishman*, 15 December 1849, *Irish People*, 23 April 1864, 20 May 1865, and *Irish Canadian*, 15 January 1868.

52 [New York] *Nation*, 22 December 1849.

53 See, for example, John Balfe to Lord Clarendon, n.d. [May 1848], Clarendon Papers, box 53, Bodleian Library, Oxford University.

54 Duffy, *Four Years of Irish History*, 765–6; Breen, *Cappoquin Rebellion*.

55 *Irish American*, 27 January 1850.

56 Quoted in [New York] *Nation*, 1 December 1849.

57 [New York] *Nation*, 12 January 1850.

58 [New York] *Nation*, 2 March 1850.

59 [New York] *Nation*, 9 March 1850.

60 *Boston Pilot*, 23 March 1850. For accounts of the disruptions, see [New York] *Nation*, 23, 30 March 1850.

61 [New York] *Nation*, 30 March 1850.

62 [New York] *Nation*, 20 October 1849.

63 Quoted in Conor Cruise O'Brien, *Memoir*, 155.

64 [New York] *Nation*, 18 May 1850.

65 *Irishman*, 13 January 1849.

66 McGee to Bella Morgan, 28 June 1849, CUA, PO30 HA256, folder 10.

67 [New York] *Nation*, 18 August 1849. Duffy had mixed opinions about James, regarding him as talented, hardworking, and likable, but warning that he was too materialistic: "Beware, beware, beware," Duffy told McGee, "of his turning into a mere American money-grub"; see Duffy to McGee, 18 August 1849, *Irish Monthly*, 1883, 494.

68 *Nation*, 6 July 1850.

69 Duffy to McGee, 18 April 1850 [misdated 1849], in Duffy, *My Life*, 2:23–4.

70 *Nation*, 6 July 1850; [New York] *Nation*, 15 June 1850.

71 Duffy to McGee, 14 October 1849, *Irish Monthly*, 1883, 496–7; see also Duffy to McGee, 18 August 1849, *Irish Monthly*, 496.

72 [New York] *Nation*, 30 June 1849; see also 7 April 1849.

73 [New York] *Nation*, 8 June 1850.

CHAPTER ELEVEN

1 *American Celt*, 31 August 1850. Isabel Skelton asserted that the warning came from Colmen O'Loghlen, one of Duffy's defence lawyers; however, she provided no evidence to support her claim. See Skelton, *Thomas D'Arcy McGee*, 182.

2 *Boston Pilot*, 6 July 1850; *American Celt*, 31 August 1850.

3 The first column, under the heading "Foreign Department. Superintended by Thomas D'Arcy McGee," appeared in *Boston Daily Times*, 26 August 1850; the columns appeared on almost a daily basis until 19 October 1850.

4 *American Celt*, 31 August 1850.

5 See, for example, Burns, "Thomas D'Arcy McGee," 223.

6 *American Celt*, 31 August 1850. In later versions of "Salutations to the Celts," "world-divided Gaels" became "sea-divided Gaels." See Sadlier, *Poems of Thomas D'Arcy McGee*, 135–6.

7 *American Celt*, 31 August 1850.

8 For McGee's earlier writings on the subject, see *Nation*, 28 November 1846; [New York] *Nation*, 29 September 1849, 27 April 1850.

9 *American Celt*, 12 October 1850; see also 26 October 1850.

10 *Nation*, 24 August 1850.

11 On Howe's mission to London, see Beck, *Joseph Howe*, 2:34–5.

12 *American Celt*, 12 April, 2 August 1851.

13 *American Celt*, 19 October, 21 December 1850; see also [New York] *Nation*, 30 March 1850.

14 *American Celt*, 19 October, 21 December 1850.

15 *Nation*, 26 April 1851.

16 *American Celt*, 15 February 1851; see also 5 April 1851.

17 On the Encumbered Estates Act, see Donnelly, *Great Irish Potato Famine*, 162–8. For McGee's subsequent views on the subject, see *American Celt*, 26 March, 7 May 1853, and 7 April 1855.

18 *American Celt*, 21, 28 September 1850.

19 *American Celt*, 25 October 1851; see also 1 November 1851.

20 *Nation*, 21 February 1852.

21 *American Celt*, 4 January 1851; see also *American Celt*, 14, 21, 28 September, 5 October, 2 November, and 28 December 1850.

22 *American Celt*, 28 December 1850.

23 McGee, *History of the Irish Settlers*, 44, 51, 120.

24 Ibid., 142–7, 188.

25 Ibid., 136.

26 Ibid., 15–16, 104–5, 185, 196.

27 *American Celt*, 27 May 1854.

28 *American Celt*, 5 April 1851.

29 See *Nation*, 1 September 1849: "This Roman love of truth, honesty, and resolute self-dependence, must be taught to our people."

30 [New York] *Nation*, 9 March 1850.

31 The Compromise of 1850 attempted to reconcile North-South divisions through five key measures: California would enter the Union as a free state; Texas would give up its territorial claims to the West and would receive $10 million in compensation; the status of slavery in the Utah Territory would be determined by territorial legislatures; slavery would continue in the District of Columbia, but the slave trade across its borders would be stopped; and a new Fugitive Slave Act would make it easier for slave catchers to do their work.

32 *American Celt*, 9 November 1850. For similar views among the United Irishmen, see Wilson, *United Irishmen, United States*, 135–7.

33 *American Celt*, 1 March 1851; Collison, *Shadrach Minkins*, 227–8.

34 The *Commonwealth*, quoted in *American Celt*, 8 March 1851.

35 *American Celt*, 8 March 1851.

36 *American Celt*, 18 January, 1 March 1851.

37 Burke, *Reflections on the Revolution in France*, 153.

38 Kerr, *"A Nation of Beggars?"* 241–81.

39 *American Celt*, 30 November 1850, and 11 January, 19 April 1851.

40 Quoted in Kerr, *"A Nation of Beggars?"* 247.

41 *American Celt*, 9 November 1850; [New York] *Nation*, 8 September 1849.

42 *American Celt*, 31 May 1851.

43 *American Celt*, 13 December 1851.

44 *American Celt*, 1 February 1851.

45 *Nation*, 18 September, 18 December 1847, 15 January 1848; Deposition of William A. Wilson, *Treanor vs Donahoe*, Minutes of Evidence, 7 February 1851, Supreme Judicial Court for Suffolk County, Mass., docket 247, f. 13, Supreme Judicial Court Archives, Boston.

46 *Boston Pilot*, 6 July 1850.

47 *Treanor vs Donahoe*, Supreme Judicial Court Archives, Boston.

48 *Treanor vs Donahoe*, in Cushing, ed., *Reports of Cases*, 231–2.

49 *Boston Pilot*, 15 February 1851.

50 Ibid.

51 *American Celt*, 7 December 1850, 1 February 1851.

52 *American Celt*, 8 May 1852.

53 McGee, "Political Causes and Consequences of the Protestant 'Reformation,'" 25.

54 *Boston Pilot*, 8 March 1851.

55 *American Celt*, 19 April 1851.

56 *American Celt*, 3 May 1851.

57 Ibid. and 10 May 1851.

58 *American Celt*, 17 May 1851.

59 *American Celt*, 31 May 1851. On Protestants cancelling their subscriptions, see *American Celt*, 7 June 1851.

60 *American Celt*, 31 May 1851; *Boston Pilot*, 7 June 1851. See also *American Celt*, 20 December 1851.

61 McGee to Urquhart, 8 September 1847, Urquhart Papers 1/J6, Balliol College, Oxford University. See also *American Celt*, 12 January 1850.

62 *American Celt*, 11 March 1854.

63 On Fitzpatrick's career, see Grozier, "John Bernard Fitzpatrick," and O'Connor, *Fitzpatrick's Boston*.

64 Merwick, *Boston Priests*, 20–40; *American Celt*, 31 December 1853.

65 *American Celt*, 31 December 1853.

66 Burke, "Thoughts on French Affairs," in *Writings and Speeches*, 8:341; *American Celt*, 17 January 1852.

67 Burke, *Reflections*, 194–5.

68 For Burke's views on parallels between the Reformation and the French Revolution, see "Thoughts on French Affairs," 341–2; for his view that Catholicism was a bulwark against revolutionary democracy, see Burke to William Smith, 29 January 1795, in *Writings and Speeches*, 9:661–3.

69 *American Celt*, 31 December 1853.

70 Balmes [Balmez], *Protestantism and Catholicity*, vii.

71 Ibid., iii.

72 Ibid., 419.

73 Ibid., 26.

74 Ibid., 44.

75 Ibid., 80.

76 Ibid., 90–1, 172. For Balmez's general argument, see 94–183.

77 Ibid., 169.

78 Ibid., 200.

79 Ibid., 205, 203–19.

80 See, for example, *American Celt*, 23 August 1851 (where McGee defended the Spanish Inquisition); 27 December 1851 (where he echoed Balmez's praise for the Jesuits); 20 November 1852 (where he repeated Balmez's view that Catholicism had strengthened the institution of marriage and had abolished slavery in Europe); and 11 December 1852 (where he followed Balmez's arguments about material progress and spiritual fulfilment).

81 Carey, *Orestes A. Brownson*, 170, 134–92.

82 Sadlier to Brownson, 14 December 1852, Brownson Papers, University of Notre Dame.

83 *American Celt*, 11 October 1851.

84 *Boston Pilot*, 8 November 1851; McGee to Brownson, n.d. [November 1851], Brownson Papers, University of Notre Dame.

85 *American Celt*, 18 November 1854.

86 *American Celt*, 26 July 1851.

87 Ibid. and 20 September 1851.

88 *Nation*, 16 August, 1851. For McGee's "sailing coffins" speech, see above, 191–2.

89 *American Celt*, 24 May, 2 August 1851.

90 *American Celt*, 2 August 1851.

91 *American Celt*, 24, 31 May, 13 September 1851.

92 *American Celt*, 20 December 1851.

93 *American Celt*, 9 August 1851.

94 McGee, *History of the Irish Settlers*, 238. See also *American Celt*, 17 January 1852.

95 *American Celt*, 13 December 1851.

96 *American Celt*, 20, 27 September, 22 November 1851; "Address to the Naturalized Citizens of Massachusetts, adopted by the Council of the Central Naturalization Society," in McGee to Brownson (n.d., November 1851), Brownson Papers, University of Notre Dame.

97 McGee, *History of the Irish Settlers*, 237–8.

98 *American Celt*, 8 November 1851.

CHAPTER TWELVE

1 Gerber, *Making of an American Pluralism*, 156.

2 Mary Euphrasia was born in Boston on 27 March 1851; the year is some-times erroneously given as 1850. See Baptism Registers, Boston Archdioc-esan Archives.

3 Mary McGee to Bella Morgan, 2 August 1852, CUA, PO30 HA256, folder 13.

4 On Timon's loan, see McGee to Moylan, 8 November 1858, James G. Moy-lan Papers, LAC, MG29 D15, vol. 1. On the priests' subscription and Bede's letter, see *American Celt*, 20 November 1852.

5 *American Celt*, 8 May 1852.

6 *Nation*, 4 September 1852.

7 *American Celt*, 16 October 1852, 22 January 1853.

8 *American Celt*, 14 August 1852.

9 *American Celt*, 21 August 1852.

10 *American Celt*, 6 November 1852.

11 *American Celt*, 11 September 1852.

12 *American Celt*, 16 October 1852.

13 *American Celt*, 2 April 1853.

14 *American Celt*, 19 March 1853.

15 *American Celt*, 23 April 1853.

16 *American Celt*, 30 April 1853.

17 *American Celt*, 19 March 1853.

18 *American Celt*, 30 April 1853.

19 This discussion of McGee's attitude to liberalism is drawn mainly from *American Celt*, 29 January and 27 August 1853.

20 *American* Celt, 1 January 1853; Buffalo *Daily Courier*, 30 November 1852.

21 *American Celt*, 22 January 1853.

22 *Nation*, 3 July 1852.

23 *Nation*, 4 September 1852.

24 See above, 107.

25 *American Celt*, 24 December 1852.

26 Meagher to Duffy, 17 January 1853, Charles Gavan Duffy Papers, NLI, MS 5757, f. 387.

27 *True Witness*, 26 May 1854; Duffy, *Four Years of Irish History*, 775.

28 McGee, "Political Causes and Consequences of the Protestant 'Reforma-tion,'" 23.

29 *American Celt*, 17 December 1853; see also 10 and 24 December 1853.

30 *American Celt*, 11 March 1854, 5 May 1855. This was also the position of Father John Roddan; see Merwick, *Boston Priests*, 31–2.

31 *American Celt*, 11 December 1852.

32　*American Celt*, 20 November 1852.

33　On the Americo-Celtic Society, see *American Celt*, 6 November 1852; on the auxiliary Irish Archaeological Society, see *American Celt*, 18 December 1852. For McGee's support of and participation in the Catholic Institutes, see *American Celt*, 13 November 1852, 28 May 1853; *Buffalo Daily Courier*, 30 November 1852; Sadlier to Brownson, 14 December 1852, Brownson Papers, University of Notre Dame; McGee, "Political Causes and Consequences of the Protestant 'Reformation.'"

34　*American Celt*, 9 April 1853.

35　*American Celt*, 14 May 1853.

36　*American Celt*, 8 January 1853.

37　*American Celt*, 14 May, 9 April 1853.

38　*Buffalo Daily Courier*, 3 May 1853; Gerber, *Making of an American Pluralism*, 159.

39　*American Celt*, 9 April 1853.

40　*American Celt*, 21 August, 2 April 1853.

41　McGee, *History of the Attempts*, 12.

42　McGee, *History of the Attempts*, 38; see also *True Witness*, 18 November 1853.

43　McGee, *History of the Attempts*, 45, 135. McGee also perpetuated the myth that Cromwell had set out "to doom all who opposed his arms or his theology in Ireland to instantaneous death"; see, in contrast, Tom Reilly, *Cromwell*, passim.

44　McGee, *History of the Attempts*, 276.

45　Ibid., 287.

46　Ibid., 102, 110.

47　Ibid., 64, 144. McGee mistakenly gave the date of Archbishop O'Hurley's death as 1582.

48　Ibid., 240.

49　Ibid., 205.

50　Ibid., 289.

51　Ibid., 335.

52　*True Witness*, 29 March 1863.

53　*American Celt*, 27 November 1852.

54　*American Celt*, 8, 15 January 1853.

55　*American Celt*, 26 March 1853.

56　*True Witness*, 5 November 1852; *American Celt*, 13, 20 November 1852.

57　Their meeting is inferred from the fact that Devlin was an active member of the Young Men's St Patrick's Association, which invited McGee to speak in Montreal.

58 *Canadian Freeman*, 14 March 1861; McGee to Mary Ann Sadlier, 9 June 1862, James Sadlier Papers, LAC, MG24 C16.

59 Sadlier to Brownson, 14 December 1852, Brownson Papers, University of Notre Dame.

60 McGee to Sadlier, 9 May 1853, Buffalo and Erie Country Historical Archives, A00-385; Burns, "Thomas D'Arcy McGee," 257–8.

CHAPTER THIRTEEN

1 *American Celt*, 11 November 1854.

2 *American Celt*, 19 August, 18 November 1854.

3 *American Celt*, 30 July 1853.

4 *American Celt*, 18 November 1854; see also 20 December 1856.

5 *American Celt*, 17 September 1853. On the Whole World Temperance Convention, see Isenberg, *Sex and Citizenship*, 99–100. For more general treatments of the women's rights movement during the mid-nineteenth century, see DuBois, *Feminism and Suffrage*, 21–52, and *Woman Suffrage*, 30–89; and Matthews, *Women's Struggle for Equality*.

6 *American Celt*, 3 June 1854.

7 *American Celt*, 11 June 1853.

8 Ibid.

9 *American Celt*, 18 June 1853.

10 *American Celt*, 11 June 1853.

11 *American Celt*, 25 February 1854.

12 *American Celt*, 25 February 1854. The quotation is from Doctor James Warren Doyle, Bishop of Kildare and Leighlin, who was one of the authors featured in McGee, *Historical Sketches of O'Connell and His Friends*.

13 *American Celt*, 25 February 1854. See also McGee, *Catholic History of North America*, 39–67.

14 *American Celt*, 25 June 1853.

15 On the Kansas-Nebraska question, see Potter, *Impending Crisis*, 160–76.

16 *American Celt*, 8 July 1854.

17 *American Celt*, 13 August 1853; see also 17 December 1853 and 10 June 1854.

18 [New York] *Citizen*, 25 March 1854.

19 Dillon, *Life of Mitchel*, 2:51–2.

20 [New York] *Citizen*, 12 August 1854.

21 *American Celt*, 22 April 1854; see also 6 May 1854.

22 *American Celt*, 26 August 1854; see also 14 January, 22 April 1854 and 22 December 1855.

23 *American Celt*, 29 April 1854.

24 *American Celt*, 16 July 1853.

25 Ibid. and 13 May 1854.

26 *American Celt*, 3 December 1853.

27 *American Celt*, 22 April 1854.

28 *American Celt*, 6 May, 3 June, 26 August 1854.

29 *American Celt*, 6 May 1854.

30 *American Celt*, 31 December 1853, 29 April 1854; see also 5 August 1854, where he described the Irish emigrant as a "voluntary exile." Ironically, when McGee had been an emigrant in 1843, he referred to himself as an exile; after he actually was an exile in 1848, he began to call himself an emigrant.

31 *American Celt*, 31 December 1853.

32 *American Celt*, 4 February 1854.

33 See, for example, [New York] *Citizen*, 17, 24 June and 1 July 1854.

34 [New York] *Citizen*, 21 January, 11 March 1854; *American Celt*, 28 January, 11 February 1854. See also Connelly, *Visit of Archbishop Gaetano Bedini*, which argues that the long-term effect of Bedini's mission was to strengthen American Catholicism.

35 [New York] *Citizen*, 12, 19, 26 August and 2 September 1854.

36 *American Celt*, 16 September 1854.

37 Ibid.

38 *American Celt*, 25 June 1853.

39 [New York] *Citizen*, 14 January 1854.

40 Jane Verner Mitchel to Mary —, Brooklyn, 20 April 1854, Meloney-Mitchel Papers, Columbia University.

41 *American Celt*, 4 February 1854.

42 *American Celt*, 27 May 1854; see also 23 August 1856.

43 *American Celt*, 7 October 1854; cf. [New York] *Nation*, 8 September 1849.

44 Knobel, *America for the Americans*, 120–1, 137–9.

45 Gerber, *Making of an American Pluralism*, 374.

46 For McGee's views about an imagined British conspiracy, see *American Celt*, 25 June, 30 July, 31 December 1853 and 28 October 1854; for his views on the role of Orangemen within American nativism, see *American Celt*, 15 July, 9, 23 September 1854.

47 *American Celt*, 9, 23 September, 28 October 1854.

48 *American Celt*, 16 September 1854.

49 *American Celt*, 27 May 1854.

50 *American Celt*, 23 September 1854.

51 *American Celt*, 13 September 1856 and 3 September, 22, 29 October 1853.

52 *American Celt*, 18 March 1854.

53 *American Celt*, 13, 20 May 1854; MacRaild, *Faith, Fraternity and Fighting*, 181.

54 *American Celt*, 18 March, 17, 24 June, 8 July, 12 August, 28 October 1854.

55 *American Celt*, 24 June 1854.

56 *American Celt*, 16 September 1854.

57 *American Celt*, 28 October 1854.

58 Brownson, "Native Americans," 281–2, 297.

59 Ibid., 286; Brownson, "The Know-Nothings," 301–80.

60 Brownson, "Native Americans," 285; Brownson, "The Know-Nothings," 322.

61 Brownson, "Native Americans," 287.

62 Ibid., 282–4.

63 *American Celt*, 9 September 1854.

64 *American Celt*, 15 July 1854.

65 *American Celt*, 30 December 1854.

66 McGee, *Catholic History of North America*, n.p., see also *American Celt,* 7 April 1855. In true ultramontane form, he fully subscribed to the dogma of the Immaculate Conception, which Pope Pius IX proclaimed in December 1854.

67 McGee, *Catholic History of North America*, 9.

68 Brownson, "The Know-Nothings," 322.

69 McGee, *Catholic History of North America*, 77–89, 118–20, 134–5.

70 *American Celt*, 21 October 1854.

71 *American Celt*, 5 August 1854.

72 *American Celt*, 19 August 1854; see also 12 August 1854 and 21 October 1854.

73 *American Celt*, 2 September 1854.

74 *American Celt*, 9 September, 14 October, 4 November 1854.

75 *American Celt*, 11, 18 November 1854.

76 *New Era*, 14 November 1857.

77 *American Celt*, 18 November 1854.

78 *American Celt*, 30 December 1854.

79 *American Celt*, 8 November 1851, 8 January 1853.

80 *American Celt*, 18 June 1853; Keep, "Irish Migration to Montreal," 92.

81 *American Celt*, 18 June, 20 August 1853.

82 For Irish Catholic Canadian criticisms of his position, see *American Celt*, 3 September 1853 and 15 April, 13 May 1854.

83 *American Celt*, 15 April 1854.

84 *American Celt*, 24 June 1854; *New Era*, 19 January 1858.

85 *American Celt*, 5 August 1854.

86 *American Celt*, 18 November 1854.

87 *American Celt*, 16 December 1854.

88 *American Celt*, 9, 16 December 1854.

89 *American Celt*, 9 December 1854.

90 *American Celt*, 14, 21 April 1855.

91 *American Celt*, 9 December 1854.

92 *American Celt*, 23 December 1854.

93 *American Celt*, 9 December 1854.

CHAPTER FOURTEEN

1 Mary McGee to Bella Morgan, 21 July 1856, CUA, PO30 HA256, folder 15.

2 *American Celt*, 29 December 1855.

3 Davis, *Revolutionary Imperialist*, 318–19.

4 *American Celt*, 13 January 1855.

5 Mary McGee to Bella Morgan, 23 March 1855, CUA, PO30 HA256, folder 14; *American Celt*, 29 December 1855.

6 *American Celt*, 21 April 1855.

7 Ibid.

8 *American Celt*, 27 October 1855.

9 *American Celt*, 14 April 1855.

10 *American Celt*, 31 March 1855.

11 *American Celt*, 7 April 1855.

12 *American Celt*, 21 April 1855.

13 *American Celt*, 31 March 1855. On Sadleir's career, see O'Shea, *Prince of Swindlers*.

14 *American Celt*, 14, 21 April 1855.

15 *American Celt*, 31 March 1855.

16 *American Celt*, 21 April 1855.

17 *American Celt*, 7 April 1855.

18 Ibid.

19 Ibid.

20 *American Celt*, 14 April, 12 May 1855. The "northern nightingale" was Jenny Lind, the Swedish singer who had taken America by storm earlier in the decade.

21 Brownson, "Know-Nothings," *Quarterly Review*, July 1855, 409–10; *American Celt*, 11 August 1855.

22 *American Celt*, 23 August 1856.

23 [New York] *Citizen*, 17 November 1855.

24 *American Celt*, 23 August 1856.

25 *American Celt*, 8 September 1855.

26 *American Celt*, 28 April 1855.

27 Mary McGee to Bella Morgan, 23 March 1855, CUA, PO30 HA256, folder 14, and 21 July 1856, folder 15. Rose was beginning to walk in July 1856, so she was probably born between July and September 1855.

28 McGee returned on 20 April 1855; see *Boston Pilot*, 5 May 1855. For his continuing attack on nativism, see *American Celt*, 12 May 1855.

29 *American Celt*, 3 February 1855.

30 *American Celt*, 9, 16 June, 7 July 1855.

31 *American Celt*, 16 June 1855, 5 April 1856.

32 *American Celt*, 11, 18 August 1855; Deusner, "The Know Nothing Riots in Louisville," 122–47.

33 *American Celt*, 15 December 1855.

34 *American Celt*, 24 May 1856; see also 7 June, 2 August (where McGee reported that Herbert had been acquitted of the murder), and 13 December 1856. The Herbert-Keating affair, of so much importance to McGee, has received no attention from historians of the Irish in America.

35 *New Era*, 9 July 1857: "Assassins go at large, or are elected to Congress; they even become heroes among their savage associates."

36 *American Celt*, 28 June 1856.

37 *American Celt*, 6 September, 25 October 1856.

38 *American Celt*, 9 August 1856; see also 6 September 1856.

39 *American Celt*, 13 September 1856.

40 *American Celt*, 8 November 1856.

41 *American Celt*, 11 October 1856.

42 *American Celt*, 19 May 1855.

43 *American Celt*, 5 April 1856; see also 25 August 1855.

44 *American Celt*, 12 April 1856.

45 *American Celt*, 23 June 1855.

46 *Lehigh Register*, 24 September 1856; *American Celt*, 27 September 1856.

47 *American Celt*, 27 September 1856.

48 *American Celt*, 27 October 1855 (on Free Love), 10 May 1856.

49 *American Celt*, 10 May 1856.

50 McGee to Bella Morgan, 9 February 1844, CUA, PO30 HA256, folder 5; [New York] *Nation*, 20 October 1849; *American Celt*, 16 October 1852, 3 May 1856.

51 *Boston Pilot*, 27 January, 10 February, 6 October 1855.

52 Wilson, *United Irishmen, United States*, 156–7.

53 *American Celt*, 18 August 1855, 2 February 1856.

54 *American Celt*, 27 January, 3 February, 8 September 1855.

55 *American Celt*, 27 January, 23 June 1855.

56 *American Celt*, 23 June 1855; see also 27 January, 8 September 1855, and 8 March 1856.

57 *American Celt*, 3 February, 25 August 1855.

58 *American Celt*, 23 June 1855.

59 *American Celt*, 19 May 1855.

60 *American Celt*, 23 June 1855.

61 *American Celt*, 16 June, 22 September 1855; see also 19 January 1856.

62 *American Celt*, 22 September 1855; see also 14, 21 April, 12 May, and 9 June 1855.

63 *American Celt*, 4 August 1855.

64 Ibid.

65 See, for example, *American Celt*, 3 February and 10 March 1855.

66 *American Celt*, 29 September 1855.

67 *American Celt*, 10 March, 9 June, 28 July 1855.

68 *American Celt*, 10 November 1855. On Kirwan's origins, see the letter from "Crossmaglen" in *American Celt*, 27 November 1852.

69 *True Witness*, 10 August 1855.

70 *American Celt*, 10 November 1855.

71 *American Celt*, 26 January 1856.

72 *American Celt*, 5, 12, 19 January 1856; *Catholic Citizen*, 7 February 1856.

73 *American Celt*, 12 January 1856.

74 *American Celt*, 23 February, 15 March 1856. For the Canadian delegates, see *American Celt*, 2, 9, and 16 February 1856. The numbers are based on McGee's final estimate in *American Celt*, 15 March 1856; for his previous estimates, see 23 February and 8 March 1856.

75 *American Celt*, 9 February 1856; Clerk, "Diary" (handwritten notes by T.P. Slattery), CUA, PO30 HA261, folder 12.

76 *American Celt*, 23 February 1856; Clerk, "Diary," CUA, PO30 HA261, folder 12.

77 Clerk, "Diary," CUA, PO30 HA261, folder 12.

78 *American Celt*, 23 February 1856.

79 *American Celt*, 1 March 1856. For the splits in the Astor House Convention, see [New York] *Citizen*, 15 December 1855.

80 *American Celt*, 1 March 1856.

81 *Metropolitan* 4 (May 1856): 251–3. Mary Ann Sadlier's *Con O'Regan* ran in the *American Celt* between 5 January and 28 June 1856. On the plans for St Patrick, see *American Celt*, 12 April and 10 May 1856.

82 *American Celt*, 31 May 1856.

83 *American Celt*, 23 February, 16, 30 August 1856.

84 *American Celt*, 30 August 1856.

85 *American Celt*, 18, 25 October 1856.

86 *American Celt*, 13 December 1856.

87 Browne, "Archbishop Hughes and Western Colonization," 277; Burns, "Thomas D'Arcy McGee," 299; *American Celt*, 30 August 1856.

88 Byron, *Irish America*, 54–5; Akenson, *Small Differences*, 102. This does not mean, however, that most mid-nineteenth-century Irish immigrants to the United States settled on the land; see Doyle, "The Irish as Urban Pioneers," 36–59.

89 Hughes to James Roosevelt Bayley, n.d., quoted in Browne, "Archbishop Hughes and Western Colonization," 271; Hughes, "The Nebraska Irish Colony," in *Complete Works*, 2:754.

90 *Boston Pilot*, 27 January 1855. The letter was probably written by the Reverend J.S. Ballantyne, who had told Brownson a few weeks earlier that he intended "to commence an attack on M'Gee ... for his foolish twaddle about the Irish exodus from the U.S."; see Ballantyne to Brownson, 24 November 1854, Brownson Papers, University of Notre Dame. In *Boston Pilot*, 5 May 1855, the author of the letter was described as a "reverend correspondent."

91 *Boston Pilot*, 17 March 1855; see also 10 February 1855.

92 *Boston Pilot*, 15 September 1855; see also 10 February, 16 June, 7, 28 July, and 6 October 1855.

93 *Boston Pilot*, 5 May, 16 June 1855.

94 [Toronto] *Globe*, 11 February 1856.

95 *Boston Pilot*, 7 July, 18 August 1855; see also 15 September 1855.

96 *Boston Pilot*, 15 September 1855.

97 *Boston Pilot*, 6 October 1855.

98 *Boston Pilot*, 15 September 1855.

99 *Boston Pilot*, 18 August 1855.

100 [New York] *Freeman's Journal*, 1, 22 March 1856.

101 Compare Hughes to Brownson, 29 August 1856 (Brownson Papers, University of Notre Dame), with *American Celt*, 3 May 1856, in which McGee wrote of encountering "a wire-pulling plot worthy of the lowest party managers" during a recent lecture tour.

102 *Metropolitan* 4 (December 1856): 652–5.

103 Ibid., 653; Hughes to Bayley, quoted in Browne, "Archbishop Hughes and Western Colonization," 271.

104 Hughes to Bernard Smith, 23 March 1858, and Hughes to James Roosevelt Bayley, n.d., quoted in Browne, "Archbishop Hughes and Western Colonization," 282, 271–2.

105 *Metropolitan* 4 (December 1856): 661.

106 *American Celt*, 23 February 1856; *New York Herald*, 27 March 1857.

107 *New York Herald*, 27 March 1857.

108 See *Metropolitan* 4 (December 1856): 652.

109 Hughes, "The Nebraska Irish Colony," in *Complete Works*, 2:751–5; Browne, "Archbishop Hughes and Western Colonization," 276.

110 [New York] *Citizen*, 10 November 1855.

111 [New York] *Citizen*, 1 December 1855.

112 See, for example, *American Celt*, 11 April 1857, in J.J. O'Gorman Papers, LAC, MG30 D20, folder 10.

113 *American Celt*, 22 September 1855.

114 *American Celt*, 12 July 1856.

115 *American Celt*, 11 August 1855.

116 *American Celt*, 7 July 1855.

117 Quoted in Browne, "Archbishop Hughes and Western Colonization," 279.

118 On Irish politics in New York's Sixth Ward, for example, see Anbinder, *Five Points*, 145–71.

119 The best modern synthesis of the Irish in the United States is Kenny, *The American Irish*. See Byron, *Irish America*, for the Catholic Irish in Albany.

120 For a good overview of the Catholic Irish in Canada, see McGowan, "Irish Catholics," 734–63.

121 Senior, *Orangeism: The Canadian Phase*, 21–2, 28–9, 54–6.

122 Clarke, *Piety and Nationalism*, 19.

123 See, for example, McGee, *The Irish Position in Republican and British North America*, 13.

124 Darroch and Ornstein, "Ethnicity and Occupational Structure," 305–33.

125 Akenson, *The Irish in Ontario*; Akenson, *Being Had*, 37–107; Toner, "Occupation and Ethnicity," 155–65; Darroch, "Half Empty or Half Full?" 1–8.

126 *American Celt*, 11 October 1856.

127 *American Celt*, 20 December 1856.

128 McGee to Charbonnel, 10 July 1856, Archives of the Roman Catholic Archdiocese of Toronto, CAH01.01.

129 *American Celt*, 9 August 1856.

130 *American Celt*, 16 August 1856.

131 *True Witness*, 5 September 1856.

132 Circular letter from M.P. Ryan, Marcus Doherty, H. Kavanagh, and James Donnelly, 27 November 1856, CUA, PO30 HA253, folder 12; McGee to Sadlier, 14 October 1856, James Sadlier Papers, LAC, MG24 C16.

133 Father McCullough to Father Patrick Dowd, 27 February 1857, Father Patrick Dowd Papers, St Patrick's Basilica, Montreal; Clerk, "Diary," quoted in Keep, "Irish Migration to Montreal," 111–12.

134 McGee to Sadlier, 14 October 1856, Sadlier Papers, LAC, MG24 C16.

135 McGee to Moylan, Easter Monday 1857, James G. Moylan Papers, LAC, MG29 D15, vol. 1.

136 McGee to Dr Mackenzie, New York, n.d., Public Archives of Nova Scotia.

137 Duffy, *Four Years of Irish History*, 775.

138 Burns, "Thomas D'Arcy McGee," 373.

139 *Nation*, 12 June 1847; *American Celt*, 18 November 1854.

140 *American Celt*, 11 October 1856; see also 13 September 1856.

Bibliography

MANUSCRIPT SOURCES

Archives of the Archdiocese of Kingston, Ontario
    Bishop Edward John Horan Papers
Archives of Ontario
    Charles Clarke Papers
Archives of the Roman Catholic Archdiocese of Toronto
    Charbonnel Papers
Balliol College, Oxford University
    Urquhart Papers, 1/J6
Bodleian Library, Oxford University
    Clarendon Papers
Boston Archdiocesan Archives
    Baptism Registers
    Bishop's Journal, vol. 3
Buffalo and Erie County Historical Archives, MSS A00-385
Columbia University Rare Book and Manuscript Library
    Henry J. Browne Papers
    Meloney-Mitchel Papers
Concordia University Archives
    Thomas D'Arcy McGee Collection, P030
Dublin Diocesan Archives
    Paul Cullen Papers
Library and Archives Canada
    Brown Chamberlin Papers, MG24 B19
    Mercy Ann Coles Papers, MG24 B66

John A. Macdonald Papers, MG26A
Thomas D'Arcy McGee Papers, MG27 I E9
Henry Morgan Papers, MG29 D61
James G. Moylan Papers, MG29 D15 I
Charles Murphy Papers, MG27 III B8
Archdeacon O'Brien Papers, MG24 C20
J.J. O'Gorman Papers, MG30 D20
James Sadlier Papers, MG24 C16
National Archives of Ireland
Fenian Briefs 1865–69
Outrage Reports 1848, box 1514
National Archives of the United Kingdom
Irish Coastguard Establishment Books
National Library of Ireland
Charles Gavan Duffy Papers, MSS 5756–7, 5886
Griffith's Valuation 1853
Hickey Collection, MS 3226
James Fintan Lalor Papers, MS 340
Warrant for the Arrest of Thomas Darcy McGhee [sic], MS 7910
William Smith O'Brien Papers, MSS 438–42, 445–6
Young Ireland Miscellaneous Letters, MS 10,517
Public Archives of Nova Scotia
McGee to Dr Mackenzie, n.d.
Royal Irish Academy
Charles Gavan Duffy Papers, MS 12 P15, P19
Correspondence Book of the Irish Confederation, MS 23 H41
Proceedings of the Council of the Irish Confederation, MS 23 H44
St Patrick's Basilica, Montreal
Father Patrick Dowd Papers
Supreme Judicial Court for Suffolk County, Mass.
Treanor vs Donahoe, Minutes of Evidence, 7 February 1851, docket 247
Trinity College Dublin
1641 Depositions, County Antrim, MS 838
John Blake Dillon Papers, MS 6455
Reports of Informants, MSS 2037–40
University of Notre Dame
Orestes A. Brownson Papers

NEWSPAPERS

American Celt [Boston, Buffalo, New York], 1850–56
Boston Daily Times, 1850
Boston Pilot, 1842–46, 1849–51, 1855
Canadian Freeman [Toronto], 1858, 1860–61, 1864, 1868
Citizen [New York], 1854–55
Daily Courier [Buffalo], 1852
Daily News [Quebec], 1868
Dublin Evening Mail, 1865
Dublin Evening Post, 1848
Freeman's Journal [Dublin], 1845–56
Freeman's Journal [New York], 1844, 1849, 1856
Globe [Toronto], 1856, 1863
Guelph Evening Mercury, 1868
Hartford Daily Times, 1843
Irish American, 1849
Irish Canadian [Toronto], 1864–66, 1868
Irish Felon [Dublin], 1848
Irishman [Dublin], 1849
Irish People [Dublin], 1864–65
Irish Tribune [Dublin], 1848
Irish World [New York], 1878
La Minerve [Montreal], 1861
Lehigh Register, 1856
Limerick Reporter, 1848
Montreal Gazette, 1864, 1867
Montreal Herald, 1861
Montreal Pilot, 1845
Montreal Transcript, 1845
Mount Alexander Mail [Castlemain, Australia], 1868
Nation [Dublin], 1845–54
Nation [New York], 1848–50
New Era [Montreal], 1857–58
New York Daily Tribune, 1848
New York Herald, 1857
Ottawa Citizen, 1863

Peterborough Examiner, 1863
Peterborough Review, 1863
Times [London], 1848–49
True Witness [Montreal], 1853–59
United Irishman [Dublin], 1848
Wexford Independent, 1840–43, 1847

PRINTED SOURCES

Adams, William Forbes. *Ireland and Irish Emigration to the New World from 1815 to the Famine*. New Haven: Yale University Press 1932

Akenson, Donald Harman. *The Irish Educational Experiment: The National System of Education in the Nineteenth Century*. London: Routledge & Kegan Paul 1970

– *The Irish in Ontario: A Study in Rural History*. Montreal & Kingston: McGill-Queen's University Press 1984

– *Being Had: Historians, Evidence, and the Irish in North America*. Port Credit: P.D. Meany 1985

– *The Orangeman: The Life and Times of Ogle Gowan*. Toronto: J. Lorimer 1986

– *Small Differences: Irish Catholics and Irish Protestants, 1815–1922. An International Perspective*. Montreal & Kingston: McGill-Queen's University Press 1987

– *The Irish Diaspora: A Primer*. Port Credit: P.D. Meany 1993

Anbinder, Tyler Gregory. *Five Points: The 19th-Century New York City Neighborhood That Invented Tap Dance, Stole Elections, and Became the World's Most Notorious Slum*. New York: Free Press 2001

Anderson, Olive. *A Liberal State at War: English Politics and Economics During the Crimean War*. London: Macmillan 1967

Baker, William M. *Timothy Warren Anglin 1822–96: Irish Catholic Canadian*. Toronto: University of Toronto Press 1977

Balmes, Jaime Luciano. *Protestantism and Catholicity Compared in Their Effects on the Civilization of Europe*. Baltimore: John Murphy 1850

Banim, Mary. *Here and There through Ireland*. Part 1. Dublin: Freeman's Journal 1891

Beattie, Seán, ed. *Thomas D'Arcy McGee: A Commemoration 1998, Recalling the Escape of D'Arcy McGee to America, September 1848*. Carndonagh: Tremone Historical Society 1998

Beck, J. Murray. *Joseph Howe*. 2 vols. Montreal & Kingston: McGill-Queen's University Press 1982–83

Berger, Carl. *The Sense of Power: Studies in the Idea of Canadian Imperialism, 1867–1914*. Toronto: University of Toronto Press 1970

Berthoff, Rowland T. *British Immigrants in Industrial America, 1790–1950*. 1953. Rpt, New York: Russell & Russell 1968

Billington, Ray Allen. *The Protestant Crusade, 1800–1860: A Study of the Origins of American Nativism*. 1938. Rpt, Gloucester, Mass: Peter Smith 1963

Bourke, Austin. *"The Visitation of God?" The Potato and the Great Irish Famine*. Dublin: Lilliput Press 1993

Brady, Alexander. *Thomas D'Arcy McGee*. Toronto: Macmillan 1925

Breen, Anthony M. *The Cappoquin Rebellion, 1849*. Thurston, Suffolk: Drecroft 1998

Brown, Malcolm. *The Politics of Irish Literature from Thomas Davis to W.B. Yeats*. Seattle: University of Washington Press 1972

Browne, Henry J. "Archbishop Hughes and Western Colonization," *The Catholic Historical Review* 36 (October 1950): 257–85

Brownson, Orestes A. "The Know-Nothings," *Quarterly Review* (1854–55). In *The Works of Orestes A. Brownson, Collected and Arranged by Henry F. Brownson*, edited by Henry F. Brownson, 18:300–80. Detroit: Thorndike Nourse 1885

– "The Native Americans," *Quarterly Review* (July 1854). In *The Works of Orestes A. Brownson, Collected and Arranged by Henry F. Brownson*, edited by Henry F. Brownson, 18: 281–300. Detroit: Thorndike Nourse 1885

Burke, Edmund. "Mr. Edmund Burke's Speech, November 3, 1774." In *The Writings and Speeches of Edmund Burke*, vol. 3, *Party, Parliament, and the American War, 1774–1780*, edited by W.M. Elofson with John A. Woods, 64–70. Oxford: Clarendon Press 1996

– *Reflections on the Revolution in France and on the Proceedings in Certain Societies in London Relative to that Event*. 1790. Rev. edn, edited by Conor Cruise O'Brien. Harmondsworth: Penguin Books 1968

– "Thoughts on French Affairs." In *The Writings and Speeches of Edmund Burke*, vol. 8, *The French Revolution*, edited by L.G. Mitchel, 338–86. Oxford: Clarendon Press 1989

– *The Writings and Speeches of Edmund Burke*, vol. 9, *Part 1: The Revolutionary War, 1794–1797. Part 2: Ireland*, edited by R.B. McDowell. Oxford: Clarendon Press 1991

Burns, Robin B. "D'Arcy McGee and the New Nationality." MA dissertation, Carleton University 1966

– "Thomas D'Arcy McGee: A Biography." PHD dissertation, McGill University 1976

Byron, Reginald. *Irish America*. Oxford: Oxford University Press 1999

Cameron, Edward. *Memoirs of Ralph Vansittart*. Toronto: Musson 1924

Canada House of Commons. *Debates. First Session – First Parliament*. Ottawa 1867

Canada, Province of. Legislative Assembly. *Journals*, 25 Feb. – 1 June 1858.

Carey, Patrick W. *Orestes A. Brownson: American Religious Weathervane*. Grand Rapids: William B. Eerdmans 2004

Carte, Thomas. *The Life of James, Duke of Ormond; Containing an Account of the Most Remarkable Affairs of his Time, and Particularly of Ireland under his Government*. 6 vols. 1735. Rpt, Oxford: University Press 1851

Cavanagh, Michael. *Memoirs of Gen. Thomas Meagher: Comprising the Leading Events of His Career Chronologically Arranged*. Worcester, Mass.: Messenger Press 1892

Chapman, Malcolm. *The Celts: The Construction of a Myth*. New York: St Martin's Press 1992

Clarke, Brian. *Piety and Nationalism: Lay Voluntary Associations and the Creation of an Irish-Catholic Community in Toronto, 1850–1895*. Montreal & Kingston: McGill-Queen's University Press 1993

Collison, Gary. *Shadrach Minkins: From Fugitive Slave to Citizen*. Cambridge, Mass.: Harvard University Press 1997

Connelly, James F. *The Visit of Archbishop Gaetano Bedini to the United States of America (June, 1853 – February, 1854)*. Rome: Università Gregoriana 1960

Conyngham, David Power. *The Irish Brigade and Its Campaigns*. 1867. Rpt, New York: Fordham University Press 1994

Cottrell, Michael. "St. Patrick's Day Parades in Nineteenth-Century Toronto: A Study of Immigrant Adjustment and Elite Control." *Histoire sociale/Social History* 25 (May 1992): 57–73

Cushing, Luther S., ed. *Reports of Cases Argued and Determined in the Supreme Judicial Court of Massachusetts*. Vol. 9. Boston: Little, Brown 1866

Darroch, Gordon. "Half Empty or Half Full? Images and Interpretations of the Catholic Irish in Nineteenth-Century Canada." *Canadian Ethnic Studies* 25, no. 1 (1993): 1–8

Darroch, A. Gordon, and Michael D. Ornstein. "Ethnicity and Occupational Structure in Canada in 1871: The Vertical Mosaic in Historical Perspective." *Canadian Historical Review* 61, no. 3 (1980): 305–33.

Davis, Richard. *The Young Ireland Movement*. Dublin: Gill & Macmillan 1988

– *Revolutionary Imperialist: William Smith O'Brien*. Dublin: Lilliput Press 1998

Deusner, Charles E. "The Know Nothing Riots in Louisville." *Register of the Kentucky Historical Society* 61 (April 1963): 122–47

Deuther, Charles George. *The Life and Times of the Rt Rev John Timon, the Roman Catholic Bishop of the Diocese of Buffalo*. Buffalo, NY: The author 1870

Dillon, William. *Life of John Mitchel*. 2 vols. London: K. Paul, Trench 1888

Doheny, Michael. *The Felon's Track: A Narrative of '48 Embracing the Leading Events in the Irish Struggle from the Year 1843 to the Close of 1848*. 1849. Rpt, Dublin: M.H. Gill 1951

Donaldson, Dixon. *Historical, Traditional, and Descriptive Account of Islandmagee*. Whitehead: Dixon Donaldson 1927

Donnelly, James S., Jr. *The Great Irish Potato Famine*. Phoenix Mill, Gloucestershire: Sutton Publishing 2001

Doughty, Arthur G., ed. *The Elgin-Grey Papers, 1846–1852*. 4 vols. Ottawa: J.O. Patenaude 1937

Doyle, David Noel. "The Irish as Urban Pioneers in the United States, 1850–1870," *Journal of American Ethnic History* 10 (Fall 1990/Winter 1991): 36–61

DuBois, Ellen Carol. *Feminism and Suffrage: The Emergence of an Independent Women's Movement in America 1848–1869*. Ithaca: Cornell University Press 1978

– *Woman Suffrage and Women's Rights*. New York: New York University Press 1998

Duffy, Charles Gavan. *Four Years of Irish History, 1845–49: A Sequel to Young Ireland*. London: Cassell, Petter, Galpin 1883

– *Young Ireland: A Fragment of Irish History, 1840–45*. London: T. Fisher Unwin 1896

– *My Life in Two Hemispheres*. 2 vols. London: T. Fisher Unwin 1898

Ellmann, Richard. *James Joyce*. 1959. Rev. edn. New York: Oxford University Press 1982

Evans, R.J.W., and Hartmut Pogge Von Strandmann, eds. *The Revolutions in Europe, 1848–49: From Reform to Reaction*. Oxford: Oxford University Press 2000

Feldberg, Michael. *The Philadelphia Riots of 1844: A Study of Ethnic Conflict*. Westport, Conn.: Greenwood Press 1975

Ferguson, Lady. *Sir Samuel Ferguson in the Ireland of His Day*. Edinburgh & London: William Blackwood and Sons 1896

Fogarty, L. *James Fintan Lalor: Patriot and Political Essayist*. Dublin: Talbot Press 1918

Foster, William. *Canada First; or, Our New Nationality; An Address.* Toronto: Adam, Stevenson 1871

Gaustad, Edwin Scott, and Philip L. Barlow. *New Historical Atlas of Religion in America.* New York: Oxford University Press 2001

Gerber, David A. *The Making of an American Pluralism: Buffalo, New York, 1825–60.* Urbana & Chicago: University of Illinois Press 1989

Goheen, Peter G. "Symbols in the Streets: Parades in Victorian Urban Canada." *Urban History Review* 18 (February 1990): 237–43

Gordon, Michael A. *The Orange Riots: Irish Political Violence in New York City, 1870 and 1871.* Ithaca: Cornell University Press 1993

Grattan, Thomas Colley. *Civilized America.* London: Bradbury & Evans 1859

Gray, Peter. *Famine, Land, and Politics: British Government and Irish Society 1843–1850.* Dublin: Irish Academic Press 1999

Grozier, Richard. "The Life and Times of John Bernard Fitzpatrick: Third Roman Catholic Bishop of Boston." PHD dissertation, Boston College 1966

Gwynn, Denis. *Young Ireland and 1848.* Cork: Cork University Press 1949

Haines, Robin F. *Charles Trevelyan and the Great Irish Famine.* Dublin: Four Courts Press 2004

Handlin, Oscar. *Boston's Immigrants: A Study in Acculturation.* 1941. Rpt, Cambridge, Mass.: Belknap Press of Harvard University Press 1979

Harvey, Daniel Cobb. *Thomas D'Arcy McGee, the Prophet of Canadian Nationality, being an account of how Thomas D'Arcy McGee, by precept and example, strove manfully to convert the abstract idea of Canadian nationality into a compelling sentiment of tolerance and goodwill among sects and races, of faith, hope, charity, and neighborliness among individuals.* Winnipeg: University of Manitoba 1923

Hassard, John R.G. *Life of John Hughes, First Archbishop of New York.* 1866. Rpt, New York: Arno Press 1969

Higham, John. *Strangers in the Land: Patterns of American Nativism 1860–1925.* 1955. Rpt. New Brunswick, N.J.: Rutgers University Press 1988

Houston, Cecil J., and William J. Smyth. *The Sash Canada Wore: A Historical Geography of the Orange Order in Canada.* Toronto: University of Toronto Press 1980

– *Irish Emigration and Canadian Settlement: Patterns, Links, and Letters.* Toronto: University of Toronto Press 1990

Howell, Wilber S. *Eighteenth-Century British Logic and Rhetoric.* Princeton: Princeton University Press 1971

Hughes, John. "Reflections and Suggestions in Regard to What Is Called the Catholic Press." *Metropolitan* 4 (December 1856), 652–61

— "Address to the National Brotherhood of St. Patrick." In *Complete Works of the Most Rev. John Hughes, D.D., Archbishop of New York*, edited by Lawrence Kehoe, 2:527–8. New York: Lawrence Kehoe 1866

— "Lecture on the Antecedent Causes of the Irish Famine." In *Complete Works of the Most Rev. John Hughes, D.D., Archbishop of New York*, edited by Lawrence Kehoe, 1:544–58. New York: Lawrence Kehoe 1866

— "The Nebraska Irish Colony." In *Complete Works of the Most Rev. John Hughes, D.D., Archbishop of New York*, edited by Lawrence Kehoe, 2:751–5. New York: Lawrence Kehoe 1866

— "The Question of Ireland." In *Complete Works of the Most Rev. John Hughes, D.D., Archbishop of New York*, edited by Lawrence Kehoe, 2:793–4. New York: Lawrence Kehoe 1866

Ignatiev, Noel. *How the Irish Became White*. New York: Routledge 1995

The Irish Monthly: A Magazine of General Literature. Vol. 11. Dublin: M.H. Gill & Son 1883

Isenberg, Nancy. *Sex and Citizenship in Antebellum America*. Chapel Hill, NC: University of North Carolina Press 1998

James, Simon. *The Atlantic Celts: Ancient People or Modern Invention?* London: British Museum Press 1999

Jensen, Richard J. "'No Irish Need Apply': A Myth of Urban Victimization." *Journal of Social History* 36 (2002): 405–29

Jones, Peter. *The 1848 Revolutions*. Burnt Mill, Harlow: Longman 1981

Jones, William. "On the Musical Modes of the Hindus." In *The Story of Indian Music and Its Instruments: A Study of the Present and a Record of the Past; Together with Sir William Jones' Celebrated Treatise in Full*, edited by Ethel Rosenthal. New Delhi: Oriental Books Reprint Corp. 1970

Keep, George Rex Crowley. "The Irish Migration to Montreal, 1847–67." MA dissertation, McGill University 1948

Kendle, John. *Ireland and the Federal Solution: The Debate over the United Kingdom Constitution, 1870–1921*. Montreal & Kingston: McGill-Queen's University Press, 1992

Kennedy, Liam, and David S. Johnson, "The Union of Ireland and Britain, 1801–1921. In *The Making of Modern Irish History: Revisionism and the Revisionist Controversy*, edited by D. George Boyce and Alan O'Day, 34–70. London: Routledge 1996

Kennedy, Liam, Paul S. Ell, E.M. Crawford, and L.A. Clarkson. *Mapping the Great Irish Famine: A Survey of the Famine Decades*. Dublin: Four Courts Press 1999

Kenny, Kevin. *The American Irish: A History*. Harlow: Longman 2000

Kerber, Linda K. "The Republican Mother and the Enlightenment: An American Perspective," *American Quarterly* 27 (1976): 187–205

Kerr, Donal A. *"A Nation of Beggars?" Priests, People, and Politics in Famine Ireland, 1846–52*. Oxford: Clarendon Press 1994

Kinealy, Christine. *This Great Calamity: The Irish Famine, 1845–52*. Dublin: Gill & Macmillan 1994

Knobel, Dale T. *"America for the Americans": The Nativist Movement in the United States*. New York: Twayne 1996

Koseki, Takashi. *Dublin Confederate Clubs and the Repeal Movement*. Tokyo: Institute of Comparative Economic Studies, Ireland-Japan Papers no. 10, Hosei University 1992

Lambkin, Brian. "Moving Titles of a Young Ireland Text: Davis, Duffy, and McGee and the Origins of *Tiocfaidh Ar Lá*." In *Ireland: Space, Text, Time*, edited by Liam Harte, 103–11. Manchester: Manchester University Press 2005

Lewis, Jan. "The Republican Wife: Virtue and Seduction in the Early Republic." *William and Mary Quarterly*, 3d Series, 44 (October 1987): 689–721

Loughlin, James. "Allegiance and Illusion: Queen Victoria's Irish Visit of 1849." *History* 87 (October 2002): 491–513

MacCartney, Donald. "The Writing of History in Ireland, 1800–1830." *Irish Historical Studies* 10 (September 1957): 347–62

MacDermott, Martin. *Songs and Ballads of Young Ireland*. London: Downey 1896

MacDonagh, Oliver. *The Emancipist: Daniel O'Connell 1830–47*. New York: St Martin's Press 1989

McGee, James E. *The Men of '48. Being a Brief History of the Repeal Association and The Irish Confederation; With Biographical Sketches of the Leading Actors in the Latter Organization, Their Principles, Opinions and Literary Labors*. Boston: D. O'Loughlin 1881

McGee, Thomas D'Arcy. *A SPEECH Delivered Before the Repealers of Watertown, Mass., and the Adjoining Towns, on the REPEAL OF THE UNION, Friday Evening, Nov. 10, 1843*. Boston, 1843

– "The Priest Hunter: A Tale of the Irish Penal Laws." *Catholic Expositor and Literary Magazine* 4 (December 1843): 264–9

- *Eva MacDonald: A Tale of the United Irishmen, and Their Times*. Boston: Charles H. Brainard 1844
- *Historical Sketches of O'Connell and His Friends*. Boston: Donahoe & Rohan 1845
- *The Irish Writers of the Seventeenth Century*. Dublin: James Duffy 1846
- *Memoir of the Life and Conquests of Art Mac Murrough, King of Leinster, from A.D. 1377 to A.D. 1417: With Some Notices of the Leinster Wars of the 14th Century*. Dublin: James Duffy 1847
- *Memoir of Charles Gavan Duffy, Esq., as a Student, Journalist, and Organizer*. Dublin: W. Hogan 1849
- *A History of the Irish Settlers in North America, from the Earliest Period to the Census of 1850*. 1851. 6th edn. Boston: P. Donahoe 1855
- *A History of the Attempts to Establish the Protestant Reformation in Ireland, and the Successful Resistance of that People. (Time: 1540–1830)*. 2nd edn. Boston: Patrick Donahoe 1853
- "The Political Causes and Consequences of the Protestant 'Reformation': A Lecture." New York: D. & J. Sadlier, 1853
- *The Catholic History of North America*. Boston: Patrick Donahoe 1855
- *A Life of the Rt. Rev. Edward Maginn, Coadjutor Bishop of Derry, with Selections from His Correspondence*. New York: P. O'Shea 1857
- *Canadian Ballads and Occasional Verses*. Montreal & Toronto: John Lovell and William C. F. Caverhill 1858
- *The Irish Position in British and in Republican North America*. Montreal: Longmoore 1866

McGowan, Mark G. "Irish Catholics." In *Encyclopedia of Canada's Peoples*, edited by Paul Robert Magocsi, 734–63. Toronto: University of Toronto Press 1999

McManus, Antonia. *The Irish Hedge School and Its Books, 1695–1831*. Dublin: Four Courts Press 2004

[MacNeven, William]. *An Argument for Independence, in Opposition to an Union*. Dublin: J. Stockdale 1799

MacRaild, Donald M. *Faith, Fraternity, and Fighting: The Orange Order and Irish Migrants in Northern England, c. 1850–1920*. Liverpool: Liverpool University Press 2005

McSkimin, Samuel. *The History and Antiquities of the County of the Town of Carrickfergus*. Belfast: J. Smyth 1823

Madden, Richard R. *The United Irishmen: Their Lives and Times*. 3 vols. 2nd edn. Dublin: J. Duffy 1858

Malcolm, Elizabeth. *"Ireland Sober, Ireland Free": Drink and Temperance in Nineteenth-Century Ireland*. Dublin: Gill & Macmillan 1986

Marsden, William. *The History of Sumatra*, 3rd edn. 1811. Rpt, Kuala Lumpur: Oxford University Press 1966

Matthews, Jean V. *Women's Struggle for Equality: The First Phase, 1828–1876*. Chicago: Ivan R. Dee 1997

Meegan, Brendan, and Jenny Meegan. "Thomas D'Arcy McGee and His Sisters and Brother in Ireland, America, and Australia: Their Mother's Grave in Wexford." *Journal of the Wexford Historical Society* 20 (2004–5): 56–74

Merwick, Donna. *Boston Priests, 1848–1910: A Study of Social and Intellectual Change*. Cambridge, Mass.: Harvard University Press, 1973

The Metropolitan: A Monthly Magazine, Devoted to Religion, Education, Literature, and General Information. Baltimore: J. Murphy 1853–59

Miller, Kerby A. *Emigrants and Exiles: Ireland and the Irish Exodus to North America*. New York: Oxford University Press 1985

Mitchel, John. *The Last Conquest of Ireland (Perhaps)*. 1861. Rev. edn., edited by Patrick Maume. Dublin: University College Dublin Press 2005

Monk, Maria [pseud]. *Awful Disclosures, by Maria Monk, of the Hotel Dieu Nunnery of Montreal: As Exhibited in a Narrative of Her Sufferings during Her Residence of Five Years as a Novice, and Two Years as a Black Nun, in the Hotel Dieu Nunnery at Montreal*. New York: T.B. Peterson 1836

Morse, Samuel. *Foreign Conspiracy against the Liberties of the United States*. New York: Leavitt 1835

Mythen, Seán. *Thomas Furlong: The Forgotten Wexford Poet*. Ferns, County Wexford: Clone Publications 1998

Nowlan, Kevin B. *The Politics of Repeal: A Study in the Relations between Great Britain and Ireland, 1841–50*. London: Routledge & Kegan Paul 1965

O'Brien, Conor Cruise. *The Great Melody: A Thematic Biography and Commented Anthology of Edmund Burke*. Chicago: University of Chicago Press 1992

– *Memoir: My Life and Themes*. Dublin: Poolbeg Press 1999

Ó Cathaoir, Brendan, ed. *Young Irelander Abroad: The Diary of Charles Hart*. Cork: Cork University Press 2003

O'Connell, Maurice R., ed. *The Correspondence of Daniel O'Connell*, vol. 7, 1841–1845. Dublin: Blackwater Press n.d.

O'Connor, Thomas H. *Fitzpatrick's Boston, 1846–1866: John Fitzpatrick, Third Bishop of Boston*. Boston: Northeastern University Press 1984

– *The Boston Irish: A Political History*. Boston: Northeastern University Press 1995

O'Driscoll, Robert, and Lorna Reynolds, eds. *The Untold Story: The Irish in Canada*. Toronto: Celtic Arts of Canada 1988

Ó Gráda, Cormac. *The Great Irish Famine*. Basingstoke: Macmillan Education 1989

– *Ireland Before and After the Famine: Explorations in Economic History, 1800–1925*. Manchester: Manchester University Press 1993

– *Black '47 and Beyond: The Great Irish Famine in History, Economy, and Memory*. Princeton: Princeton University Press 1999

O'Shea, James. *Prince of Swindlers: John Sadleir M.P. 1813–1856*. Dublin: Geography Publications 1999

Owens, Gary. "Popular Mobilisation and the Rising of 1848: The Clubs of the Irish Confederation." In *Rebellion and Remembrance in Modern Ireland*, edited by Laurence M. Geary, 51–63. Dublin: Four Courts 2000

Paine, Thomas. *Rights of Man, Part Second*. In *The Life and Major Writings of Thomas Paine*, edited by Philip S. Foner, 1:345–485. 1948. Rev. edn., Secausus, NJ: Citadel Press 1974

Phelan, Josephine. *The Ardent Exile: The Life and Times of Thos. D'Arcy McGee*. Toronto: Macmillan 1951

Potter, David M. *The Impending Crisis, 1848–1861*. New York: Harper & Row 1976

Quinlan, Michael P. *Irish Boston: A Lively Look at Boston's Colorful Irish Past*. Guilford, Conn.: Globe Pequot Press 2004

Rees, Alwyn, and Brinley Rees. *Celtic Heritage: Ancient Tradition in Ireland and Wales*. London: Thames & Hudson 1961

Reilly, Tom. *Cromwell, An Honourable Enemy: The Untold Story of the Cromwellian Invasion of Ireland*. London: Phoenix Press 1999

Robinson, Gertrude. *David Urquhart: Some Chapters in the Life of a Victorian Knight-Errant of Justice and Liberty*. Boston & New York: Houghton Mifflin 1920

Ross, George W. *Getting into Parliament and After*. Toronto: W. Briggs 1913

Sadlier, Mary Ann, ed. *The Poems of Thomas D'Arcy McGee*. New York: D. & J. Sadlier 1869

Saville, John. *1848: The British State and the Chartist Movement*. Cambridge: Cambridge University Press 1987

Schama, Simon. *A History of Britain: The British Wars, 1603–1776*. Toronto: McClelland & Stewart 2001

Senior, Hereward. *Orangeism: The Canadian Phase*. Toronto: McGraw-Hill Ryerson 1972

— *The Fenians and Canada*. Toronto: Macmillan 1978

Shaw, Richard. *Dagger John: The Unquiet Life and Times of Archbishop John Hughes of New York*. New York: Paulist Press 1977

Skelton, Isabel. *The Life of Thomas D'Arcy McGee*. Gardenvale, Que.: Garden City Press 1925

Slattery, T.P. *The Assassination of D'Arcy McGee*. Toronto: Doubleday 1968

— *"They Got to Find Mee Guilty Yet."* Toronto: Doubleday 1972

Sloan, Robert. *William Smith O'Brien and the Young Ireland Rebellion of 1848*. Dublin: Four Courts Press 2000

Solar, Peter. "The Great Famine Was No Ordinary Subsistence Crisis." In *Famine: The Irish Experience 900–1900: Subsistence Crises and Famines in Ireland*, edited by E. Margaret Crawford, 112–33. Edinburgh: J. Donald 1989

Stearns, Peter N. *The Revolutions of 1848*. London: Weidenfeld and Nicolson 1974

Stewart, A.T.Q. *The Narrow Ground: Aspects of Ulster, 1609–1969*. London: Faber & Faber 1977

Taylor, Cliona. "A Fatal Affray in Toronto: The Murder of Matthew Sheedy and the St. Patrick's Day Riots of 1858." MA research paper, University of Toronto 2005

Taylor, Miles. "The Old Radicalism and the New: David Urquhart and the Politics of Opposition, 1832–1867." In *Currents of Radicalism: Popular Radicalism, Organised Labour, and Party Politics in Britain, 1850–1914*, edited by Eugenio F. Biagine and Alastair J. Reid, 23–43. Cambridge: Cambridge University Press 1991

Tolkien, J.R.R. "English and Welsh." In *Angles and Britons*. Cardiff: University of Wales Press 1963

Toner, Peter M. "The Rise of Irish Nationalism in Canada, 1858–1884." PHD dissertation, University College Galway 1974

— "Occupation and Ethnicity: The Irish in New Brunswick." *Canadian Ethnic Studies* 20 (1988): 155–65

Trial of Patrick James Whelan for the Murder of the Hon. Thos. D'Arcy McGee. Ottawa: Desbarats 1868

Vance, Norman. "Celts, Carthaginians, and Constitutions: Anglo-Irish Literary Relations, 1780–1820." *Irish Historical Studies* 87 (March 1981): 216–38

— *Irish Literature – A Social History: Tradition, Identity, and Difference*. Oxford: Blackwell 1990

Virgo, Seán. *Selected Verse of Thomas D'Arcy McGee*. Toronto: Exile Editions 2000

Walsh, Francis Robert. "The Boston Pilot: A Newspaper for the Irish Immigrant, 1829–1908." PHD dissertation, Boston University 1968

Whyte, Robert. *The Ocean Plague, or, A Voyage to Quebec in an Irish Emigrant Vessel: Embracing a Quarantine at Grosse Isle in 1847 with Notes Illustrative of the Ship Pestilence of that Fatal Year*. Boston: Coolidge & Wiley 1848

Wilson, David A. *United Irishmen, United States: Immigrant Radicals in the New Republic*. Ithaca: Cornell University Press 1998

– "The Fenians in Montreal, 1862–68: Invasion, Intrigue, and Assassination." *Eire-Ireland* 38 (Fall/Winter 2003): 109–33

– "Whiteness and the Irish Experience in North America," *Journal of British Studies* 44, no. 1 (2005): 153–60

Woodham-Smith, Cecil. *The Great Hunger: Ireland 1845–1849*. 1962. Rpt, Toronto: Penguin Books 1991

Index